RISE
AND
FIRE

ALSO BY SHAWN FURY

Keeping the Faith: In the Trenches with
College Football's Worst Team

RISE AND FIRE

THE ORIGINS, SCIENCE, AND EVOLUTION

OF THE JUMP SHOT — AND HOW IT

TRANSFORMED BASKETBALL FOREVER

SHAWN FURY

FLATIRON
BOOKS
NEW YORK

www.flatironbooks.com

The Library of Congress Cataloging-in-Publication Data is available upon request.

ISBN 978-1-250-06216-1 (hardcover)
ISBN 978-1-250-06217-8 (e-book)

Our books may be purchased in bulk for promotional, educational, or business use. Please contact your local bookseller or the Macmillan Corporate and Premium Sales Department at 1-800-221-7945, extension 5442, or by e-mail at MacmillanSpecialMarkets@macmillan.com.

First Edition: February 2016

10 9 8 7 6 5 4 3 2 1

FOR MY DAD, PAT FURY, WHO NEVER LET ME WIN BUT TAUGHT ME

THE JUMP SHOT THAT FINALLY HELPED ME BEAT HIM.

AND FOR MY MOM, CEES FURY, WHO STILL THINKS EVERY SHOT I

TAKE WILL FIND NOTHING BUT NET.

CONTENTS

RISE
AND
FIRE

INTRODUCTION

New York City's Inwood Hill Park covers 196 acres on the northern tip of Manhattan, about twenty-five minutes on the subway from Times Square. Visitors roam Manhattan's largest remaining ancient forest in this park, a green paradise unlike any other place in the city, home to springs, swans, rock caves, salt marshes, and, some longtime residents say, ghosts. In 1626, Dutchman Peter Minuit bought Manhattan Island from Native Americans. A plaque in the park marks the supposed and disputed location of the infamous real estate transaction. In the middle section of Inwood Hill Park, tucked next to the baseball diamonds and the tennis courts, you'll find one of the city's hundreds of outdoor basketball courts, home to thrilling full-court five-on-five showdowns between superb young athletes and hard-to-watch half-court one-on-one battles between middle-age teachers who are one torn ligament away from permanent retirement.

The Inwood Hill Park court has never been one of New York City's famous playground venues, like Rucker Park or the Cage at West 4th Street, courts that earn headlines and make or ruin reputations. Filmmakers haven't created documentaries focused on Inwood Hill Park's players or games. The court isn't even the most famous playground in the area. About ten blocks away, in Monsignor Kett Playground, the court that's commonly called Dyckman Park attracts some of the top players in the city during an annual summer tournament and boasts a bit of historical heft—Kareem Abdul-Jabbar grew up in the area and played there when he was a kid and still went by the name Lew Alcindor. I live five minutes from Inwood Hill Park, and on a 73-degree September day the court remains the perfect spot for a thirty-eight-year-old has-been with no quickness who still loves the game and, above all, still loves to shoot. City schools are in session so the court sits empty when I arrive just past noon. I remove my sweatshirt, perform a cursory leg stretch, pull my $22 Target ball out of my duffel bag, test it with three dribbles, palm it in case this is the day I throw down the first one-handed dunk of my life, and walk toward one of the court's four baskets. Two of them have nets, two of 'em don't—and nobody voluntarily shoots on one without the cords.

Out on the court, I'm a bit uneasy in my elements, at times feeling out of place as I shoot alone. No one looks twice at an out-of-shape forty-year-old man in tan shorts who strikes a solitary figure on a driving range, pounding away on a bucket of balls with the driver he received for Christmas. But how many times do you see an adult alone in a public park at a basket, shooting some hoops for the hell of it? In the suburban backyard, on the basket he constructed out of love for his three kids? Sure. At the YMCA as he waits for the other goggles-wearing, knee-brace-sporting, noon-hour warriors to arrive? Of course. But it feels a bit strange to perform as a solo act on an outdoor court, taking four dribbles before every free throw and firing 23-footers from behind the three-point line.

I'm here for the exercise. Running for running's sake has always seemed like a punishment and holds no appeal for me. Chasing after an errant shot remains more enjoyable than pedaling on a stationary bike. Mostly I'm here because I love the game. And there's nothing I love more about basketball than the jump shot. When kids pick up a basketball, the first thing they do is throw it in the air. They fire a shot, often before they dribble. Even if it's on a Nerf hoop, anyone with a ball and a target wants to shoot. Growing up in Minnesota, I learned to shoot on a hoop attached to my neighbor's garage and in my small town's park, on a basket six inches too high. I spent countless hours playing on those baskets and hundreds more shooting at my grandpa's farm, drilling jumpers on the basket my dad and his brothers attached to a white barn decades earlier. In the winter I would wear two pairs of gloves—thin ones I called my shooting gloves—and shovel snow off of the city park's concrete court in zero-degree Minnesota weather, all so I could practice my shot. Throughout those years I probably won a thousand imaginary NBA titles and a hundred fictional high school state championships with my jump shot. At first, like everyone who starts shooting as a kid, before I developed the consistent form and performance that comes with age and height, I shot from the hip, heaving the ball instead of shooting with proper mechanics, hoping and praying for good results instead of expecting them. As I grew and matured and learned to shoot from above my head while leaving the ground—the coordinated actions finally creating a fundamentally sound and effective form—the jump shot became my first love during my days playing high school and college ball.

And now, out at this New York City park, as I self-consciously jog after shots that bounce off the rim and roll to the far side of the court, I find a rhythm. Starting with little four-foot bank shots, I follow with free throw line jumpers. Dribble out and launch threes from the baseline. Head to the top of the key for a straight-on three. Come off the dribble for a 15-foot pull-up jumper. Now do it while dribbling to the left. Hope that no one's watching. Ignore them if they are. Because today, roughly thirty-four years after I first picked up a ball, there's still nothing like being on a court—inside or outside, with teammates or alone—firing away with the jumper.

Rise and Fire celebrates the jump shot, examines its origins, explores its fundamentals, and honors those who dominated the game with it. Consider it a love letter to basketball and the jump shot, and a profile of how it changed the game. The jumper remains the most important play in basketball. When the first jump shooting pioneers introduced the shot, it changed the sport. Experts still debate who invented the jumper. No single correct answer exists. But no one debates the impact the shot had on the sport. Players no longer found themselves earthbound. Defenses controlled the game in the early years, or, perhaps more accurately, subpar offense ruled. To adapt, players jumped to get their shots over the raised hands of defenders, and at the same time rose above the game's conventions. Basketball was never the same. The jump shot created offense, excitement, fans, and legends. Games that formerly ended with scores fit for a football field soon saw both teams reach triple figures.

In the decades since, the jumper expanded its dominance, becoming the most prevalent shot, the toughest to perfect, and the most important to master. Basketball styles change, and the jumper has always led the charge. It increased scoring in the 1950s. Great guards used it to win titles for and against great big men in the '60s. High-scoring gunners shot their way to absurd numbers in the 1970s. The midrange dominated the '80s. And today the three-pointer dictates pace and strategy, as even the game's big men gravitate farther away from the basket. No one knew what to make of the jumper when it first arrived, and the same was true for the three-pointer. But eventually people saw the power in both.

Along the way, jumpers created the game's most memorable moments, from high school to the pros. The movie *Hoosiers* celebrates the underdog, hard-ass coaches, tough-talking tutors, and Indiana high school basketball, but it ends with a jumper by the monosyllabic Jimmy Chitwood. The movie fictionalized and immortalized the real-life 1954 Indiana state champions. But the movie ending was true to life—Milan's Bobby Plump hit a 15-foot jumper at the buzzer that looked very much like the one on the big screen. Many people call the Kentucky-Duke Regional Final in 1992 the greatest college game in history. Its unforgettable ending? Christian Laettner draining a 15-foot buzzer-beater to cap a perfect shooting performance in a near-perfect game, a shot that made all of Kentucky—and at least one Duke teammate—bawl. Michael Jordan's leaping ability earned him millions of dollars and Phil Knight billions, but his jumper sealed his legacy. Perhaps the three most memorable shots of his career were jump shots. As a skinny freshman at North Carolina—where TV announcers called him Mike for part of the season—he emerged onto the national scene with the game-winning jumper from the left side against Georgetown in the 1982 NCAA title game. Seven years later, now a global icon with the Bulls, his jumper, known as The Shot, over a helpless and eternally tormented Craig Ehlo in the Eastern Conference playoffs gave Chicago a series victory and provided photographers with another unforgettable Jordan moment—his leap and fist pump on the sidelines in front of shattered Cleveland fans. And finally, in 1998, a time when an aging Jordan didn't leap as high or fly as far or sky much at all, his slight push-off and jump shot over Bryon Russell in Game 6 of the NBA Finals gave the Bulls their sixth NBA championship.

This book highlights the greatest shooters of all time at every level and from every era, from the Hall of Famers who changed the NBA to the little-known legends who only ruled in high school but are remembered forever. I researched everything involving the jump shot, from the techniques of the most accurate shooters to shooter's gyms. I spoke with as many great shooters as I could find. I spent time talking with players involved in the greatest shooting duels, and players who made thousands of shots but can't forget a devastating miss. While researching I traveled to fourteen states, from Georgia to California, sat in the living rooms of great shooters from the '50s, and worked on drills with NBA shooting coaches. One morning I talked on the phone with Kenny Sailors, an early jump shot pioneer out of Wyoming, one of the last of the original shooters who was still alive when I worked on the book. At ninety-three, hard of hearing, having told his story hundreds of times, Kenny's enthusiasm for the jump shot, which he first took eighty years before our chat, was still obvious. When I finished talking with Sailors, his friend Bill Schrage, who helps him with interviews and operates a Web site dedicated to Kenny's career, told me Kenny sported a smile as he left for lunch at his assisted living facility in Laramie. The grin wasn't because of the meal. Memories of the jump shot still make Kenny smile. Millions know the feeling.

Rise and Fire is about the secrets of the shot and the superstitions of the players who live by it. It's a sentimental, historical, personal, scientific, and critical examination of the jumper. This book is not an encyclopedia of every great shooter. That book would run 10,000 pages. But it profiles many of the shot's masters. A path connects the first shooters to modern marksmen, and I wanted to explore that road and show how basketball got from point A to point B, from the set shot to the jump shot and beyond.

Coaches preach about team defense, rebounding, boxing out, sharp cuts, hitting the open man, switching on defense, running the floor, filling the lane, getting a hand up, looking up, fighting through screens, moving the ball, and shuffling your feet. These are all important things, and I'm sure, occasionally, defense, pure defense, wins championships—but only if there's someone capable of making shots. My favorite saying in basketball has always been "Great offense beats great defense." I also believe it, as do many of the shooters featured in *Rise and Fire*. Go ahead and play tight defense—a locked-in shooter won't even notice.

This is a biography of the shot everyone tries the first time they pick up a ball and the one they shoot on lonely city playgrounds long after they're past their prime. This book details the evolution of one shot—and how it revolutionized a sport.

PART ONE

IN THE BEGINNING

ONE

ORIGINS AND MYSTERIES

It's a tribute to Wendell Smith's rich life and groundbreaking career that his possible role as one of the inventors of the jump shot didn't even make the first paragraph of his obituary. Smith remains best known for the crucial role he played when Jackie Robinson integrated baseball in 1947. A longtime sportswriter and sportscaster, Smith, a Detroit native, recommended Robinson to Brooklyn Dodgers general manager Branch Rickey. He accompanied Robinson during his first season with the Dodgers and cowrote Robinson's autobiography. Throughout his career, Smith wrote about segregation in baseball, but he was also a general columnist and respected boxing scribe. Right out of college he worked for *The Pittsburgh Courier*, one of the most prominent African American newspapers in the country, and in Chicago he wrote for newspapers and anchored on WGN. Smith was the first black sportswriter to receive the J. G. Taylor Spink Award for his contributions to baseball writing, given posthumously in 1993. People who didn't know Smith's story learned about him in the 2013 Robinson biopic *42*, in which actor André Holland portrayed the writer, who's shown in the movie sitting in the stands with his typewriter.

Smith died in 1972 of pancreatic cancer at the age of fifty-eight. But Smith's obituary from UPI included a line that didn't appear in most stories about him, and it didn't come until the sixth paragraph. "An athlete himself in both high school and college, Smith was credited with taking basketball's first jump shot while playing for West Virginia State." When his old paper *The Pittsburgh Courier* covered Smith's funeral—about 200 people attended, including Chicago sports legends Gale Sayers and Billy Williams—its story waited until paragraph seven to reveal Smith's historic achievement on the hardwood: "He earned a bachelor of science degree from West Virginia State College in 1937 and was a star for the basketball and baseball teams. He was credited with introducing the one-handed jump shot to the game of basketball, but it was in the field of sportswriting that he earned his reputation and his living."

Introduced the one-handed jump shot? Took the first jump shot? What day? Where was the gym? Who was the opponent? And did he celebrate when he swished the shot or curse when it rimmed out? The mentions in those stories provide just two hints of the odyssey awaiting anyone who attempts to track down the first jump shooters. Just when you think you've found a unique nugget that perhaps unearths the first shooter . . . four more names of early shooters emerge from the archives. Forget about finding the absolute first. Historians have debated the question of who took the first jump shot for decades, but fresh claims about the original shooters still emerge from old sources, thanks to a newly discovered tattered newspaper from the 1920s or a dusty school yearbook from the '30s. Or a forgotten obituary from the 1970s. A dozen people might have invented the jump shot, or a hundred—but no one patented it. The early shooters operated in isolation, independent of each other, mostly away from what little media existed. We know some names—John Cooper, Joe Fulks, Kenny Sailors, Glenn Roberts—but others like Barney Varnes, Jimmie James, and Belus Smawley also made claims, some of them even legitimate, about being the first jump shooters. But finding the first is impossible. A fourteen-year-old Nebraska boy might have picked up a ball one summer morning in 1930 and jumped into the air while shooting at a basket attached to a red barn and never thought of it again after getting called over to finish his chores. A college player in Maine might have found himself six inches off the ground while shooting with two hands above his head and realized he did something wrong when the coach benched him. A black professional player on a barnstorming tour in the Midwest might have jumped on every 15-foot shot he took in an exhibition game inside a dance hall and thought nothing of it because that's how he played the game every night: in the air. And, yes, it's possible future sportswriter Wendell Smith, best known for his skills on the baseball diamond in college and his passion for social justice in and out of press boxes, took the first jump shot—although he probably didn't.

"You'll never get to the pioneer, the absolute Adam of jump shooters," author John Christgau told me during a visit in his Northern California home, and if anyone should know, it's Christgau. He spent years working on his 1999 book, *The Origins of the Jump Shot: Eight Men Who Shook the World of Basketball*. Christgau traveled to about a dozen states and identified eight players who were among the first to leave the ground. Fifteen years after the book's publication, people still e-mail Christgau every week about a great-uncle who took the first jump shot in high school or a grandfather who made the first jumper in junior college. Hunting for the original jump shooter presents a fun challenge, but discovering a single creator isn't as important as learning why the first players went into the air. Whether those innovators jumped because they went against taller players or because they expressed creativity while growing up in rigid households, their inventions helped the game evolve, ushering in changes that turned basketball from a boring, low-scoring affair into an exciting, high-scoring game. They were artists and rebels, altering a game controlled by scientists and conformists.

James Naismith invented basketball in 1891, but it basically took forty years before players began shooting jump shots of any kind, sixty-five before they became a common sight, and more than *seventy* before people realized the shot wasn't going to ruin the game. Set shots ruled. And that's because coaches and instructors ruled the game. For years players shot with two hands on the ball, feet nailed to the floor, metaphorically only because the law didn't allow coaches to take a hammer out on the court and make it literal. Variations included underhanded shots and shots taken from the chest. Shooters could step into a push shot and occasionally lift a leg. In his book *Big Leagues: Professional Baseball, Football, & Basketball in National Memory*, Stephen Fox highlighted books published by famed college coaches Walter Meanwell from Wisconsin, Illinois's Craig Ruby, and Kansas legend Phog Allen. Fox revealed how each coach described the shots of the day.

Meanwell called it a one-hand push after a high jump, with the ball banked off the backboard. Ruby called it a two-hand shoulder shot: a player moving away from the basket, toward the left sideline, jumping off his left foot to face the hoop and shooting with both hands from a point to the right of his head. Allen called it a push arch shot: the player with the ball springing up and back off his rear leg, extending his front leg in protection, and shooting a soft, loopy ball to the rim.

Fox noted these shots were "glorified layups, mainly used close to the basket after a lateral jump off one foot instead of a vertical, two-legged leap."

Physical educators played a big role in the development of basketball—they're the ones who first taught the game and contributed to its growth around the country. Author Bob Kuska has written several books about the game's early years. "If you were going to win, there was a very scientific way to play basketball," he says. "All the coaches bought into it. The prominent coaches bought into it. It very much trickled down to the players that if you're going to play, you have to play in a very scientific way. You can go back and look at the textbooks—if you're going to shoot a shot from afar, you've got to come to a complete stop and you have to have both feet on the ground."

Improvising players—not coaches drawing it up on a chalkboard—invented the jump shot, creating a weapon that defied rules and angered coaches who feared a future where the jumper allowed individuals to trump the team. Through passing and screens, players worked themselves open until they had a clear look at the basket and an opportunity to shoot—with two hands, feet on the floor. Jump shots worked against tough defenses, but that was part of the problem: Coaches didn't want players taking contested shots, not when their offenses were designed to move the ball until someone was wide open—even if a play now existed that worked against any defender.

Unlike many trends, the jump shot started in small towns and migrated to the big cities. The early jump shooters did not inspire an immediate revolution—the jump shot confused teammates who were unable to duplicate the jumper when they tried it on their own and were fearful of the coach's wrath if they succeeded. The early jump shooters persisted through doubts, benchings, raised voices, and eyebrows, sticking with their aerial theatrics, fully aware of how the jumper changed their own games, even if they couldn't fathom how the shot would alter an entire sport.

When I talked with Kuska, he said finding the first shooters wasn't as important as who popularized the shot. Taking a jump shot in isolation made a player a pioneer, but not necessarily a revolutionary. Still, while it's impossible to find the Adam of shooters—or the Eve—the stories of the innovators shed light on how they changed the sport for the better. But, before getting to those players and their tales of childhood hardships, poverty-stricken upbringings, rebellious natures, accidental discoveries, and war heroics, we should first recognize a player who *did not* invent the jump shot—but changed the game forever with his shooting.

Even hard-core basketball fans struggle to name the players most identified with the early days of the jump shot. To many, their knowledge of basketball history begins around the time Wilt Chamberlain and Bill Russell started dominating the NBA. The jump shot was just always there, wasn't it? When I started working on this book, I had never heard of men like Glenn Roberts or John Burton. I knew nothing of their accomplishments, and I'm not alone. But if you took a poll of fans who had some knowledge of the past and asked them to name the first person to take a jump shot, the leading response—after a few seconds of contemplation and an acknowledgment that they're not sure—would probably be, "Hank Luisetti." Many people have heard of Hank Luisetti, even if their knowledge of him is a bit hazy.

Luisetti, a San Francisco native, starred for Stanford in the 1930s. A high-scoring forward in a low-scoring era, Luisetti famously scored 15 points against Long Island University on December 30, 1936, in a 45–31 victory at New York's Madison Square Garden. At the time, each region played a distinct brand of basketball. Many thought East Coast ball—with its countless passes, weaves, and deliberate style—was the proper way to play the game compared to West Coast teams that relied on a faster pace of play and more freedom. As Fox wrote in *Big Leagues,* "Skeptics called it the avalanche system, pell-mell, wild and woolly, racehorse, fire-horse basketball." Stanford and Luisetti fit in with their left coast brethren. Luisetti unleashed his running one-handed shot against Long Island, baffling his foes and simultaneously stunning and delighting the crowd, all while helping Stanford snap LIU's 43-game winning streak. In later years, Luisetti said a player for LIU told him he got lucky the first time he made his one-hander but "didn't say a word when the next one dropped in." Francis J. O'Riley wrote in *The New York Times*, "Some of his shots would have been deemed foolhardy if attempted by any other player, but with Luisetti doing the heaving, these were accepted by the crowd as a matter of course." That crowd consisted of a record 17,623 fans, with many more unable to get into the famous arena. Stanford's six-foot-three Italian star played like that for years out west, but doing it in the media capital changed the game. Not everyone appreciated Luisetti's flamboyant, whirlwind style. A great passer and driver who attacked from all angles, Luisetti played with a flair that was foreign and infuriating to longtime watchers. In addition to the one-handed shot, Luisetti passed behind his back and sometimes hovered in the air on drives, long before the concept of hang time entered the basketball world.

Veteran coach Nat Holman, an early star player in the game's history, said after Luisetti's display, "I'd quit coaching before I'd teach a one-hand shot to win a game. Nobody can convince me a shot that is more a prayer than a shot is the proper way to play the game. There's only one way to shoot—the way we do it in the East. With two hands." Years earlier, Holman complimented the East Coast way of playing basketball, because if players didn't have a wide-open set shot, they resisted firing from a bad angle. Instead, "He throws the ball back to one of his mates, and the play is started over again." Those days were dying, a fact Luisetti brought home in New York.

Luisetti learned his move on the playground, battling older, taller players (a theme that appears over and over with the early shooters). Stanford coach John Bunn encouraged his trendsetting star, confident the results—

Luisetti set numerous scoring records and was the first college player to get 50 points in a game—spoke louder than the complaints. The LIU game turned Luisetti into a celebrity. Two years later he starred with a young Betty Grable in *Campus Confessions*, a "comical campus romance" about a dean's son who becomes a basketball player but struggles academically and . . . well, it failed to win an Oscar.

But the fame he garnered from the one-handed shot outlasted movie stardom. Others shot one-handers earlier, but as Kuska explained, no one popularized it like Luisetti, who took full advantage of the Big Apple stage. But he didn't create the jump shot. When Christgau researched his book, he telephoned Luisetti, who died in 2002 at the age of eighty-six. "I never had a jump shot," Luisetti told Christgau. "I admired the jump shot, but I never had one. I had the running one-hander, and that was it." Throughout his life, Luisetti downplayed the idea that he invented the jump shot, sometimes in stories that carried headlines crediting him with that very accomplishment. He once explained, "I didn't jump and shoot at the height of my jump, the way they do now. I'd let the ball go right near my face; I'd push and shoot, off my fingertips."

So if it wasn't Luisetti, who were some of the first classic jump shooters? The Naismith Memorial Basketball Hall of Fame unofficially recognizes Glenn Roberts as one of the originators, although in a profile of the star from tiny Emory & Henry, the Hall notes, "There is of course no absolute proof that Glenn Roberts was the first person to shoot the jump shot. He was simply the first to use the new shot to reach such high-scoring exploits." Meanwhile, the NCAA's archives honor John Cooper, a star forward for Missouri in the early 1930s.

Both Roberts and Cooper grew up in rural settings—Roberts in Virginia, Cooper in Kentucky. Roberts lived on a farm with his folks and six brothers and attended school in Pound, a town of 150. He graduated from high school in 1931 and led his team to a state championship. In college at Emory & Henry—a small Methodist school in the Virginia mountains—Roberts averaged more than 19 points per game, in an era when many teams barely scored 20 points. He often outscored opponents by himself. At college, he played in an indoor gym for the first time. His hometown of Pound only had outdoor courts. Mud made it impossible to dribble on these courts and missed shots at one hoop in town meant the ball disappeared down an incline. Accuracy became a necessity. The youngsters from Pound played what could be considered a version of the classic playground game 21—when it's every man for himself and whoever gets the ball tries to score against the other players, no matter if it's seven guys playing or twelve. Roberts once explained, "By starting to jump as high in the air as I could after recovering the ball and releasing the ball after jumping out of reach of the others, I got the ball to the basket consistently, and before long I even succeeded in making some baskets without depending entirely on luck."

Roberts didn't care if he found himself surrounded by defenders. One writer noted, "He pivots, leaps high, wheels about in midair and cuts the darned thing loose. Swish!" Writers admired his ability to take contact while hanging in the air. Six-foot-four and a husky 180 pounds, he "moved like a flyweight" and always kept his composure. This all happened before the elimination of the center jump after every basket, a primary reason basketball scores usually resided somewhere in the 20s or 30s. Competing mostly against smaller colleges, Roberts maintained his scoring feats whenever Emory & Henry faced tougher competition. Following a 28–25 loss against Richmond, the newspaper complimented Roberts, a "remarkable center who leads all of the state's scorers by so many points it's no contest. Nor could the Spiders stop him last night. They gave him lots of personal attention but the rangy pivoteer, who has his strange backward, half turning shot down almost to perfection, scored a dozen points."

At that same time, Cooper excelled at the University of Missouri, after spending his childhood shooting on dirt courts, just like Roberts. He took his early shots on a hoop attached to the side of a Kentucky smokehouse. Cooper discovered the jump shot by accident—he went up to catch a pass, didn't see anyone to dish off to, and fired the ball at the basket. This led to the development of his twisting jumper. Putting down roots in the lane—the three-second rule didn't exist, much to the anger of Cooper's opponents—Cooper faked his shot for several seconds while keeping his feet planted before finally leaping with his back to the basket, turning, and shooting over the frustrated defender. A crafty, patient scorer, the six-foot

Cooper employed the maneuver perfectly against bigger foes. Cooper re-called, "My feet left the hardcourt surface, and it felt good. It was free and natural, and I knew I had discovered something." Cooper's college coach, George Edwards, didn't know exactly what Cooper discovered, but he knew it didn't belong on a basketball court—not at the University of Missouri. Edwards benched Cooper, telling him he should never shoot it again. Cooper listened at first, but he eventually brought it back, and Edwards relented. The impact was obvious—his average of nearly 11 points per game in 1932 was the school's highest for nearly twenty years, which says a lot about the style of play back then, but also about the effectiveness of his jumper, launched with two hands above his head.

If George Edwards didn't know what to make of Cooper's jump shot, opposing coaches didn't have a clue about stopping it. A newspaper story detailed Cooper's "perfect shot, a jump and half-turn that brings Cooper around facing the basket. He takes passes near the free throw circle with his back to the goal, jumps up and does an about-face in midair, scoring with the orthodox push." His coach, now fully behind the jump shot, said "legal defense against the shot is virtually impossible." An Associated Press reporter called it a "bewildering jump-turn shot." Kansas's Phog Allen—a first-rate basketball scientist, a man who learned the game from Naismith—spoke about the unfairness of the shot.

In one 1932 game, Missouri defeated Kansas 26–22, just another ex-ample of the low-scoring affairs that dominated that era. Cooper scored 18 of Missouri's points, his jump shot giving him a distinct offensive edge. The game desperately needed ten players on the court with John Cooper's advanced skills. At one point in the game, Missouri guards held the ball for 11 minutes, passing it back and forth. Bored Kansas players sprawled out on the floor, either from sleepiness or in protest, while angry fans fired pennies onto the court.

Roberts's and Cooper's basketball greatness was limited to college, al-though Roberts spent one season with the Akron Firestone Non-Skids. Owing to his work as a researcher, instructor, and author of textbooks on the subject, Cooper is sometimes called the father of biomechanics—which goes nicely with being one of the fathers of the jump shot. Coo-per's long career in academics had Indiana naming its kinesiology graduate program after him. Roberts and Cooper didn't know about each other during their playing days. Perhaps if they had, they could have become pen pals, writing about the difficulties of being different—and so much better—than everyone else on the court. But they weren't alone in not realizing jump shooting comrades played in different parts of the country. None of the early shooters knew about the others. And many of the shooters didn't realize anyone cared about their talents until nearly sixty years after they first left the ground.

John Christgau's *Origins of the Jump Shot* was published in 1999. But the inspiration for the book came nearly five decades earlier, when Christgau played high school basketball in Minneapolis and watched a college basketball star named Myer "Whitey" Skoog leap off the court, kick his legs back, and take a jump shot, all while the crazed crowd at University of Minnesota games shouted "Fire, Myer! Fire, Myer!" At his high school practice, Christgau tried the shot. Teammates asked him why the hell he kicked his legs out. He didn't know, only that Whitey Skoog did it. Fascinated by Skoog and the jump shot, Christgau developed a lifelong love of the game, and of the jumper. He played for a high school coach who discouraged the shot—the man wanted players shooting a set shot . . . underhanded, using two hands and sweeping one leg back. "How would I get a shot off shooting down there?" Christgau says. "That's when I began to become independent." Following high school, Christgau bounced around, attending Gustavus Adolphus and then the University of Minnesota, where he tried out for the team, but was one of the last players cut. Instead he left the Midwest, went into the service, and later played ball at San Francisco State. Christgau remained on the West Coast, teaching, then writing. He lives in Belmont, California, in a home filled with floor-to-ceiling bookshelves, and enjoys a picturesque if uneasy view. The house sits along the San Andreas Fault, and a few days before my visit fires raged after a large earthquake in nearby Napa County.

Christgau was on the mend during our visit. Earlier in 2014 a dangerous infection forced doctors to amputate his left leg below the knee. He showed me the "peg leg" he hobbled around on. After he got sick, doctors warned him the infection could travel to his heart and kill him. "You cut my leg off or I die? Yeah, take my leg off. I don't need it anymore. My jumper went a long time ago."

The eighty-year-old Christgau primarily writes about sports and history (everything from a game between the Lakers and Globetrotters to a history of the P-51 Mustang fighter plane), although he's eager to write a comic novel. But the jump shot book generates the most interest from readers—in the form of compliments and challenges. Christgau happily corresponds, though he doesn't partake in quarrels. "The people I covered were early jump shooters, and they were early within certain regions. The earliest? Who knows?" And their lives were interesting beyond just their on-court accomplishments. Christgau profiled eight players who fit his criteria, men whose exploits he could document through newspapers or by talking to others who observed the pioneers taking a jump shot: His idol Skoog, John Burton from California, East Coast star Bud Palmer, Indiana's Dave Minor, Kentucky's Joe Fulks, Johnny Adams from Arkansas, North Carolina's Belus Smawley, and Wyoming's Kenny Sailors.

Three of the players—Burton, Fulks, and Adams—all carried the same nickname: Jumpin'. It was not a golden era for creative nicknames in basketball, with the only debate being whether they were known as Jumpin' or Jumping Joes and Johns.

Christgau interviewed six of the eight players—Adams and Fulks had died decades earlier. In Christgau's descriptions of each player's first shots, the sense of wonder jumps off the page, as if the shooters were six miles off the ground instead of six inches. Relying on instinct and creativity, they broke free from the invisible shackles that kept players grounded. An accomplished ski jumper, Skoog left the floor in a northern Minnesota high school game in 1944, and "it was as if he had lifted off the lip of a ski jump, and now there was that familiar Boom Lake sensation of both triple-speed and slow motion. At the edge of his vision, instead of the wood palings of the ski jump flying by, he could see the colorful trails left by streaking jerseys. Meanwhile, despite the noise in Memorial Hall, he was in a cocoon of silence and floating."

Beyond the on-court similarities, Christgau found off-court connections among his eight players, threads he believes played a role in their upward paths. "The family structure. Three or four or maybe even five of them came from single-parent families," he says. "Three or four or five of them had absolutely devout mothers who just hammered religion into them." On the court the players enjoyed freedom and the opportunity to express themselves in ways that were impossible at home or in church, because while coaches weren't always the biggest fans of the jump shot, at least the good Lord never delivered a ruling against it.

Several players expressed amazement when Christgau contacted them, surprised anyone remembered their contributions. Even Bud Palmer's accomplishments were largely forgotten, although he remained famous in another field. Palmer's jump shot carried him to a great career at Princeton and then to the captaincy of the New York Knicks. Following his playing days, he became a respected broadcaster, calling everything from hockey to golf to basketball to ice skating. Christgau interviewed Palmer in Colorado, where the two talked about Bud's dynamic jumper, which he preferred shooting off of the dribble and which so confused his first coach with the Knicks, it led to a temporary banishment to the bench.

Dave Minor, an Indiana high school star and one of the first black players signed by the NBA, was "thrilled to have somebody suddenly recognize him after forty years." Minor starred at Froebel High School in Gary, Indiana. He was known as "The Wheelhorse of Steel City" (now that's a nickname!). After Minor unleashed his jump shot off of two feet, some of his teammates tried following his lead. One game the fed-up Froebel coach called timeout and, Christgau wrote, screamed at the players, "No one shoot that damn shot! Except Minor. The rest of you shoot two-handed." Minor led Froebel to the 1941 state semifinals in Indiana, including a victory over powerful South Bend Central, coached by John Wooden.

One of my favorite chapters focused on John Burton. Longtime coach Pete Newell credited Burton with taking the first jump shot on the West Coast. He attended San Francisco State, becoming the first player in school history to score 1,000 points. Burton only went about five-nine, 135

pounds, but he became a scoring sensation thanks to the jump shot. He had come a long way from his reaction the first time he took one, when, Christgau revealed, Burton asked himself, "What the hell did I do?" But Burton also thought, "I'm a little man in a big man's game. But now I have a shot nobody can touch." He was thrilled to talk to Christgau about his youth, family, and his jumper, which he shot, Christgau wrote, with the ball "centered off his nose before he dropped away his left hand and released the shot."

My own hunt for the early jump shooters wasn't as dramatic as Christgau's, though I discovered intriguing tales. I also learned the danger Christgau detailed in his book, when his own search "threatened to expand with infinite possibilities." Every deep dive into a newspaper's archive turned up new information about early shooters and early forms. I read about a man named Charles Diven Jr., who competed for the University of Pennsylvania in the 1930s and was nicknamed "the Chucker," a nod to his given name but also, perhaps, his playing style. In 1938, Penn's student newspaper wrote about the five-foot-eight, 135-pound Diven discovering "a new shot for his repertoire, a leaping two-handed overhead try from the vicinity of the foul line." *Sports Illustrated* featured Diven in an item, but he didn't recall if he made a jump shot—even early chuckers fired so many shots the details blurred. When reading about Hank Luisetti's one-handed shot I stumbled upon players who utilized that form before him. Conley Watts came out of Utah with a one-hander in the early 1930s, ignoring his coach's advice to use two hands. And in 1985, sportswriter Bill Jauss wrote about Blair "Barney" Varnes, an Illinois judge who "is widely credited with inventing basketball's one-hand shot." Varnes shot it in the 1920s, including on a Chicago team owned by George Halas. One peer told Jauss, "I was accustomed to seeing the underhand shot or the two-hand set shot. Here was Blair Varnes with his one-hand shot, way ahead of his time."

And then there's a Massachusetts man named Alvin "Jimmie" James. News accounts most often called him Jimmie James, but sometimes papers spelled his first name Jimmy—sometimes it was spelled both ways, on the same crowded sports page, about three columns apart. A 1975 feature in

Lowell's *The Sunday Sun* profiled James, who was "in his 70s" at the time. The headline read, "Westford man 'invented' one-handed jump shot," and included a picture of James in a plaid jacket, with large-rimmed glasses, surrounded by memorabilia and photos of his basketball teams. James supposedly took his shot while starring at Springfield College in 1928, when he led the team to an 18–2 record. According to the *Sun*, James displayed his jump shot during a game that season on March 2, when Springfield faced Connecticut. A Springfield paper back in 1928 supposedly wrote:

> *The Connecticut crowd was amazed to see Jimmie James' one-hand jump shot. After the game the coach of the Conn. team commented that he had never seen this before and that he thought the day might come when more basketball players would be shooting the same way. At this point one could say without fear of contradiction that Jimmie James is the greatest basketball player in Springfield history to date.*

One could have said that and it might have even been true. But those lines do little to solve the mystery of Jimmie James's shot. The problems with the 1975 story looking back on James's career begin with the date of the game. Springfield did finish its 1928 season against Connecticut, but the game took place on February 29, a Wednesday, not March 2. It was a leap year, and accounts of the game appeared in the March 1 papers. I read through four of the Springfield newspapers from that time and didn't find the above description of James's shot. He scored 18 points in a 39–36 defeat, but none of the accounts mentioned him shocking the crowd with his leaping exploits. That doesn't mean it didn't happen; it just means it didn't happen on March 2, and I couldn't find the story. James likely had some newspaper clippings when the *Sun* wrote about him in 1975, and perhaps the papers noted his jump shot exploits a few days after the game in question. The *Sun* story quoted a letter from former Harvard player Ken Dorn, who said James was "years ahead of his time." A one-handed shot would qualify. So maybe James was the first or maybe it was like Luisetti—not a real jump shot, but a real one-hander. There could be a dozen more players like Jimmie James out there, their stories hidden away in card-

board boxes filled with old newspaper clippings, their contributions as forgotten as the exact form of their innovative shot.

One reason it's impossible to find the first jump shooter is that many of the players back then didn't get the type of media coverage their peers received. Many of the jump shot pioneers were white players, but we know about them because some record exists of their accomplishments, even if they're just brief mentions in newspapers. Gena Caponi-Tabery wrote in *Jump for Joy: Jazz, Basketball, and Black Culture in 1930s America*, "The jump shot was an anomaly on the courts where white players dominated, which makes its path there easier to trace." Black players were taking jump shots too, but "with spotty reporting from the weekly black press and no reporting on white sports pages, there remains very little historical record of the way black ballplayers actually played the game." Caponi-Tabery tells the story of Cumberland Posey, who played for Penn State and Duquesne. In the late 1930s, two decades after his playing days, Posey reminisced about his career and wrote in *The Pittsburgh Courier* about winning a game with a "one hand shot through the nets." Caponi-Tabery asks, "Was it a dunk? Or was it a one-handed shot similar to Hank Luisetti's? Was it a jump shot? We can't know."

Author John Edgar Wideman tackled the black-white issue in his one-of-a-kind style in his book *Hoop Roots*. Wideman played ball at Penn. He made the All-Ivy team—a good scorer, tough under the boards. One chapter in *Hoop Roots* is titled "Who Invented the Jump Shot (A Fable)." A short story, the piece cuts between the present—a seminar room hosting an academic crowd of stiffs investigating who invented the jumper—and an imagined night inside a car in 1927 with the early Harlem Globetrotters. (The story ends with the lynching of a black man who inadvertently invented CPR while trying to save a young white girl—the crowd leaving the Globetrotters game misinterpreted the lifesaving measure.) But early in the tale, Wideman writes:

> *The title of the session let the cat out of the bag. It broadcast two faulty*
> *assumptions—that at some particular moment in time the jump shot*

*appeared, new and as fully formed as Athena popping from the head
of Zeus, and that a single individual deserved credit for originating
the jump shot. "Who Invented the Jump Shot" would be a pissing contest. And guess who will win. Not my perpetually outnumbered,
outvoted, outgunned side. Huh-uh. No way. My colleagues of the
Euro persuasion will claim one of their own, a white college kid on
such and such a night, in such and such an obscure arena, proved
by such and such musty, dusty documents, launched the first jump
shot.*

Let's go back to Wendell Smith—Jackie Robinson confidant, famous
journalist, baseball star at West Virginia State, and, possibly, an early jump
shooter. I could not find any mention of Smith taking a jumper in the
newspapers that covered West Virginia State in the 1930s. Although
that doesn't mean much; as Caponi-Tabery wrote, it's not like the media
delivered dispatches from every contest. Smith wrote a few stories about
the school's basketball team for *The Pittsburgh Courier* after he left college,
but he never scribbled a first-person essay describing what it was like
shooting a jump shot. But maybe he was just humble. I wrote to John
Simms, West Virginia State's sports information director, to see if
the school had any information about Smith's basketball days. Smith
belongs to the school's Hall of Fame, but for his baseball exploits. The
archives didn't hold any old reports about his jump shot. Simms and his
staff discovered a couple of team pictures with Smith on the hoops team—
the stylish coach in an overcoat, the players somber and serious, posing
outside the school, all of them wearing the kneepads that were common
back then. I'm not sure where UPI got the information about Smith's jump
shot that it included in his obituary. And if he did shoot a one-hander, he
didn't necessarily introduce it to the game.

But he certainly could have been part of the jump shot fraternity. Players introduced the jumper to their towns or cities or regions, but getting
the game to absorb the shot, to embed it in the normal flow so it wasn't a
freakish occurrence, took years. Writers ridiculed the shot and coaches
fought against it, fearful of losing control. Think about what a jump
shooter could do: Create. No more would teams rely solely on intricate,

highly structured patterns that featured weaves, nonstop player movement, and constant passing. Coaches designed those motion offenses, and players followed the rules, until the jumper gave individuals more power. The jump shot was changing the game, but it had not yet revolutionized it, not when many of the original shooters didn't even know about each other. But one terrible event brought jump shooters from across the country together: World War II.

CHAPTER

TWO

JUMP SHOOTING MARINES

Without World War II, maybe the jump shot still would have made its way around the country, becoming a national phenomenon instead of a regional rarity. But it would have taken a few more years, perhaps more than a decade for this to happen. Because there was no television coverage, the early jump shooters were unaware of one another, oblivious to their aerial partners spread across the country. The war brought players from across the United States together, and those soldiers competed on military bases in every service branch. Now, often for the first time, the early jump shooters spotted their own kind, each deployment bringing them in contact with others like them. They realized they weren't alone in pushing against the game's tradition. No longer did a player from the South think he was the only player shooting a jumper, not when he played ball on a base with a player from the West who possessed the same shot. And other players in the military, who never saw any jump shots back home, also watched this new breed of shooter. When their time in the service was done, they returned home with tales of the jump shot and, in some cases, a desire to rise off the court themselves. Bob Kuska said the military became a "mixing bowl" of the styles played throughout the country. He interviewed a high school coach in Washington, D.C., who told him, "The first time I saw a jump shot I was in the Navy. We were out in Hawaii. We had this interservices squad. We played a team from the West Coast. Man, those guys were jumping up in the air. We didn't know what the hell to do."

No one kicked ass in those days—on the basketball court and in more important endeavors—like the Marines. Specifically, the basketball team stationed at the Marine Corps base in San Diego. Before sending the men off to war, the Marines cobbled together a strong outfit with some of the top players in the country and faced everyone from college squads to industrial league teams. In 1943–44, the Leathernecks went undefeated in 35 games, clubbing teams such as Southern Cal and a strong Dow Chemical. Two of the great early jump shooters led the Marines—Joe Fulks and Kenny Sailors. In a 1943 preview of the USC game in the military branch's newspaper *Marine Corps Chevron*—enlisted personnel got first dibs on 2,000 available seats—the writer lauded Fulks for "pouring points through the hemp at the rate of 10.7 per game." With two of the great scorers of their time on the team, the success of the Marines surprised no one. Fulks eventually became the first NBA player to dominate with the jump shot, while Sailors, who also enjoyed a fine professional career at stops like Cleveland, Providence, and Denver after the war, is considered the creator of the modern jump shot.

Writers sometimes called Fulks the Babe Ruth of basketball. The same way Ruth was so far ahead of his time in the 1920s, so Fulks was in the 1940s. His prime only lasted a few seasons, during a time when few people cared about the NBA, years when it wasn't even actually called the NBA.

Born in 1921, Fulks came from Birmingham, Kentucky, in the western part of the state where poverty reigned. The iron-mining industry had died long before, but moonshiners still plied their trade. As a kid, John Christgau wrote, Fulks watched the Birmingham high school team—with fewer than twenty-five boys in the school—make it to the state tournament, led by a player named Robert Goheen who shot a variation of a jump shot with two hands and later returned to the school to coach Fulks and teach him his favorite trick. Because they often couldn't afford real basketballs, Fulks and his buddies stuffed socks with toilet paper, sawdust, or other materials they scrounged up. Fulks developed into a standout player in high school, but he wouldn't finish his career in Birmingham. A TVA-constructed dam on the Tennessee River submerged Birmingham and surrounding towns, eventually erasing them from existence. With the town facing extinction, Fulks's father, Leonard, moved the family, with the promise of work luring him to Kuttawa, a Kentucky river town about fifteen miles from Birmingham. Town elders found a job for Leonard because they wanted his son on the basketball team, which sparked controversy and accusations of recruiting, likely from opposing schools who weren't pleased with facing the powerful team Kuttawa constructed with Fulks and other transfers. Fulks ignored the distractions and turmoil—which included hearings about his eligibility in front of the Kentucky State High School Athletic Association—and proved unstoppable, thanks to his turnaround jump shot. Christgau notes the shot did not involve Fulks getting much air, writing, "As for his jumping ability, western Kentucky observers laughed and said with characteristic drawls that you could hardly slip a shingle under his feet on his jump shot."

After carrying Kuttawa to the state tournament, Fulks put together a nice college career at Murray State in western Kentucky before joining the Marines, becoming the leading scorer on the perfect team at the San Diego base. When the Marines defeated Dow for their 31st consecutive victory, Fulks scored 14. Sailors added 13, the two jump shot artists combining to outscore their opponent in a 43–25 game. A few weeks earlier the Marines crushed USC 46–26 behind Fulks's 12 points.

Following his service days, Fulks made his professional debut with the Philadelphia Warriors in 1946, in the first season of the Basketball Association of America, one of two early pro leagues that became the NBA. (The BAA merged with the National Basketball League to form the NBA. The NBA—the name—didn't exist until the 1949–50 season, but for historical records, the NBA begins with that initial season of the BAA. With only eleven franchises at the outset, no shot clock, shaky and shady league finances, and players who worked summer jobs when the season ended, professional basketball—which was also segregated at the time—barely resembled today's game.) Standing six-four or six-five, depending on his posture, the stoop-shouldered Fulks became a sensation. He shot with his arms extended over his head, making him impossible to stop without fouling. One writer marveled, "Big and agile, Fulks makes most of his points from the pivot post. He has a one-hand jump shot that is difficult to stop. He leaps into the air from around the foul circle and, having unusual control of the ball while doing it, he zips in the points." With the corkscrew shot, he made "basket tossing look as easy as eating strawberry shortcake." Another scribe believed he owned "the shooting eye of a well-drilled bluegrass feudist." When he led the Warriors past Chicago for the 1947 BAA title, the losing Stags were said to suffer from a case of "the Joe Fulks jitters." Often shooting without seeing the rim, Fulks sometimes shifted the ball to a different hand at the last second before releasing it. Defenders were better off playing off of him—the closer they guarded him, the better he shot.

His big hands and long fingers gave him great control. He was usually expressionless as he went about his business, and opponents thought they could stop him by getting him angry. It sometimes worked, but more often defenders felt helpless. "Since I most want to win," he said, "I shoot. The trouble with a lot of good basketball players is that they don't shoot enough." Fulks's jumper—which writers thought he converted more than shots near the basket—awed his teammates, perhaps to Philadelphia's detriment. One scout said the other Warriors fed Fulks too much, passing up layups for his longer jump shots. That didn't bother Fulks. Great shooters ooze confidence, and Fulks was the first NBA player whose confidence was obvious to anyone in the stands, a player who believed it was better to shoot with someone on him than pass to an open teammate who couldn't get the ball anywhere close to the rim.

In his younger days, Christgau himself watched Fulks play against the Lakers when the Warriors traveled to Minneapolis. "We all thought he was a joke," he says. "He shot every time he got the damn ball. He was shot crazy, and at the time I don't think we fully appreciated just what he was doing. He was such a negative figure in our heads that I never looked close enough back then to see this guy had a jump shot."

That jumper destroyed scoring records. As a twenty-five-year-old rookie, he averaged 23.2 points and led the Warriors to the BAA championship. The next-best scorer averaged 16.8. (More evidence of how different the game was then: Bob Feerick led the league in shooting at 40 percent. Fulks was 12th at 30.5. But thanks to the jump shot, those percentages went up and up.) With his playoff total, Fulks broke the record for most points by a pro—as far as anyone could tell. In that era, tracking records proved difficult. Writers believed he broke a mark set by Willie Kummer, who scored 1,404 points in an old pro league way back in 1912.

The greatest night of Fulks's basketball life came on February 10, 1949. With only 1,500 fans in attendance in Philadelphia—a winter storm and looming transit strike were partially to blame—Fulks set a single-game record with 63 points against the Indianapolis Jets. That season Fulks engaged in a battle for the BAA scoring title with George Mikan. No longer was Fulks chasing the records of pro players from a prehistoric era. Here he went against the NBA's original dominant big man, a player who changed the game. It was Mikan's overwhelming physical dominance against Jumpin' Joe's jump shot, the giant against the contortionist. On January 27, 1949, an AP story headlined "Mikan Issued Challenge by Joe Fulks" detailed the fight. The story began, "Look out Mr. Mikan. Joe Fulks is shooting your way and he has a 'record' look in his eye."

"Tell George Mikan he isn't the scoring champion of the Basketball Association of America yet," Fulks said.

Three days later, Mikan gave his rebuttal, scoring a BAA single-game record 48 points against Washington. But that simply gave Fulks another mark to shoot for—and shoot down. He had 49 points by the end of the third quarter against Indianapolis on his record-setting night. Fulks added 14 more in the fourth to finish with an astonishing 63, hitting shots with one and two hands, from all angles. The 63 points came on 27 field goals—and an arm-exhausting 56 attempts. Even the Indianapolis players cheered. Jets coach Burl Friddle rushed over to shake Fulks's hand at the end of the game. Fulks told reporters he didn't know how many points he was scoring in the game, but "I knew I was hitting good and that something was going on by the way the crowd kept yelling, 'Shoot, shoot.'"

In the end, Mikan won the scoring war—he averaged 28.3 to Fulks's 26—but NBA people remembered Joe's one-night explosion long after everyone forgot who finished first in average. A decade later, the *Sporting News* twice wrote pieces speculating about the chances of anyone breaking Fulks's mark. In 1957, Red Auerbach said the record "may last another nine or ninety years. Unless Wilt Chamberlain comes into our league and some night gets red-hot against a team that is off its game. And Wilt's teammates would have to be feeding the ball to him." Two years later, on the tenth anniversary of Fulks scoring 63, the *Sporting News* revisited the record, noting more than 2,500 NBA games had gone by without anyone breaking it. The record fell a few months later, when Elgin Baylor scored 64 points in November 1959. Baylor later broke his own mark with 71 points. Then Wilt Chamberlain came into the league and fulfilled Auerbach's prophecy with 100 points.

Fulks slowed down after 1949, the third straight year he averaged more than 22 points. He retired after the 1954 season—when he averaged 2.5 points. His accomplishments faded from view, and his records disappeared, followed by memories of his innovation. Fulks moved back to Kentucky and worked in a prison. He died in 1976, murdered by Greg Bannister, the twenty-four-year-old son of the woman he was seeing at the time. A night of drinking concluded with a 3:30 A.M. argument about a pistol, a verbal fight that ended when Bannister killed Fulks with a shotgun blast to the neck. Fulks was fifty-four. Bannister claimed the gun went off by accident, and he only served a few years in prison. Christgau wrote that no one from the Warriors attended Fulks's funeral, and he was "buried quietly in a small cemetery just outside the Marshall County town of Briensburg, Kentucky, alongside the relocated graves of the dead from Old Birmingham."

By the time I started working on my book, almost all of the early jump shot stars were gone. Glenn Roberts died in 1980, John Cooper in 2010 at the age of ninety-eight. Belus Smawley, Bud Palmer, John Burton—the early pioneers died years or decades earlier. But Kenny Sailors, the man whose jumper most closely resembled the modern jump shot, was still alive, still (relatively) healthy, and still happy to tell his story to anyone who asked. Because he was one of the last of the old jumping guard, more people started talking with Sailors about his impact on the game, especially after the turn of the century. Profiles appeared in New York papers and in *Sports Illustrated* as writers and fans hunted for information about a player whose exploits were forgotten for many years, a shooter whose jumper from 1946 resembled those of players from 1976 or 1996.

Kenny's hearing was failing during our chat in October 2014, but that was about the only physical limitation in his life—aside from the normal aches experienced by anyone three months away from a ninety-fourth birthday. His mind remained sharp, his humor intact.

Genetics helped Sailors make his remarkable discovery. If he stood just a few inches taller than his brother, Bud, when they were teens, Kenny wouldn't have had reason to leave his feet for a jump shot. The Sailors boys lived with their mom on a Wyoming farm. Bud, five years older, was a star athlete in school. He also stood six-foot-five, which in 1934 made him about seven or eight inches taller than his little brother. Christgau wrote, "How could these two be brothers? Side by side they looked unrelated, the one tall and deliberate in each of his movements, the other darting and spontaneous." Bud and Kenny played ball against each other at their farm, going one-on-one whenever they weren't busy with crops or feeding the animals. They played on a homemade backboard attached to a windmill. Whenever they went at it, Bud, in the tradition of all older brothers, refused to take it easy on Kenny.

Finally, one day in 1934, Kenny dribbled up to Bud. Instead of attempting a set shot Bud could easily block, Kenny jumped and shot. His brother, Christgau recounted, would later "laugh deeply and insist that his little brother's first awkward jump shot hadn't reached the backboard, or even hit the windmill." But the result of the shot ultimately didn't matter—the fact that Kenny even took it was the amazing part. Standing there together, both of them realized that shot was something special. Bud told him, "Kenny, that's a good shot, if you can develop it."

"I started because of that big old bum of a brother of mine," Kenny tells me with a laugh. "Then I became aware of the fact that I could shoot this shot over just about anybody no matter how tall they were."

Bud played at the University of Wyoming and the family moved to Laramie, while Kenny continued to carry the lessons from that day in 1934 with him for the rest of his life. Kenny followed his brother to Wyoming, carrying the Cowboys to great heights behind his jump shot. His jumper didn't just benefit his own point total—when he went in the air Sailors often dumped passes off to teammates for easy shots if a defender turned toward the basket for a rebound. His dribbling skills set up all of that. Defenders didn't know if he would pass or hit a pull-up jumper, a basic move in today's game, but a startling one in the early 1940s.

Wyoming arrived in New York City for the 1943 NCAA tournament as a relative unknown entity—even after Hank Luisetti opened the eyes of the Eastern basketball world with his performance in 1936, people still doubted teams and players from the West. Western teams were sideshows—curiosities, but not contenders. When the Cowboys came to New York, famous Madison Square Garden promoter Ned Irish liked dressing them up for the big-city folk, putting the basketball players in cowboy hats and boots, just another part of the never-ending Times Square show. But once the Cowboys actually took the court, they schooled the East Coast powers and impressed the basketball establishment— thanks to their jump shooting star. Wyoming defeated Georgetown 46– 34 to win the NCAA championship. Sailors, the only player in double figures, scored 16. The Cowboys weren't finished. At the time the NCAA Tournament was nothing like it is today. The National Invitation Tournament (NIT)—which is now only a consolation prize for teams who can't make the NCAA event—had been around longer and ruled the college landscape, thanks to the glamour that came with hosting the event in New York City (the 1943 NCAA tourney was the first time it was held in NYC). St. John's won the NIT title in 1943 and met Wyoming two nights after the Cowboys' victory over Georgetown in a battle for bragging rights. Against another East Coast power, Wyoming won 52–47. Sailors scored 11 in that game, but the points hardly showed his overall impact.

His overall floor game surprised and thrilled. Writers struggled to describe what they watched. Normal words didn't suffice, not even the overblown verbiage common in the newspapers of the day. Sports reporters expanded their worldview to find comparisons. The *Sporting News* raved after the St. John's game, "He put on a two-night display that was a combination of Sonja Henie in an ice ballet, Sid Luckman quarterbacking and forward-passing and Leopold Stokowski directing a symphony orchestra. One expert left the Garden the night of April 1, exclaiming, 'Sailors is just out of this world.'" The rapturous coverage in the *Sporting News* didn't end with that passage. "He dribbled up the floor with one hand, using the other to direct his teammates. If it can be said a man has 'beautiful' hands, Sailors has them. Once at quarter-court, he used those hands like a virtuoso, and the Wyoming team responded to every move. Sailors was like a coach in action." He riddled defenses with his passes, disrupted the opposition's offense with his steals, and "sank those amazing one-handed shots from quarter-court."

Sailors grew to about five-ten, meaning he still required the jump shot against bigger opponents. He remembers only having a jump shot blocked once—and that was from behind, never by a defender in front. The jump shot he took a decade earlier had evolved, but still hadn't been refined. But the victory over St. John's was the last he'd play in college for two seasons. Having enlisted in the Marines, Sailors contributed to the unbeaten team at the San Diego base before going overseas. But even in the middle of the war, "I thought about the shot," Kenny says. "Even in the foxhole over there in the South Pacific. I thought about it a lot."

When the fighting ended, Sailors returned to Wyoming to complete his college eligibility. By 1946, the shot he first took in 1934 had been fine-tuned and finely crafted. "The last thing I had to work out," he says, "was to stop my forward movement and go straight up. I was getting called for the offensive foul" as he dribbled and went forward on his shot. Sailors now dazzled with the jump shot that would look more familiar to today's fans, although players are constantly refining and the game's always evolving. Partially influenced by Luisetti, whom he watched in a tournament, Sailors kept his left hand to the side on the one-hander. "I brought the ball up on the right side, and then I held the ball over my head, about four inches over my head and just out in front a little ways." He shot it at "the apex" of his jump, a leap that was about 36 inches by some estimates, his dribble creating a type of rocket fuel he used to launch himself off the court.

Wyoming didn't win another national championship after Sailors returned, but his jump shot became immortalized. In another game at Madison Square Garden, Sailors took one of his normal jump shots in a game against Long Island University. A few weeks later, *Life* magazine published a picture of Sailors in the air, firing the shot. It's a great picture, perfectly timed. At the top of the key, Sailors pulls up for a jumper. The

LIU defender raises his right arm, but Sailors hovers high above. Nothing impedes his view of the basket. His feet look at least two feet off the ground. The other players—teammates and defenders—stare up, waiting for him to release the ball. They look like they're watching someone play a different sport. No one else rose off the floor, not with this grace, honed with twelve years of practice. The picture depicts Sailors at the top of his leap, the ball in his right hand, the guide hand positioned perfectly on the side, right before he'd drop it away. It was a routine jumper for Sailors, but having the photographer capture it at that perfect moment froze it in time, preserved it for history—and changed the future.

Life sold millions of copies and all of those readers saw Kenny Sailors taking a jump shot. Kids saw it and tried duplicating the play. The picture in *Life* became the most famous photo of Sailors's jump shot, but it wasn't the only photo that displayed his rare skill. Pictures from a February 1943 game against Brigham Young University show Sailors in midair, firing the one-handed shot as he rises. *The New York Times* ran one after Wyoming's victory over St. John's in 1943 at MSG. It captures Sailors shooting from the wing, perhaps eyeing a bank shot with all eyes again on him as he flies above everyone else. The cameras also filmed Sailors shooting in February 1946, a month after the picture in *Life*, against Utah State. In that one Sailors looks even higher off the ground, perhaps achieving that 36-inch vertical. A Utah State defender trails Sailors but can do nothing to stop him. In the picture it looks like he's trying to shove Sailors on the leg, perhaps hoping to disrupt the form that is practically textbook—despite no one knowing what picture-perfect jumpers actually looked like for another decade.

Unlike many of his fellow innovators, Sailors received mostly encouragement from his coaches when it came to his jump shot. It was only when Sailors became a pro that he encountered resistance. Dutch Dehnert coached Sailors during Kenny's first year with the BAA's Cleveland Rebels. The old coach didn't approve of Sailors's dribbling abilities, and his reaction to the one-handed jump shot was even more extreme. Kenny remembers Dehnert saying, "Sailors, where'd yuze get that leapin' one-hander?" Dehnert benched Sailors, although he offered to teach him the two-handed set shot. At five-foot-ten, Sailors knew he'd have no chance of getting a shot off in the pros if he remained rooted to the floor and shot with two hands from his chest or above his head. One of Kenny's team-mates told him his days in the BAA would end soon if he didn't get a chance to play that first season. Sailors went to the Cleveland GM and asked for a trade. But Dehnert was already on his way out. Under new coach Roy Clifford, who had no issue with Sailors taking his jump shot, Kenny started and averaged nearly 10 points a game as a rookie, and the young guard's career finally took off.

Kenny's best seasons came in 1949 and 1950, when he averaged 15.8 and 17.3 points per game. The fourth-leading scorer in the league in 1950 when he played for Denver, Sailors also averaged four assists, a high number for the era. Many considered him the best ball-handler in the league—people said he was faster going up the court with the drib-ble than most people were running without the ball.

Sailors retired after the 1951 season. He worked as an outdoors guide in Wyoming, dabbled in politics, and then moved to Alaska in 1965, where he lived with his family for nearly thirty-five years. He coached in Alaska, but he was off the basketball grid. His role in the jump shot received little publicity in the Lower 48. Others got their credit while Kenny lived in the wilderness. But in 1990, Sailors went to the Final Four in Denver and spoke at an event about his old jump shot. He was next to the UNLV team, the eventual national champions. "These kids were looking at me, this little runt, like, how did he ever invent the jump shot?"

Sailors didn't think about being a pioneer when he actually was one. Only years after he retired did people talk with him about it. Only decades later did they recognize his spot in basketball history and how, like so many others from small towns or rural areas, something that came naturally to him seemed like such an unnatural creation. "Eventu-ally I think that got through to me that I was a little bit different with my jump shot," he says. "That it was something that hadn't been used like that before."

Agreeing with historians, Sailors says it's impossible to find the first person who took a jump shot—and he never claimed to be that player. But he was proud of his groundbreaking role as the early owner of a more modern jumper. Others acknowledged his importance, like legendary coaches Ray Meyer, Bobby Knight, and Joe Lapchick. The early jump shooters could fit on an evolutionary chart, like the one that tracks the progress of humans. On the far left, the set shooters. Players like John Cooper and Glenn Roberts with their twisting two-handers make an appearance, as does Luisetti in 1936 with his running one-hander. A bit farther down on the right we find Kenny Sailors and his one-hander, shooting the ball off the dribble, shooting at the top of his jump.

The game continued to evolve—it never stops, of course. But as the 1950s arrived, the jump shot finally found a home in basketball, more than sixty years after Naismith invented the game. It arrived on—and off—the hands of John Cooper, Glenn Roberts, John Burton, Wendell Smith, Bud Palmer, Conley Watts, Joe Fulks, and Dave Minor. And, of course, Kenny Sailors. All of those players—and many more—changed the game they loved. But many others hated the shot. They knew with the arrival of the jump shot, basketball would never be the same.

THREE

1950s: NAYSAYERS AND TRENDSETTERS

Basketball fans divided into two camps by the end of the 1950s: those who thought the jump shot made the game exciting, and those who believed it destroyed the game. Call it the Joan Crawford School of Basketball against the Grizzled Columnist Camp. And for anyone who appreciates basketball today and enjoys watching athletes soar to the rim or rise for 24-foot jump shots, just know this: You're siding with Team Mommie Dearest.

In 1957, *Sports Illustrated* asked coaches, celebrities, and divas, "Do you think that old-time, low-scoring basketball—before Hank Luisetti popularized the one-hand jump shot—was a better and more interesting game than it is today?" It seems like a trick question—who wants low-scoring basketball?—but the answers varied. Jerry Berns, a partner in the famous New York City restaurant 21, said, "Yes. Overofficiating has taken the defense out of basketball. The game has changed into a contest of basket shooting—you shoot and then I shoot. The team with the most accurate shooters usually wins. The only defense against the jump shot is considered a foul by the officials." But Joan Crawford—a "movie star" from "West Los Angeles," as *SI* noted—believed, "From the spectator's point of view, today's game is much better, although much harder on the players. It particularly appeals to young boys the ages of my children. Any sport that appeals as strongly to spectators as basketball does today will be a success, but it must be full of action."

Not everyone shared the *Queen Bee* star's view, and they couldn't keep up with the changing game. By the latter part of the decade, players like Joe Fulks and Kenny Sailors had company in their jump shooting fraternity. More players dedicated themselves to learning the jump shot, and as more of them perfected it, scores shot upward, along with the excitement level. But some people thought the jump shot was unfair, that it robbed the game of teamwork. Now a single player dribbled and launched from anywhere. Those early fears of coaches like Nat Holman had come true. In 1956, future Pulitzer Prize winner Jimmy Breslin worked as a humble syndicated sportswriter, and he wanted to know what happened to the game he loved:

> What's ruining basketball is the jump shot. Nearly all your big scorers have it. It's impossible to stop, and the way the modern player can shoot, you wonder how he ever misses. . . . The jump shot today is the bread and butter part of basketball. It requires no team effort. Just a guy who can jump and shoot with made-in-a-laboratory accuracy.
>
> It has driven basketball's main feature almost out of the game. That's the give-and-go play, the sport's version of the hit and run. In the pros, only Philadelphia and New York practice it to any extent. Around the rest of the nation, the jump shot does it all.

Newspaper Enterprise Association sports editor Harry Grayson took a cue from his colleague and drinking buddy Breslin and delivered his own criticisms in 1957. Under the headline "Jump Shot Leaves Fans Yawning as Cage Scores Mount," Grayson wrote:

> Basketball today, however, is doing a fine job of killing itself. One word sums it up: repetition. Shoot and score, then throw it up again—that's all they're doing except in isolated cases from coast to coast. The jump shot is the big thing. Kids are coming out today with deadly eyes. They get any place near the basket and up they go. . . .
>
> The jump shot is virtually impossible to block. The combatant today in college basketball hardly knows basketball at all. All his practice time is put into this shot. By the time he is a varsity starter, he is a tall, quick-moving boy who can shoot. That is fine, but where

does it leave the game? The jump shot has stripped all technique
from the sport. Give-and-go used to be the heart of the contest. . . .
The rules should be changed, however, so that plays requiring bas-
ketball sense would count more than just a jump shot.

Basketball still toiled in the background of the American sports scene
at this time, and stories like those from Grayson and Breslin didn't help,
especially because they criticized the play that made the game better. Baseball ruled, and boxing captivated the country more than Naismith's
game. Football got its greatest game ever with the Colts beating the
Giants in the 1958 NFL title game in New York, a contest that captured the
public's imagination and kick-started a league that became a cultural jug-
gernaut while basketball struggled for positive attention from the media
and fans. But several players used the jump shot during those years to
change basketball, winning championships and breaking scoring records,
although the sport's stars didn't receive nearly the accolades of athletes
like Mickey Mantle in baseball or Johnny Unitas in football. Inventions like the 24-second shot clock also played a crucial role in changing
the game's very nature, forcing teams to attack on offense for an entire
game and creating a demand for players who could create scoring opportunities instead of holding the ball in a stall. The 1950s was the first decade
since the jump shot's introduction in the 1930s when multiple players
turned the jumper from a freak shot into an unstoppable one. Men like
Bob Pettit, Bill Sharman, Frank Selvy, George Yardley, and Paul Arizin
made their mark on the '50s and beyond—and all the while, fans, writers, coaches, and even some fellow players still looked on in disbelief, or
maybe even envy, at the aerial shooting skills. Years before people believed
the dunk wrecked the game, many thought the same thing of the jump
shot. Thankfully for the game's future, progress won. The jump shot in
the 1950s still set people apart, but it didn't isolate them like it did when
coaches refused to let so many players use it in the 1930s and '40s.

In the same *Sports Illustrated* issue that quoted Crawford, Arizin—a
star with the Philadelphia Warriors—told the magazine, "I like this game
fine. Can you imagine what would happen if we went back to the old style
of play? The action would be so much slower that it would be almost

boring for the fans, and our crowds would be cut in half. Sure it's harder on the players. So what? We like it."

Arizin, who went by the nickname Pitchin' Paul—you really expected a nickname that didn't start with the letter P?—didn't even play basketball in high school and he attended Villanova mainly to study chemistry. At the time he also played ball in independent leagues around Philly. In the Catholic League, the teams competed on a narrow floor primarily used for dances, which made Arizin slip often when he attempted hooks or drives. "So one day I began jumping and shooting," he said. "I didn't slip, and I was having success with the shots. So you see it was more a matter of expediency than anything else." With the jump shot in his arsenal, Arizin drew the attention of Villanova coach Al Severance, who'd heard about a player with a Joe Fulks–like jumper. He brought Arizin onto the team. Four years later, the player who couldn't make his high school team earned All-American status and led the nation in scoring.

Like Sailors and Fulks, Arizin served in the Marines and dominated on military teams, just as he did at Villanova and in the NBA, where he won two scoring championships and a title with Philadelphia. Arizin bridged the gap between the early stars of the NBA and the players who set records that would never be matched. Pitchin' Paul played with Jumpin' Joe at the end of Fulks's career and teamed with Wilt Chamberlain during the early stages of the Big Dipper's reign. Before joining forces with Chamberlain, Arizin's jump shot helped him dethrone George Mikan as the NBA's top scorer, averaging 25.4 in 1952, and ending Mikan's three-year run as the league's leader.

The great jump shooters of the era led the NBA in scoring for four years in a row in the late 1950s, until Chamberlain entered the league and made a mockery of all previous records. Pettit—the first great big man jump shooter—led in 1956, followed by Arizin. In 1958, Yardley, playing for Detroit, became the first NBA player with 2,000 points in a season, thanks to his jumper, until Pettit again broke that record the following year, with his own accurate shot 15 to 18 feet from the basket.

These scoring eruptions—and how they occurred—bothered more people than just some observers and cranky writers. Even one of the greatest players of the 1950s didn't like the jump shot's influence. Bob Cousy became the NBA's first magician, a passing wizard who won six championships. He used flash, but also fundamentals, a showman who entertained while winning. If anyone would appreciate the impact of the jump shot, you would think it would be a revolutionary like Cousy. But in March 1963, a month before his final game for the Celtics, Cousy complained to the Associated Press, "I think the jump shot is the worst thing that has happened to basketball in ten years." Cousy's objections? "Any time you can do something on the ground, it's better," he said, sounding very much like a coach who would have enjoyed benching Kenny Sailors or Bud Palmer. "Once you leave the ground, you've committed yourself." Jump shot critics discouraged players from flying into the air because they feared the indecision that came when someone left their feet. They feared the bad passes from players who jumped with no clear plan of what they'd do in the air. Staying grounded meant fewer mistakes. It was simply a safer way to play the game, if not as exciting.

Cousy spent a decade playing in the same backcourt with one of the great jump shooters of the era, making his objections sound even stranger. How could anyone who watched Bill Sharman shoot for so many years think the jumper was anything but great?

"Sharman was the standard in the 1950s," longtime Boston sportswriter Bob Ryan tells me. "In terms of a technician, he was the standard." A great all-around athlete, Sharman also played professional baseball—he was on the bench for Brooklyn when Bobby Thomson hit his game-winning homer to win the 1951 pennant for the New York Giants. On the basketball court, with his jump shot, Sharman broke Hank Luisetti's college conference scoring records.

NBA official Lou Eisenstein once said Sharman's jumper is "so accurate he disillusions the other team." Consider his teammate Cousy among the disillusioned. He hated playing Sharman in H-O-R-S-E. Forget trick shots—Sharman kept it simple. "H-O-R-S-E is supposed to be fun," Cousy said, "but he was so businesslike. He'd just keep taking 15-footers and never miss."

Off the court, Sharman became known as the consummate gentleman, appreciated for the handwritten notes he sent players, fans, and writers. On the court? "He was a mean, tough bastard," according to

Cousy. And another Celtics teammate, Tommy Heinsohn, said, "Sharman was the most tenacious son of a bitch I ever met." Sharman once broke the nose of a player named Andy Phillip, and the six-one Celtics star sent the six-nine Noble Jorgensen into the stands with a right-hand punch.

With the jump shot growing in popularity in the 1950s, basketball began learning about the concept of "gunners," players whose shooting skills made them stand out on the court. Shooters often had reputations as players who cared only about stats instead of the team. Sharman, that tenacious son of a bitch, pushed back against that idea. He told the *Sporting News* in 1958, "I don't like to hear fans say that this guy or that guy is a gunner . . . and only thinks of himself . . . or that all shooters are selfish players. I'm a shooter. A shooter is paid to shoot. He helps the team by shooting. Take [Bill] Russell's case. Does he say to one of us, 'I'll take this rebound and you take the next?' Certainly not. He gets all the rebounds he can. That's his job and he's helping the team." In his role as a shooter, Sharman averaged more than 20 points three times for the Celtics as Boston won four titles over his final five seasons.

Following Sharman's retirement, he earned respect as one of the great teachers of the game, especially of the jump shot. His 1965 book, *Sharman on Basketball Shooting*, became a seminal text. His old backcourt partner Cousy—who worried about the jump shot's influence—still contributed to the classic book, writing in the introduction, "Rebounding, passing and defense may be important aspects of basketball. But the entire game still revolves around putting the ball through the hole. If he can't impress the coach with his shooting, the average player never gets a chance to display his other talents." Sharman himself wrote:

There are many reasons given why shooters in basketball today are much better scorers than a few years back. Better coaching, improved equipment, rule changes, improved methods of employing the fast break, and so on, are all major factors, but I feel sure most coaches will agree that the development and utilization of the jump shot has been the greatest factor for the increase in scoring. It has left the defensive man a great burden.

Coaches had no idea how to alleviate that burden for beleaguered defenders once more players shot the jumper. Joe Lapchick told *The New York Times* in 1954, "The way these fellows shoot nowadays, it's impossible to stop them. . . . When you get a fellow coming down court at full speed and still able to throw in a one-hander from off his ear, what can you do? And then by way of making things worse, we now have the jump shot, the greatest of all basketball inventions."

The two great scorers in college basketball in 1954, Frank Selvy and Bob Pettit, showed the power of the greatest of all basketball inventions. Before 1954, no Division I college player averaged more than 30 points in a season. Pettit however—the six-foot-nine forward at LSU—averaged 31.4 in '54. His mark, good enough to break records any other year, didn't even come close to leading the country. Instead Selvy, the six-foot-three guard at Furman, pumped in an unheard-of 41.7 points per game. (And here's the jump shot's effect: In twenty-six seasons after Selvy and Pettit broke the magical 30-point-per-game mark, twenty-five of the nation's leading scorers averaged at least 30.)

As pros Pettit far surpassed Selvy, becoming a ten-time member of the first-team All-NBA squad. At the time of Pettit's retirement in 1965, no one had scored more points in NBA history. He's considered one of the all-time great power forwards, a position he practically invented, a six-foot-nine force who shot like a little man and rebounded with the ferocity of a seven-footer. Selvy, meanwhile, became best known for missing a shot at the end of the seventh game of the 1962 NBA Finals. But at Furman, Selvy put up numbers that remained unmatched until Pete Maravich strolled onto the LSU campus more than a decade later.

A Corbin, Kentucky, native, Selvy grew up playing on a dirt court overlooking a hill. As with old Glenn Roberts in his small town, accuracy proved crucial for Corbin kids, who didn't want to chase wayward shots that bounced down the hill. He dreamed of playing for the University of Kentucky, but coach Adolph Rupp thought Selvy was too small. By the time he left Corbin, he'd grown to his full height, and Rupp now wanted him. Instead Selvy stuck with Furman in South Carolina, a struggling program he made into a respectable one. Furman won three games his freshman year—when he didn't play varsity—but 18 as a sophomore when he made his debut.

He made history on February 13, 1954, when he became the only Division I player to score 100 points, in a 149–95 romp over Newberry. Several carloads of people from Corbin made the 250-mile trip to Greenville, South Carolina, for the game, including Selvy's mother, who had never before seen her son play in college. Just 2 minutes, 43 seconds into the game, Newberry guard Bob Bailey fouled out, proving the difficulty of defending the great jump shooters. Selvy had 94 points with 30 seconds left in the game, scored four quick points, and hit a long shot near midcourt at the buzzer to reach the magical 100-point mark. One teammate said the final shot "was one of his rainbows, and it went right through the basket like dust."

A few weeks before his 100-point game, Selvy commented on Bevo Francis, an NAIA player at tiny Rio Grande College who scored 113 points in one game. "Good gosh, it's almost unbelievable," Selvy said. "I could never make that many a game." He was right, but not by much. For the game, he hit an incredible 41 of 66 from the floor and 18 of 22 free throws, his 100 points breaking the record of 73. In the decades that followed, Selvy downplayed his accomplishment on that rainy night in front of 4,000 people. "I'm not real proud of that," he said. "If it was against a real good team I would've been."

Tireless and prolific, Selvy played every minute of every game as a senior and appeared on every All-American team, along with Pettit, who put up big numbers—if not triple figures—at Louisiana State. The two phenoms eventually ended up on the same NBA team. Baltimore picked Selvy with the first choice in the 1954 draft, while the Milwaukee Hawks took Pettit with the second selection. Selvy impressed early in Baltimore, but the franchise folded after fourteen games, and the league dispersed the players to other teams. Selvy partnered with Pettit in Milwaukee, temporarily creating a high-scoring tandem. Three years before Harry Grayson decried the jumper's influence on basketball, the veteran writer described Selvy's various shots in an admiring 1954 column:

Hurried, he goes into the air, bends his body backward. The shot gets off—heads for the ceiling. This trajectory removes any possibility of a defender blocking it. As it soars upward it begins to float softly at the basket. It has no spin at all, and when the ball comes down it searches for every break the rim can give it. When Selvy has time, he advances at the basket slowly, then goes up for the same type of shot with either hand, except his body is laid out for the basket. The minute he gets the ball off, he starts a wild scramble for the basket and a possible rebound.

Selvy's best season in the NBA came in his first year. He averaged 19 a game, but never again scored more than 14.7, as he served as a journeyman with the Hawks—who relocated to St. Louis—the Knicks, Nationals, and Lakers. Early in his second season, Selvy was called into the service. He missed nearly two seasons and lost his touch. While in the military with an armored unit, he suffered a knee injury that bothered him the rest of his career. "Maybe it was a form of arthritis," he said, "but I don't know for sure. And the doctors can't find anything wrong with me, but to this day my knee stays sore all the time and swells up. It's hurt my jump shot for sure." In 1958, Selvy admitted he used the set shot more because of his injuries. When Selvy lost his jump shot, he lost his edge.

Unlike Selvy, Pettit never struggled. The only time he didn't make the All-NBA first team came in his final year—when he made the second team. Pettit's jump shot advanced the game. Following Pettit's MVP season in 1959, his St. Louis teammate Ed Macauley said, "He's the perfect player for today's style of basketball. The big man with the grace of the little fella. He has great strength and great spring and he can shoot."

The son of a Louisiana sheriff, Pettit primarily played with his back to the basket at LSU, but upon entering the NBA he fully developed his jump shot. In a column he wrote in 1963 about his college days, he noted how he once took "nothing but hook shots, but now I had to develop new shots from the corner. So I started concentrating on the shot that has revolutionized the game of basketball—the jump shot." By the time Pettit penned the newspaper story, the jump shot had become "virtually the only shot I attempt, usually from just about any sensible position on the court."

He also beefed up, from 205 pounds to 230, in the process becoming one of the first players to use weight training. Coaches believed weights hurt a player's shot, but Pettit proved them wrong. Pettit's Hawks were the only team that kept the Celtics from capturing ten straight championships, instead of the eight they did win in a row. But before the Hawks interrupted the Boston dynasty, they first played victim when the Celtics started their run of dominance. Boston defeated St. Louis in seven grueling games in the 1957 Finals, giving Cousy and Bill Russell the first of many titles to come.

That series came down to Game 7 in Boston. Whether caught up in the pressure of the moment or because of the St. Louis defense, the Hall of Fame backcourt of Sharman and Cousy endured atrocious shooting days. Sharman made only three of 20 shots. Cousy was even worse, making two of 20. But rookie Tommy Heinsohn scored 37 points and grabbed 23 rebounds, and fellow rookie Russell went for 19 points and 32 boards. The teams exchanged the lead 38 times in Game 7, with Pettit leading St. Louis with 39 points and 19 rebounds. He also drained two clutch free throws to send the game into overtime. In the second overtime, the Celtics took a 125–123 lead with two seconds left. St. Louis player-coach Alex Hannum devised a brilliant, ridiculous strategy for the final seconds. The Hawks had to go the length of the court. On the inbounds pass, he would throw the ball all the way down the court, off the backboard, and into the hands of a Hawks player for a last-second shot. Remarkably, everything worked—except the final shot. Hannum's line drive traveled down the court. It hit off the backboard with tremendous force. Pettit grabbed the ball near the basket, but didn't have control as he shot it. The ball rolled around the rim and fell off. Boston claimed its first world title.

The Celtics enjoyed the type of stability Pettit only dreamed about with his own franchise. When Russell won his eleven world championships, he played for two coaches: Red Auerbach and himself, when he served as player-coach. Pettit played for ten coaches in eleven seasons, and even served as a player-coach himself in 1962, going 4–2. Blame St. Louis owner Ben Kerner, a friend of Pettit's who did his star no favors with his impatience. Despite the chaos that always surrounded the franchise, Pettit kept St. Louis in contention. And in 1958, he delivered one of the great games in NBA history as he brought a title to St. Louis. With the Hawks again engaged in a tight series against Boston—a bad ankle hobbled Russell—Pettit scored 50 points in Game 6 to lead St. Louis to a 110–109 win and a 4–2 victory. It was the only time from 1957 to 1966 Boston didn't win the Finals. Pettit exploded in the fourth quarter, scoring 19 of St. Louis's final 21 points, including a tip-in that gave the Hawks a three-point lead with 16 seconds left. In the winning locker room, Pettit sat exhausted, his head in his hands for thirty minutes. "I have only a vague memory of the last few minutes of the game," he said, "and I have no idea how I got to the dressing room."

Despite performances like that Game 7 effort, Pettit didn't always receive the publicity he deserved. He played in the same city as Stan "The Man" Musial, and in St. Louis, not even a basketball immortal could ever surpass a baseball god. With Russell winning titles, and Chamberlain breaking the scoring records Pettit once held, his accomplishments got overshadowed. For his career Pettit averaged 26.4 points and 16.2 boards. In two different seasons he played with broken bones in his arm, one time during that 1957 season when he fractured the ulna bone in his left forearm after a hard foul by Boston's goon-for-hire, Jim Loscutoff. Columnist Jim Murray said Pettit was the equivalent of a singles hitter, making it difficult for him to earn attention. "Instead of cracking it like a Baylor, he just jumps and swishes through a 12-to-15 footer. He hasn't made a basket in years farther than he could spit." George Yardley was the first to score 2,000 points in a season, but Murray explained that when it came to prolific scoring campaigns Pettit "was the first to make them commonplace."

Pettit retired in 1965 at the age of thirty-two, leaving the NBA to work in a bank. In his eleven seasons he changed basketball, proving the jump shot was the ultimate weapon for all players, not just guards. That's what so many, whether columnists or legends, feared.

To Joan Crawford's enjoyment, the game moved forward, thanks to the players rising vertically. But before venturing into the 1960s, to an era when jump shots by Jerry West, Oscar Robertson, and Sam Jones decided games controlled by Russell and Chamberlain, it's worth first taking a look at everything that goes into a jump shot, the weapon that people hated before they accepted it and celebrated it. A jump shot isn't just influenced by practice and talent. It's about the tools of the trade—the basket, ball, and gym. The jump shot has come a long way since its creation, but only because everything else about the game has also changed since Naismith put up his peach baskets.

FOUR

BUCKETS, BALLS, AND SHOOTER'S GYMS

I spent most of my time as a kid shooting at the park in the southern Minnesota town of Janesville, population 2,000. I had a neighbor who had also put a basket on his garage, and I knocked in shots that hit the brown door and removed the paint. But the basket that lingers in my memory was at my grandpa's farm. Grandpa Fury liked to say, "Give me five shooters on the court, and I'll beat anyone." Grandpa was born in 1913, died in 1999 and, except for his days in the Army in World War II when he fought in Europe and won a Silver Star, he spent his life in southwestern Minnesota. He never coached basketball. But his beliefs about shooters put him about thirty years ahead of his time.

During every visit to my grandpa's, I would spend hours out at the basket, on the uneven grass surface that made dribbling nearly impossible. The fan-shaped white backboard was attached right to the white barn. Shooting along the baseline—not that it had a real baseline—meant adjusting to the roof. The basket's tight rim rarely produced friendly bounces. In the winter, when the net froze, it captured the basketball. Rain brought mud, and that completely eliminated dribbling. This was not a court to learn ball-handling; it was a court to learn shooting. I spent hours and hours there shooting with my dad or playing two-on-two games with my uncles Mike and Jerry. Grandpa sometimes watched, standing off to the side in his blue overalls. He wouldn't say much, didn't pick a favorite, although a grandson always knows who his grandpa wants to win. As I got older I liked to show off a bit, moving farther and farther away from the basket, closer to the lake the basket overlooked, closer to the other barns, closer to the long gravel driveway. Every so often—maybe once a year—he'd say, "Nice shot, Fury," or give a smile when another jump shot found the net. Then he walked away. The dominant image I have of my grandpa in my head isn't from his final days in hospice or even him sitting at the kitchen table smoking his pipe and talking about farming, baseball, or how Republicans were ruining the world. I picture him outside, watching me shoot, perhaps thinking if things worked out in a different way and he coached and directed that mythical team of five shooters, I'd be a good one to have on it. I spent more time at my city park and the neighbor's than I did on Grandpa's basket—he lived two hours away—but the farm hoop is the basket that helped me fall in love with the game.

All shooters have one of those, whether it's inside an old high school gym or attached to an old barn. A basket draws kids to the game and later conjures memories of moments spent shooting alone or of games in front of packed houses. Basketball started with James Naismith's peach baskets, and more than a century later there's still no greater thrill than watching a shot go through the bucket.

I imagine it's been like that since the very first game in basketball history, in December 1891, when Naismith organized eighteen players for a game in Springfield, Massachusetts. That was probably also the first time a player complained about a basket, ball, rim, net, floor, gym, or lighting affecting a shot. No record exists of anyone officially whining about the surroundings or the equipment, but one truth that has existed since the inception of basketball was surely true that first day as well: A shooter's never at fault when he misses. Based on the results of that first outing—a 1–0 game; the only basket was most likely made by William Chase, supposedly from 25 feet—players probably directed nothing but complaints at Naismith in the moments after the game. "What's with the lighting in this place?" "It's impossible to get a good bounce on those ridiculous peach baskets." "No one can shoot with that lump you call a ball."

Shooting is about mechanics and confidence—the order of importance varies, according to different shooters. But a jump shot isn't just about the skills and self-esteem of the offensive player or the savvy and quickness of a defender. Everything on a court, whether it's outside in a park with a chain net or inside a 50,000-seat dome, affects a shooter. And that was the case even when players took set shots and never dreamed of ever leaving the floor.

This might seem strange considering basketball is always played on a 10-foot rim. Games happen away from the elements. This isn't baseball, where quirks exclusive to parks—fast turf in the infield, giant walls in left, deep fences in center—play a crucial role. This isn't football, where the weather—rain in Tampa, wind in Chicago, snow in Green Bay—alters games. Yet the color of the seats behind the baskets or the length of the nets can throw off or help a shooter. The phrase "shooter's gym" best sums up the idea that certain places are more receptive to the jump shot, but even those two words don't reveal the entire role played by outside influences or, in this case, inside ones.

Great shooters make more excuses than anyone. That's what confidence does—it convinces players they bear little responsibility for missed shots. The greats are so attuned to every nuance, they notice when anything is off, or are creative enough to pretend something is wrong even when it's not. It's like Tiger Woods leading the field in complaining about the speed of the greens.

When Michael Jordan returned to the NBA in 1995, humbled by baseball, hungry to reign again in basketball, he struggled in his new home, the United Center in Chicago. He established scoring records from the confines of Chicago Stadium until retiring in 1993. Jordan always appreciated the old NBA arenas. He loved shooting in the Boston Garden, where he set the playoff scoring record, and every trip to New York's Madison Square Garden became a one-man show. In April 1995, as he prepared to play in Boston Garden, he said, "I like the old buildings. I know they don't have the facilities or the skyboxes. I understand that this is a business. But I miss them. Boston Garden is the last place you can really call a stadium. It is the last place that feels like a home to me." The old stadiums provided an intimacy the modern-day palaces with their massive suites couldn't match, with everyone in the crowd seemingly right atop the court. The buildings were louder, messier, dirtier, smaller, but they also worked better for shooters. Those old stadiums had fewer distractions in the crowd, fewer people milling around, perhaps some looser rims. Jordan always felt fans were too far away in Chicago's new arena. "A lot of it is shooting background. You like to have the fans close. I still don't feel right at the United Center."

Jordan first made terrorist-like threats about his new home after Orlando eliminated the Bulls in 1995. Even into 1997, after Jordan led the Bulls to the best record in NBA history in 1996, he took digs at the new digs. "I still want to blow it up. I haven't fallen in love with it yet." Management declined the modest remodeling suggestion, and the team won three straight titles. Jordan's teammates shared his view. One of the best shooters ever—Steve Kerr—voiced his concerns. "In Miami, the ball kind of sticks to the glass, then comes off the way it is supposed to. Here, it slides. Maybe it's because of the ice under the floor, or because it is usually very dry in here." These are the concerns of a man who has mastered everything else about shooting, but could still pinpoint a problem no one in the stands and very few players would notice. Piling on, Kerr added, "This is the worst gym I have ever shot at."

Shooting is not as easy as the greats make it look. From junior high school to the NBA, these elements affect jump shots: the ball, the gym (gym meaning arena, stadium, dome, cracker box, and everything in between), and the basket. Learning about the jump shot means learning about everything that surrounds shooters, and everything they use.

Start with the ball, even if Naismith didn't. Since the game of basketball hadn't been invented until Naismith organized his pickup affair, an actual basketball didn't exist, either. When William Chase made the only shot in that first game he did it with a soccer ball. A real basketball came about three years later, when Albert Spalding and his company constructed one. Early basketballs resembled modern basketballs only in that they are all members of the ball family. As Robert W. Peterson wrote in *Cages to Jump Shots*, the early ball was originally a "leather-encased pumpkin somewhat larger than today's molded ball, with laces along one side creating a bulge that made shooting and dribbling an adventure." Players received some breaks back then with ball-handling because double-dribbling was originally allowed. But no rule made shooting easier. Original basket-balls "were pretty lumpy," says Dan Touhey, a former Spalding employee who now runs his own company called PSI 91 in, fittingly, Springfield. Early basketballs contained soft spots and bubbles and were not much more than a rubber bladder with leather covering the panels. Seamless basketballs helped, about forty years after the game's invention.

Shooters are touchy when it comes to the ball. Too heavy and it's like shooting a medicine ball; too light and it's like shooting a Ping-Pong ball. Shooters search for a ball that's just right, and it doesn't matter if it's in a game at the Y or the NBA Finals. Basketball science didn't change much after seamless balls for another sixty years, until companies made composite basketballs that are cheaper to produce because the leather is synthetic instead of the real thing. In 2006, the NBA made the dra-matic change from the leather ball to a microfiber composite model. It was a risky move. Spalding worked for nearly a decade on the new ball—the NBA was the last league to use leather. The company promised the ball delivered a superior grip and didn't need breaking in. The ball promised consistency. Instead it created chaos.

In preseason, Shaquille O'Neal said it was like "one of those cheap balls you buy at the toy store, indoor-outdoor balls." Eventually, and fatally for any chance the ball had of sticking around, players said the ball cut their fingers. As proof they displayed bloody digits. Steve Nash wore bandages. Dallas owner Mark Cuban told *Newsweek*, "You should see the hands of the coaches who work with the players. They are far, far worse." The com-plaints about the cuts developed later in the season, as if the ball devel-oped self-awareness and took action against the players, slicing them for their insubordination (there also might have been some exaggeration about the physical damage, since cuts weren't reported at other levels that used the ball). No one was quite sure what caused the cuts, although Nash said the composite ball was "friction-ey," with abrasions developing over time after constant exposure to the ball. By late 2006, Dan Touhey found himself under siege. As vice president of marketing for Spalding at the time, Touhey took all of the calls from reporters, who gleefully detailed the corporate and league debacle. In the ball's defense, scoring went slightly up in the few months it appeared in NBA games, and shooting percentages weren't adversely affected. But the outrage from the players, who felt blindsided by the change, overwhelmed any rational statistics.

Touhey chuckled that he still had "some scars and welts" from the fiasco, although most of those were emotional and weren't physically caused by Spalding's composite ball. At the height of the controversy, as stories about open wounds shared space with game recaps, Touhey spoke with *Newsweek*: "All I can say is that . . . we are working with the NBA on a daily basis to ensure that the product on the floor is the best possible." Finally, on December 11, with the future of the league at stake—or at least the fingers of its players—Commissioner David Stern scrapped the ball and announced the leather ball would return by January 1. The dreaded words "New Coke" described Spalding's new ball, but the company survived, as did Touhey's pride (his departure from Spalding came years later). Eight years after the firestorm, Touhey says, "It was challenging because we really felt like we had a better ball that we made, and today a hundred percent of all high schools and colleges are using a very similar ball. It's only the NBA who's really using a leather ball."

Spalding had mailed a ball to every player months before the season, but Touhey wondered if anyone opened a box. Touhey regrets not having the players more involved in the development of the ball. That was a "huge lesson that I took away," says Touhey, who now spends more time with athletes than he ever did at Spalding. He receives immediate market research from the people who actually use the products for their livelihood. "And because of that, you never want to touch the tools of the trade without getting feedback. Even if there's a fear of change, at least give the player the opportunity to experience that change to the product over and over and over again."

When companies conduct research, basketball players don't always know how to communicate what it is that they want. Maybe the pebbles feel a bit high or it's too hard or too soft or doesn't quite bounce the way it should. Figuring out these sentiments through a questionnaire filled out by players is impossible. "It's so feel-driven," Touhey says, as anyone who's spent five minutes at a pickup game bouncing, squeezing, and shooting six basketballs to find the right one knows. So companies manufacture several basketballs—ones that are "outliers on certain characteristics" like inflation or texture. Then the researchers ask for opinions from players, and they do it by handing them the actual product.

How soft should a ball be on a scale of one to ten, one being the softest?
"Six."

Well, here's a ball the company thinks is a six, dribble it around and see what you think.

"It's trial and error," Touhey says.

The old ABA created the best ball ever for shooters: their red, white, and blue model. Not only did the colors stand out, the ball looked magnificent coming out of the hands of a shooter. It looked great on television—the few times the games appeared on TV. ABA player Gene Littles once said, "As a guard, what I liked about the ABA ball was the color. It was a special feeling to take a long shot and watch those colors rotate in the air and then see the ball with all those colors nestle into the net. It made your heart beat just a little faster when you hit a 25-footer with the ABA ball."

Basketball technology advances, though the basics stay the same. The next frontier includes embedded sensors that measure backspin and arc, among other things. Touhey sees more developments coming with this smart-ball technology. The basketballs will own longer memories than the players, reminding shooters of every make and miss, every brick and swish. Shooting a computer chip doesn't seem as much fun as shooting a red, white, and blue ball. But if it provides shooters with an edge—and does minimal damage to limbs—players will give anything a shot, as long as it gives them a better one.

Players think a lot about where they shoot. Larry Bird devoted 16 of the 259 pages in his autobiography, *Drive,* to arenas. He wrote that even as a kid in Indiana, when he went somewhere to shoot, "The first thing you did when you got there was look at the basket, the rims and the backboards." Much of the chapter focused on specific arenas. New Jersey's Brendan Byrne Arena had "too much open space and too much glare." Bird loved shooting in San Antonio's HemisFair Arena because "the lighting is perfect and you seem to get every roll. I even like the type of basket supports they have. The basket never shakes when you shoot."

So what is a shooter's gym? An arena is a gym. A stadium is a gym. A dome possessing zero charm but filled with 60,000 people is a gym. Basketball players refer to their stages as gyms. For the 2012 Olympics, London constructed a basketball arena with 12,000 seats. After the United States defeated France, Kevin Love complained about the place, "I always feel like a shooter's gym is far more condensed." The London arena—gym—was too spacious.

Confines were once much tighter. Games took place in cages, which is why, even today, basketball players are sometimes called cagers, especially by seventy-seven-year-old former sports editors still working part-time at their old newspaper. The cages went up partly because under original rules, when a ball went into the stands, whichever team reached the ball first gained possession. Today the rule would lead to lawsuits after every game, but even then people saw the problems. So, fences went up on sidelines and baselines, keeping the players caged, and the raging masses on the outside. The cages were originally made out of wire mesh, and later rope netting. As time went by, the cages also kept fans from going after the players—instead they took their cheap shots when the player went against the boundary. *Cages to Jump Shots* author Peterson discovered a newspaper from the 1920s describing the chaos of early pro ball. "Gladiatorial combats of the ancient Romans pale into insignificance compared with the rowdyism rampant among some of the fans and some of the players. . . . The games are not fit places on some occasions to take a lady, certainly not the sort of contest they should like to witness." Cages stuck around until the 1930s, which is probably when the phrase "shooter's cage" went out of style, if it ever existed at all.

Shooters didn't benefit from proper structures, even after the cages went extinct. In his 1937 book, *Better Basketball*, Phog Allen wrote, "Strong, bright lights glaring down from the ceiling directly above the baskets are abominable. When shooting, a player's glance is always upward and the glare from such lights completely demoralizes his scoring technique."

In a shooter's gym, fans sit close to the court, but not too close. The color of the seats affects shooters. Players once complained about L.A.'s Fabulous Forum because the orange and yellow seats threw them off. In the 1991 Finals—a few years before he discovered the joy shooters get from blaming bad games on the arena—Michael Jordan said of The Forum, "I played here in the Olympics when the colors were lime green, so I don't think [the color scheme] has any effect." The old arenas Jordan loved provided intimacy, perhaps because they weren't built for basketball in the first place. Boxing and hockey ruled when places like Chicago Stadium and the Boston Garden opened. As basketball facilities, they proved ideal for most shooters. In Boston Garden, Leigh Montville wrote, "The seats hung over the court, two balconies creating a vertical intimacy that architects of modern arenas somehow cannot seem to find."

Architects do worry about how players shoot in arenas, although skyboxes, suites, and modern entertainment concerns are of more interest. Colleges and pro franchises think more about the citizens who fill the skyboxes than the great shooters who fill the seats. Still, architects do what they can to help, but they often start at a disadvantage because their jobs aren't just about creating ideal homes for shooters. Brad Clark of the firm Populous has worked on several basketball arenas, including Amway Center in Orlando and Georgia Tech's home gym. Clark says other sports complicate an architect's basketball jobs—a multisport facility could be built more with a hockey team in mind. Or an aisle runs center with the basket and people walking up and down end up in the sightline of the shooter. With HDTV, today's buildings have much higher light levels and "a whiter light on the actual floor than a lot of the old hockey barns would have had. A lot of the old buildings had a pretty dim feel to the court." Dim can be good, at some level.

Constructing a perfect shooter's gym from scratch is difficult, because everyone's definition varies. It needs to be small but not too small, light but not too bright. One shooter's dream gym is another's nightmare. "Iconic basketball arenas—in a way," Clark says, "they probably had as much to do with the teams that played in them as it did the building." In other words, a shooter's gym needs shooters. But when even players like Michael Jordan and Larry Bird express favorites, there's something to the theory that some places are built for shooters and some aren't. You know a shooter's gym when you see one—and when you miss your shots or make them.

Stories of improvisation and ingenuity litter the origin tales of many great shooters, from Rick Mount slicing the bottom out of a peanut can and shooting his first baskets on it, to Travis Grant using a five-gallon bucket. Steve Alford threw Ping-Pong balls into a Pringles can as a little boy. Shooters can develop touch—that elusive, hard-to-define quality—on any type of contraption, whether it's a regulation basketball rim, a homemade cylinder, or a throwback peach basket. Although once they do, they become much pickier about where they shoot.

Shooters believe no two baskets are exactly the same. Tight rims can affect a shot, as can the backboard. Even the nets—or lack of them—play a role in how a shooter plays. The basket's always been 10 feet, although ever since Naismith happened to put his peach baskets at that height, people have talked about changing it. This usually stems from concern over the dominance of tall players or the dunk. Raise the hoop and skill will return to the game, some say, apparently not realizing ugly shooting would instead terrorize basketball.

In 1942, Phog Allen said "tall freaks" and "glandular goons" were wrecking the game. Twelve-foot baskets, Allen believed, meant "skyscraper players will be swept off the court. In that case they would be expected to play the game instead of merely standing beneath the baskets as tall towers of defense." Allen was friends with Naismith, but that didn't mean he hesitated when speaking out. "When Doctor Naismith hung his peach baskets 10 feet from the floor half a century ago, he didn't mean that his height would prevail down through the ages. He fixed this height merely because it was comfortable in the low-ceiling YMCA at Springfield, Mass." Allen's ideas failed to gain support. Regrettably, the phrase "glandular goons" also fell out of favor.

Curious about steps that could be taken to blunt the power of the game's tallest towers, the NBA experimented with a 12-foot hoop in a 1954 regular season game, earning the award for most dubious timing. The

Minneapolis Lakers and Milwaukee Hawks played with the new, higher goals shortly before the end of the regular season, as the Lakers—who eventually won the NBA title—hunted a Western Division championship. Despite the game coming at a crucial phase of the season, the NBA believed it was the right time to mess around with one of the most basic parts of the game, all because dominant big men created a type of moral panic usually reserved for people scared that youngsters would indulge in the type of drugs needed to come up with this idea. March 7, 1954, was a *very* strange night in the Minneapolis Auditorium. The game featured other changes, in addition to the higher baskets. As Stew Thornley wrote:

> *The rules for the March 7 game called for no free throws to be shot during the first and third periods. Instead, they would be held "in escrow" and shot at the end of the period. In the first quarter, the free throws were to be totaled and canceled out. (For example, if Minneapolis was entitled to 10 shots and Milwaukee to seven, the Lakers would shoot three.) At the end of the third quarter, all free throws earned would be shot.*

The Lakers won 65–63. The most feared big man at the time, George Mikan, missed his first 12 shots, so it did limit the tall, bespectacled wonder—and everyone else. Lakers coach John Kundla observed, "Nobody could hit the darn thing. The guys who usually couldn't shoot were the ones who hit the most. And the big guys still got the rebound."

If you want to mess with a shooter, don't bother raising the basket two feet—an inch or two up or down does the trick. When the Celtics beat San Antonio in a 1977 playoff game, Louie Dampier, who made the most three-pointers in ABA history before going to the NBA, complained about a worker raising the basket before the game. "We had been warming up for 15 minutes," he explained, "when they brought out their measuring stick, decided the basket was low and they cranked it up slightly. Maybe that's why all our shots were falling short in the first half." It again shows the delicate sensibilities shooters possess. Before that game, Dampier shot tens of thousands of jumpers in his life. His form was as natural to him as his walking gait. Yet a small change in the minutes before the start of the game possibly affected his shot.

While the height stayed the same on baskets, backboards have always changed. Coaches love to tell their players to use the glass, but that literally wasn't always possible—glass backboards didn't gain widespread use for several decades. Instead the boards were made of wood or metal. As with many basketball-related advances, Indiana was ahead of its time. A story in 1926 enthused "glass backboards hanging from the roof of the livestock pavilion at the state fair grounds will enable spectators at the finals of the state high school basketball to see every play. Wooden uprights and wood backboards at previous tournaments have obstructed the view of persons at either end of the court."

Backboards came in different sizes and materials. Wooden rectangular boards, metal fan-shaped boards, glass rectangles. A man named Richard Morey is often credited with inventing the glass backboard. In 1950, a headline in Maine's *Lewiston Evening Journal* read: "Inventor of Glass Backboard Fighting for Job as Teacher." The story noted Morey's "transparent reflector backboard permits arenas to sell hitherto unsalable seats at either end of the court. It is his chief source of income." Perhaps not surprisingly, considering that most every advance in the game annoyed him, except for the mandatory use of jockstraps, Phog Allen hated glass boards. He called them "clearly illegal" in 1942 and could not believe the NCAA would determine a national champion while using them.

A year earlier college coaches fought with the rules committee over the implementation of fan-shaped boards, the kind you might see in a rural town's old elementary school gym that still has a stage bordering the court. The fan-shaped boards were supposed to cut down on the rebounding dominance of big men—again, tall freaks never got any love from the powers-that-be. Coaches wanted the wood rectangles, believing the smaller-shaped fans led to too many "shots missing the basket entirely and thereby results in an exceptional number of outside balls which automatically slow up the game."

Glass boards did, however, help fans in the stands. As basketball became a game where offense finally ruled—thanks, in large part, to the jump shot—these innovations increased the sport's appeal. Not many people cared if they couldn't see the basket in a 26–20 game. But when scores pushed into the 50s, 60s, and far beyond, it became important for the crowd to see where the ball ended up when it left the jump shooter's hands. Debate raged about whether players shot better with the glass boards. One columnist wrote in 1938 that clear glass boards "present a poorer target than does the non-transparent surface, throwing players used to the regular backing way off form. It is reported that large colleges and universities which have used them have shoved them into the [garbage]." Brandeis University lost a game against Belmont Abbey in 1954, a defeat one writer blamed on late afternoon sun rays that "shone right through the glass backboard of the basket for which Brandeis was shooting."

To learn more about backboards, rims, nets, and everything else that goes into a basket, I spoke with Dan Shaw about some of the equipment changes over the years. An engineer, Shaw worked for Spalding for years before starting his own sporting goods company in Utah called Mountain States. In a fascinating story about the basketball rims New York City uses on its playgrounds—they were still made by hand—*The New York Times* described Shaw as an engineer and "expert on the history of basketball rims."

Shaw didn't grow up playing basketball, but he knows everything there is about the equipment used to make a basket. When Shaw watches a game he intently studies the baskets even more than the action, a craftsman looking for signs of weakness or a change in a piece of equipment's normal behavior. Unlike Dan Touhey and the composite ball, Shaw rarely hears complaints about rims. "Some people might say, 'Well, the units are kind of wobbly,' but they're really not." Perception trumps reality for those players or coaches, who want to blame the basket or an outside force for a poor shooting night.

Stiffer NBA rims are one reason, Shaw believes, that some prolific college scorers struggle when they reach the pros. When rims are tested with a tool that measures the elasticity, "The actual assisted reading on an NCAA rim has to be 35 to 50 percent, and people argue as to what it really means. It has to do with the entire system, not just the rim, but the only one you could adjust is the rim. The higher the number, the looser the rim. The looser the rim, the more forgiving it will be for shooters." (In *Hoosiers*, the filmmakers admitted on a commentary to loosening the rims during a famous scene where Jimmy Chitwood drained a series of shots on an outdoor hoop.)

The NCAA uses flex rims, which, Shaw says, "means if you hit it with one pound of pressure, it flexes a little bit. If you hit it with 100 pounds, it flexes a lot. All the rims flex down to 17 degrees." But in the pros, "It stays perfectly horizontal until someone puts 200 pounds of pressure on it." A college shooter hitting the front of the rim will get it to flex just a bit, giving his shot a better chance to fall. "If you hit an NBA rim in exactly the same spot, exactly the same angle, the rim doesn't move, and the ball bounces out." Over the years, coaches tried manipulating practice rims to help their shooters in games. When Loyola of Chicago won the 1963 title and made history with four black starters, reporters noted the 15-inch rims the team used in practices. Loyola coach George Ireland discovered an innovation by a South Dakota man named Paul Marschalls, who trimmed the 18-inch rim down to 15. Ireland figured if his players could make shots on the smaller rims, the larger ones should have been easy. "I don't know where he makes these things," Ireland said. "Maybe in his basement, but I liked the idea right off. It has made us a better shooting team."

Shaw also designed nets for the NBA, even though "I didn't know anything about nets when I started it." The shell of a net is nylon, but the top half is supposed to be stiff so it doesn't flip up and hang under the rim. The bottom half needs flexibility, so the ball slows down when it comes through it. "Basically what I ended up with was monofilament in both parts," Shaw says. "I had braided monofilaments and then I took the braids and braided them together for a top part. In the bottom part I just used the same monofilament but I didn't braid it at all so it was still very flexible." Unfortunately, the design takes away from the thrill of flipping a net on a swish and leaving it hanging on the rim, the ultimate proof for a player he hit the perfect jump shot, especially when it occurs during a game and the action stops while officials fix the stuck cords, giving the crowd time to appreciate the purity of the disruptive shot. When former Indiana star Steve Alford practiced as a kid, he never left a shooting session until he flipped the net. On rare occasions it can still happen with the newer net, as overuse sometimes makes the cords more flexible. But for the most part, at least in this case, technology has robbed shooters of a thrill known only to those who make a perfect shot.

The net on the basket out at Grandpa Fury's farm rarely hung up on the rim, although not because of a lack of swishes. The stiffness of the net, exposed to the prairie weather, prevented it from flipping. That feature didn't prevent me from wearing out the basket. I remember shooting under the summer sun and into the winter wind, alone and with Grandpa watching. Those mental images will remain vivid, long after I lose the physical ability to consistently make a jump shot.

One day baskets might be 12 feet high, and a basketball might be made out of an entirely different material that emerges from a lab. But one thing will never change: Those who can hit their shots from deep will always remember the basket where they changed from a mere player into a true shooter.

FIVE

1960s: BIG SHOTS, BIG MEN

Giants ruled basketball in the 1960s. Blessed by genetics, these were not the talentless glandular goons Phog Allen feared, not when they displayed offensive and defensive skills that made their size only one part of their greatness. Wilt Chamberlain and Bill Russell towered over the entire decade, one with unmatched scoring and rebounding, the other with rebounding and defense. From 1957 to 1973, either Russell or Chamberlain appeared in every NBA Finals but one. The only year one of them didn't make the Finals, Kareem Abdul-Jabbar led Milwaukee to the championship in 1971. The iconic plays from that era remain Wilt's finger-rolls and fadeaways, Russell's blocks and outlets, and Kareem's dunks and—when the establishment took that away from him through absurd legislation—the skyhook that gave defenders nightmares for twenty years.

But the jump shot, and the players who used it to carve out Hall of Fame careers in the shadows of mountains, played a vital role. And in a handful of cases—a miss here, a make there, a lucky roll, an unlucky bounce—jump shots defined the legacies of the greatest players of the 1960s, including the giants who battled for supremacy.

Four players—Oscar Robertson, Jerry West, Sam Jones, and Hal Greer—became four of the greatest shooters of all time during the years of Russell and Chamberlain. Those four guards monopolized the All-NBA Team backcourts in the 1960s, with immortals West and Robertson controlling the first team, and the other two a notch below. With West and Robertson setting records, it was easy to overlook Greer and Jones. But each of the four great guards of that era played starring roles in some of the most important moments in the NBA, games that changed basketball history. Key figures in the game's evolution, these players grew the game's popularity. As great as Russell and Chamberlain were, it was harder to identify with the two towering figures. But on the playground, everyone could be Oscar or Jerry. All four players starred with the jump shot—West rising off the dribble; Robertson faking and shooting; Greer a midrange maestro; and Jones off the glass. A few shots and games altered seasons and legacies, fairly or unfairly. All of the games involved Robertson, Jones, Greer, or West. And all involved the jump shot.

SAM JONES: WINNER, BANK SHOT ARTIST

By the time his Celtics career ended in 1969, two numbers defined Jones: His 9–0 record in Game 7s, and his 27.1 points per game average in those games. It was an unexpected career for a player the Celtics knew nothing about when they acquired him. Jones grew up in segregated North Carolina. For years as an adult he never went to movies because of the memories from his childhood, when blacks had to sit in the balcony at the theater. After high school Jones stayed home, attending North Carolina College. Red Auerbach took him in the 1957 draft despite never watching Jones play in school. The Celtics leader put his faith in the recommendation of former Wake Forest coach Bones McKinney, who raved about Jones. When the Celtics drafted him, Jones was "a little mad, a little glad." Boston had just won a league title. Jones figured the Celtics had little use for an unknown rookie, and he instead debated taking a teaching offer in North Carolina. He asked the school to up its salary offer by $500. When the school declined, Jones headed to Boston. The fates of West, Chamberlain, and Russell would have changed if one Southern school administrator hadn't been so tight with the budget. Once Auerbach watched Jones in camp, the coach realized he had an underrated talent, even if Red didn't yet know it was Hall of Fame talent. Still, even in the early days, Sam's speed and spirit impressed.

Perhaps the most remarkable aspect of the Celtics dynasty, which produced eight straight championships and eleven titles from 1957 to 1969, is that they lost two Hall of Fame backcourt players and never faltered. It's a tribute to Russell, the anchor, the one irreplaceable player. But it also shows the greatness of Sam Jones and his eventual backcourt mate, K. C. Jones. Early in their careers, the Jones Boys came off the bench, backing up playmaker Bob Cousy and sharpshooter Bill Sharman. The change of pace left opponents "panting and puzzled." A one-point Celtics lead quickly grew to 10 with Sam and K.C. on the floor, a 10-point lead swelled to 20.

Sam eventually became a starter, and 1962 became a breakout year. The player who averaged just 4.6 as a rookie and 10.7 in his second year averaged 18.4 in 1962. Against Philadelphia and the dominant Chamberlain in the Eastern Division Finals that season, Jones hit a soft jumper with two seconds left in Game 7, giving Boston a 109–107 victory. Jones scored a team-high 28 points. It was no surprise Jones hit a shot that tormented Chamberlain, the only player who could match Jerry West and Elgin Baylor story for story at late night bar sessions about what it was like losing in heartbreaking fashion against the Celtics. Chamberlain tied the game with a basket and free throw that completed a three-point play, but as usual, Jones got the final shot—and made it count. It was nothing new. The Celtics guard loved taunting Chamberlain throughout their careers. Two decades after Cousy retired, he talked about Jones routinely holding the ball on the perimeter and telling Chamberlain, "Come and get it, Wiltie, baby, come and get it." As Wilt dutifully ran out for the block, Jones released his jumper and yelled, "Too late, too late."

Jones's shot against Philadelphia carried Boston into the 1962 Finals. The series featured the Lakers against the Celtics, the matchup that became an annual event during the 1960s, a one-sided battle that always ended with Boston cheers and L.A. tears. But the entire decade could have played out in a different way if one shot had found the net instead of bouncing off the rim. That one shot—by Lakers guard Frank Selvy in the final seconds of Game 7—remains the most memorable missed shot in NBA history. But without Sam Jones's heroics one game earlier, the series never would have even gone to seven games.

The Lakers took a 3–2 series lead, with a chance to clinch the championship in Los Angeles. Instead, an early Lakers lead disappeared in the third quarter, thanks to Jones. He hit 17 of 27 from the floor for 35 points, including five early baskets in the third quarter, when Boston out-scored L.A. 34–16. During the third-quarter barrage, Jones reached into the past and broke out his old set shot. He didn't use the set often, but from long range it made occasional appearances. Lakers coach Fred Schaus said after the 119–105 Boston victory, "Sam Jones killed us. He tore us up." Game 6 set the stage for Game 7 and Selvy's miss, which set the stage for the decade that followed, from West's and Baylor's greatness never being enough against Boston to Sam Jones being the quiet man who always came through for the Russell-led Celtics.

In Game 7, Boston took a late four-point lead on its home court. Selvy, the man who once scored 100 points in a college game before serving as a valuable role player in deference to the greatness of West and Baylor, scored four points in the final minute to tie the game at 100. On the final possession of regulation, Los Angeles had a chance to win the game—and the championship. Hot Rod Hundley took the ball for the Lakers and looked for West. With the great Lakers shooter covered, Hundley passed to Selvy on the left side, about four feet from the baseline, maybe 12 feet, if that, from the basket. At the last second, Bob Cousy challenged Selvy's shot. On the grainy video, the shot looks good when it leaves the former Furman star's hand. Lakers fans watch the replay to this day and believe they can bend history to their will and make it fall. It would have been the greatest shot in NBA history—there's never been a buzzer-beater in Game 7 of the NBA Finals. Instead the ball came off the rim, and Russell engulfed the rebound with two hands. Boston won 110–107 in overtime. Decades later Hundley talked about still calling Selvy, waiting for his old teammate to pick up, then saying, "Nice shot, Frank," and hanging up.

Jones scored 27 in that Game 7—Russell had 30 points and 40 rebounds for the Celtics while Baylor (with 41 points) and West (with 35) carried the Lakers. Jones hit the layup in overtime that put Boston up for good, a shot that contributed to the reputation he already owned for being the man the Celtics relied on in the clutch.

Selvy's wayward shot in the final seconds proves legacies are decided by single plays, that one shot changes how we view history. If Selvy's shot falls, the Lakers win the championship, Boston's streak of NBA titles ends at three, and West and Baylor win a title in their second year as partners and don't spend the rest of their careers together in a tortured pursuit of a championship. If Selvy's shot falls maybe the entire decade changes—perhaps the Lakers become the team that always wins the close games. Instead Boston's dominance continued—and Sam Jones made Red Auerbach look like a genius for taking a chance on him in the 1957 draft.

Following the 1962 season, Jones's scoring average kept rising, peaking at 25.9 in 1965. Now people knew Jones not just for his sprinter's speed and dancer's balance—his peers always talked about how Jones glided around the court, a picture of grace at six-foot-four—but for his steady jump shot, which always seemed to become more accurate when the fourth quarter rolled around. Sam's teammates yelled at him if he didn't shoot enough; even on the ultimate unselfish team, the players knew some shooters occasionally needed a touch of selfishness. The *Sporting News* once described Jones's jump shot being "more deadly than the asp." And while Auerbach never put Jones in the same class as West and Robertson—their all-around games set them apart—he added, "As a shooter, he's every bit as tough to guard."

One shot set Jones apart, a shot you first heard about from your grandpa or seventh-grade coach: his bank shot. Old-timers *love* talking about the Sam Jones bank shot because so few players use it. Tim Duncan's a bank shot artist, Scottie Pippen displayed a deft touch off the glass, and Kobe Bryant and Dwyane Wade employ it on the wing. But why don't more players use the backboard (or, depending on the age of the person complaining, bangboard)? The interesting thing about reading old accounts of Sam's bank shot is no one else did it back then either. He was always an anomaly. In a profile, *Sports Illustrated* wrote, "Sam is one of the few professionals (Gene Shue is another) who expertly use the backboards on medium-range shots; the fashion today is to aim for the front rim of the basket." Not that he was an objective observer, but Auerbach claimed Jones created one of the four offensive weapons that revolutionized the game: George Mikan's inside play; Cousy's playmaking; Kareem's skyhook; and Jones's bank shot. "He made it popular, and he made it an art," Auerbach said.

Jones revealed when he came into the NBA, "Nobody was using the bank shot. I felt it was like making a layup." It felt like that because that's how the famous bank developed. Back in North Carolina, Jones struggled with the most basic shot of them all: the layup. When he started using the backboard on those short shots, they went in. Every player learns that skill, but Jones was nearly alone in realizing he could also use the backboard as he drifted farther out on the court. The same principles still applied, from a foot away or 15. No matter where he stood, he picked a spot on the board. It became a trademark, his name an adjective you can still hear today when an announcer compliments a player for hitting a Sam Jones bank shot. Jones made the bank shot look easy, but if it was, more players would have done it before he arrived in the league in 1957, and more would have done it after he retired. The failure of current players to use the backboard on jump shots isn't an indictment of the modern game. It's proof of the greatness of Sam Jones, a player who basically brought the bank shot to the NBA—and took it with him when he walked away.

HAL GREER: MR. 15-FOOTER

Like his contemporaries, Hal Greer experienced heartbreak against the Celtics, first when he played in Syracuse, then in Philadelphia after the franchise relocated. In the 1965 East Finals, Greer threw the inbounds pass John Havlicek famously stole to clinch the game with the Celtics ahead by a point.

The Sixers finally got their revenge in 1967, winning the NBA title with one of the best teams in league history. On March 8 of that year, in a game at the dreaded Boston Garden, the Sixers won the East title during the regular season with an overtime victory over the Celtics. Philly trailed by 15 points in the third quarter before starting its comeback. In overtime, Boston tied the game at 113, but Greer won it with a jump shot in the final seconds. Following the victory, Greer's teammates hoisted him on their shoulders and celebrated with beer in the locker room. Greer's winning shot confused writers, who couldn't agree on the distance of the game-ending bomb. One paper called it a 40-foot set shot, which seems improbable. Others called it a 25-foot jump shot. Regardless of the distance and exact form, it was a credit to Greer's toughness that he was even on the court for the shot. With five minutes left in the fourth quarter he suffered painful cramps in his right leg. He remained in the game, determined to get the Sixers past their toughest rival. A few weeks later, the Sixers defeated Boston again, this time in the playoffs, with a dominating 140–116 victory in the clinching game.

Philly went on to win the NBA Finals, breaking Boston's eight-year grip on the championship and capping a season that saw the Sixers go a record 68–13. Not surprisingly, Chamberlain led the team in scoring that season with 24.1 points per game, but Greer followed at 22.1. In the playoffs Greer took over, leading Philly in scoring at more than 27 per game. Greer, the man who owned, in Hall of Famer Dolph Schayes's opinion, the best midrange jump shot in the game's history, finally earned recognition.

Greer emerged from segregated West Virginia, becoming the first black player at Marshall College. Although he stood only six-foot-two, Greer once spent a season playing center. Despite his college credentials, when Greer came to Syracuse in 1958, unsure of his future, he didn't unpack his bags. But even as a rookie he displayed explosive scoring ability, relying on a jump shot that ensured his spot in the league. Greer loved shooting from inside the top of the key. His coach Alex Hannum said, "He's so good on his jumper that it startles you when he misses." Greer even used the jump shot on his free throws, something most basketball players stop when they're teenagers. But Greer hit 80 percent of his career free throws.

Rarely did Greer express his emotions on the court. After he scored his 20,000th point, a reporter wrote, "It was the first time some had seen Hal smile since the yearbook picture was taken." None of the Big Four guards in the 1960s displayed much anger or happiness on the court. Maybe it was the times; men didn't hug their sons, and stars didn't smile or gesture on the basketball court, no matter if they scored 40 or four. They contained everything inside, sometimes to their detriment, as seen by the internal demons that nearly destroyed Jerry West. Jim Murray said West wore "the perpetually startled expression of a guy who just heard a dog talk," and wrote of Sam Jones, "He looks as if he just heard Paris fell." Greer fit in with his dour peers.

He always looked ready for battle, or like he'd just engaged in one. Instead of an NBA guard, he looked more like an NFL running back preparing for 40 carries right up the gut. In addition to the normal tape on his ankles, Greer wore a knee brace, sported a heavy thigh pad, and played with a pad on his elbow. The armor never slowed him down. Occasionally Greer exploded for 40-plus-point games, even for 50. As a rookie he scored 39 in a half against Boston, on his way to 45 points. But mostly he just produced a steady stream of 20-point outings, each one looking the same, whether in agate form in the newspaper box score or visually on the court. Opponents found it easy to overlook him, right up until the moment he drilled four or five straight shots. Teammates called Greer Mr. 15-Footer. One time against the Knicks, Greer shot a 16-footer to win the game, but the ball only went 10 feet. After the game-losing airball, his coach, Jack Ramsay, cried for a foul. "Hal Greer can't miss the basket like that, the shooter he is."

Billy Cunningham, Greer's teammate who won an NBA title while coaching Philly, said Greer's jump shot "was as good as anybody's who ever played the game. I think the beauty of Hal Greer's game is that he knew where he was most effective, and he never shot the ball from an area where he was not completely confident and comfortable. He never went outside of 18–20 feet maximum, but he was deadly, and he had the ability to get to that spot."

It took until 1967 for that deadliness to finally result in a championship for Philadelphia. When people think about Philadelphia's 1967 season they likely think about that title validating the seven-foot-one Chamberlain's decade-long quest for a championship—and forget that Mr. 15-Footer played the starring role.

OSCAR: BASKETBALL'S METHODICAL MASTER

Oscar Robertson didn't suffer as many memorable defeats as Jerry West at the hands of the Celtics, but he, too, understood the frustration of battling a team that could put five Hall of Famers on the floor at once while keeping a handful more on the bench. In the 1963 Eastern Finals, in the seventh game, Robertson scored 43 points for Cincinnati. As always, it proved futile against Boston. Sam Jones scored 47 points to lead Boston to a 142–131 victory. That's what happened throughout the 1960s: No matter what anyone did—no matter how many points Wilt Chamberlain scored, no matter how many jumpers Jerry West drained, no matter how many hanging floaters Elgin Baylor coaxed into the net, no matter how many midrange shots Hal Greer drilled, no matter how many triple-doubles Oscar Robertson posted—Boston almost always won. Far from being a sign of weakness in those great players who came up short against the men in green, it was testament to Boston's strength. Nothing could detract from the individual greatness of the players who measured themselves against the ultimate team. And in Oscar, basketball welcomed its first ultimate weapon, a player with no weakness.

Robertson first drew attention for his superior play as a teen at Crispus Attucks in Indianapolis, an all-black school created because the city— the strongpoint for the Ku Klux Klan—wanted all of the black students in one school. From that shameful legacy of racism emerged the greatest high school basketball team ever in Indiana, in a state known for producing once-in-a-lifetime prep basketball teams. Robertson's team defeated Dick Barnett and his Gary Roosevelt squad in the 1955 state title game, making Attucks, as far as anyone could tell, the first school in the nation to win a state championship with five black starters. Attucks did this a decade before Texas Western accomplished the same thing in the NCAA Tournament. In his senior year, Robertson led Attucks to a repeat championship and the first unbeaten season in Indiana history. A high school teammate of Robertson's remembered an opposing player crying and the kid's dad telling him, "You might as well stop that crying. Because can't nobody beat them. You ought to be glad you ever played against them."

Even as a teenager Robertson played like a man ahead of his time. He never wasted a movement. Economic and efficient, Oscar seemed to have mapped out every game in his head before the jump ball, and getting 35 points and 10 assists was as easy as following the directions he'd already mentally diagrammed. One writer observed in 1970, "Oscar's points were like short putts. He faked so many guys that he had all day to shoot a soft jump shot or had enough time to walk up a stepladder and lay it in."

His all-around game made people talk about him being one of the best ever. In 1968, future *New York Times* columnist Ira Berkow speculated about Oscar's place in hoops history, writing, "Oscar Robertson can do more things better on the floor than anyone who has played the sport since Dr. Naismith got a brainstorm in the 1890s." At the time, Robertson carried career averages of 30 points and 11 assists. Because he did everything so well, it was easy to overlook his shooting. He beat defenders with the dribble or while just holding the ball, faking them out of position, patiently waiting for a slight opening, then rising for a jumper.

Robertson earned a long-sought NBA championship in 1971, manning the backcourt for the Milwaukee Bucks while Kareem Abdul-Jabbar dominated in the frontcourt. In the final game of a four-game sweep over Baltimore, the old guard from Indianapolis displayed the old touch. Robertson scored a game-high 30 in the 118–106 victory. He made 11 of 15 from the floor, moving deliberately around the court, knocking in jump shots with the ball high above his head. By that time he carried more weight, the "Big O" nickname becoming more accurate with each passing year. But that didn't lessen his skills or impact. And it took Robertson to prove that even a giant like Kareem—the heir to Russell and Wilt, with the most unstoppable shot in the game's history—needed help from the smaller players, with an assist from Oscar's jump shot.

Late in Game 4 of the Finals, Robertson scored his final basket of the night on a turnaround he'd hit thousands of times in his life, dating back to those days at Crispus Attucks. With Milwaukee in command 106–91, Robertson took control of the ball on the right side. Facing Baltimore's Kevin Loughery, he dribbled with his right hand before turning his back to the basket. Methodically he backed his way closer to his target. At times like that, Robertson looked like a thirty-five-year-old man bullying his ten-year-old son in the family driveway. Pounding the ball into the floor, Robertson finally turned on his right shoulder and launched his favorite jump shot. Loughery contested the shot, but could only watch it fall through the net. It was the perfect way to end Robertson's night, and the perfect way to cement his only NBA title. Because while Robertson's all-around brilliance made him one of the game's greats and helped

Milwaukee to that championship, the "Big O" was never better than when he launched his sweet "J."

JERRY WEST'S HEARTBREAK

The 1969 series between Boston and Los Angeles was one of the most memorable in NBA history, but the quality of play was mostly terrible, with too many turnovers and too many missed shots. The Celtics and Lakers both employed aging stars, and both teams lost depth when expansion franchises in Phoenix and Milwaukee entered the league for the 1968–69 campaign. At the conclusion of the seven-game war, Frank Deford wrote in *Sports Illustrated* that any of the losers from recent Finals could have beaten the Lakers or Celtics, "ravaged by time and expansion as they were."

But the finality of the affair made the seven-game battle unforgettable. The Celtics dynasty ended—Boston went 34–48 the following season. Wilt Chamberlain and Bill Russell met on a court for the last time. Game 7 was Russell's final game. Sam Jones's, too. One thing didn't end: Jerry West's misery. Five times previously the Celtics defeated the combination of West and Baylor. Los Angeles added Chamberlain in 1969 and enjoyed home-court advantage over a Celtics team that only went 48–34. It was supposed to be L.A.'s year, a coronation for West and Baylor.

The Celtics struggled throughout the regular season, a tired, injured team on its last legs, primarily because their veterans rarely had two healthy ones. Jones suffered a groin injury that limited him on both ends of the court and robbed him of his speed. In the *Sporting News*, Jones talked about the frustration he felt about how the Celtics handled his injury. "I really felt I was being rushed, but I didn't argue," he said. "I tried and it hurt. But when someone who is paying your bills tells you to play, and you know you're not coming back next year, you play."

Jones knew he was retiring at the end of the season—he took a coaching position at Federal City College in Washington, D.C. Always known for his endurance, Jones now conserved energy, a veteran move for someone who knew he could no longer run like a rookie. His wife, Gladys, told a reporter, "I still hear people say my husband paces himself too much in games. And maybe they're right. I know Sam feels there is only so much in him, and that he's got to spread it around." All the Celtics wanted that year was to make it to the Finals. They wanted to survive the long regular season simply so they'd have a chance to win a short playoff series.

The shot that defined the 1969 Finals didn't have the potential of ending the series—it wasn't like Selvy's in 1962. This shot came in Game 4. The home teams won the first three games of the Finals, with the Lakers holding a 2–1 lead entering Game 4 in Boston. In a ragged game with 50 turnovers, the Lakers forged an 88–87 lead with just 15 seconds left. But Boston's Em Bryant stole the ball from Johnny Egan, giving the Celtics one last shot at victory. Egan claimed he was fouled. I asked veteran columnist Bob Ryan—who was seated behind the basket—about the play. "Oh God yeah, it was a foul. They mauled Egan. Mauled."

Jones missed a potential go-ahead shot with seven seconds left, but the Celtics retained possession, giving them one more chance to win, one more chance to break the hearts of the Lakers. The Celtics hadn't made a field goal in four minutes. They looked old. They were old—Jones and Russell were both thirty-five. But on the Lakers' radio broadcast, Hot Rod Hundley—who probably saw Frank Selvy's shot fall off the rim every time he visited the Garden—told listeners, "Neither one of them has scored a basket this quarter, but still, it's got to go to Sam or Havlicek." Russell, the player-coach, didn't necessarily think Jones should be a choice, despite a career built on late-game heroics. Since Jones was retiring, Russell didn't want Jones remembered for missing a shot at the end, apparently forgetting Jones built a career on *not* missing those shots.

Russell ultimately settled on a play suggested by Havlicek and Larry Siegfried, a set the two used to win a game during their days at Ohio State. Havlicek took the inbounds pass, and Jones moved to his right, utilizing a triple pick. Jones stumbled, but still caught Havlicek's pass. He threw up perhaps the ugliest shot of his career, shooting off the wrong foot from about 18 feet. Deford wrote that when Jones shot the ball, Russell cursed, believing it didn't have a chance. Every fan in the stands with a Boston accent probably did the same. The ball hit the rim a few times before finally bouncing in for the winning points. After the game, Jones said, "I thought to shoot it with high arc and plenty of backspin, so if it didn't go in Russell would have a chance for the rebound." The only issue with Jones's plan: Russell wasn't in the game. Siegfried said, "What the hell. You make a shot like that, you're entitled to blow smoke about arc and backspin and things like that."

West scored 40, but Boston held Chamberlain and Baylor under double figures. A morose West hosted reporters in the decrepit locker room and expressed a pessimistic view, as if he knew the Celtics more than evened the series. Everything he'd experienced in the past prepared him for the future. "I guess when the good Lord wants you to win, you win," he said. "A defeat like that is hard to take. I don't know. I must be a loser. I really don't want to talk about it. We played dumb basketball and got beat, that's all that matters."

Throughout the 1969 Finals, the Celtics were helpless against West. Boston put Bryant on him, and Deford wrote it "was sheer disaster as West just shot over him at will." In the first five games of the Finals, West scored 53, 41, 24, 40, and 39 points. But in Game 6 he battled a bad hamstring and scored only 26 as the Celtics evened the series. "We won that game because we held West 13 points under his average," Havlicek said. "I seriously doubt we could have accomplished it if he was sound."

Game 7 remains the most devastating loss in Lakers history, and probably the greatest victory for the Celtics. Of all the championships they've won—the seventeenth came in 2008 against, of course, the Lakers—nothing quite compared to Game 7 in 1969. As a Lakers fan who wasn't even alive, I can still recite the famous details, as if I watched it happen in another life. Take the balloons. Those damn balloons. Lakers owner Jack Kent Cooke wanted thousands of balloons in the rafters at The Forum, ready to be released when the Lakers vanquished the Celtics. Instead they turned into the greatest motivational material in NBA history, with Boston players vowing to make the Lakers pay for their hubris.

Boston grabbed a quick 24–12 lead. The Lakers sliced the deficit to three at halftime, but the third quarter was another L.A. disaster, with the Celtics leading 91–76. Jones, who scored 24 points, fouled out in his final NBA game. The great warrior Russell, in his final NBA game, scored just six. And the Lakers still couldn't win.

West rallied the Lakers, but another lucky jump shot sealed the victory for Boston. With the Celtics leading by a point with a little over a minute left in the game, Don Nelson caught a deflection and took a shot, almost as an afterthought. The ball bounced off the back of the rim, went high in the sky, grazed the strings on Jack Kent Cooke's balloons in the rafters, and fell gently through the net. Another jump shot that changed history. Another jump shot that tortured the Lakers. West went for 42 points, 13 rebounds, and 12 assists in the 108–106 loss. His greatest individual performance came in L.A.'s worst defeat. He's the only member of a losing team to win a Finals MVP. He got a car out of the deal, a consolation prize for eternal torment. Surely the Celtics of the 1960s never enjoyed a more satisfying victory—the franchise and its fans have gotten mileage out of those balloons for five decades—but even after the emotional victory, the thoughts of the conquerors from the East turned in an unlikely direction: to Jerry West. Russell found him and held his hand. Havlicek told West he loved him. Jerry West was now winless in six trips to the NBA Finals. "I guess it just wasn't meant for me to be a member of a championship team," he said. "Maybe there'll be another year, another chance. I don't think so right now."

Of course West got another chance, as did the Lakers. The basketball gods savored bedeviling West with another opportunity. And inevitably it ended in defeat. The following season—the Lakers' losses in the Finals came one after the other in the 1960s and '70s—the Knicks defeated L.A., again in a seven-game fight. The series also produced the most memorable shot of West's career. At the end of Game 3 in L.A., with the Lakers trailing by two with three seconds left after a Dave DeBusschere jumper, West fired a shot that was, according to various reports, anywhere from 55 to 63 feet away. It went in, setting off a delirious celebration at The Forum. The Knicks won in overtime, but West's shot was all anyone talked about and maintains its spot as one of the all-time answered prayers. Chamberlain shoved West in the back in a celebratory gesture as they returned to the bench, but the man who made the shot didn't even smile— partly because he still had work to do, but also because, as crazy as it sounds, maybe the shot was . . . routine? It took luck. Yes. West could have shot the ball forty-nine more times from the same spot and missed every one. But somehow, when West made the shot, it seemed more like skill, as if only Mr. Clutch could produce that play at that moment. Maybe he practiced it in the off-season. Or maybe he only needed one attempt. *Of course* Jerry West made a 60-footer at the buzzer. Who thought he would miss?

It also seemed fitting that the most memorable shot of West's career occurred during a defeat, just as his Game 7 triple-double against the Celtics in 1969 happened during a loss. For more than a decade, nothing West did in the purple and gold was good enough in the Finals. As Deford wrote, "All told, he has scored almost 30,000 points. If in five particular games he had scored 10 more points he would have won one NCAA and four NBA championships."

When West and Wilt finally won a title for L.A., it came when both were far below their peak powers. The 1972 Lakers won 33 straight games and beat the Knicks for the championship. The victory didn't include a poetic finish—it didn't end with West knocking down a 20-footer from the top of the key at the buzzer in the clinching game. It didn't come against Boston. But it made West a winner, even though he proved for a dozen years he already was one, no matter what the scoreboards said—and no matter what he said about himself in so many dejected postgame postmortems. West didn't seem to know what to do with himself, how to celebrate after so many years of mourning. Finally he told reporters, "The feelings I have now are private ones—I'm at a loss for any more words. I'm going to go home and lock the door."

More than a decade after Sam Jones played a major role in leading the Celtics to ten of the eleven titles the franchise won between 1957 and 1969, a decade after his jump shot—off glass or otherwise—provided the firepower that Boston needed nearly as much as Russell's defensive intimidation, he still hadn't been elected to the Naismith Hall of Fame. Neither had Hal Greer, whose only sin as a player consisted of coming along at the same time as West and Robertson. Jones and Greer toiled in the background in a decade ruled by two otherworldly perimeter talents—and the two giants who reigned over the whole league. Overshadowed during their playing days, it continued into retirement.

In 1979, Bob Ryan wrote a piece urging voters to honor the pair. The 1981 exclusion was especially confusing. That year, the Hall inducted Thomas Barlow (a pro back in the 1920s and '30s), Ferenc Hepp ("the father of Hungarian basketball"), former NBA commissioner Walter Kennedy, and Arad McCutchan (a longtime coach at Evansville). Finally in 1982 Greer earned induction, Jones in 1984. After being chosen, Greer said, "It's a little tarnished because it took a little longer than I thought. It should have happened much sooner." When Jones went in two years later, he thought about skipping the ceremony. Auerbach said, "My first reaction is they waited too long. After all, they've elected guys before him who couldn't carry Sam's pants." Jones went, and while he didn't reveal why he thought about staying home—he said his mom and kids persuaded him to go—he did say, "It would have made me very happy if the Celtics had gone in as a team, because that's what we were—a great team, not great individuals." Jones expressed a sincere thought—the Celtics built their dynasty on the concept. And there's no question that even without their great individual shooter from North Carolina, the Celtics would still have been a great team—but they wouldn't have been the most dominant franchise in NBA history.

Jerry West told Frank Deford in 1969, "I've reached a point where nothing will satisfy me but the very best. I can only settle for that from myself. I used to think so much about scoring, but I'm just no longer interested in points. I scored a lot against Boston because that happened to be the way to win. I really don't think they have anyone to guard me. But I've always wanted to be appreciated for being more than a shooter."

He received that all-around appreciation. Jerry West is now known for so much more than his shooting. There's the defensive prowess—a combination of a blanket and a cat, someone wrote—and the famous dribble, immortalized in the NBA's logo, and the way he dealt with terrible defeats against the Celtics, and the triumph in 1972, and the ability to play through broken noses and torn muscles, and the teams he constructed as one of the great general managers. Very little is unknown about Jerry West, especially after his autobiography, *West by West: My Charmed, Tor-*

mented Life, detailed his battles with depression, internal demons, and his hatred for his father, a man he once thought about murdering so he could stop the physical abuse. Above all, people appreciated his ability in the closing seconds of games, which gave him just one of the nicknames he disliked, even if it fit so well: Mr. Clutch.

But even with all of that, a Jerry West jump shot remains, for many people, the picture of basketball perfection. That jump shot solidified his clutch credentials, for while he won games with dramatic layups—like against the Celtics in the 1962 NBA Finals—and hit an occasional 60-footer at the buzzer, the majority of his game-tying or game-winning shots came via his jumper. There's Jerry West, taking three dribbles to his right, pounding the ball into the hardwood on the final one, bringing it up and rising for another jump shot and another two points as the clock strikes zero.

Those skills as a shooter still impress, forty years after he took his final shot. A YouTube video emerged of West at a camp in 2013. With kids seated around him, West, wearing slacks and a blue golf shirt, made shot after shot while talking about arc and the placement of his elbow. He didn't jump—he was seventy-five years old after all—but the form and the results looked like they did when he won the scoring title in 1970. "I haven't shot a basketball, probably in two years," he told the campers. "Once you learn how to do it, you won't ever forget it."

One morning in October 2014, my phone rang, and the voice on the other line—familiar from the dozens of interviews I'd watched over the years—said, with a touch of the old West Virginia drawl, "This is Jerry West." I'd been trying for weeks to get a chance to talk with West about shooting—about the jump shot in general, about his jumper in particular. For a man who turned his life into an open book—one reviewer said his autobiography was "front to back, a purge and a dirge"—and who has been the subject of thousands of articles, there isn't a lot of new ground to cover in an interview. But I focused on the jump shot during our conversation because West is one of the great technicians and possesses the ability to pick apart his own shot with the same critical eye he's used on his psyche. It's not an area that has been written about as much as so many other aspects of West's career: his difficult upbringing in West Virginia, the heartbreaking losses, the Oscar rivalry, the relationship with Elgin, his coaching days, his depression. But West is one of the first players people think about when they think about the jump shot. By the end of his career he wanted to be known as so much more than a shooter—but his skills as a shooter always remained his defining characteristic, especially with the game on the line.

"Honestly, I never had anyone to teach me anything," he says. "I pretty much did things that seemed right and natural. To me, when you're young like that, all you do is experiment anyway. You see what you can do or you can't do because you weren't exposed to the same things that kids are today. . . . There's a way that they can copy things today where you were sort of on your own then."

Being on his own, and alone, helped West become a great shooter. One year he broke his foot in high school. Stuck in a cast, West practiced shooting from one spot. Roland Lazenby wrote about the process in his book *Jerry West* and quotes West's sister Barbara: "He would move to another position the next night. And I'm just convinced that he became a master shooter because of that. Seeing him shoot, one would see the right arm out and the left with his hand under his elbow, lining up everything."

In the same way so many kids wanted to own Mickey Mantle's swing in the 1950s and '60s—whether they lived in New York or 3,000 miles away—so countless kids wanted Jerry West's jump shot. His great lift—Jim Murray wrote that West jumped so high on the shot he'd need the fire department to retrieve him—and a quick release made even the tightest defense meaningless. Fred Schaus, who coached West at West Virginia University and again with the Lakers, marveled during his star's professional days, "Watch him. You will see a guard right on top of West and apparently easily able to stop him. But before the man can even get off the ground, Jerry has gone up quickly, fired and is on his way down again."

But no matter how many times a young player went to the park in 1966 to emulate Jerry West, it might not have done much good. Nature plays a major role in shaping great shooters, West believes, no matter how long they nurture their jumper. "You've got a couple of fingers on your hand," he tells me, "that if you don't have the right touch there, I don't care who you are, it's not going to go in. I don't care what kind of formula, it's not going to go in the same." Shooting is like "opening and closing a door. You don't open and close a door if your elbow's sticking out." West says anyone can teach the jump shot, but "if you put them in a game could they make it? The answer's probably no because they couldn't get open."

Though he was only about six-foot-three, West excelled by creating his own shot. In the early years of the West-Baylor partnership, the two stars played a two-man game the likes of which the league has never quite seen before or since, each man taking turns dominating—Baylor with a game ahead of his time (in addition to the aerial ability, Baylor possessed tremendous passing skills), and West with his efficiency and versatility. During one shooting display, opposing coach Alex Hannum wondered, "What can you do about that? He came down and fired before any of his players were past center court, but it didn't make any difference. When he has a hot hand, you can just forget it and go home."

West thinks shooting is a "mechanical thing that you don't want to be mechanical. You don't want to have to think about it." In other words, all the practice that goes into developing a shot only becomes a perfect weapon when it becomes second nature, when a player doesn't dwell on all the lessons learned on the practice court. Working on a shooting stroke during lonely nights on the court—when the only audience noise is in the shooter's head as he makes an imaginary game-winning shot—pays off when there's an actual defender.

"It's just reactionary in terms of when someone's in front of you," he says. "That's the real secret to somebody being an extraordinary player or a good player. There's not very many extraordinary players in this league. There's a few, but not many." West always messed around with "little things" on his shots, "stupid little shooting drills that I used to do that I didn't see anyone else do." Those drills included working on tough angles. He enjoyed going behind the backboard along the baseline because "you have to be able to shoot the ball straight or otherwise you're going to hit the corner of the board. If you don't have the right arc on it, you're going to hit it."

West's tales about his drills and the backboard reminded me of a story written by Rus Bradburd, who once ran West's son Jonnie and NBA player Earl Watson through dribbling drills in California. Jerry stopped by and asked to say a few words about shooting. West, in his sixties at the time, demonstrated by making shot after shot. Bradburd rebounded, an easy job as the ball fell through the net each time. West told his son and Watson, "You've got to practice enough so you know every spot on the floor." Bradburd wrote about West going to the corner, out-of-bounds, behind the three-point line. "From that angle," Bradburd explained, "a shooter can barely see the rim. You're actually behind the backboard, and need to get just the right arc and release—there's zero margin of error." Bradburd moved out from below the basket to the wing, where he anticipated the ball coming off the rim. West instead made three in a row.

But in our talk, West returned to the theme of making shots in game situations, when a defense does everything to stop shooters. "It's a fast, quick game and a game that's built on people crowding you, people trying to take away the best thing that you do." As he got older—as the physical scars added up, in addition to the mental ones—he learned more efficient ways of shooting and getting free. In warm-ups, West liked taking only one or two dribbles, left or right, simulating his favorite move, although he admitted not wanting to take too many shots in pregame, maybe "eight or 10. I just didn't need it," he says, because all of the practice he put in when he was alone on his days off meant there wasn't much more to do before a game when he needed to be on in front of an audience.

The actual shot is simply the final act in a performance that also takes place away from the ball. "To really prosper in the game you have to be able to learn how to get open. It takes a lot of instinct, it takes a lot of practice. Takes reading defensive players and how they react to you." Early in his career West resented receiving screens when he had the ball, believing his quickness and jumping ability—and those instincts—allowed him to get any shot off. "When you're younger, you don't even know anyone's in front of you." West had "kind of a unique brain that I knew how people were going to try to play me. But it wasn't because we had all these teaching aids and all these scouting reports. The game was in many ways light-years behind where we are in terms of scouting players, all the statistical things that people see today. They can chart those all they want to, but the right player's going to figure out how to do it. Trust me."

Fans did trust West, putting their hopes and faith in him for fourteen seasons, especially when the Lakers needed a basket in the closing seconds. Mr. Clutch sometimes resented the name—he told Deford people could taunt him with it if he missed—but it was his own fault for coming through so often fans needed to call him something other than Jerry. I asked if his thought process—if the way his unique brain worked—changed when attempting game-winning shots. "Honestly, I felt it was easier to score later in the game because players are almost always in positions that are not as advantageous for defensive players. But I've always been kind of crazy when it comes to confidence."

The Lakers great maintained that late-game confidence throughout his career. Plenty of Hall of Famers lost those skills, including Bob Cousy. Long after Cousy retired, he spoke about West's ability in the clutch in his later years. The misses stack up in a player's mind, creating doubt for the first time. Players hesitate and become aware of everything that's at stake. They're older and smarter, but they were better in the clutch when they were younger and dumber. "I found that the more experience I had, the more it magnified the pressure in that situation," Cousy said. "Early in my career I always wanted the ball, but year by year, the fear of missing started to creep in. Near the end of my career, I always looked to set up Sam Jones in that situation, but Jerry always wanted that responsibility."

Throughout his final years in the league, West proved how much he still wanted the game in his hands in the closing seconds, never abdicating his spot among basketball's late-game royalty. Late in the 1972 All-Star Game, he delighted the Forum crowd with a game-winner in the final second. Calling the game as an analyst on television, West's old rival and admirer Bill Russell simply said "two points" when the winning jumper from the top of the key was only halfway to the basket. Against Golden State in a 1973 playoff game, in a game that saw him score 11 of his 17 in the fourth quarter, he hit a 15-footer to give the Lakers a win. In his final year, in January 1974, West, having missed the previous fourteen games with an abdominal muscle pull, won a game against Kansas City with another 15-footer at the buzzer.

As we spoke, West occasionally sounded almost apologetic for the confidence he expressed in his game, and in his jump shot. "This has nothing to do with me sounding cocky or arrogant. I'm just telling you how I felt personally. . . . I didn't want anyone else to shoot a shot that was going to decide a game. I really didn't. It was just the crazy confidence that I felt at that time. My last three years of my career I felt I really had lost my physical edge because of a knee injury I had. Again, it didn't deter my confidence, that's for sure."

Toward the end of our call, I mentioned a theory from a shooting coach named Paul Hoover. He believes introverts make better shooters than extroverts. Hoover thinks introverts retreat to their own worlds on the practice court. This pays off because they're so focused on improvement. They build force fields that deflect distractions. West didn't make a universal proclamation about the theory, but about himself, he said, "Frankly I was quiet and shy. I was very quiet and shy. I wasn't one of those boisterous people at all."

A quiet kid who internalized so much it nearly destroyed him. But the story of Jerry West has always been about that internal struggle, a fight that produced so much pain, but also played a role in making him one of the best ever. His perfectionism drove him. The demons nearly killed him. Longtime L.A. sportswriter Mitch Chortkoff once told Lazenby, "The lunatic part cannot be denied, because that was a part of him, but all that emotion is what made him great."

And he was never greater than at the buzzer. "I didn't feel pressure," he says. "I just felt it was something I'd done so many times as a kid playing by myself. Everyone wants to be known as someone that when the game is close, they want to be known as the player who's going to go out and make those kinds of shots."

That's what people remember. Generations know about West's performance in the clutch, moments defined by a jump shot that helped define an era dominated by giants. Jerry West on the move with the dribble remains the NBA logo, but Jerry West shooting a final jumper—from 20 feet out on the wing, with the game on the line and a defender in his face, with 15,000 fans standing in anticipation, all of them convinced the shot will rip through the net—remains the basketball ideal.

PART TWO

THE JUMP SHOT TOUR

CHAPTER
SIX

LEGENDS, TRAGEDIES, AND FAMILIES

In October 2009, I started playing in a pickup basketball league in New York's Washington Heights neighborhood. It's mostly a group of old guys and an old lady, and the talent ranges from the really good to the really bad. Over the years, I've become friends with many of the players, but on that first night I walked into the gym as a stranger. I went up with my dad, who was visiting. While I played he watched, just as he'd done since I was five years old. I had a good night—after some early struggles I found my range and hit my jump shot, a few of which won a couple of games.

During a break, Chris, a young guy from the neighborhood, who was about twenty and the best player there—an unselfish point guard with quickness, a gorgeous floater, and a sharp passing eye—asked my dad where we were from.

"Minnesota."

"I knew it!" Chris said. "I knew he was from Minnesota. Those Minnesota guys love to shoot those threes."

When Chris said Minnesota he probably meant we represented all of the Midwest, since my home state itself isn't known for having legions of great shooters. The reputation for, say, Indiana being home to players with great jump shots happens to rub off on us Minnesotans as well. But Chris is right: Certain areas develop reputations for producing certain types of players. As he talked to my dad, Chris added that New York City point guards like to drive the ball to the hoop. But the Big Apple's also been home to sharpshooters. All of the states have players who were known for their jump shot, even if their exploits never took them outside the borders.

Take Louisiana, home to the all-time leading high school scorer in the nation's history, Greg Procell. He only stood five-foot-eleven, but he scored a staggering 6,702 points in tiny Ebarb, a community near the Texas border that's home to only a couple hundred people. That total couldn't have happened anywhere else because schools in Louisiana played more games than in any other state in the country. As a senior in 1970, when he scored 3,173 points, Procell played 68 games; in other states, teams usually play between 20–25 games each season. But he averaged 37.2 per game in his career. People in Louisiana still talk about his jumper. His college coach, Tynes Hildebrand, told Jeré Longman of *The New York Times* in 2002, "He was short, slow and couldn't jump, but I tell you what, not many people in the world ever had a better shooting eye than Greg." Longman wrote about Procell, who grew up in poverty, becoming a marksman early in his life by shooting his dad's beer cans into a "rusted foot tub." Procell's range left opponents searching for defensive solutions, and even impressed himself. He once scored 100 points in a single game. Years later he lamented, "I was born too soon. If we had that three-point line when I was playing, I might have scored 150 points one night."

Louisiana's neighbor Mississippi produced two gunners who put on one of the greatest shows in Southeastern Conference history. On March 4, 1989, Greenwood native Gerald Glass scored 53 points to lead the University of Mississippi to a 113–112 victory over freshman sensation Chris Jackson, who starred as a prep in Gulfport before leaving the state for Louisiana State University. Jackson scored 55 in the losing cause.

Jackson, who converted to Islam in the NBA and became Mahmoud Abdul-Rauf, was one of the greatest pull-up shooters the game's ever seen. As a freshman at LSU, Jackson averaged 30.2 points, with games of 53 and 48 early in the season. But late in his record-breaking debut campaign, his 55 weren't enough against another Mississippi kid—Glass, who transferred to Ole Miss after attending Division II Delta State. He lived in the Mississippi Delta and says players from the area didn't get respect, nationally or from people in the state. Glass showed he belonged at the top levels by averaging 28 per game in 1989. His battle against Jackson on the Mississippi campus is thrilling to watch today, Jackson flaunting a quick release on his jumper, Glass utilizing a strong post-up game and light touch on his midrange shot. Watching the game today it's hard to believe two players from any state will again engage in that type of shootout, in an era when many college games end with both teams scoring only in the 50s.

Kentucky has manufactured as many shooters as anyone, from early stars Joe Fulks and Frank Selvy to more modern players like Darrell Griffith, a man known as Dr. Dunkenstein who became an NBA pioneer with his three-point shooting. Bird Averitt also came from Kentucky. The left-handed Bird led the nation in scoring in 1973 during his days out west with Pepperdine, relying on a high-arcing jumper that reached the skies.

When Bird won the 1973 scoring crown, he edged a player from another California college, a player whose lasting legacy is that of being one of the best players to never play in the NBA. And so on this tour of the jump shooting landscape, we'll head to the coast, to meet a player who became a California legend, but could have ruled the entire basketball world.

LOS ANGELES'S UNFORGETTABLE, FORGOTTEN PHENOM

Back when Raymond Lewis embarrassed opponents on playgrounds and in gyms around Los Angeles, people didn't even need to say his whole name to discuss his exploits. In 1978, Lewis was still a young man but had already become a central figure in "Whatever Happened to . . ." stories. *Sports Illustrated* spoke with NBA assistant Bob Hopkins, who said, "In Los Angeles he is a legend. You say Raymond, they say Lewis. You say Lewis, they say Raymond." By 2001, when Lewis died at forty-eight, he'd been widely forgotten by fans across the land, even in his home state, in the city he ruled as a teenager. For those who saw him play on a regular basis, it was an unfathomable ending, because they always remembered watching him, dribbling through entire defenses and firing from all over the court.

Jerry Tarkanian desperately wanted Lewis to play for him at Long Beach State, and in his book *Runnin' Rebel* called the star guard "the greatest player I ever recruited." Tarkanian raved, "It was his ability to shoot with a man right on top of him that made him so great. A lot of players can shoot, but Lewis had all the moves to get the shot off." Many of those who knew Lewis always wondered if his life would have been different—better— if he'd played for Tark like he planned, before a new Corvette brought him to a different school and started him on a path that ended in ruin, on and off the court.

The facts about Raymond Lewis, phenom, California legend, one of the best players to ever come out of L.A., one of the best players to never play in the NBA: Between 1969 and 1971 the six-foot-one guard led Verbum Dei, the small private school in the Watts neighborhood, to three consecutive California Interscholastic Federation Southern Section championships. After committing to Tarkanian and Long Beach State, he instead attended Los Angeles State, a little-known school with no basketball history that Lewis put on the map in his two years. As a freshman he averaged 38.9. As a sophomore he scored 32.9, second-best in the nation. In his most memorable game he led Los Angeles State to an upset victory over Tark's Long Beach club, scoring 53 points. He entered the NBA draft in 1973. The Philadelphia 76ers took him with the eighteenth and final pick in the first round. He signed a contract, without an agent. At camp, the legend goes, he destroyed Doug Collins, Philly's top pick in the draft, the number one choice overall. In one game, so the legend continues, he scored 60 against Collins—in one half. Upset that Collins made more money, he left camp. Lewis never made an NBA team. Instead he ripped opponents in summer league games and on the playground. He was the best player and shooter many saw, but they never saw him in the ultimate league. Lewis became a substance abuser and an alcoholic, convinced the league blackballed him. He died in middle age, devastated by old scars.

Those are the broad strokes; the details are even more heartbreaking. He died without money, mostly alone after a leg infection went untreated. Eventually he required an amputation, but he originally resisted. *Los Angeles Times* columnist Bill Plaschke spent time in the hospital with Lewis in his final days, and wrote about Lewis telling his own brother-in-law, "I can still go down to the corner and shoot the ball. If my leg is gone, I can't do that." He finally agreed to the procedure, but died from complications after the surgery. He was the player with everything, who ended up with nothing.

His former high school teammate and good friend Randy Echols tells me, "The jump shot can take you a long way. It can take you a very long way. On the other hand, here's a guy with one of the most prolific jump shots, in my opinion, in the history of the game, but never played one minute of professional basketball. He was a tragedy as much as a prodigy."

In August 2014, I met with two men hoping to tell the entire story of Raymond Lewis—the prodigious player and the tragic human. Dean Prator, who even at sixty maintains his linebacker's build, went to school in Southern California at the same time as Lewis. Prator started the Web site raymondlewis.com in 2005. He put magazine and newspaper stories online, along with his contact information. People wrote with testimonials about Lewis's high school days or memories of the time he took on thirty of the top streetball players in L.A. in a single day in one-on-one games—and went 30–0. "I just wanted to give him a home," Prator says, "where people could actually read or talk about him." Through the Web site, Prator connected with filmmaker Ryan Polomski, and the two have spent years on a documentary. Together they've researched and interviewed family, peers, and rivals, telling the story of a player who scored 73 points as a freshman in college on 30-of-40 shooting, in a season where he hit nearly 60 percent of his shots. "You can find centers, all they do is dunk, and they don't shoot 60 percent," Prator says. "And he's doing it long range." Simply finding footage of Lewis became the most difficult part of the project. "Raymond was considered a mysterious, phantomlike figure," Polomski says, "and it even held true in his archival film history. No film footage existed of this guy. His college stuff disappeared. High school stuff disappeared. I spent two full months looking for film footage, full-time forty hours a week, running around, reading, going through people's attics, calling people, chasing people down until we found something."

I visited Prator and Polomski on a day that they were filming at Solar Studios in Glendale, California. They spoke to a young UCLA player who'd only heard stories about Lewis; a cousin of Raymond's; former NBA guard Reggie Theus; and current University of Washington coach Lorenzo Romar, also a former pro. Romar arrived with his wife, who sat and listened with the rest of us as he told tales of Lewis handling him in games throughout Southern California. With the cameras focused on him, Romar grew animated recapping the time Lewis lit up Michael Cooper—the wiry Laker and five-time NBA champion Larry Bird considered his toughest defender—for 56 points in summer league, an electric performance in a packed gym that included a Lewis clear-out and jump shot that had fans running out of the joint in disbelief and excitement.

No one stopped Lewis, whether in a formal setting between rival teams or an informal playground battle. When Echols—a six-foot-four star who handled the rebounding and defense while Lewis scored the points at Verbum Dei—played against Lewis, "Raymond's jump shot was so quick, the release was so quick, you'd get exhausted. So I said I'm going to let him go around, and then as he goes for the layup, I'm going for the block, and that would piss him off." Imagine a jump shot so lethal a foe preferred letting him shoot a layup.

Lewis turned Verbum Dei into a national power. The basketball team brought joy to a Watts neighborhood ravaged by riots. Verbum Dei intimidated opposing teams. Echols remembers, "You have an all-white team coming into South Central Los Angeles. A gym full of very combustible people. Very hot atmosphere. That alone would psyche them out in addition to sometimes it would take them five minutes to even cross half-court." In warm-ups, Verbum players sometimes wore apple caps with the little brim and dunked in the layup line. "That would scare the hell out of opponents," Echols says. As a senior, Lewis and Verbum Dei defeated unbeaten Crescenta Valley for the California Interscholastic Federation championship. Verbum Dei won 51–42 behind Lewis's 18 points, although he only made 9 of 25. But in front of 11,151 at the L.A. Sports Arena, Lewis left no doubt about the identity of the best player on a court he shared with future Division I talent, including Crescenta star Bill Boyd, whose dad, Bob, coached at Southern Cal. "He kicked our ass," Bill says, noting Lewis's floor game as much as his shooting.

Many of Lewis's friends, fans, and rivals believe his downfall began when he attended Los Angeles State instead of Long Beach State. Tarkanian worked for years to land the superstar guard, cultivating a relationship with Lewis—and his teammates. He got Echols and Lewis summer sanitation jobs, and one day, Echols says, he came home to find "some white guy with an apron on bending down in my mother's oven, pulling out chicken thighs. I'm like, what the hell?" It was one of Tark's boosters, a supporter of Long Beach State's basketball team, operating on the theory that if the school landed Echols, maybe they could also get Lewis. Instead, L.A. State trumped Long Beach with cars and cash. Lewis told *Slam*'s Paul Feinberg in 1994 the decision came down to "more money. I ain't gonna lie about nothin'. I love Jerry Tarkanian, he's a very special man in my life. . . . It hurt me [to turn down Long Beach], that I chose money over someone caring about me and [making] sure that I made something out of my life. I chose a car, a Stingray, I chose $2,000 a month in my pocket. To live." Echols left for Arizona, but when he returned to visit his friend, he immediately relayed his concerns. "Tark was certainly no pinnacle of ethics," Echols says, but he believes that the towel-chewing coach known as the Shark could have controlled the excesses. Tarkanian later said Lewis would have made it in the NBA if he played for him. Echols found Lewis at one stage with a little mobile van, a Lincoln Continental, a De Tomaso Pantera, and a "damn limousine. I said, 'Raymond, you don't even have anywhere to park these cars. What are you doing with all this shit?'" Lewis assured Echols everything was fine—and on the court, he was right.

Following his sensational freshman year, Lewis's sophomore season was just as spectacular, the highlight coming when he scored 53 in L.A. State's 107–104 victory over once-beaten, third-ranked Long Beach State in February 1973. *Sports Illustrated* once wrote Lewis was a "whirling, swirling sleek machine with the ball who shoots 59 percent from the floor and has a spin-around move that makes others look infirm and obsolete." Lewis told the magazine, "There is no one in college who can turn me off one-on-one. There probably is a whole defense that can, but I haven't seen it yet."

That confidence didn't disappear when he went to Philadelphia in 1973 and proceeded to attack top pick Collins in rookie camp. When Feinberg profiled Lewis in *Slam*, he mentioned one Philly columnist writing, "Lewis, on the other hand, was doing everything but talk. . . . You watched him closely for flaws. . . . You saw absolutely none on offense. He could do it all and do it so much better than the next best, he was in a class by himself." Ed Ratleff, an All-American at Long Beach State when Lewis scored 53 in that upset, played with Collins on the haunted 1972 Olympic team. He says Collins remains a "dear friend," but tells me, "Raymond Lewis is better than Doug. It wasn't even close. I hate to say it, but it wasn't even close. I'm serious, that's how good he was."

Lewis grew upset at the respective contracts for the two picks. His convoluted three-year deal was worth a total of $190,000, with Lewis eligible to make more money in the 1980s, but only if he stayed in the league. Collins signed a deal that paid him $200,000 annually. Lewis eventually left the Sixers. A year later he sat on the bench for the Utah Stars in the ABA, waiting for a game, when Philly informed Utah it would sue if Lewis stepped on the court. In 1975 Lewis returned to camp for Philadelphia. He left again, returned, and finally left for good, becoming that phantomlike figure, impossible to pin down, his motivations and actions increasingly inexplicable. Over the next decade he went to several NBA camps, but he never landed a roster spot. He became convinced teams conspired against him, but at various times he left before anyone could cut him. Lewis's failure to appear in the NBA was a combination of a league and teams being unsure what to make of an occasionally troubled star, and a superstar unable to deal with the fact that pro ball was about much more than just having the best jump shot on the court.

Echols—who went on to a long career in politics before entering the business world—says, "I told him, 'Look, okay, you were misled about your contract. Yeah, you busted 60 on him in a half. But you have a signed contract. You'll be Rookie of the Year, then you can renegotiate. Go out there and average 20, 25, and maybe have a 40-, 50-point game here or there. . . . You will be in the NBA. You will be playing. Then you can renegotiate. Right now you cannot.'" Lewis believed his unmatched skills on the court would one day sway suitors, convince them to take a chance. The shooting touch never abandoned him. At one NBA tryout, veteran Billy Paultz raved, "Offensively he's as good as any guard I've ever seen. He has an automatic jump shot. He's not afraid to go against anybody."

Lewis dreamed big, making it even tougher when his career became a nightmare. Echols remembers the two of them driving around Baldwin

Hills as teens, parking the car outside Ray Charles's house, drinking malt liquor, and watching Diana Ross and other singers and movie stars walk in. "He had stars in his eyes." For those who saw him, it remained inconceivable that he never reached the top of the basketball world.

Echols says Lewis "grew even more resentful" as the years went by and his glory faded further into the past, and he confronted a future without basketball. He suffered from alcoholism and substance abuse. Echols still recalls Lewis's unmatched tenacity on the court, a trait that couldn't survive away from it. "The intensity, the mental strength was there, until he was broken."

In the *Slam* piece, Feinberg wrote, "What Lewis would really like, is for someone to make a movie about his life, to get the message out there. Perhaps all that's missing is the upbeat Hollywood ending." Lewis didn't get that ending. But basketball fans might still one day get the movie.

When I left the studio where Prator and Polomski filmed, the future of the project remained unknown, despite the dozens of interviews, hundreds of hours of research, and thousands of dollars they'd put into it. Funding, distribution, footage, politics—documentaries are a brutal business. But the pair had maintained their passion, determined to tell the story of Raymond Lewis, the player who was so good, and whose shot was so true, everyone knew him by just one name.

THE BIG APPLE'S BEST

Between the two of them, Howard Garfinkel and Tom Konchalski possess insight on every great player in New York since the 1950s. Garfinkel founded the Five-Star Basketball Camp, which, over the decades, welcomed players like Michael Jordan, Isiah Thomas, and LeBron James. Konchalski lives in gyms during the winter and summer, watching hundreds of high school games while writing scouting reports for his *High School Basketball Illustrated* that he mails to college coaches throughout the land. Publications like *The New York Times* and *New York* magazine have touted his skills as one of the premier evaluators in the country. College coaches everywhere listen to Garfinkel and Konchalski when they opine about basketball talent. When I spoke to them about the best shooters to come out of New York, both men first mentioned two players: Tony Jackson and Roger Brown, a pair of Brooklyn kids, the former a 1957 Thomas Jefferson High School grad who set a city scoring record, the latter a 1960 Wingate graduate who broke that mark three years later.

"Tony was incredibly consistent, a beautiful touch, the best I ever saw," Garfinkel told me over lunch at a Midtown deli. Konchalski raved about Jackson's deep shooting, and mentioned the same for Brown. "Intergalactic range. He shot from distances that would have sort of ridiculed the NBA three-point arc," he says. "Roger Brown totally reinvented himself as a player. He wasn't great playing off the bounce when he was in high school. But he had deep, deep range, and when he came to the ABA they called him the 'Man of a Thousand Moves.'"

But neither he nor Jackson made the NBA. Both players got entangled in the gambling scandals of the early 1960s, and the top professional league blackballed them. They didn't throw games or shave points, but overzealous investigators hounded them, and timid executives made examples out of them. Jackson failed to report a bribe offer—he passed it off as a joke—while Brown associated with the scandal's ringleader, the notorious game fixer Jack Molinas, who eventually went to prison. Brown later won a lawsuit against the NBA, but still never played in the league.

Jackson at least enjoyed a full college career at St. John's. His coach, Joe Lapchick, told reporters during Jackson's sophomore season, "This is the most talented basketball player New York has had since the Garden started basketball twenty-five years ago. I've never seen a greater long jump shooter, and he has the ability to get up there and hang and then shoot from the hanging position." Denied a spot in the NBA, Jackson became a marksman in the American Basketball League. In his first year, he made 141 "home runs," as three-pointers were called. Future sportswriter Peter Vecsey grew up in New York City at the same time as Jackson and Brown. More than fifty years later, the writer best known for his acerbic barbs talks up their abilities with a touch of awe. Jackson boasted a "flawless shot, just perfect touch, perfect form, long range, midrange pull-up, whatever. People never heard of him. Ask anybody who saw him play back in those days, they'll tell you in a second how good he was."

Vecsey graduated in 1961, a year after Brown left Wingate. Brown's graduating class included future fellow Naismith Hall of Famers Connie Hawkins and Billy Cunningham, three extraordinary forwards from one city. The Brown-Hawkins rivalry thrilled New York. Hawkins, a strong inside presence who became known for his high-flying skills, played with better teammates, but with Brown, Wingate proved dangerous. The superstars met in the city semifinals in Madison Square Garden. Brown won the individual matchup, outscoring Hawkins 39–18. Hawkins guarded Brown with little success, fouling out in the third quarter. But Hawkins's Boys High team used its superior depth and won 62–59, on its way to the city title. In 2010, Vecsey wrote in the *New York Post*, "Hawkins came into the building as the nation's most hyped-up child prodigy, yet wasn't even Brooklyn's finest by the time he fouled out with one second remaining in the third quarter after fruitlessly chasing Roger Rabbit far beyond and below the arc." Hawkins told Vecsey, "Why would I want to look back fifty years and think about that game? That was the biggest game of my career and he lit me up. If the three-point shot was in existence, he would've had 50. He kept going further and further back. The guy killed me!"

Hawkins and Brown ruled the city, but were ultimately done in because of their loose association with sleazy New York characters. When news of the scandal broke in 1961, both found themselves banned from college, Hawkins at Iowa and Brown from Dayton. Brown spent the next six years—the prime of his career—in exile. A husband and wife took Brown into their Dayton home, an act that helped him maintain his sanity and dignity. He played in AAU leagues, but before he landed in the ABA with Indiana in 1967, he worked the night shift on an injection machine at a General Motors plant. Originally reluctant to play in the new league, Brown became one of the most beloved players in Pacers history. In 1980, five years into his retirement, he told *The New York Times*, "What it comes down to is that I died and came back to life in the ABA."

Behind Brown, the Pacers won three ABA championships. With the ABA employing the three-point line, he proved the perfect player for the renegade league, perhaps one reason he stayed even after he earned vindication against the NBA. During the 1970 campaign, Brown averaged 23 points on 50 percent shooting. At one point in 1970 he talked about briefly losing confidence in his stroke, telling the *Sporting News*, "I stopped shooting completely and started driving all the time. I figured it was a better percentage to shoot from two feet than 20." If six years out of the game failed to rob Brown of his confidence, a shooting slump wasn't going to last. When Indiana faced Los Angeles in the Finals, he played with an injured knee that required cortisone shots. In the key Game 4, Brown made 18 of 29 shots on his way to 53 points, 13 rebounds, and six assists. Indiana took a 3–1 lead, and L.A. coach Bill Sharman—the old Celtics sharpshooter who recognized a fellow marksman—told reporters, "They call him the Elgin Baylor of the ABA. But he actually goes out farther to shoot." Two games later, Brown scored 45, including three three-pointers in the fourth quarter, to lead Indiana to the title.

Indiana always leaned on Brown in the closing seconds, confident he could get any shot he needed, convinced every shot would fall. Pacers coach Slick Leonard used to say in the huddle, "Get the ball to Roger, and let's go drink beer."

In the 1972 ABA Finals, when Indiana defeated New York, Brown battled Rick Barry, three years before Barry would lead the Warriors to an NBA championship. Leonard told *Sports Illustrated* in 1997, "It's hard to say who won the duel, but we won the series. Now Rick's in the Hall of Fame, and nobody remembers Roger." That article ran after Brown died of liver cancer at the age of fifty-four. It took sixteen years before he joined Barry in the Hall of Fame.

In the same way Dean Prator and Ryan Polomski are trying to bring Raymond Lewis's story to the basketball masses, the legend of Roger Brown benefited from the work of a filmmaker. Ted Green, a former news-paperman in Indianapolis who became a documentarian, made 2013's *Undefeated: The Roger Brown Story*. Green talked with many of Brown's teammates, coaches, and the folks in Dayton who befriended Brown after the scandal. He heard from legends like Julius Erving and Kareem Abdul-Jabbar about Brown's dominance in high school and the ABA.

At lunch in Indianapolis, I spoke with Green about Brown, a player the filmmaker knew little about until stumbling upon his story. Green tracked down footage of Brown's ABA days, but for a professional league, little television coverage existed. So while people saw more of Brown as the

1970s progressed, they missed him at his finest, when he was both the Man of a Thousand Moves and a superior shooter. Green says, "A lot of people say, and I'm with this, that really Roger Brown is the best player of the first half of the ABA, and Julius Erving was the best player of the second half. When I sat down with Julius, and he was saying that Roger was just as good as he was, I even stopped and said, 'I've got to take a timeout because please don't just tell me what you think I want to hear. Are you really saying this?' He looked me in the face, and he said, 'I'm telling you that right now.'"

New York's playgrounds have been the setting for more classic basketball tales—tall ones and otherwise—than any college or NBA arena. Rick Telander's *Heaven Is a Playground*, Pete Axthelm's *The City Game*, and Vincent Mallozzi's *Asphalt Gods* are just three of the iconic books about streetball. But on a court where players live to take one another off the dribble so they can finish at the basket and talk trash to the defender, what's the role of the jump shot? Is a sweet J as respected as a violent jam?

"Mine is," says Keydren Clark, a New York City native who won two NCAA scoring titles at Saint Peter's, thanks to a gorgeous jumper that created instant offense for a playmaking guard who's not quite five-foot-eleven. Because Clark played at obscure St. Peter's in Jersey City, New Jersey, many aren't aware of his exploits, despite his 25.9 career average. Even in New York, people who watch him light it up in summer leagues might not know the man they're watching is named Keydren Clark. They might know him as the Adventure Begins, a nickname he earned after several impressive shows at Rucker, because doing it just once isn't enough to earn a moniker. Or they might be like me when I watched Clark in northern Manhattan and knew him as Wet Those, because his shot is as pure as water. Or fans might simply recognize him as Kee-Kee, his shortened given name, which is economical and true, like his jumper.

I've seen Clark all over the city, but I also watched him during his workouts at the Gauchos gymnasium in the Bronx, where he went through drills and played pickup games. Clark uses streetball to stay in shape. A professional overseas, Clark's jump shot has helped him make a living out of the game he learned in Harlem. Clark says fans watching a playground game don't always appreciate his style, "but real basketball minds understand. People say, 'Make him drive, he can only shoot.'" But as Clark notes, if defenders fear his jumper, they'll play tight on him, and then he can show his entire arsenal. "If I can shoot out here, and you have to play me, I can drive." So for those who want to become great drivers to the basket, always remember: A sweet jump shot from outside makes it easier to penetrate inside.

New York playgrounds have always hosted players who made their reputations with their jumpers as much as their ball-handling, including Joe Hammond, aka "The Destroyer." A great shooter, Peter Vecsey acknowledges, but "you can't believe all the myths attached to him, all the stories. Please don't believe all the stories."

But that's so hard to do on the playground! The stories make it so fun. Like the one about hotshot Jack Ryan, who Hall of Famer Chris Mullin— left-handed owner of one of the smoothest jumpers ever—said was the best shooter he'd seen who wasn't in the NBA. That's the story, whispered about on courts from Manhattan to Brooklyn. Whether Mullin said it is unknown, according to Jack Ryan himself. One sweltering day I met with Ryan at the Brooklyn court he played on as a kid, and he said that tale came from a guy he played against who "wrote his own self-biography and said Chris Mullin was talking about me. Chris never said that to me. I don't know if it's true." What is true is the television show *Rescue Me* included a line of dialogue that referenced him. Denis Leary practically spits in disgust when another character suggests a player could rival Ryan. And Justin Timberlake has talked for years about playing Ryan in a biopic.

Even in high school, Ryan earned a reputation on the playgrounds. His high school coach told *The New York Times* Ryan was the best prep player he ever saw—and the most disappointing. A college career never materialized, despite numerous opportunities ruined by bad grades or demons; his community college team tossed him from the squad for showing up drunk at practice. Vecsey even helped Ryan get a workout with the New Jersey Nets. Nearly thirty years old at the time, Ryan impressed the coaches, but not enough to make the team. At one stage he worked in a fish market. For a decade he seemed destined to be another story of another great player on the playground who flamed out on real courts and in real life. Finally, though, he found a way to make a living with his prodigious skills, when the Harlem Wizards brought him in, making him the only white player on the all-black team, which plays much like the more famous Globetrotters. Eventually Ryan went off on his own, becoming a solo hoop wizard—the phrase is in his e-mail address—who performs ball-handling tricks at arenas across the country and at birthday parties and bar mitzvahs.

But even today, at fifty-three, when he drives his car into the city from his New Jersey home and pulls his bike out of the trunk and rides around to various outdoor courts, it's the street that brings out the best in Ryan. He has always enjoyed the outdoor atmosphere, especially at the famous West 4th Street courts. "Everybody knows in my family, when I die, burn my ashes, and sprinkle me all over that court," he says. The playground becomes his theater. "I've always been a showoff, a ham. They see a little white guy do something, they go nuts. I feed off that. I didn't want to go where nobody's watching. I wanted to go to West 4th." The passion hasn't dissipated, even as those he played with during his younger, wilder days accepted a more sedentary life. "All my friends are like, 'Dude, I lost the love. I didn't want to play anymore. I didn't want to get injured.' I still have it in me where I don't want to score 20 points on you—I want to score 50 points on you."

And usually it's his jump shot—that one Chris Mullin may or may not have bragged about—that helps him score 50. Ryan has won outdoor shooting contests, and still plays against guys thirty years younger who have no chance of stopping him, not when he releases his shot from the top of the key, the wing, or the baseline. One of his street tricks involves purposely firing a shot off the side of the backboard, retrieving the ball after the defender turns his back, and calmly knocking in a jumper. On the day we met, I watched him do it against five baffled kids who were similarly enthralled by the ball-handling tricks—spinning basketballs on his fingers and head—Ryan performs at his shows. When it comes to the jumper, the environment doesn't matter to Ryan. "Some people say, 'I can't shoot outdoors.' I hear people say that all the time about themselves. It's a rim. It's the same size. With shooting, it's all about focus."

The playground demands that focus because of all the distractions that surround players—windy weather, physical opponents, belligerent fans, loud announcers, bent rims, unforgiving asphalt, long memories. For those who concentrate, and possess skill, a lifetime of fame, if not fortune, awaits.

Bevon Robin moved to New York from Guyana when he was nine. He became a hero of high school ball in 1996 with a last-second shot that won a city title against a team led by future NBA star Lamar Odom. But it was his performance and focus as a young man at Rucker—featured in Mallozzi's *Asphalt Gods*—that earned him his nickname: The Eye of the Tiger. "I had a demeanor where I couldn't get one of those flashy names," he says. "I always had this mean look." When Robin made a name, and nickname, for himself at Rucker, "There weren't too many guys shooting a ball in streetball to that effect. Everybody wanted to go to the hole." Robin—like Keydren Clark—stocked the flashiest of moves in his arsenal, but "I didn't waste any motion, I didn't dance around. It was bing-bing and I'm to the basket or bing-bing pull-up." He didn't talk much trash, but not saying a lot on the court doesn't mean a player lacks confidence. Robin always believed he'd get his points. "I come in the park, and it's all about business. I'm going to eat. I felt like I'm going to roam around, and I'm going to eat sooner or later." In 2000, Robin led his team to the coveted Rucker title. Mallozzi described the championship game in *Asphalt Gods*:

> With the crowd in a terrible tizzy and apartment lights from the Polo Grounds projects flicking on at the kind of alarming rate that made the dark buildings light up like huge, brick switchboards, the Tiger pounced again. Late in the first half he took a pass from a tall, lean teammate named "African Slinky," then drained his fourth three-pointer of the evening to give the Posse a 27–20 lead.

Robin's competitive career and dreams of a life in the pros came to a halt when he collapsed from a heart condition while playing a game and nearly died. Paramedics shocked him with paddles and saved his life. He now trains players, but still tests his own skills in lower-key settings. I watched him on a Saturday afternoon in a three-on-three tourney, where he was one of the older players, unlike when he lit up Rucker while winning MVP. The jump shot stood out, a smooth, easy stroke in a series of rough, hard games. At the end of the tournament, we lingered on the Harlem playground. We talked about those days more than a decade ago, and how his game has changed, even if the jumper that brought him fame and a name on the most famous playground court in the country remains the same. "I joke with people now," he says. "I'm not the Eye of the Tiger anymore, but I'm a cat and I can still scratch the shit outta your ass."

MINNESOTA'S FIRST FAMILY

Are shooters born or made? Not even great shooters agree on an answer. Maybe they're born with a certain touch that appears when a player picks up a ball, or maybe thousands of hours of practice create something where genetics failed. But in northern Minnesota, in the small town of Chisholm, in an area of the state known for hockey and iron ore, if you were born into the McDonald family, you were made into a shooter.

The McDonalds—the coaching dad Bob, the statistician mom Darlene, and the sharpshooting kids Mike, Paul, Sue, Tom, Judy, and Joel—never sent anyone to the NBA. But the McDonalds are one of the great basketball families in the country, for their exploits on the court and on the sideline. In many ways the jumper started the family on the path to basketball greatness.

It begins with Bob, who retired in 2014 at the age of eighty after fifty-nine years as a high school coach. He won 1,012 games, the most in Minnesota history. All six kids enjoyed outstanding playing careers. All six used the jump shot to accumulate impressive and occasionally staggering totals. The youngest son, Joel, graduated in 1991 with 3,292 points, a career record for Minnesota at the time. Tom graduated in 1982 with 2,221 points. The oldest child, Mike, finished in 1975 and scored 853 (and has dealt with a lifetime of people asking, so, why so few points?). Paul graduated in 1976 with 1,425 points. And don't forget the girls. Sue graduated in 1980 with 1,962 points while younger sister Judy finished in 1984 with 2,152 points. All six then became head coaches, whether in high school or college. While none of them will challenge the family patriarch's record, they've also put up impressive numbers after replacing their basketball uniforms with suits and sweaters. Three of the boys have won more than 400 games. Between the old man, the kids, and the grandkids, the McDonalds have won more than 2,500 games.

In May 2014, I visited with Bob, two months after his retirement. "What a strange life," he says. "Is there anybody that could match that exact scenario?" That scenario McDonald spoke about had nothing to do with basketball. Instead he meant his life, from the time he was born to a young woman who left Minnesota to give birth in a home for unwed mothers in Buffalo, New York, to being raised back in Minnesota by his Croatian grandmother. When he talks about a strange life he means learning English when he went to kindergarten, because pretty much all he knew was his grandmother's native tongue. He talks about a lifetime spent searching for his real father.

But when he talks about anyone matching an exact scenario, it's also doubtful there's been a basketball family like his. Many families produce multiple great players or kids who become coaches. But to have one of the winningest coaches in the country in the same family as six kids who broke numerous scoring records while winning state championships before embarking on their own coaching careers? No families match that.

Before he became a coach, McDonald also starred at Chisholm High School. After a brief stay at the University of Michigan, he excelled at Hibbing Junior College and the University of Minnesota Duluth. At Hibbing, McDonald played with Dick Garmaker, who went on to an All-American career at the University of Minnesota and played with teams like the Lakers and Knicks. McDonald and Garmaker led Hibbing to a second-place finish in the national tournament. More importantly, Garmaker taught him the power of the jump shot. Garmaker developed a potent jumper, back when it remained something of a gimmick. McDonald says, "I haven't truthfully seen anybody, to this day, that would have the innate ability, animalistic ability to do what he did. He had a weapon that nobody else had. I can still picture him shooting because I tried to copy him—but nobody could copy him. Everything I look at in basketball, after I played with him, was geared to having kids play like him, even on a high school level, try to teach them to fade, and his fakes—all of the things he used so many times."

To play for Chisholm you needed ball-handling skills and the ability to shoot. Especially the McDonald kids, who started early. "As soon as you were well behaved enough and potty-trained, you were the water boy," Paul says. When it came to shooting, Bob drilled them on shots from four to five feet. Then they moved farther out. "I just remember halfway cussing him out under my breath," Joel says. "I'm so sick of shooting ten-foot jump shots. Come on! Eventually you look back and say, that's exactly what we should have been doing. If you can't knock down those when you get them, you're not going to be able to bank on anything else."

Movie fans know about Chisholm—in *Field of Dreams*, Kevin Costner and James Earl Jones travel there in search of an old baseball player named Moonlight Graham, portrayed by Burt Lancaster. Doc Graham, the man who never got to hit in a Major League game, was a real-life friend of McDonald's. For me, growing up in Minnesota, Chisholm meant basketball and the McDonalds. If you thought of the town you thought of the family. Bob developed a reputation as a disciplinarian—players wore ties to games and sported short haircuts. But on the court, he encouraged freedom. "I don't think Dad ever told anybody not to shoot," Tom says, "because I think all Chisholm guys could shoot. If they couldn't, they were sitting on the bench."

Chisholm became known for its full-court pressure, fast break, and patterned offense. Too many coaches, especially early in McDonald's career, believed holding the ball equaled discipline. Not Bob. "It was a mentality," he says. "At Chisholm, we wanted to score." Aggressive teams resulted in angry opponents as Chisholm won by 40 or 50 or 60 points. Even the school song contained lyrics about "see them rolling up the score, now hear them shout for more, more, more," although Bob himself wasn't the lyricist. Chisholm didn't just beat up on overmatched kids from mining towns. McDonald's teams took down giants—like future NBA player Mark Olberding, a six-foot-nine man-child Chisholm handled in a state title game, and Kevin McHale, one of the great big men in NBA history, a superstar at rival Hibbing. Between 1973 and 1975, Chisholm never lost a regular season game and won two state championships behind the oldest boys, Mike and Paul. Joel won a state title in 1991. Tom's team finished as the state runner-up in 1982.

The toughest adversary for the McDonalds was Hibbing, Bob Dylan's old hometown, located just five miles from Chisholm. When Mike and Paul played, McHale led Hibbing, and years after he faced Chisholm, McHale joked about the dread he experienced being chased around the court by five guys with crew cuts who were coached by a guy with a crew cut. Hibbing's coach at the time, Gary Addington, remembers, "You're playing in a box surrounded by a balcony and people are hanging over the balcony and hollering into your huddle into timeouts and everything else." To prepare, Hibbing practiced on smaller courts to replicate Chisholm's cramped gym and against seven players to simulate the suffocating press. "But you could never really re-create the atmosphere," Addington says. "Once you get all those people in the gym, it was pretty nuts over there."

One of the main basketball nuts was Darlene McDonald, Bob's wife of more than forty years who died of cancer in 1997, two weeks before her sixty-third birthday, three weeks before Joel's wedding. As the statistician, she sat in the balcony behind the basket. There's a spot still dedicated to her. "You never thought, hey, how come I only got two assists?" Mike says. "You never questioned because you knew she had it right." And she told refs when they got it wrong. Throughout his career—those remarkable fifty-nine years on the bench—Bob insists he never received a technical. Darlene never got one either, but one game a ref, finally fed up with her harping from above, flipped her the finger.

It all made for a great show. Chisholm games became spectacles. See Tom score 51! Watch Joel score 40! Marvel at Paul dominating inside and outside, in a home gym where he never lost a game, not from fifth grade through twelfth grade. And arrive early for the pregame warm-ups. During Mike and Paul's era, Chisholm borrowed the pregame routine of Bill Musselman's Minnesota Gophers, who put on a Globetrotters-like show before each game. The Chisholm players spun the ball on their fingers and noses, dribbled between their legs, and threw behind-the-back passes. Mike scored pregame baskets by bouncing the ball off his forehead. Even the opposition watched. Bob encouraged the theatrics. So did Mom. "She was a hard-core fan," Joel says. "She was a proponent of that Chisholm attitude, she really was. She wanted to kill everybody as much as possible, and write as many stats as she could fill up the stat sheet with."

"You either liked us because in the hippie era we had short hair and suits and ties and did some things that were avant-garde or you hated us," Paul says. "There was no in-between."

The Chisholm teams, and the McDonald kids, walked into gyms with big targets plastered on their blue jerseys. Hibbing—where Joel has coached for more than fifteen years and Bob now lives with his second wife, Carol—once greeted Joel the player with a poster that depicted a tombstone with the words, "R.I.P., Joel," a sign that would bring the authorities today. The kids fed off the crowd's energy, whether from their own fans or in an enemy gym. Looking back, Tom expressed some regret at his cockiness, when he wagged his finger after baskets. Tom says he would never let his players get away with those antics, but his tough-guy dad allowed it. The fifty-year-old Tom still plays, often against players from Paul's college team. Both brothers live in Ely, in northern Minnesota. When Paul's young guys face Tom, he confounds them with his shot and fakes. They call him Old School, and he uses his dad's old tricks. Well into his thirties, Bob played in a Chisholm rec league, before he ruptured his Achilles. "I remember just the competiveness, and he could shoot," Tom says. "All over the floor."

Bob always had a good jump shot—lessons he learned from Garmaker—but the boys exceeded him. Still, they aren't certain who takes the title of best shooter. Paul once made all 11 of his field goal attempts and all 11 of his free throws in a game. In their high school days Tom might have had the best jumper. After college Joel perhaps possessed the deepest range. Today the boys maintain their sibling roles. Paul still shows his class clown persona; Tom's more serious, yet still a great athlete; Mike gets Bob animated in conversation, the same way he once antagonized his dad in a practice by questioning an offensive set, a move his father greeted with a literal kick to his ass. Joel serves in the caretaker's role for Bob, living in the same town, helping him with appointments and interviews, the boy who was spoiled as a kid by his mom—in his words and those of his older siblings—but as an adult watches over the dad who started the family's basketball adventure.

The McDonalds aren't one of the most accomplished basketball families just because of the men. Both Sue and Judy displayed skills that set them apart from their peers, at a time when girls sports had just begun in Minnesota. Girls basketball became an official sport when Sue, four years older than Judy, was in eighth grade. In Sue's senior year Judy joined her on the varsity. Both scored with their jumper, and Judy used hers to lead Chisholm to the 1984 state championship. When it came to teaching the game he made his life's work, Bob taught his girls the same way he taught the boys. He made Judy dribble in the dark in the basement. Sue remembers going to the gym to learn the jump shot, and "we weren't going to leave until I had it down. I cried, and I pouted. But it worked. I knew how to shoot a jump shot by the time we were done. He knew that to get anywhere, a set shot wasn't going to cut it."

Unlike their brothers, Sue and Judy didn't get to play for their record-breaking dad—not officially. When the girls program started with an inexperienced coach, Bob sat in the stands and passed notes to a manager who delivered them to the girls coach. When the coach read them in the locker room, the girls recognized their dad's trademark black marker. One game, the girls actually played for Bob, when the girls coach had an illness. Predictably, Chisholm won—by a large margin.

Years after the kids graduated and established their own coaching careers, they gathered at Paul's basketball camp. Bob arrived as a guest counselor. Before he allowed Sue and Judy to teach the kids, "My dad had to check our jump shots," Judy says. "He was like, 'Come on, get out here, I've got to see if you guys can still shoot it.'"

"Could you?" I asked Judy.

"Yeah, we passed the test."

The McDonald children wondered how their dad would handle retirement. He paints. He watches his grandkids play ball. And, perhaps, for a few years, he will still travel to Croatia. Since the late 1980s, McDonald has taken more than twenty trips to the country. Each time he brings a couple of his children and several grandkids. They explore the country and visit with old relatives, the ones whose kin stayed behind when the grandmother who raised Bob left for America. He still speaks Croatian, the language of his youth, and plays tour guide. His coaching days are over. But Bob McDonald, the man who taught his kids the one shot that paved the way for a lifetime in basketball, still has a few lessons to teach.

Chris, the only young guy in my old-man basketball league in upper Manhattan, never knew about the McDonalds of Minnesota, but their jump shooting exploits wouldn't have surprised him. We played every Wednesday night, and anytime I got on a hot streak from outside, Chris again talked about Minnesota and its shooters. He just figured everyone from the state shot three-pointers. He wasn't quite right about my home state—if anything, Minnesota's more known for the big guys it's sent to the NBA, like Kevin McHale.

But there's no doubt the Midwest, all of it, carries a reputation of being home to great shooters. Outsiders might wonder, what else is there to do *but* learn to shoot? And so this tour across the country will spend extra time in two states in particular—Iowa and Indiana. Of course Indiana, home to Oscar Robertson, Larry Bird, Steve Alford, Louie Dampier, and thousands more. But as we'll see, no one else from Indiana ever shot like Rick Mount and Jimmy Rayl. Or produced a shot more memorable than Bobby Plump's. First, though, a stop in Iowa, and a trip back to 1968, when two girls ahead of their time played in the game of the century—and used jump shots folks still marvel at half a century later.

SEVEN

DENISE, JEANETTE, AND THE GAME OF THE CENTURY

The 1969 NBA draft produced one of the great sports trivia questions: Who was the first woman ever selected in the NBA draft? The answer is Denise Long, a five-foot-eleven scoring sensation from Whitten, Iowa, population 185, give or take one or two people. Denise's exploits caught the attention of San Francisco Warriors owner Franklin Mieuli, who dreamed of starting a women's professional basketball league and thought her talent and fame could anchor it. During the 1969 draft in New York City, Mieuli selected Denise in the thirteenth round. The publicity blitz altered Denise's life—appearances with Johnny Carson and on the *Today* show followed, along with opportunities to travel the country, showing off her basketball shooting skills at a time when many states didn't even allow girls to play high school sports.

For NBA fans today, Denise Long is a footnote. But in Iowa, her legend lives. At one time she was the all-time leading scorer in girls basketball in the country. Folks in Iowa still remember her 111-point regular season explosion and her 93-point state tournament game. They remember her hook shots, her layups, and her jump shot, a little fadeaway that always seemed to find the net. Mostly people remember the game Denise played on March 16, 1968, when she led Union-Whitten to the state title with a 113–107 victory over Everly. Denise scored 64 points in the overtime victory—and wasn't the leading scorer in the game. Jeanette Olson, another scoring legend from a small town in Iowa, led Everly with 76 points.

I love great shooting showdowns between scorers, when everyone else on the court seemingly disappears. The only thing better than watching a great shooter get hot is watching two do it in the same game. And for Denise and Jeanette, the jump shot was their primary weapon. Most players in the game took nice, polite set shots. Jeanette looked futuristic—highlights of her rising off the floor would fit in perfectly with clips from any college game today. Denise matched her basket for basket, if not point for point—Jeanette's 76 points included a 24-of-25 performance from the free throw line. By the time the two met in the state finals, the jump shot had only been widely accepted for about a decade. But Jeanette Olson and Denise Long were decades ahead of their time.

In the summer of 2014, I enjoyed separate visits with Denise Rife and Jeanette Lietz, one a pharmacist in Wichita, Kansas, the other a retired teacher in northern Iowa. We talked about their lives, families, travels, and, befitting two women in their sixties who were superb athletes putting strain on their bodies in their younger years, hip replacement surgeries. And we talked about the March night when they were still Denise Long and Jeanette Olson, the two most famous girls basketball players in Iowa—and the country. On that Saturday, their two teams played in front of nearly 14,000 people in Veterans Memorial Auditorium in Des Moines and in front of tens of thousands watching on television—the game was broadcast to nine states. Fans in Iowa still call it the game of the century, a common enough title in sports, but in Iowa if you say those words no one thinks about a football game between Nebraska and Oklahoma or a basketball game between UCLA and Houston. They think about Union-Whitten against Everly, which is another way of saying Long vs. Olson. That's how newspapers touted the showdown. On game day, *The Des Moines Register*, in an all-caps headline stretching across the top of the sports page, wrote, "OLSON DUELS LONG IN TITLE GAME." The game exceeded the hype, earning its place as the best game fans in Iowa ever witnessed—in a girls basketball tournament or otherwise, and in the twentieth century or any other. The day after Denise's 64 points helped Union-Whitten outlast Jeanette's 76, the *Register* again ran an all-caps headline, this one touting the team result: "UNION WHITTEN WINS IT: 113–107!"

Iowa girls played six-on-six basketball at the time, three forwards on one end scoring, three guards on the other who took their position's title literally and only played defense. The setup made it possible for great scorers to put up absurd numbers—Denise broke the national scoring record with 6,250 points, which lasted until 1987, when an Iowa girl broke it. Six-on-six basketball ended in Iowa in the early 1990s. It was time. But the legends who played six-on-six haven't been forgotten, partly because of the scoring numbers but also because girls basketball achieved mythical status in Iowa. Think about football in Texas. Or the state hockey tournament in Minnesota. Or basketball in Indiana. That was the six-on-six girls state basketball tournament in Iowa. At schools where the boys and girls played doubleheaders, many fans left after watching the girls, leaving the boys with a half-empty gym.

The state held its first girls basketball tournament in 1920. Six-on-six basketball became a phenomenon in Iowa, mostly in the small towns. The state tournament transformed into a must-see event, either in person or on television. Small-town farm girls became celebrities in Des Moines; some wore wigs when leaving their hotel to avoid overbearing fans. Growing up in southern Minnesota I watched the six-on-six event each March, marveling at the pageantry—men in tuxedos sweeping the floor, Hall of Fame introductions featuring the announcer reciting astonishing feats by girls who were now middle-age or elderly ladies as they walked onto the court: "In 1948 she averaged 46.2 points per game . . ." At one end of the court hung a large electronic map of Iowa, with blinking lights indicating the sixteen teams in the tournament. When a team lost, the light got extinguished. National media flocked to Iowa—look at these farmers and their daughters and how they love that game of basketball! *Sports Illustrated*, *The New York Times*, *The Wall Street Journal*, the *Chicago Tribune*, and TV networks filed reports from the tournament. Iowa turned down a request from ABC's *Wide World of Sports* to broadcast the event because Wayne Cooley of the powerful Iowa Girls High School Athletic Union refused to relinquish control over the production, which was as extravagant as anything the major networks could have created.

But even Iowa hadn't seen a game like the 1968 finals. Everly came in unbeaten. Union-Whitten entered with one loss, which came when the coach sat all the starters. Jeanette led Everly to the 1966 state championship and a third-place finish in 1967. Fans anticipated the matchup for months before it actually happened. On YouTube, a user posted numerous old championship games from the six-on-six tourney. For the 1968 game, presented in black-and-white, the user simply described it as "THE Game! Denise Long. Jeanette Olson. What more can you say?"

Growing up in Whitten, in an old house that was once home to a hat shop and meat market, Denise Long seemed destined for stardom. Union-Whitten coach Paul Eckerman spotted potential in Denise, placing—and raising—expectations on a kid who was ready for basketball greatness, if not the attention that came with it. Denise says, "I remember in seventh grade the coach was teaching his civics class, and he had me come up in front, and he had me stand there and he said to the rest of the class, 'This girl is going to break all the records in the state of Iowa and set all kinds of records, and they won't be broken for a long time.'" Eckerman didn't want anything standing in the way of his prophecy. One day he saw Denise get knocked off her horse. He made her sell the animal she loved. The external pressures on Denise were exceeded only by her internal drive. For three to four hours a day, she practiced at the town park. One night, she says, she bundled up and ventured out when it was 11 degrees below zero. She used a frozen ball. She couldn't dribble. But she could still shoot. An editor from a small newspaper drove by and witnessed Denise in the cold. He wrote an article about the dedication it took for someone to go out in the elements and work on their game. In 1970, the town renamed the park after Denise.

Revenge also motivated Denise. Year after year she watched her sister Dana's team lose in the tournament before Union-Whitten made it to state. Denise vowed to change that. It became her mission in life, transformed her into a basketball machine, and a scoring one. From her first game as a freshman, Denise brought a frightening intensity to the games. When I met Denise and Dana—along with their husbands—in Kansas for lunch and coffee, forty-six years after the title game, I told Denise the story about Bill Russell supposedly vomiting before most of his games. She identified with the combination of nerves and resolve. "The night before games, I was never relaxed. Anytime we went on bus rides to the game, all the other girls would be laughing, talking, and just chattering. I would have red blotches up on my cheek. I couldn't talk. I wouldn't talk. I wouldn't say a word to anybody. To me it was life-and-death." Instead of hurting her game or making her nervous, "The more I felt apprehensive about it, the more I felt foreboding, the better I did."

Up in northwest Iowa, growing up on a farm about five miles outside Everly, Jeanette Olson displayed the same dedication to her craft, but with a different personality. At the 1968 state tournament, Denise remembers sitting in the stands and seeing Jeanette a few rows away. Denise idolized Jeanette, the year-older star who had already been to multiple state tourneys, won one title, and seemed at ease with being the star of the greatest show in town. Jeanette told her, "Denise, come sit by me, I don't bite." Denise says, "I was very shy. She was very relaxed. We had different temperaments."

Jeanette shot at her farm for an hour a day, no matter the weather, firing shot after shot, first on gravel, then on a slab of cement. In seventh grade she missed practice the day the coach showed the kids the basics of the jump shot. Instead her older brother taught her the jumper. "You go to church, you go to school, and maybe an occasional movie," she says, "but you're pretty much just there on the farm, and so we just practiced basketball." Jeanette played against her brothers and received no mercy. Eventually Jeanette drove into town. The custodian let her into the gym, where she perfected her craft. She combined her height—five-ten—with superior leaping ability, making her impossible to stop.

Jeanette owned a more classic shooting form than Denise, a purer jump shot. When Denise was a sophomore, coach Eckerman told her she was good but needed to work on her jump shot. "Because Jeanette had a jump shot, and I was going to have to get one." Jeanette jumped several feet off the court, a vertical leap that set her apart in 1968. Her shooting elbow was always straight, her guide hand perfectly placed on the side. Iowa broadcasting icon Jim Zabel called her the "jump shot specialist."

During my lunch with Denise, her husband, Dan, marveled, "Have you seen pictures with Jeanette being like three and a half feet off the ground? She was amazing. No wonder she has to have hip replacement surgery."

The Everly basketball team wore skirts and bloomers—"I loved our uniforms," Jeanette says. "They were cool." Photos captured Jeanette's red-and-white uniform flaring out as she rose for her gorgeous shot. During my visit to the Estherville, Iowa, home of Jeanette and her husband, Doug, I asked her to drag out some scrapbooks that looked like they hadn't been pulled out much this decade. "I don't know why I'm holding on to them all this time," she says. "It's probably time to let them go." But as we sat on the couch and turned the pages and read the old newspapers of Jeanette's accomplishments and saw some pictures of her jumper, the retired schoolteacher said, "There's my jump shot, and I've got another picture that's even better. On some of them my form is really, really good. And with my vertical jump . . . not to brag. Sorry." The Midwestern reticence is misplaced. The only time Jeanette Olson should have ever apologized for her jump shot is if she told a defender, "I'm sorry—you can't stop this."

She led Everly—home to about 700 people at the time—to the 1966 state title as a sophomore. Early that season Jeanette suffered a knee injury and missed five games. Jeanette occasionally limped on the knee. She looked wounded and defeated—and then routinely scored 40 points. It was a little like Jim Brown limping back into the huddle after every carry, then ripping off eight more yards. One paper called her Jeanette O-Granny Olson. I read part of that story to her and Doug.

"She shoots like her life depends on scoring points. She's basketball's Jekyll and Hyde. A crippled, limping string-bean sophomore and a standout prospect for most valuable player. Old granny will rock again."

"Oh, God," Jeanette says.

"Walks like she needs at least one cane. Sometimes it looked like she was using her last ounce of strength to get back to midcourt. But put a basketball in her hands and you've got a wildcat. If she's in as much pain as she appears she's headed for a nursing home."

"Haven't got there yet, have you, Jeanette?" Doug asks.

"No. Thank you very much."

In the 1966 finals, with Everly trailing 49–48 with less than four minutes remaining, Jeanette hit a jump shot and scored eight quick points in a 65–55 victory. Following the game, her mom told a newspaper Jeanette wore out at least three basketballs over the previous summer, even though Jeanette "was out in the fields with the rest of us pulling weeds out of the soybeans."

Two years later, as the season progressed, it became clear Everly and Union-Whitten were the two best teams. Entering the state tournament, Jeanette averaged 58.7 points, Denise 61.6. In a regular season game against Dows, Denise scored 111 points, although she believes it was 112— the scorekeeper incorrectly credited one of her free throws to another Union-Whitten player. (One point in a 111-point outing seems like just adding another buck to a millionaire's checking account, but 112 would have been a state record; as it was, Denise tied the mark.)

In Everly's opening state game, Jeanette set a new tournament record for most points in a game with 74 (breaking the old record of 69). The mark lasted twenty-four hours. In Union-Whitten's debut, Denise made 32 of 46 from the floor and 29 of 31 free throws to score 93 points. Vince Coyle wrote in the Ames newspaper, "As the first quarter wore on you were not so much aware of the fact that you were at a state tournament game as you were of the fact that you were watching a great artist at work." Anticipation about a showdown between the two shooting sensations that built over the course of the year became a frenzy as reporters, fans, and even the other teams waited for the two best teams—and players—to emerge from the initial field of sixteen.

When it finally arrived, the *Register* and other papers touted the Olson vs. Long showdown. *Sports Illustrated* covered the 1968 tournament, although the story didn't run until February 1969. Large color photos of Jeanette in her skirt shooting her jumper and Denise in her green uniform going up for a shot ran with the story. The *SI* feature admired one newspaper that profiled the final with a headline that read, "MISS OLSON, MEET MISS LONG."

At the outset, Jeanette—battling strep throat—held up her end, hitting shots from the baseline, the wing, and the lane, oblivious to the defenders and pressure of the moment. Following a made basket in six-on-six, one official fired the ball to half-court and a fellow referee, who then quickly passed it to the other team. When Union-Whitten drilled a basket and Everly took possession, Jeanette started with the ball at midcourt. She'd pass and cut or work to get the ball back. Players were only allowed two dribbles—this was offensive efficiency in its purest form, although creatively stifling. With two bounces Jeanette covered large swaths of the court, getting wherever she needed. Denise started slow. On her early scores, she banked her shots, something she almost never did with her jumpers or shots from close to the basket. Fortunately for the Cobras, Cyndy Long, Denise's cousin and frequent shooting partner at the park, was hot early. With Everly putting two, sometimes all three, defenders on Denise (she was literally being covered by every opposing defender on the court, and given the two-dribble rule, it wasn't a bad strategy), Cyndy found herself open from 15 feet away. She fired her set shot without hesitation and with great success. By the time the game ended she'd scored 41 to complement Denise's 64—but it was those early shots that proved key.

Then Denise finally took over and became fully engaged in her great duel. After a slow start she exchanged baskets with Jeanette while Union-Whitten took a double-digit lead.

Down on Everly's offensive end of the court, another all-state Union-Whitten player, guard Carol Hannusch, attempted to contain Jeanette. Carol came to Union-Whitten her senior year, transferring from Gilbert, Iowa. (Did shady recruiting happen in Iowa girls ball? Yes.) I called Carol because I wanted to know what it was like playing basketball and never being able to shoot. The concept fascinates me. The whole point of playing basketball is to score, or so those of us who were perhaps a bit weaker on the defensive end tell ourselves. A kid picks up a ball and shoots and a lifelong love is born. Yet every year hundreds of players in Iowa willingly surrendered the chance to shoot. Carol was an outstanding all-around athlete and physically strong—she set national shot put records as a teenager. She fired half-court and even full-court passes to Union-Whitten's forwards, often hitting Denise for an easy layup. Her outlet passes looked more like the work of Wes Unseld or Kevin Love than of any seventeen-year-old girl. But still . . . how did she handle not being able to shoot? "I liked defense, I really did," she says. "And I didn't practice like the girls at forward. They worked on it all the time. You don't get as much glory on defense, I suppose, but I loved it." (That attitude by guards stuck down on the defensive side wasn't universal. During her career, Jeanette dealt with teammates who weren't always supportive of her high-scoring ways. But Everly coach Larry Johnson told Jeanette to shoot, demanded she shoot. She worked on her shot every day, while others picked up a ball for the first time each year on the first day of practice. Why wouldn't the team rely on her?)

Carol played Jeanette as well as anyone could, bodying her on the majority of her shots. Jeanette didn't even seem to notice. "I knew I was doing well," Jeanette says, "but I'd done well all of the other games for the most part, too." Six-on-six meant an offensive wizard was helpless to do anything on the other end against someone just as talented. They were scoring machines sent out to destroy. But gazing down on the other end, they were spectators, just like the 14,000 people in attendance. It allowed time to appreciate a rival's skills, as Denise did while watching Jeanette.

"I was totally entertained," Denise tells me, the mental pictures as clear as they were forty-six years earlier. "She was mobile, she could reverse pivot and go in different directions. She could jump. She didn't need a pick. She was just artistically beautiful to watch."

Union-Whitten led 53–47 at halftime—at least on the scoreboard. In reality, the official scorekeeper messed up the score in the first quarter, giving Union-Whitten too many points and taking points away from Everly. Coach Larry Johnson noticed the mistake in the first half, but even after a long delay, the score remained three points off. Finally during the halftime break, newspaper reporters and radio announcers convinced the scorekeeper he made a mistake. Instead of being a 53–47 game, it was actually Union-Whitten holding a 52–49 advantage. The scoreboard was corrected in time for the third quarter. The mistake annoys Jeanette to this day.

Everly trailed 101–95 with less than 45 seconds left in the game before Jeanette hit two jumpers to narrow the deficit to two. Then, after a Union-Whitten turnover, Jeanette caught a pass near midcourt and got fouled on the play, giving her a one-and-one at the free throw line. There were three seconds on the clock. Following a timeout, as Jeanette stood at the line, announcer Jim Zabel called her a "pressure ballplayer," with "the weight of the world on her shoulders." Jeanette first tells me she wasn't scared—"Well, a little nervous," she says with a laugh—but instead thought, "We're going to get this and win it."

Neither shot touched any part of the rim—two perfect swishes, putting both teams in this game of the century over the century mark. The teams tied at 101, Hannusch tried another of her long passes for Union-Whitten. An Everly defender intercepted it. In the longest three seconds in Iowa girls basketball history, Everly made two passes and got the ball again to Jeanette, just above the free throw line, 16 feet from the basket. She rose one more time, just like she'd done ever since learning to shoot on the family farm. A Union-Whitten defender put a hand up, but it was a useless gesture. It wouldn't affect the shot. Jeanette released the ball— and watched it go in and out.

"It rolled out. Dang!" she says five decades later, probably still surprised a shot she made thousands of times in her life didn't fall on one of her final shots as a high school legend. Although shocked at the late-game collapse, Union-Whitten still took control early in the overtime—and Denise finally felt comfortable. "That's when I finally had the most confidence," she says. She scored at her normal pace throughout the game, but early in the showdown Denise didn't feel right. For the first time in her career all that tension she felt in the moments leading up to a game— that sense of foreboding—didn't fully disappear when she stepped on the court. At one point as Denise stood on the free throw line, an Everly defender came up and said, "Miss it, bitch." And she did. The moment almost proved overwhelming, until she overwhelmed one more defense. Before the overtime, with her team having just blown a six-point lead in the final seconds, and with her teammate who fouled Jeanette nearly "suicidal" in the huddle, Denise told the girl the foul "doesn't matter because we're going to win anyway." Denise won the jump ball from Jeanette, and on the first Union-Whitten possession banked in a short shot. On the next possession, Denise dished off to Cyndy for a layup. Union-Whitten took a four-point lead it wouldn't lose.

Jeanette's and Denise's final numbers: 76 points on 26 of 41 from the field and 24 of 25 from the free throw line for Jeanette; 64 points on 27 of

38 from the floor and 10 of 12 free throws for Denise. For the tournament, Denise scored 282 points in four games, Jeanette 258, both marks shattering the old record of 200.

Newspapers from around the country—from Spokane to San Antonio—picked up the wire reports of the game. That exposure created fans for Denise and Jeanette far beyond Iowa. Letters poured in. Denise got them from the Naval Academy, Jeanette from writers at the Chatsworth, Georgia, newspaper seeking a local paper with a recap of the game. A mother wrote about her daughter coming home and saying Jeanette had the neatest jump shot. And a man who said he was older than sixty requested a picture of Jeanette—"a small one; I will enlarge it." (He also wanted her to call him Jack, because all his friends did, and said he kept his mind young by writing to college girls. Celebrity has its downside.)

Jeanette graduated in 1968, but Denise returned for one more season of unparalleled scoring. She averaged nearly 69 points per game as a senior, but Union-Whitten failed to repeat as champions, getting upset in the state semifinals. The pressure built for Denise. Even after the 1968 championship, when she fulfilled her dream, she says she remembers "a dead-end feeling, like what can you do now?" That ambivalence stayed with Denise for the next several decades, as she alternated between wanting basketball to be the only thing in her life to wanting it expelled from her life. Then, in 1969, in the spring, the San Francisco Warriors called her high school.

Denise took the call in the school office. She thought it was a joke—drafted? Young people associated that word with the Army in 1969. But, yes, it was the San Francisco Warriors. NBA commissioner Walter Kennedy thought it was a joke too, and not a particularly humorous one. He disallowed the selection, removed it from the record book. (That's why in some records Denise is not listed as the first woman drafted in the NBA. New Orleans took Lusia Harris in 1977. But, for you trivia buffs, Denise was first.) Mieuli—the charismatic, bearded, motorcycle-loving owner—admitted the Warriors didn't want to use Denise in an NBA game, but in a women's league. "We weren't trying to belittle the draft or the caliber of players available in the late rounds."

Already an Iowa legend, Denise became a national celebrity. She traveled to New York and appeared on *The Tonight Show* and *Today*. During her cross-country travels, she met Jack Dempsey, Gene Tunney, Bob Hope, and, perhaps her—and her mom's—favorite, the dashing and charming Robert Wagner. Appearing on TV with Carson brought to life a dream Cyndy expressed years earlier, during a break at the Whitten park. As the girls sucked on lollipops and chewed sour apples, Cyndy, perhaps thinking about a life outside Whitten, as if she knew Denise's skills could take her far beyond the town's boundaries, said, "Wouldn't it be neat if you could get on the Johnny Carson show and tell everybody about girls basketball?"

Mieuli previously had wanted to start a women's league, but didn't know where to find players. A writer from *Sports Illustrated* told him about the high-scoring stars of Iowa girls basketball, specifically Denise Long. He made a trip to see an all-star game. The high level of play surprised him, and he knew he had a player who could now anchor his new league based out of California. The Longs picked him up from the Des Moines airport and took him to Whitten. They toured the town—two main streets, one going east–west, the other north–south.

"Is this all of it?" Mieuli asked Denise and Dana.

"I told him you could run through the town in less than a minute," Denise says.

Mieuli—who joked he shook all 187 pairs of hands in Whitten— "promised to take care" of Denise when she headed west. Sister Dana, a former high-scoring forward herself, picked up a roster spot in the league too, and both players became stars in Mieuli's California creation. The owner imported Iowa's six-on-six rules, seeking the high scores—and record-breaking scorers—that attracted fans to the game in the state. Mieuli, forty-nine years old when the Long sisters moved to San Francisco, treated the two like royalty. "We were his pets," Dana says. "He was a lot of fun and a lot of fun to be with. He was kindhearted." Mieuli gave eighteen-year-old Denise a purple Jaguar during her time in California while Dana received an emerald-green Cadillac Eldorado. They took trips out on his yacht, toured Haight-Ashbury, and he introduced them to movie stars and athletes. He gave them season passes to all the pro teams in the Bay Area. Dana and Denise sat next to Jerry Lucas at a banquet

and watched the NBA legend memorize a phone book. They met Willie
Mays at a Giants game and got a lift from Willie McCovey. A picture in
the Santa Cruz paper showed Denise dribbling toward the basket against
Nate Thurmond, San Francisco's six-foot-eleven Hall of Fame center.

Just like they did when chronicling her high-scoring games, national
writers again covered Denise. Some reporters wrote sarcastic pieces, others
were amused. Some were protective, others admired Denise. Some were
just plain sexist. Ed Levitt of *The Oakland Tribune* wrote:

> *I never met a woman basketball player I liked—until I spotted De-*
> *nise Long going up to stuff one through the hoop. It was love at first*
> *shot. Denise is different. She's a long-limbed 19-year-old beauty with*
> *medium brown hair and dark brown eyes. She's not exactly a Raquel*
> *Welch. But can Raquel sink a basketball from 40 feet out? . . . I don't*
> *care how well Al Attles coaches or Joe Ellis shoots, 10 young, shapely*
> *gals bouncing around in skimpy suits must be more appealing to the*
> *eye than some rugged he-man basketball team.*

The league consisted of only four teams, all of them named after Bay
Area clubs: Giants (Denise's team), Raiders, 49ers, Athletics (Dana's team).
The original plan for games called for the eight-minute quarters that were
the standard in six-on-six basketball. At one time Mieuli wanted the teams
playing the first three quarters prior to the NBA game, with the last quarter coming at halftime of the men's pro game, a bizarre scheme meant to
spread out the entertainment for fans. Despite living in a radically different
home and playing in radically different environments, Denise still scored
with ease. She poured in 51 points in her first game and averaged 45 for
the season.

Denise lasted just a year, and the league died shortly after her departure. She returned to Iowa, beginning an odyssey where she played basketball and left the game, only to return and leave again. Denise played
overseas in South Korea, Japan, and the Philippines on a tour, and appeared at camps and exhibitions with NBA players. On the front page of
the June 30, 1970, edition of *The Des Moines Register*, the paper reported
about ground forces in Cambodia, and an explosion that rocked the Drake

University campus. Those stories shared front-page real estate with a piece about nineteen-year-old Denise's retirement. It was the first of a series of articles over the next decade that chronicled her disillusion with the game, although stories about her desire to return were mixed in. A 1972 story headlined "Dream World Gone for Denise Long" included her saying, "I loved the limelight, the attention and everything, but I hated it too." She freely admits not enjoying the game as much when she played in front of a few hundred folks compared to more than 10,000, a sentiment Jeanette echoed when talking about her own post-high-school playing career. "I just didn't want to play in front of nobody," Denise says. "It made me lose interest. Because that always inspired me, to play in front of people who cared."

Her celebrity stature in Iowa smothered her. She heard people whisper her name when they spotted her at the movies in a darkened theater. At one college, she received up to a dozen obscene phone calls a night. They only stopped when Denise—who became a born-again Christian in the early '70s—quoted Scripture and talked about Jesus as her savior. The callers hung up and finally gave up. Denise attended several colleges in the decades that followed, searching for peace and her place in the world, but eventually established a career in pharmacy. Today the good memories of her days as a superstar stand out over the difficult ones. She has her faith, and a job she hopes to retire from soon—the grueling weeklong schedules have taken a toll.

When it came to playing basketball after high school, Jeanette, like Denise, was a victim of her time. Few college opportunities existed for women basketball players in the 1960s. Jeanette attended John F. Kennedy College and became a top player at the Nebraska school, which qualified for an AAU tournament. Jeanette was also set to represent the United States at the Pan Am Games until another knee injury, this one severe, ended that dream. She became a teacher and coach in Iowa, finally settling down in Estherville with her husband, Doug, and their blended family of seven children.

Denise and Jeanette saw each other occasionally over the decades, at gatherings or when they'd get honored at the state tournament. They'd say hello but that was about it. Both suffered physically. Jeanette's knee problems led to a knee replacement, and later she received a hip replacement. (She was born with a hip displacement that didn't start affecting her until she was in her forties and spending long days on her feet as a teacher. So her vertical, as impressive as it was, didn't seem to be a factor in the eventual surgery.) A month after I visited Denise, she was scheduled for her own hip replacement surgery. She considered calling Jeanette about what to expect.

While Jeanette's jumping days ended with her surgery, a great shooter never loses her touch. During our visit, she talked about the recent time she played her elementary-school-age grandson in Around the World, a game where shooters move to various spots on the court. It was not shocking that she won the game. But the youngster only knew her as Grandma, and grandmas don't shoot like that. "Big mistake," Jeanette says. "I got a little too competitive. I thought, 'What did I do?' I felt sorry." The kid took the loss hard.

"Your brothers didn't let you win," I pointed out.

But that's what siblings do. Grandmas are different. Jeanette still looked chagrined about her grandson's disappointment. The regret over the youngster's bruised ego seemed greater than the pride she had about her old shooting stroke remaining potent.

One day the kid will learn: Getting beat in a shooting game by your grandma on the basketball court is embarrassing—unless your grandma was once the unstoppable Jeanette Olson.

I read one more letter of Jeanette's before I left, a note Denise mailed her a few days after the 1968 title game. Denise wrote, "This letter will probably be very short because I'm writing it in English class, which is the last period of the day and I want to get it out (mailed) today." In the note, Denise congratulated Jeanette and talked about her term paper—which she was far behind on—that focused on dreams. She told Jeanette, "I think you're the best B.B. player I've ever seen and I mean that. There'll never be a player like you—never. Just because you didn't win the state championship, it didn't take any points away from you being the greatest player because you are. I want you to know that too, ok? I just felt privileged to be able to stand beside you on the all-tournament team." The note goes on for two pages, cursive, written at the end of a school day by a teenage girl who was one of the most famous people in Iowa, intended for a rival, peer, and fellow actor in a game that wasn't even a week old, but would be remembered forever.

Two months after my visit with Jeanette, I showed Denise a copy of the letter as we sat in Starbucks. "She's still got a letter? Wow." Denise read the note. When she finished she placed it on a table. About ten minutes later she leaned over and picked it up. Holding it a few inches from her face to help decipher her own words from long ago, she read it again.

"Isn't that something," she finally said, the same thought people in Iowa and far beyond have always had about that March night in 1968 when small-town teenagers Denise Long and Jeanette Olson put on the greatest shooting display they'd ever seen.

EIGHT

THE ROCKET AND THE SPLENDID SPLINTER

Take a trip to Indiana during basketball season. Stop in at four or five high school games, catch a Purdue vs. Indiana battle, spring for tickets to a Pacers game, visit the Indiana Basketball Hall of Fame. At each stop ask people to name the greatest player to come out of the state. Most will say Oscar Robertson or Larry Bird. Ask them to name the most dominant high school player, and George McGinnis and Damon Bailey enter the conversation. But ask them about the greatest shooter, and the names you'll hear most often are Jimmy Rayl and Rick Mount. They're the quintessential Indiana legends, two shooting savants from a state where shooters became the primary export, two stars separated by seven years, bonded by their accomplishments and shooting strokes.

Today both Rayl and Mount live in the towns where they became famous—Rayl in the Kokomo home he lived in as a high school star, Mount in Lebanon, a block from his old house—and both maintain an aura more than five decades after their shots captured the public's imagination. Old-timers tell stories about their most famous games and shots, of jumpers made from 25 feet or even 35, of 40- and 50-point games, and young people know all about their talents, the tales passed down through generations.

Both are grandpas now, although only one looks the part. Rayl, who graduated from Kokomo High School in 1959 and won Mr. Basketball in Indiana before setting scoring marks at Indiana University, has thinning white hair and glasses. He walks with a slight limp and experiences some short-term memory problems—aftereffects of a mild stroke. Mount, who graduated from Lebanon High School in 1966 and won Mr. Basketball before setting scoring marks at Purdue University, had just wrapped up another one of his shooting camps when I visited, clinics highlighted by his lectures and his personal displays of shooting greatness. The phrase "former schoolboy legend" seems permanently attached to Rayl and Mount, even as one experiences life in his seventies and the other approaches it. Visitors still stop by often to see Rayl—Dick Enberg, who called Rayl's games at Indiana, has dropped in. I visited with Jimmy and his wife, Nancy, who watched Jimmy going back to his days as a high school star and recalls some moments from her husband's career that even the former Hoosier has forgotten.

Mount still looks a bit like the schoolboy who went from a statewide phenomenon to a nationwide sensation when he appeared on *Sports Illustrated*'s cover in high school, his golden hair and golden touch intact. I met him on a Friday, an hour after his camp ended. He wore his camouflage shorts, black basketball shoes, and red tank top as he settled into his chair with lunch from Arby's. Still sweating, he looked more like a sixteen-year-old kid winding down after a tournament game than a sixty-seven-year-old camp director. His wife, Donna, was out. But like Nancy with Jimmy, Donna has seen all of Mount's famous games, dating back to when they were high school sweethearts, has heard all the stories, and has watched Mount occasionally struggle as he transitioned from the boy everyone in the state loved to a man who didn't always find peace in his hometown.

Both players have spent decades talking about each other. In November 1965, as Mount prepared for his senior season at Lebanon, Rayl had been out of high school for six years and finished his All-American career at Indiana two years earlier. Kokomo writer Bob Ford called Mount "the most exciting basketball player to hit the Indiana high school ranks since Jimmy Rayl."

Upon Mount's induction into the Indiana Basketball Hall of Fame in 1992, David Kasey wrote, "Rick 'The Rocket' Mount smiles as someone asks him again for the one millionth time, 'Who's a better pure shooter, yourself or Jimmy Rayl?'" Mount replied then, "Why can't we both just be remembered as great shooters? Why does one of us have to be better?" Other Indiana legends offer their own opinions. Bobby Plump told me Mount was the best shooter he ever saw. Rayl's Indiana teammate Tom Bolyard once said, while Mount stood a few feet away at a Hall of Fame reception, "Jimmy has to be the greatest shooter in the history of Indiana." John Wooden simply said they were the two best.

For his part, Rayl didn't express his opinion outright. He once told a writer, "I know people think he's the greatest shooter who ever played in Indiana. Some say I was. It's too silly to worry about. But I will say one thing. I shot farther out than Mount did, for what that's worth. Rick didn't have the range I did, but he had his corner shot. I'm not putting him down in any way, shape or form, but maybe I was just a little bit crazier. I had a coach who would let me do them." But when I ask Rayl if he was as good as anyone, he says, "As far as shooting, yeah, I was."

When I talk with Mount about the comparison, he says, "That's why they make barbershops, all the little cafés that serve coffee, and little pubs, so you can all go in there and argue about it. Was Rick Mount better than Jimmy Rayl or was Jimmy Rayl better than Rick Mount?" Mount eventually provided an answer, but it didn't come when I asked directly about Rayl. Instead, it was when I asked Mount to name the best shooter he ever faced, and if any were better than him. I suppose I was leading the witness.

"I'm the best shooter that ever played," he says. "People say, 'Oh, really?' The first thing I tell them, I say, 'I believe that, and I'll take it to my grave. I believe I was the best.'" Mount thinks owning that arrogance is a requirement for anyone who wants a roster spot in the argument; there's only one right answer if anyone asks if you're the best there's ever been. He tells me, "If I asked you, if you and I were great shooters, and I said, 'Are you the best shooter that ever played?' You say 'no,' I wouldn't think much of you. If you asked me that, if I said, 'No, I was probably the tenth best,' you wouldn't think much of me, would you? You wouldn't be right here. You'd probably close that book up and get your ass on the plane and get out of here."

Adults lost their minds when they watched Rayl and Mount shoot. The *Sporting News* wrote of Mount at Purdue, "Fans yelled at Mount's teammates to give him the ball. If he held it for a few seconds they yelled at him to shoot, creating amazing pressure. If Rick missed, they'd groan. But when Rick scored, there was sheer ecstasy. More than 54 percent of the time, this ecstasy and accuracy blended into the greatest love affair that ever descended from a balcony. Not even Juliet was so enraptured by Romeo."

Rayl inspired actual poetry, not just ecstasy. One of Rayl's most memorable games came against Muncie Central in 1959. Late in the game, Rayl—competing with a 101-degree fever—hit his face on the side of the scorer's bench. He left, but returned with a patch that nearly covered his swollen eye. Knocking in jumpers and the game-clinching free throws, Rayl scored 45 in a 79–77 victory. It was a great performance regardless. The aftermath sealed the legend. Indiana sportswriter Corky Lamm wrote, "Sickly, spindly Jimmy Rayl, caught a Bearcat by the tail, wouldn't let him out alive, shot him dead with 45." During my two weeks in Indiana, four people recited the poem to me, without prompting, a testament to the staying power of Rayl's legend, if not the Hoosier State's love of poetry. This effect on grown men lasted long after Rayl stopped playing ball. In a 1983 column, Bob Ford described covering Rayl:

During the winter of 1958–59 my weight ballooned to 185 pounds, my pants size went to 38 and our grocery bill, thanks to my enormous appetite, resembled the tab for the Korean war. All summer and fall the sewer had been belching, threatening to make our basement a disaster area. The Roto-Rooter man spent more time at our house than his own. The eaves on the east side of the house had begun to sag. The roof developed a leak over the corner of the living room. The furnace became violently ill. The screen on the patio had more holes in it than John Dillinger's alibis. The old Buick needed new tires and the kids needed new shoes. The dog, the hamster and the parakeet all died within a period of three months. But there were, I figured, a couple of pluses. We were all healthy . . . and Jimmy Rayl was coming back for his last year of basketball at Kokomo High School.

Rayl's jumper did what his physique never could: Intimidate. People called Rayl the Splendid Splinter, and if it seemed presumptuous to give a skinny high school kid the same nickname as the greatest hitter in baseball, just remember: Jimmy Rayl would have kicked Ted Williams's ass in H-O-R-S-E. Rayl stood about six-two and weighed, depending on which program you consulted or newspaper you read, anywhere from 135 to 145 pounds. One writer said he looked like the before picture in a muscle-building ad. If he'd gone flat on his back someone could have slipped him under the door at the packed Kokomo gymnasium. Sportswriter Bob Collins once called Rayl "the physical marvel, 6-foot tall, 145 pounds, a nervous wreck and a human test tube for every new disease that hits town, Jimmy looks like death warmed over before any game starts." Opponents bullied him with elbows and hip checks on the court, and would have kicked sand in his face and tried walking off with his girl if they had the chance. None of it prevented him from lighting up scoreboards. Rayl surprised defenders with his quickness and confounded with his stamina—where on that thin body could he fit an engine that never stopped running?

No matter his size or age, Rayl never met a defense he couldn't conquer with his jumper. He once said, "I led my grade school in scoring. I led my church league in scoring. I could always shoot. I could always make it go in the basket." Summer months in Kokomo found Rayl playing hour after hour in a city park. "I had a rough schedule in the summertime," he tells me. "We'd sleep in late and get up and go out to the park about noon. Stayed out there. All the new players showed up about 6:30. That's when the real good games would start because the older guys would work during the day. I'm still convinced that's how you get a lot better, going against older guys." Twenty to thirty players gathered at the park, five on a team, playing half-court games. "If you lost you may not play for another forty-five minutes," Rayl says, "so you had to keep winning." Playing on baskets in the summer with chain nets didn't affect Rayl, as his jumper found the target as effectively as it did with regulation cords during the winter.

Unlike Mount—a household name as a high school freshman—Rayl's dominance snuck up on people. As a sophomore the school yearbook spelled his name "Rayles." His final two years electrified Kokomo and the fans who packed the school's historic Memorial Gymnasium. More than 7,500 people watched Rayl and his teammates, the line to get into the games stretching block after block starting as early as 3:30 in the afternoon.

The game was changing—and players like Rayl were the reason. Ford wrote in 1958, "There was a time not many years ago that if an entire team scored 45 points in 32 minutes it had done a slam-bang job. That was considered a real barn-burner . . . a real firewagon demonstration. That was before the advent of the jump shot. It was before fine gymnasiums and almost perfect equipment made it possible for a team to score as many as 100 points in 32 minutes." A superstitious player, Rayl always missed his final shot in warm-ups, figuring it helped his chances of making the first shot of the actual game. Once the games started, Rayl never stopped shooting—or scoring. Under the direction of his coach, Joe Platt, who encouraged his star's gunning, Rayl shattered school and conference scoring records as a senior, averaging 29.6 points and finishing with 1,632 in his career.

The most famous game Rayl played in as a high school phenom ended in a loss. At the end of the 1959 regular season, Kokomo faced New Castle in a game known as the Church Street Shootout. It took place in New Castle's old gymnasium, which the school stopped using the following year when it moved into the biggest field house in the country, with room for 10,000. On that night, New Castle beat Kokomo 92–81. Even more memorably, Ray Pavy outscored Rayl 51–49. The game isn't as famous in Indiana as Milan's 1954 victory over Muncie Central, but it's surely one of the four or five most well-known games in the state's history. A fellow guard, Pavy didn't possess Rayl's skills as an outside shooter. Instead he scored from all over, with sharp instincts around the basket. "He wasn't a pure shooter like Jimmy Rayl," one writer noted. "Who the hell is?"

Despite the loss at the end of the regular season, Kokomo cruised through the playoffs, relying on Rayl's knack for late-game heroics. In the first round of the semistate—in a game featuring a showdown between Rayl and his future Indiana teammate Tom Bolyard—Kokomo defeated Fort Wayne South, the defending state champions, 92–90. Rayl outscored Bolyard 40–33, with the final, winning points coming when Rayl drove to his right and launched a shot estimated to be 30 feet out. It flipped through the net with two seconds left, giving Kokomo the win. Pandemonium ensued. Rayl later said there were "folding chairs flying through the air." Kokomo advanced to the state championship game against

Crispus Attucks. Oscar Robertson was long gone, but Attucks remained powerful, crushing Kokomo 92–54. Rayl still broke Oscar's record for most points in the final four games, scoring 114.

Rayl went a hundred miles south of Kokomo to Bloomington, and Indiana University, where he played for Branch McCracken, leader of the famed Hurryin' Hoosiers. McCracken eventually proved the perfect coach for Rayl—he encouraged aggressiveness on the offensive end and the Hoosiers didn't run traditional plays. "Branch never said no," Rayl has said. "I shot 48 times against Michigan State. What coach today would put up with that?" But Rayl's time in Bloomington proved frustrating the first two years. Few great scorers experienced the type of career Rayl had at Indiana, where he went from being a player who never scored, to one who couldn't be stopped, from afterthought to All-American. As a sophomore, in his first year of varsity eligibility, he scored a mere 79 points and struggled with his confidence. Everyone who thought he was too frail to make it in the Big Ten appeared vindicated. Instead, in his final two seasons, from 1961 to 1963, Rayl became one of the most explosive scorers in conference history, although he remained the same malnourished figure he'd always been (a *Sporting News* story in 1962 noted he'd gained ten pounds, which put him at 145).

Twice Rayl scored 56 points for the Hoosiers—no one else in Indiana history has scored more than 48 in a game. The first time occurred against the Minnesota Golden Gophers. In the first game between the two teams in the 1962 season, Minnesota won 104–100. The rematch took place in Indiana, and the Hoosiers won 105–104. The Gophers took the lead with two free throws in the final seconds. McCracken wanted the Hoosiers to call timeout. Instead Indiana got the ball to Rayl. He dribbled up the court, dodged defenders, and won the game with a shot that was described in various reports as being from 16 feet, 25 feet, 30 feet, and a "few paces" past the midcourt stripe. With each year that passes, another foot gets added. McCracken said, "That was the greatest exhibition of outside shooting I have ever seen." Players hoisted Rayl onto their shoulders, and the fans did the same. Rayl's 56 points broke the Big Ten record at the time. Since it came in overtime, and because Roger Maris had just set a home run record and denigrating records was sort of a popular pastime, people suggested Rayl's mark deserved an asterisk, because the previous record of 52 came in regulation. Rayl removed any need for nonsensical punctuation a year later, when he again scored 56 points, this time against Michigan State, this time in regulation.

Rayl says he's grateful he played for McCracken in college and Joe Platt in high school. He thought about shooting the second he got his hands on the ball in the backcourt, and once he passed midcourt his trigger finger started itching. "They wanted you to shoot. These coaches today act like you're stealing money if you shoot too many shots."

Like Rayl, Rick Mount was a self-taught shooting genius, even though his dad, Pete, was perhaps the most heralded player of his time. Pete led Lebanon to a runner-up finish in the 1943 state tournament (when Rick broke the school scoring record, it was Pete's old mark he crushed). While Pete didn't teach Rick the actual mechanics of the jump shot—he'd been a set-shooter during his high school days—he still played a key role in his son's development. He wouldn't let Rick shoot on a 10-foot hoop until he was ready. It all started with a peanut can and a tennis ball, until Rick progressed to a volleyball and eventually a basketball on a regulation hoop. Mount still gives his dad credit and preaches the same tactic to young shooters today. He sees too many kids screw up their jump shots at an early age by launching regulation basketballs on regulation baskets before they're physically capable. "I didn't have bad habits." Rick shot the tennis ball with his two power fingers, and he still uses them when shooting a basketball all these years later. When he talks about shooting, he says you could put a glass on a table and give him a little plastic golf ball and he'd drop it in. "Because people try to throw it in there like a dart. It's flat. What you've got to do is get arc and it will go in." I get the feeling Mount carries a career 98 percent mark when he crumples up a piece of scratch paper and shoots it into a garbage can from eight feet with the same motion and stroke he's used on a basketball court for fifty years.

He relied on strong wrists and mastered the art of falling away as he knocked in his jumpers. In his four years as a starter at Lebanon, his career low was 11 points. Remarkably consistent, Mount averaged 33.1 points per game both as a junior and as a senior. He scored 57 in one game. The story goes that Mount's high school coach, Jim Rosenstihl, got the job because the previous coach made it clear he wouldn't start Mount as a freshman and the school replaced him. Rosenstihl became Mount's biggest fan, a tireless promoter who took advantage of the sharpshooter's talents from long-distance whenever possible. The coach was also responsible for getting the outdoor courts built where Mount worked on his game for hundreds of hours in the summer sun.

The Memorial Park court became the centerpiece of the Mount legend—he worked as a lifeguard at the nearby swimming pool and took 200 shots during his breaks, using ice cream as payment for the kid who rebounded and passed for him. At the end of his shift, he returned for five hours of full-court ball. Players came from all over the state to play at the park, eager to take on the budding legend. Mount rarely showed emotion on the court, whether it was on the playground or in a high school game. The occasional lapse occurred, but for the most part he followed the lesson taught by his dad. "He always told me, 'Don't do any talking to other players. They call your mom a whore, you want to punch them, no— don't do that. Stay levelheaded, relax, and do your own thing. They'll be asking to get out of the game because you've knocked down six or eight straight shots.'"

Mount carried supreme confidence in himself, no matter the setting. The carnival came to Lebanon each year for Fourth of July, with its rides and games, all of it taking place near Mount's favorite outdoor court. The carnival included a basketball shooting game. Over the years, kids asked Mount to shoot for them. He happily obliged, but he was never fully prepared for the event and never seemed to put on the type of shooting show folks from Lebanon were accustomed to watching on a real basketball court. It bothered him that he couldn't dominate with his jump shot on the carnival attraction. At one fair, Mount, determined to conquer the contest, finally told a friend, "Tonight, I'm cleaning him out."

That year Mount treated the carnival game like it was a real basketball game. He put on his basketball shorts and Chuck Taylors and went to the park, his park, to shoot for thirty minutes. He worked up a sweat.

"You're probably the first person ever that practiced before a carnival shooting game," I say.

"You go there with your shirt tucked in, you got your penny loafers on, no socks, you can't get loose."

For fifty cents, a player had to make four shots, two if they paid a dollar.

"Here's fifty cents," Mount says. "Boom, boom, boom, boom, four in a row. I said, 'I'll take that big bear up there.'" Mount gave a little girl the stuffed prize. A crowd gathered to watch Mount on the hot summer day, the same way they did on cold January nights. Little kids asked their dads to win them a stuffed bear, and the dads asked Mount to step in and win it for them. The worker had about twenty bears. At one point Mount backed up.

"And I start shooting off the dribble, from about 20 feet." He went left with two dribbles, and right. "I looked down the midway, and all these kids are walking with these great big bears."

"What in the hell is your name?" the worker asked.

"Rick Mount."

"Son of a bitch—I should have made you stop a long time ago."

(Mount isn't the only famous shooter whose mythical status benefited from tales of midway dominance. Friends of Pete Maravich talked about the time he left a carnival worker on the boardwalk in Daytona, Florida, hurting for inventory when he participated in a shooting game that involved him moving farther out with every shot. Any skepticism about these two tales stems from one thing. No one else—from the Hay Daze carnival in Janesville, Minnesota, to the Texas State Fair—has ever won any prize while shooting those basketballs that are too big to fit into those tiny rims. Everyone fails at carnival basketball, and everyone knows the disadvantages going in. Foolish shooters still line up with dollar bills in their hands. The contestants joke about the overinflated balls or the bent rims, but somehow they convince themselves they can win that big stuffed animal for a date or a little kid, believing their shooting skills can overcome stacked odds. Most everyone's wrong. Mount and Maravich were right.)

While Rayl looked sickly when he played at Kokomo, no high school star looked as stylish as Mount. A lean six-foot-four, Mount wore his hair short with a "pointed forelock," an "inverted triangle that bisected his forehead" and was called the Cobra. During his senior year in 1966, he became an actual cover boy, when *Sports Illustrated* made him the first male high school athlete from a team sport to appear on its cover. The story, written by a then young, now legendary Frank Deford, alerted the nation about the jump shot Indiana schoolkids already imitated. Mount's life changed forever with the cover. Coach Rosenstihl "came down to my sixth-hour class," Mount recalls. "He says, 'Here's the deal. *Sports Illustrated* in two weeks is coming here.' . . . I said, 'I'm not doing it.' He looked at me and he says, 'You're doing it.'" Rosenstihl knew a great promotional opportunity when he saw it. Mount worried about team chemistry and jealousy.

Mount appeared on the February 14 cover with a red barn in the background, a basketball in his right hand, a slight smile on his face, the cover line reading, "Brightest Star in High School Basketball." Some people in town didn't like the story. "They thought it made us look like a hick town," Mount says, "but we were!" The *Sports Illustrated* story made Mount a national icon, a tough role for any teenager, especially a quiet one who was just learning the more shots he made, the more people wanted from him, and the more some people resented him.

Mount couldn't write the storybook ending his senior year. His shooting stroke didn't betray him, but his body did. At semistate, Mount produced his greatest game in the first contest, when he led a furious fourth-quarter rally against Logansport. Trailing by 12 in the fourth quarter, Lebanon came from behind thanks to Mount's 20 points in the final eight minutes. He finished the game with 47 points and 15 rebounds in Lebanon's 65–64 victory. One reporter wrote, "The final score read 65–64 Lebanon, but when you say Lebanon you might as well say Mount. He is Lebanon."

That night, with a trip to Indianapolis on the line, where he'd get the chance to win the title that eluded his father, Mount carried Lebanon to a double-digit lead over East Chicago Washington. But in the fourth quarter, leg cramps crippled him. He didn't make a field goal in the final eight minutes, left the game at one point, and barely functioned as his calves seized up. Lebanon lost 59–58. Mount still scored 29. Fans and reporters thought a healthy Lebanon would have advanced, but maybe there wasn't any chance of that. It was the third straight weekend Mount fell victim to leg cramps, the Indiana tournament schedule—two games in one day in regionals, semistate, and the finals—doing him no favors. "There wasn't Gatorade or water," Mount says. "At the hotel I wasn't thinking about drinking ten gallons of water. I was just having a couple Cokes." (Cramps plagued Mount into his college years. A doctor wanted to put an inner sole in his shoe to help. Mount resisted, believing the sole would make him a quarter of an inch taller, meaning his shot would be off by the same amount.) By the time that final agonizing game ended, Mount had scored 2,595 points in his prep career. More than the records, Mount left behind memories—of a pure stroke and perfect shot.

At Purdue, Mount set the Big Ten career scoring record—since broken—and he remains the leading scorer in school history. As a sophomore he averaged 28.5 points and upped it to 33.3 as a junior, second in the nation behind Pete Maravich. In his final year, he scored 35.4 per game. His first official game at Purdue came against the UCLA Bruins, the defending national champions. The game was the first in Purdue's Mackey Arena. A few weeks before the game—perhaps the most anticipated one in school history—Mount broke a bone in his foot. The injury limited him all season, but especially in that game—it robbed him of his lateral movement, and he couldn't rise for his jump shot in the same fashion. Mount still scored 28 points. But he missed a potential go-ahead free throw in the final minute, and one of his baseline jumpers fell off the rim in the closing seconds. UCLA rebounded and Bill Sweek buried a shot at the buzzer to give the Bruins a 73–71 victory.

While his career started with a defeat, Mount remained an icon for his three years at Purdue, thanks to his famous jumper. He was deadly off the dribble with a good first step. "They put those guys with long wingspans on me," he says. "They couldn't guard me, either." His high release made it difficult for anyone to alter his shot. "Coming down off transition, a couple of dribbles, boom, I'd score off that." A scout told the *Sporting News* in 1968: "The boy has a great eye as well as a great knack for the ball. When it moves he moves with it, and his range stretches from one end of

Yellowstone to the other." Nothing escaped Mount's shooting gaze, as he analyzed everything from the mechanics to his environment. During a game against Iowa, he stared at the rim during warm-ups and finally told his coach, George King, "The rim of the basket isn't level. It's a little high in front." Iowa officials denied it, but eventually someone climbed up on a ladder with a tape measure and discovered the rim was off by half an inch.

Few teams or players contained Mount and his jumper, even when people said they did. The *Sporting News* wrote a piece on Penn and guard Dave Wohl in 1971, a year after Mount left Purdue. The story said Wohl held Mount to just nine points in a game one year earlier. Wohl did hold Mount to nine points in a holiday tournament—in the first half. After only hitting three shots in the opening 20 minutes, Mount scored 28 in the second half—37 for the game—as Purdue rallied for an 88–85 victory.

Like Rosenstihl in Lebanon, coach King needed to balance team chemistry with Mount's dominance at Purdue. King once said Mount was allowed to shoot as much as he wanted. "After all, I tell them if you're playing on a football team, you don't send a tackle on an end sweep." Mount tells me, "Guy says, 'Man, you were a selfish player, weren't you?' I said no. If you can't shoot and you're gunning it up there, that's a bad thing. It was a good thing for my team. The shots I took, they look tough, but they weren't tough shots for me."

The individual scoring exploits combined perfectly with the other elements on the team during Purdue's 1969 season, when the Boilermakers won their first Big Ten title in twenty-nine years. Purdue led the nation in scoring at more than 94 a game. Mount's finest moment came in the Mideast Regional Final. Marquette was on its way to upsetting Purdue for the right to go to the Final Four until Purdue rallied for a one-point lead. Marquette's Ric Cobb missed a potential game-winning free throw with two seconds remaining, sending the game into overtime. With the game tied Purdue called timeout with 26 seconds left. King diagrammed a play that provided opportunities for three different players, although everyone knew only one man was the real candidate for the final shot. A pick by teammate Jerry Johnson gave Mount just enough room as he dribbled to his preferred spot in the right corner, a tidy place he should have paid rent on. Mount launched what was later called a "leaping lofter" that fell into the net with four seconds left in the game, giving Purdue a 75–73 lead (other accounts put the shot falling with two seconds).

Purdue drilled favored North Carolina 92–65 in the Final Four, with Mount hitting 14 of 28 for 36 points. Many of Mount's shots, UPI reported, came from outside 20 feet. That set up the title game, a showdown against UCLA—mighty UCLA, still led by the incomparable Kareem Abdul-Jabbar, who was still Lew Alcindor. Mount dreamed about the game for a long time. Before choosing Purdue, Mount originally picked Miami in 1966. At the time, he spoke about his desire to eventually face the big man who graduated a year before Mount and was also a high school legend before he dominated at UCLA and in the pros. Mount told the AP, "I'd like to play him in the final game of the NCAA tournament." Purdue played UCLA tough twice before—that first game of Mount's career and a 12-point loss earlier in the 1969 season. But with Kareem looking to end his NCAA career with a third title, Purdue had little chance. For Mount, the game turned into a nightmare, one of the few times the sharpshooter found nothing in the chamber. Abdul-Jabbar and Mount exchanged two baskets apiece in the early moments, but Mount then went more than 18 minutes without making a shot. He went 3-for-18 in the half as UCLA ran away with a 92–72 victory behind Kareem's 37 points and 20 rebounds. Mount got many of the same shots he'd always gotten—whether against Logansport or Iowa—but this time a seven-foot-two athletic genius jumped out on help defense. Dealing with defenders with big wingspans never usually bothered Mount, but perhaps dealing with the greatest wingspan of them all finally did.

Entering the 1970 season, Purdue expected to challenge for the national title, but injuries and suspensions cost the Boilermakers. Late in the season, Mount erupted for a Big Ten record 61 points against Iowa, but the Hawkeyes won 108–107, clinching the conference title. Mount hit 27 of 47 from the field—later research, conducted by someone watching film, revealed 13 of Mount's shots would have been three-pointers, putting him at 74 points. Iowa coach Ralph Miller later wrote in his book, "He was absolutely one of the greatest pure shooters that ever stepped on a court. He had 40-foot range and 35 was a snap. Everything else was like a layup."

His every move fascinated people in Indiana, on and off the court. When Rick and Donna got married in 1969, it was news. He told the *Sporting News* how she helped his game. At first, she went along when he practiced and kept him company. Then she retrieved the ball. "One night she asked if she could throw me some lead passes. Sure enough, she was putting the ball right where I wanted it. I couldn't believe it. I not only got a wife, but I got a practice partner, too."

Mount and Rayl had uneasy relationships with their schools after they left campus. Rayl believed Bobby Knight wanted nothing to do with Branch McCracken's players. Although Rayl says Knight was nice to him, Jimmy once estimated he'd only attended maybe five games in thirty years at Indiana because he didn't feel much affection for his old school. Some of the old Big Ten rivalries factored in. Knight played on Ohio State teams that ruled the Big Ten when Rayl starred at Indiana, although the future iconic coach was just a role player. In Rayl's home, he showed me a black-and-white picture that captures him rising for a jump shot from the left side against Ohio State; Bobby Knight looks on helplessly in the photo. Mostly Rayl didn't like Knight's coaching style. "If you like a bully, he's your man," Rayl tells me. Rayl also scoffed at Knight's disciples who recited the coach's beliefs. Indiana announcer John Laskowski agreed with Knight about squaring up to take a jump shot, and Rayl once said, "I never had a squared-up shot in my life. The guy teaching that wasn't worth shit as a player. If I had had to wait for squared-up shots, I'd probably have shot about five shots in my career." Mount experienced a bitter falling-out with Purdue, following son Rich's departure from the school in his sophomore year.

Neither man found great success in pro ball. Rayl enjoyed a good run with an AAU team out of Akron, but only played for a little more than a season with the ABA's Pacers. Both men suffered in their home states— expectations were too high, from fans and themselves. Mount suffered through an unhappy marriage with the Pacers. For the first time in his life, Mount didn't have a green light. He couldn't get off the bench. Slick Leonard, the former Hoosier star who became a beloved coach with the

Pacers, didn't have much use for either player. When he took over he got rid of Rayl. And when Mount came to the Pacers after his record-setting Purdue career, Leonard seemed to resent the move or any implication that he had to play Indiana's favorite son. Both players had their moments in the ABA, but scoring 12 or 15 points per game didn't compare to the numbers they put up in high school and college—and falling a bit short in front of the hometown fans made it even tougher. For Mount, injuries—pulled hamstrings, a dislocated shoulder—proved even more troublesome than Leonard's rotations. He was out of basketball a decade after being Mr. Basketball—just like Rayl.

Post-basketball, Rayl enjoyed more stability than Mount. Rayl became a success in Xerox's sales department until his retirement. Mount struggled to adjust to life after his final professional jump shot. He worked in insurance. An outdoors business failed. He seemed to feud with every group that once loved him, from Purdue coaches and fans to people in Lebanon. Heated arguments broke out when Rick's son, Rich, became a high school star at Lebanon. Rick stopped going to the games, convinced people wanted the Mounts—any Mount—to fail. *Sports Illustrated*'s Tim Layden wrote about a near-brawl between Mount and an old high school teammate at Memorial Park. Some folks in town thought Mount was clinging to past glory, unable to move on with his life. The relationship between town and legend still isn't healed—Mount worked with both the girls and boys basketball teams at the high school at various times, but that fell apart. An avid hunter, Mount once owned a gun shop. In the 1980s he gave an interview and said, "I'd like to run the gun shop until I'm about 50 years old and then move to the high timber country of Michigan, build me a cabin, grow me a beard and live off the land. My wife won't go with me, so I'll have to take my dog and my gun and my bow and arrow and live off the land."

That didn't happen. Instead, and to no one's surprise, Rick Mount still lives off his jump shot, the same one that brought him adulation and fame as a teenager.

Mount still calls his old gym home, although Lebanon High School left the place decades earlier for new facilities. But the gym where Rick Mount became a legend hosts his shooting school each summer. In the parking lot I saw the trailer for the Rick Mount Shooting School. Painted black with an image of a basketball in the center, it features phone numbers for the camp and a photo of Mount as a young player shooting a jumper, his wrist bent, the perfect form again on display. Mount hauls his Shoot-A-Way—a contraption that brings the ball back to the player through a bucket and down a rack—in the trailer. In late June 2014, I walked into the gym on the second day of the three-day camp. This was basketball heaven. I was watching Rick Mount shoot jump shots. Imagine watching Hemingway hammer away on his typewriter, or Scorsese shout directions behind the camera.

Modern amenities don't exist in Memory Hall—if you watched Rick Mount play a game in 1966 and didn't step in the gym again until 2014, you wouldn't notice much change. The brick walls and the hard bleachers that encircle the floor remain. About a half dozen parents sat in the stands, which held 2,200 and more back when Mount played and the fire marshal worried about a disaster at every game. The stage doesn't exist anymore, replaced by a wall and mural that celebrates some of the great moments in school history, including the 1912 state champs. Mount's visage appears in the lower right corner, with a quote from coach Rosenstihl calling Mount "naturally one of the greatest shooters to ever play the game."

Three dozen campers ate lunch as I snuck in and sat down. Mount looked a bit sore during the break. He spent several minutes stretching. He grimaced. Later he talked about the medicine he takes for an atrial fibrillation, admitting it causes some issues. He can't recover like he once did. After just four shots, he flexed his arms as he tried getting loose following the short intermission, which probably never happened when he shot 40 times in school.

The kids sat around Mount as he shot free throws and delivered his life story, intermingled with musings about shooting, housing prices in Indiana in the 1950s, the state's beloved one-class state basketball tournament, Memorial Park, coaching politics in 1960s Lebanon, the free throw struggles of the current Lebanon High School team, ice cream, and corporal punishment. Mount wore a blue shirt, black shorts, black shoes, and black socks pulled up. The kids sat cross-legged, while one parent took up residence on a folding chair about ten feet from Mount, recording every word.

Mount talked about his dad, Pete, telling young Rick that if he caught him shooting on a 10-foot basket before he was ready, he'd smack him with a Ping-Pong paddle. (The paddle played a role in another father-son tale, when Rick talked about wearing his dad's silver ring he received for finishing second in the Indiana state tournament, without Pete's permission. If they hadn't realized it before, the paddling stories probably convinced the kids Mount came of age in a different time.)

As he spoke about free throws, he told the kids what to scribble down on their paper, though he encouraged them to take notes on their own, not the easiest task for teens just escaped from school. He only took one dribble on his free throws—they can take more, he said. It's all muscle memory, the result of "millions and millions of jump shots over my life," and his math might not even be far off. At one point he closed his eyes and drained some shots, a parlor trick that always impresses. Mount checked to see what the kids wrote down. One camper, maybe twelve years old, wearing glasses, failed to take the proper amount of notes. Mount later told me all the camper wrote was "bend your knees," and he wanted the youngster to take more away from the lecture than those three words. Mount made the kid do push-ups. The shooting pupil went up and down with enthusiasm. He also ran traditional basketball wind sprints—to the free throw line and back, to midcourt and back, etc.—and seemed to enjoy the punishment even more than the shooting. It's fun being the center of attention! The other kids cheered as he finished, and I got the feeling he might forget to take more notes just so he could go through the drill again.

If any kid thinks the old guy talks a bit too much about his accomplishments, Mount says, "It's not bragging. I did it." When the talk ended, the kids worked on their own shots, with Mount and his assistants guiding them. There's no scrimmaging since it's a shooting school. Mount called individual players over to his portable Shoot-A-Way basket. The campers track their progress on yellow sheets of paper, and Mount also videotapes their shots. As the kids fired away, he watched. How's the backspin off their fingers? Where's that guide hand? What's the shooting elbow doing sticking out like that?

The next day, I stopped by Mount's Lebanon home. When I asked him how much he thought the campers knew about his career, he says, "They don't know me, but their dads, and their grandpas know me." Those memories of the folks might bring the kids in, but to keep their attention Mount knows he has to impress them. "You go out there and knock down 92 out of 100 jumpers, they're going to go, 'Yeah, my grandpa was right. I'm listening to this guy.' If I shot 30 for 100, they'd say, 'What am I doing here?'" One year, about a decade ago, during one of his early camp demonstrations, Mount says he drained 96 of 100 three-pointers. And that's why he's still out in his driveway every day taking 200 shots or more. He also shoots for the cardio—"You can't get anything better"—so he takes one or two dribbles when he shoots, turning it into the type of workout he couldn't get walking or riding a bike. Age does affect a shooter—he doesn't get off the ground like he once did—but the end result never changes, not for Mount.

No one has thought about the jump shot as much as Mount, but when he actually shoots, the thoughts disappear. "I have no care in the world," he says of the moment before he releases the ball. "I think all great shooters are like that. It's all about feel. If you have to start thinking . . ."

About an hour into our talk, Mount lifted himself out of his chair, groaned, and stood up to demonstrate his form, showing the proper placement of the wrist. A scout once called Mount a basketball scientist, and while his normal lab is the court, the living room works fine. As Mount gave a lesson on how the ball should come off a shooter's fingers and how he should pivot when catching a pass, his Brittany spaniel, Buck, looked up at his owner, perhaps a bit confused by the impromptu lesson— although probably not. Life in the Mount household involves listening to the man of the house talk about the jump shot. Mount later expressed bewilderment that no one from Lebanon attends the camp. Kids come from Chicago, Indianapolis, Florida, and Texas—but not his hometown. The old wounds between the city—which once had a sign proclaiming it the home of Rick Mount—and its former favorite son linger.

Three days after spending time with Mount, I traveled to Kokomo to visit with Jimmy and Nancy Rayl, who was a year behind Jimmy in high school. The Rayls have dealt with terrible tragedy. Their son Tim died in a car accident in 1997 at the age of twenty-five. Jimmy's endured numerous health problems. But they persevere. Jimmy and Nancy dated for nearly eight years before getting married. Nancy joked about a friend in the church at their wedding saying that when Jimmy finally said, "I do," someone passed a dollar bill over the pew—paying off a bet they apparently lost on the ceremony's outcome. Forty-eight years later . . . it seems permanent. They live in the Kokomo home Jimmy first moved into when he was a junior in high school. When the couple returned to their hometown after living in Ohio, the house went up for sale again and the two purchased it. Jimmy has slowed down, the stroke, heart surgery, diabetes, and a hip replacement taking a toll—but he says he's starting to take care of himself now. Once up to 255 pounds, the former Splinter now comes in at 225.

Although Lebanon's old tribute to Mount at the edge of town came down years ago, a new monument to Rayl's greatness went up in Kokomo. Jimmy and Nancy took me on a tour of Kokomo—past the courthouse, near a museum honoring early auto innovator Elwood Haynes, by the site of a new YMCA, and a stop at Opalescent Glass, "America's oldest art glass company," which has been around since 1888. Jimmy rode shotgun, I took the backseat. Nancy and Jimmy narrated, and the Kokomo Chamber of Commerce couldn't find two better guides. It ended with a visit to a frozen yogurt shop owned by their son Jimbo. Eventually our drive took us past old Memorial Gymnasium, opened in 1949, filled with Jimmy Rayl fanatics from 1957 to 1959. The newest addition to the outside is a beautiful black-and-white photo montage depicting some of the great players and moments in Kokomo basketball history. And on the left side— receiving the most space—is a picture of a teenage Rayl, the kid with the jump shot that drove people crazy, holding a ball at his skinny waist. The picture's fifty-five years old, and all of that time Rayl has been aware of what the jumper meant in his life. When he was inducted into the Indiana Basketball Hall of Fame, he said, "I'm just glad I had a jump shot. I would have been nothing without it. Like Rick Mount, we were lucky to play in a time when everybody worked hard to try and develop a jump shot. We played in a time when teams liked to score a lot of points, and the fans seemed to like it a lot."

Well into middle age Rayl still displayed his abilities. In 1988, Larry Bird hosted a charity game in Indianapolis in front of 16,912 people. The event featured a three-point contest with twelve players. In the first round, the players took 10 shots from the NBA three-point line. Rayl, forty-seven at the time, made his first nine before missing. The second-best guy hit seven. The top four shooters advanced to a sudden-death round. Former Purdue standout Troy Lewis was the only player to hit his first three-pointer in that round and won the event and a trip to Paris. Rayl was the second player to hit in the final round and settled for the consolation prize, a trip to Orlando. All told, Rayl hit 10 of his 12 three-pointers. David Kasey wrote, "The longest ovation of that night was not for Larry Bird, Magic Johnson or Michael Jordan, but it was for a top Xerox sales-man from Kokomo who has a very sweet shot . . . maybe even the sweet-est shot of all."

Visits with Mount and Rayl confirm that both remain delightfully unapologetic gunners. Can't stand watching another 52–45 Big Ten game? Neither can Rayl and Mount. Can't stand watching coaches bark com-mands on every play? Neither can Rayl and Mount. Rayl has said, "My philosophy was—and still is—if you are the best shooter on the team, then shoot the ball. Teams can't score if their shooter doesn't fire away. You don't want them to shoot bad shots, but they need to shoot. I could have smoked cigarettes and played pool all summer when I was a kid if all I had to do was take three or four shots a night." For his part, Mount says, "People say, what's changed about the game? Well, you've got to pass the ball ten times before you shoot. We came right down, right off the drib-ble, maybe no pass at all, let her fly. Sometimes I'll sit and watch a college game and go, 'God, almighty!' "

Despite the age difference, Mount and Rayl did actually square off against each other. Both participated in an outdoor summer tournament in Rochester, Indiana, in 1966. Temperatures soared into the 90s. Rayl won the individual scoring battle 34–29, and his team won 77–62 in front of more than 1,000 fans. Hitting his jumper from all areas, Rayl broke the game open with 13 points in the second quarter. The fight wasn't

NINE

THE MIRACLE, THE MOVIE, AND THE MISS

Troy Lewis doesn't remember a lot of the details about the event where he met Bobby Plump, but he does recall his surprise at their interaction. "I go up to him and say, hey, Mr. Plump, my name is Troy—and he seemed so excited to meet me. I was just taken aback and I was like, no, man, you—they made a movie about *your* team." Bobby Plump and Troy Lewis have much more in common than you might think for two people who graduated from high school thirty years apart, one a five-foot-ten white kid from a town of about fifty people, the other a six-foot-four black kid from a city of roughly 65,000. Plump and Lewis both won Indiana Mr. Basketball. Both players enjoyed outstanding college careers. Neither played in the NBA, but both Plump and Lewis played some professional ball.

But what links Plump and Lewis more than anything is the shared knowledge about the power of a single jump shot, the way it can alter lives and futures—not just of individuals, but of communities. Plump made his 15-foot jump shot, Lewis missed his, and both men have lived with the memories ever since—Plump for sixty years, Lewis for thirty. The jump shots they took as teenagers stay with them as adults. *Hoosiers* immortalized Plump's shot and the Milan Miracle, but Lewis's shot was just as dramatic.

THE MIRACLE

Bobby Plump relaxed outside the restaurant Plump's Last Shot in Indianapolis, telling me the story of his shot that won the 1954 Indiana state boys basketball tournament. As Plump talked about tiny Milan's upset of mighty Muncie Central, in a state tournament that started with more than 750 teams competing, I thought about just how many times he has told this story. Plump might hold the unofficial record for telling one story the most times—especially for athletes. Plump was seventeen when he hit his title-winning jump shot on March 20, 1954. That night, for the first time, he told reporters how he did it. The next day he told the story again. And in the sixty years since, Plump has talked about Milan's victory—and his jumper from the right side—to countless groups, reporters, old men, young kids, Americans, foreigners, celebrities, friends, family, and strangers. He told the story for the first time as a crew-cut-sporting high school senior and told it to me as a white-haired, glasses-wearing senior citizen.

I met with Plump on a Saturday afternoon in Indianapolis. The seventy-seven-year-old was an hour late for our meeting at Plump's Last Shot, the family restaurant located in the Broad Ripple neighborhood. The restaurant exuded a laid-back vibe—it's a converted two-story home on a tree-lined street, visitors bring their dogs up on the patio, and the waitress called me "honey" and "sweetie pie" within thirty minutes. Plump ran late because he went into work that afternoon. He runs a financial planning company after a long career in insurance and lost track of time. He likes weekends in the office "when nobody's calling. I can get more done in an hour, hour and a half than I can all day during the week."

Plump's biography didn't end on that March night in 1954, even if the moment was frozen in time forever. He attended Butler University, worked—and played basketball—for Phillips 66 in an industrial league, endured near-death experiences, and ran businesses. All of which I wanted to hear about. But like everyone else who has met Bobby Plump, I was there primarily to talk about one moment in his life. That one shot. "Do I get tired of talking about it?" he says. "No, I don't. I think it's an honor that people would remember something that long and would want to know something from a seventy-seven-year-old, soon to be a seventy-eight-year-old."

Plump lived three miles down the road from Milan in Pierceville, a town with no more than fifty people. Milan, with a population of 1,014, felt like a metropolis at the time for the Pierceville kids. Plump was the youngest of six kids in his family, known simply as "the baby" for the first five days of his life. The family didn't get electricity until Plump was about twelve, and didn't have a telephone until after he graduated—he took the call informing him of his Mr. Basketball honor at a store. His mom, Mabel, died when he was just five. Lester Plump, Bobby's dad, taught, and later worked at A. D. Cook Pump Company to bring in more money. When Bobby was eight, his dad gave him a basketball and a backboard with a rim, which the family attached to a smokehouse. The basket wasn't 10 feet high, but that's where Bobby began developing his jump shot. Watching an older player in school named Bill Gorman shoot a jumper inspired Bobby to work on one of his own, at a time when players still relied on a set shot or a one-handed push shot. His Milan teammates would later say no defender could stop Plump's jump shot in a one-on-one situation.

The 1954 championship team got its start during the 1952–53 season, when new coach Marvin Wood—Woody, Plump still calls him—took over. Just twenty-four when he started at Milan, Wood instituted the "cat-and-mouse" offense, a slowdown that served as a sort of precursor to Dean Smith's four corners, the ball-control attack North Carolina used to spread the floor and drain the clock while frustrated defenders either chased the ball or sat back while the Tar Heels sat on the ball.

Plump was known for soft hands, that jump shot, and leadership. Wood once said, "Bobby was the go-to guy. So our opponents would do everything they could to stop him. And in the tough spots, our guys did everything they could to get him the ball, often when they should have been looking for the open man." The strategy paid off. Milan went 19–2 in the 1954 regular season. One tournament game saw Milan defeat Crispus Attucks out of Indianapolis, whose star player was sophomore Oscar Robertson. Milan played its best game of the year against Attucks, proving it could run in a 65–52 victory. Plump scored 28 and likes to say Milan was lucky that Oscar, who went on to win two state titles, was so young—but the future Hall of Famer was "already damn impressive. We knew he was going to be great."

Milan drilled Gerstmeyer out of Terre Haute in the semis, 60–48, with Plump scoring 26 points. That set up the title showdown. Muncie Central owned the tradition—the school had won four state titles, including ones in 1951 and '52. The school enrolled more than 1,600 students, compared to 161 for Milan. As far as big vs. small showdowns, you couldn't get any bigger than Muncie Central vs. Milan. Fifteen thousand people watched the game at Butler Fieldhouse. Across Indiana, people crowded around radios and televisions. In Plump's biography, *Last of the Small Town Heroes*, authors Marty Pieratt and Ken Honeywell wrote, "Journalists and sportscasters from around the state remember the game as the highlight of their careers—more spellbinding than any World Series, more exciting than any Super Bowl, more chilling than the Indy 500 or a Muhammad Ali title fight." The game was as anticipated and hyped as any in Indiana's state tournament history, and it managed to exceed all expectations.

At least the ending did.

After two straight dominating performances, Plump played the worst three quarters of his life in the greatest victory of his life. He made three shots and scored only 10 points, four of them in the final two minutes. Milan again controlled the tempo, with Wood orchestrating from the sideline, Plump directing on the court. Milan's star wasn't hitting his shots like normal—the few shots there were in the game—but Milan removed the air from the ball, leading 14–11 after the first quarter and 23–17 at halftime. The Indians lost the lead in an ugly third quarter and entered the fourth tied 26–26. Muncie Central took the lead with two free throws in the first 20 seconds. Then things slowed down.

Over the years, a story developed that Plump crossed midcourt after Muncie took the lead and held the ball for 4 minutes and 13 seconds. The story has been repeated over and over again. In fact, reporters who wrote their game stories at the time reported a similar tale. But it didn't quite go that way. Plump didn't, as the legend goes, immediately hold the ball and stall. I watched the video of the game, available as an extra on a special edition of the *Hoosiers* DVD. It's the original broadcast. The video shows that after Muncie Central took a 28–26 lead, Milan brought the ball downcourt and engaged in its cat-and-mouse offense, again passing the ball around without looking for a shot. Milan made several passes before Plump finally caught a pass with, according to the announcer, 5 minutes and 32 seconds left in the game. At first, the announcer even said it wasn't a stall, but it developed into one. On the sideline, Plump looked over and saw Wood telling him to hold the ball. He was in the midcourt circle, his defender a few feet off. And then he did stand. Motionless. His teammates loitered around the court, hands on their hips. The defensive player guarding Plump put his right hand up. Plump occasionally took a jab step or faked a pass. Otherwise he portrayed a statue in front of 15,000 people.

The plan was simple. Wood wanted to milk the clock and take the game down into the final minutes—he didn't want to give Muncie a chance to grab a bigger lead. His team had proven itself in close games over the past two years, so why not take one more game—his dream team's final game— to the final seconds? The announcer kept up with the action by saying Plump was still holding the ball. Still holding the ball. Still holding the ball. One fan told authors Marty Pieratt and Ken Honeywell the roar of the crowd "got progressively louder as Bobby held the ball. It just kept going; people were crying, praying, laughing, yelling."

Plump called timeout with 3 minutes and 28 seconds. So instead of holding the ball at midcourt for more than four minutes, it was more like two minutes. Either way, the strategy worked. Following the timeout, Milan finally went back into action. Plump, still struggling, missed an outside shot. Ray Craft tied the game with a jumper of his own and Plump's two free throws gave Milan the 30–28 lead. Craft squandered a chance to extend the lead in the final two minutes by missing an open layup from the right side. (Legendary Indianapolis writer Bob Collins joked for years, "If Ray Craft makes that shot, Bobby Plump is just another guy pumping gas back in Pierceville today.") Muncie Central took advantage and tied the game with 48 seconds. Bobby Plump's life was about to change forever.

On the Milan end, Plump dribbled around with his right hand as the clock ran down. Wood called timeout with 18 seconds. Out of the timeout, Plump again dribbled until finally making his move. He worked his way to the elbow of the free throw line on the right side, got enough space on the defender, and rose up for the 15-foot jump shot, the same type of shot he first saw in a practice a few years earlier. The shot went through with three seconds left. The crowd erupted, the buzzer went off, and Milan's players celebrated. Plump estimates he scored "probably 65 percent of my points" from where he made the winning shot. "If [the defender] would have given me an opportunity to drive, I would have gone ahead, but he was off of me." Plump says he knew the shot would go in when he released it. What Plump couldn't know was his life would never be the same. He knew how important a jump shot could be when he worked on it as a freshman—he didn't yet know the power of his most famous jumper.

The immediate aftermath provided a hint. When the team returned to Milan, a massive crowd greeted the players and coaches, overwhelming the town—an AP report put the crowd at 20,000, other reporters estimated 40,000, and even if the correct number was somewhere in between, the town of just a thousand people eagerly welcomed the visitors. The players spoke at a ceremony, as did the coaches and some big-city reporters who covered the team, objectivity going up in the same smoke that rose from a bonfire the town threw in celebration. Even an Indianapolis police officer gave a speech—Pat Stark, who unofficially adopted the team during its stay in the big city. He took them on a mini-parade through Monument Circle in Indy following the victory over Muncie Central, adding to the craziness by going the wrong way down the street, creating a temporary traffic nightmare that angered the police chief. Stark didn't care—he was caught up in the madness from the Milan Miracle. When Stark talked at the large celebration back in Milan, the boy in blue spoke of his admiration for the team, broke down into a blubbering mess, and left the stage.

Everyone loved the underdog, and Milan's championship team of 1954 became the ultimate underdog story, from the time Plump's shot went in and continuing for the next sixty years. In features about the team, the words "David and Goliath" have probably appeared nearly as many times as "Bobby Plump." But the cliché doesn't totally fit. Milan put a powerhouse team on the court in 1954—and had the added experience of making it to the Final Four the previous season. Milan had Mr. Basketball. Milan had, Plump believes, "the best backcourt in the state." Muncie Central previously won four state titles, but started three juniors and two sophomores. Yet the hysteria—which went beyond the normal levels seen in the state known for it—was warranted based on the uniqueness of Milan's triumph. No small school had won a state title since 1915—no school Milan's size ever won one again in the one-class system.

People wrote letters but addressed them to Plump, Indiana. The letters still found him. His name entered Indiana's lexicon. Nine years after his winning shot, a newspaper in Tipton, Indiana, wrote about an eighth-grade game being decided on a "Bobby Plump basket" with three seconds left. Children of the 1950s grew up wanting to be him, and children in later decades grew up hearing the stories about him and wanting the same thing. All thanks to one jump shot.

Plump went on to a record-breaking career at Butler University, scoring a then school-best 1,439 career points and 41 in a single game. Following college, Plump lived in Oklahoma when he played for the Phillips 66 industrial pro league team. After moving back to Indiana with his wife, Jenine, and his children, he got into the insurance business. The Milan Miracle was never far away. His first two children—Tari and Kelli—were born in Oklahoma. When Jonathan came along, it was back in Indiana. As Jenine prepared to give birth, the doctor expressed more interest in Bobby, wanting to talk "about Butler and Milan, and he kind of forgot about her a bit," Bobby says.

"Hey, Doctor," Jenine said. "I gotta have this baby. Would you quit talking . . ."

Plump survived several health scares with his heart over the years, but has no interest in retiring. He enjoys his work in the financial arena; a life filled with nothing but fishing, golfing, and napping doesn't appeal to him.

The one constant in Plump's life has been that jump shot. He's spoken to people from around the world. Even Eli Manning asked a teammate to get him Plump's autograph when the Giants were in the Super Bowl in Indianapolis.

The fame doesn't bother Plump—if it did he wouldn't take a seat in front of the restaurant that bears his name. Plump estimates he gave ten to fifteen speeches a year when he moved back to Indiana. "It dawned on me that this might last for a while," he jokes. "And then the movie *Hoosiers* just took it to another level."

Ah, *Hoosiers*.

THE MOVIE

Bobby Plump's quintessential Indiana story became the quintessential American underdog story when writer Angelo Pizzo and director David Anspaugh took Milan's tale, fancied up the details, and turned it into *Hoosiers* in 1986. Milan became Hickory in the movie, Marvin Wood became coach Norman Dale, and Plump became Jimmy Chitwood, the enigmatic, mute shooting genius whose jump shot wins the state championship. The American Film Institute ranked *Hoosiers* the fourth-best sports movie of all time while *Sports Illustrated* listed it as the sixth-best sports film. Both lists are wrong—there's nothing better.

Not everyone in Milan enjoyed the movie. Because *Hoosiers* was based on Milan's story—but didn't use the actual Milan story—townsfolk felt an ownership. That sense of propriety magnified the changes and omissions. Plump says only the final 18 seconds of the championship game depicted in *Hoosiers* matches the reality. Still, *Hoosiers* inspires with the underdog tale, and entertains with Gene Hackman's performance as Norman Dale, Shooter's struggles, Rade's stubbornness, Ollie's underhanded free throws, Strap's faith, the town's demands for a zone defense, Merle's heady guard play, the fervor of small-town fans, the picket fence, on-court brawls, locker-room-invading police chiefs, Jimmy Chitwood's coach-saving speech, and Jimmy's jump shot. Especially Jimmy's jumper.

I remember sitting in the theater watching Jimmy drill shots on the outdoor hoop as Dale told him he didn't care if Jimmy joined the team. Throughout the film Jimmy only misses a handful of times. Then, in the state title game, with the game tied—just as it was for Bobby Plump in 1954—Jimmy holds the ball near midcourt, dribbles toward the defender, rises, and drills the winning jump shot. The title-clinching basket in

Hoosiers proved a game-ending jump shot is the most cinematic of basketball plays, even in real life. A layup or dunk ends the game so abruptly there's no time to comprehend what's happening. The rare half-court game-winner is so unexpected, there's no real tension as the ball heads to the rim, as no one expects it to fall. A winning jump shot hangs in the air for a few seconds—enough time for players and fans to contemplate the possibilities, both good and bad. With Milan as its inspiration, *Hoosiers* had to end on a jump shot—but no basketball movie should ever end any other way.

A big part of *Hoosiers* still exists, and not just in memories. Knightstown, Indiana—a town of 2,100 about thirty-five miles east of Indianapolis—is home to the Hoosier Gym. Hickory played its home games in the little gym—it's where Norman Dale said his team was on the floor with only four players, and Shooter ordered the picket fence. But it served as a real gym at one time and became a tourist attraction, in addition to being a community center. I visited the Hoosier Gym a week before I met Plump, a belated birthday present to myself. A green road sign with white letters off Interstate 70 alerts drivers to take Exit 115 for the Hoosier Gym. The sign seems timid, the same model that announces a town no one has heard of is ten miles away, the same type of sign that reveals travelers can find lodging and gasoline at the next exit. It needs a bigger font, possibly with an exclamation point.

I pulled up to the gym at three in the afternoon. A small monument out front welcomes visitors to the community center and "Hoosier Gym." My one issue with the gym? The name. Hoosier Gym. The gym was named for the movie *Hoosiers*, not for the Hoosier State. Hoosiers Gym should be the name. The understated monument also requires an upgrade. A statue feels more appropriate. If Philadelphia can construct a statue for the fictional Rocky Balboa, why can't Knightstown create one for a *Hoosiers* character? A commissioned work. Who does the statue represent? How about Norman Dale screaming at a ref or a local hick who just yelled a suggestion from the stands? Or maybe Ollie at the free throw line—little, helpless Ollie, ball in his hands, ready to shoot his granny-style free throws. But obviously Jimmy deserves the honor of being immortalized in eight feet of bronze. Jimmy going up for a jump shot, textbook form, as he delivers the winning shot at the buzzer. Put it out in front at Hoosier(s) Gym. Children can leave handwritten notes at the base of the statue on the anniversary of the movie's release.

Folks in Knightstown built the gym in 1922. The high school played in it until 1966, when a new gym went up at the new high school. *Hoosiers* filmmakers discovered the place on a scouting trip. Now the gym serves as a shrine and a destination point for pilgrims. Walk inside and travel back in time—if not to the 1950s, at least to 1986. The lobby looks similar to how it did when Knightstown played here, except for the numerous tributes to the movie. A TV plays *Hoosiers* on a loop—when I walked in Jimmy was telling coach Dale, "I'll make it." Visitors can purchase memorabilia in the small room off the lobby. I bought five Hickory shirts and another DVD, adding to the two copies I already had at home. Hoosier Gym never welcomed a bigger mark through its old doors.

The wooden stands with gray paint look the same, as do the side baskets that still have the wood backboards. A large U.S. flag hangs vertically on the stage end, and the scoreboard lists the names of Hickory and hated Terhune, the team Hickory battles in a bloody brawl in the film. (Trivia: Jimmy Rayl's son Jimbo played for Terhune in the movie.) On the other end, a yellow banner with red letters reads, "Go Hickory. All the way!" Next to it, a black-and-white picture of the 1952 Hickory team. Narrow steps take visitors down to the ancient locker room. Famous lines from the movie remain written on the chalkboard—reminders about four passes and "Don't get caught watchin' the paint dry." Mustard-yellow bars of soap are available under the showers for . . . guests who want to pretend they just ran for two hours under coach Dale's stern direction and want to wash up before the sock hop? I didn't touch them.

The real thrill comes from stepping on the court. I spent forty-five minutes shooting, wearing my shorts, purple Lakers T-shirt, and sandals. Just being in the gym made me want to don a pair of skimpy satin shorts, maybe even the same size as Jimmy's. If I'd watched the movie before arriving, I would have written down the exact spot of every shot Hickory made in this gym, and then replicated those baskets. Instead I took my normal shots, although I made sure to reenact the picket fence play Shooter drew up for a victory. I came off the—imaginary—screens, spun the ball off the floor so it bounced back to me, and popped it in from the free throw line elbow. The crowd—in my head—went wild. Shooter wept.

After I stopped shooting, I walked into the lobby and talked with Ed Ferguson, a volunteer and Knightstown native, although he attended school at nearby Morton Memorial. Ferguson spends his days chatting with visitors and selling memorabilia. "I get no paychecks," he says. "I love this gym and us old-timers that care about the game of basketball are keeping this thing alive."

Before leaving Hoosier Gym—which people can rent for thirty dollars an hour, and was the desired wedding location for one couple—I walked onto the floor once more and sat in the bleachers for ten minutes. It was 4:30. Ed was preparing to close. I stared at the stage and the scoreboard, but mostly the floor. Jimmy shot there! And he only shot there because Bobby Plump made a shot in 1954. Sitting there, alone, I pictured the gym filled—for a real Knightstown game but primarily for *Hoosiers*. A part of me wanted to start chanting, "We want Jimmy! We want Jimmy!" to see if I could summon the spirit of Norman Dale. *Hoosiers* is timeless— kids not even born in 1986 appreciate the movie just as much as those who saw it when they were eleven. In those stands I remembered fictional games, but also my own small-town showdowns back in school. I remembered coach Dale's line about high school ball: "Most people would kill to be treated like a god, just for a few moments."

Troy Lewis knows all about being an Indiana basketball god, worshipped for his jump shot—even if he didn't get the Hollywood ending.

THE MISS

If Indiana is the unofficial basketball capital of the country, and high school basketball rules Indiana above all else, then Anderson High School's old gymnasium was the headquarters of Hoosier Hysteria. The Wigwam had room for 9,000 fans, and during Anderson's glory years, 9,000 fans attended the games. Fifty-six-hundred people owned season tickets to the Wigwam—a couple thousand more than had season tickets to the Indiana Pacers one year. Fans lined up at 3:30 in the morning, just to nab a stub that put them in a drawing that gave them a chance to win a sectional ticket.

Norm Held coached in Anderson for eighteen years. Charismatic, quotable, arrogant, he held court on Anderson's sideline. "When I was interviewed, I told the superintendent, 'I think we're in the entertainment business,'" Held says. "And he said, 'That's what I wanted to hear from you.'" One thing eluded Held: a state title. His teams finished runner-up four times in the single-class tourney. Twenty-one years after heart problems forced him to retire, Held tells me, "I was on the speaking tour, so to speak, for a long time and all people ever wanted to ask me—whether it was in Oklahoma, Texas, New Orleans, or North Carolina—all they wanted to talk about was the Wigwam."

No one enjoyed playing for Anderson and in the Wigwam more than Troy Lewis, a favorite son of the city who hasn't lived there in more than twenty years but remembers his exploits from thirty years ago as if they happened yesterday. Indiana named Lewis co–Mr. Basketball in 1984. Anderson retired his jersey number 23 when he was still in high school. Lewis went on to a tremendous career at Purdue—he left as the school's fourth-leading scorer of all time and played on some of the most beloved teams in Boilermakers history. Purdue also retired his number. Lewis owns an encyclopedic sports memory, a trait I took full advantage of when we met for dinner in Dayton, Ohio. He remembers specific practices and games—from Purdue alumni games to his elementary school days. "I can remember the first time I ever a hit a shot," he says. "Elementary school." He was "outside and I had a volleyball in my hand." He couldn't make a shot on the 10-foot hoop, but right after the bell rang he shot one that went "straight through the net. It's like that golf swing, my first time I hit that sweet spot on my golf swing, that's how it was when I saw that ball go in the net."

A man with that recall has no difficulty remembering the shot that didn't find the net, the shot that would have won a state championship. In the 1983 state tournament title game against Connersville—played in front of nearly 17,500 fans at Market Square Arena in Indianapolis—Lewis's 15-foot jumper from the right elbow bounced off the rim in the final seconds. Connersville defeated Anderson 63–62. It was Anderson's third defeat in the championship game in five years—games the Indians lost by a total of seven points. A year after the one-point loss to Connersville, Lewis's high school career ended with another one-point loss and another missed shot at the buzzer—although that occurred in semistate and the shot was from just past half-court. When I asked him which shot he thinks about more, Lewis didn't hesitate. "The state title game. Because growing up in Indiana it's all about the state championship. Playing in the Wigwam, wearing that Anderson uniform, winning state—I'm living everything that I watched growing up."

Growing up in Anderson meant living in a city dominated by General Motors. Lewis's folks worked for GM, like 40,000 other people in Anderson. "Everybody left high school and worked at GM. I mean, everybody. And every Friday and Saturday night, we went to the Wigwam or listened to the games on the radio." The auto industry supported Anderson. The city thrived. But when the auto industry collapsed, the aftershocks decimated the city. By the time Lewis entered high school, Anderson's unemployment rate reached 22 percent. Today the factories are all gone. But in good economic times or bad, residents always had basketball. The oldtimers still cling to the past—a few days before I spoke with Norm Held, a man in Florida, a former Anderson resident, called him to talk about old games.

No gym's environment matched the Wigwam's, not even after rival New Castle built a palace for 10,000. The Wigwam that Lewis played in replaced the Wigwam that burned in 1958, with a rumor rising it fell victim to an arsonist who was upset at not being able to squeeze in for a game. The gym cost two million dollars. Season tickets were passed down generation to generation. Divorced couples fought over the custody of tickets. In 1985, *Sports Illustrated* writer Bruce Newman quoted Anderson fan Belinda Kinder, who worked in the school cafeteria. "We don't have any fringe benefits, no insurance or anything," she told him, "but a couple of years ago they started making sure that all school employees would be able to buy two tickets to every Indians tournament game. They couldn't have given me anything better than that."

Lewis wanted to play in that electric atmosphere, in front of those devoted fans who'd waited since 1946 for another state championship. Lewis worshipped another Mr. Basketball from Anderson, Roy Taylor, who graduated in 1974. Taylor wore number 43, and that's the number Lewis wanted. When he got the jersey, he found out it was too roomy—the jersey numbers went up by the player's size, and Lewis wasn't big enough. Instead he received 23. A few years later, every kid in America wanted the number because of one man, but at the time, "I didn't know who the hell Michael Jordan was."

Lewis believes his maniacal competitiveness came courtesy of his grandpa on his dad's side. "I had never understood where I got it from." During a Little League game, with the bases loaded and two outs, Troy waited in the on-deck circle. A neighbor boy struck out, ending the game. "I go up and hit him in the jaw, and I said, 'You did that shit on purpose, you didn't want me to bat!' This fire I had . . . One day I told my father, 'Why am I like this?' " Troy's dad figured it came from Grandpa, who once punched a cow that wouldn't move where he wanted out on a Missouri farm.

Red Auerbach played a role in developing Lewis's shooting eye. Old television segments called *Red on Roundball* featured the legendary coach working with NBA players on fundamentals; the segments became cult classics. Red and Dr. J discussed dunking. Red and Pistol Pete performed ball-handling drills. And Lewis watched Red and Bob McAdoo talk shooting. "Red was saying you get backspin on a ball, and it's dead when it hits the rim. Bob McAdoo's shot hit the rim, and it went in and I was like, 'Oh, that's how you do it.' "

Blessed with great instincts and a deep knowledge of the game, Lewis knew how to get open and take advantage of any situation. He didn't need the quickest first step physically when he was always one step ahead mentally. Once he got the ball, he became nearly automatic from outside, but much of the real work happened before he even touched it. "Troy knew how to go from side to side and create screens and use screens to get shots," Held says. "That's the art of a good player, and he was a great one."

As a junior, Lewis did not receive a lot of publicity—certainly not as much as fellow North Central star and future Olympian Steve Alford. Indiana basketball in 1983 featured scoring outbursts from several players—every week in the North Central's Friday-Saturday battles two guys matched each other with 30 or 40 points each. Alford averaged 37 and won Mr. Basketball at New Castle. Marion's James Blackmon signed with Kentucky and averaged 31.9. And Anderson's Lewis emerged from relative obscurity and averaged nearly 30 points per game while leading his team to the state finals.

Marion and Anderson squared off in the Final Four of the state tournament at Market Square Arena. The two teams played in the afternoon game, a rematch of a regular season game that ended with Blackmon scoring 50 points in a Marion overtime victory. Before the state tournament contest, Held said, "A reporter asked me, 'What are you going to do about Blackmon?' I said, 'Heaven only knows. If he gets 50 points again, we're going to get beat.'" This time Blackmon scored 52. But behind Lewis's 42 points, Anderson prevailed. One writer called it the Indiana state tournament's "most-publicized two-man struggle of all-time." Blackmon made 24 of 47 shots from the floor while breaking the Final Four record for points, and Lewis made 15 of 28 and 12 of 13 free throws. Lewis's 42 also bested the previous mark of 40 points. Anderson won the war 89–87 in double overtime. Marion rallied from an 11-point deficit in the second half, but Blackmon's only missed free throw of the game kept the game tied at 77 with four seconds left. That sent the game into overtime, where Lewis calmly made two free throws with seven seconds to force a second extra session. Anderson survived and won on a last-second basket by David Jackson. "I knew in one stretch I was getting what I wanted, and I was in a rhythm, but I didn't really realize he was doing the same thing," Lewis says.

How good was the Blackmon-Lewis showdown? That night Connersville beat a tired Anderson and Lewis 63–62 for the title, on Lewis's missed shot at the end. But even that championship game, Logansport sports editor Carl Gustin wrote, "was simply anticlimactic. What will be remembered is the second game, not the finale, in the minds of basketball historians."

Being a basketball historian himself, Lewis certainly appreciates the double overtime victory, the back-and-forth with Blackmon. But the details from the night game, when he did everything possible to lift Anderson to its fourth state championship, only to see his final shot fall off the rim, can never be forgotten. The superstitious Lewis suffered a blow before the game, when the managers misplaced his wristbands. They tracked down a replacement pair. Lewis jokingly says that's why Anderson lost, but even new wristbands didn't cool his hot hand as Anderson took a six-point lead. Connersville tied it at halftime, setting the stage for the dramatic final eight minutes in front of 17,490 fans.

The teams exchanged the lead twelve times in the fourth quarter. With 1:56 left, Lewis gave Anderson a 62–61 lead. But Mike Heineman made a layup after a series of offensive rebounds to put Connersville back up by one. Anderson let the clock run down, content to take one shot at the championship. Twenty-nine years after Marvin Wood called timeout for Milan, and Bobby Plump beat Muncie Central, Coach Held and Lewis nearly reenacted the dramatics each step of the way. Held called timeout with 29 seconds left. Lewis was the first option—a second option didn't exist. On the floor, Anderson passed the ball around as the clock ticked down. Defensively Connersville played a two-three zone, with a pair of guards shadowing the ball out front while Anderson waited to strike with its best shooter. Lewis touched the ball with 19 seconds left but delivered a quick pass back to a teammate. On the broadcast, one of the announcers said, "We know who's going to shoot it." Everyone in the arena knew. Lewis patiently stayed on the right wing, poised for the moment he'd dreamed about since he was a little kid and listened to Anderson games on the radio. The play-by-play man said, "They are looking for Troy Lewis." Lewis finally caught the ball with seven seconds, his left foot outside the NBA three-point line, his right foot inside. With one left-handed dribble he coasted past a guard at the top of the zone. He pulled up at the free throw line elbow after a fundamentally perfect jump stop and rose for his fundamentally perfect jump shot. If you took an image of Bobby Plump from 1954 and superimposed it onto the Market Square floor in 1983, Lewis would have found himself nearly in Plump's footsteps. When Lewis jumped, another Connersville defender stepped up to challenge. He put both hands near Lewis's face. Lewis says he never saw the rim, but the shot felt good. The ball left Lewis's hands with four seconds left. Just like Plump's shot—just like every cinematic jump shot, in the movies or in real life—it hung in the air for a second, the fate of two teams resting on its flight path. As Plump's shot went through the net with three seconds, so

Lewis's bounced off the rim at three seconds. A Connersville player secured the rebound as the final seconds went off the clock.

As Lewis watched Connersville celebrate, cameras caught him on the other end, finally turning away from the opposition, his left hand on his face, his head pulled back in anguish. Following the game, a TV reporter asked Held about other options on the final play. One reporter wrote Held snapped, "We didn't have a second shooter. Did you see a secondary shooter out there?" Thirty-one years later, Held tells me, "He was the best shooter in Indiana. You're going to take it down to the wire and win or lose on one shot. It just didn't go in."

Even with that final miss, Lewis put together the greatest single day in the state finals. His two-game total of 76 points broke the Final Four record.

Despite the heartbreak, Lewis still had one more year to win a championship. Anderson entered his senior year ranked first. Lewis averaged 35 points per game in sharing Mr. Basketball honors with Delray Brooks. Anderson only lost one regular season game and entered the tournament as favorites. But in semistate, Lake Central shocked the Indians 60–59. This time, Lewis didn't get a good late look at the basket, just a long heave that again bounced off the rim. A picture in the paper showed Lewis facedown on the court, his younger brother, Rico, and teammate Jeffrey Jackson providing comfort. "I felt like my world kind of ended," he says. "I couldn't fathom this was it. I'm thinking, 'I worked my whole life to have this opportunity.' Even though I was sprawled out on the floor, I wasn't crying. The whole time I was mumbling to myself, 'I can't believe it's over. I can't believe it's over.'"

A few minutes after Lewis said this, I told him about my last high school game, a six-point loss to the eventual state champions in Minnesota, in the days of a two-class state tourney. Even as I talked with him about it, I recognized the absurdity of comparing my humble if successful senior season with that of a guy who was named Mr. Basketball in the top basketball state in the country, of comparing my defeat with his misses against Connersville and Lake Central. But that helpless feeling did compare. Several years earlier I wrote a newspaper piece about my final game, focusing on the fact I still dream in my sleep—"experience a nightmare" would be more accurate—about that loss about once a week. I told Lewis about how I went home after my final game, saw my parents, and kept saying, "I don't want it to be over," just about the same words Lewis said. The reason those words linger is because something we'd been working on for nearly twelve years was over. Little kids dream of playing high school basketball. They play with friends in the summer, go to camps, and more than anything find a basket and shoot alone, envisioning the final shot to win state. That's the scenario. All of that work and then it . . . ends. Lewis kindly indulged my reminiscing, with the same ease Bobby Plump displays with eager visitors; superstars are used to these interactions with commoners. But no matter the school or the team or the player, the feeling of helplessness when it all ends in a loss is universal.

Unfortunately for Lewis, he experienced that sensation several more times during a record-setting career at Purdue. At West Lafayette, Lewis teamed up with Todd Mitchell and Everette Stephens to form a group affectionately called the Three Amigos. As seniors, Lewis said of the group, "We've got so much in common. Music, TV shows, women . . . not the same women, the same type of women." On the court, they complemented each other—Stephens the point guard, Mitchell the strong forward, and Lewis the scorer. The three-pointer came into college basketball Lewis's junior year, and he became one of the top long-distance shooters in the country, his ability to get open carried over from his Anderson days. Stephens once told the *Sporting News*, "He leaves me in awe sometimes. He can be off-balance. He can maybe get shoved. But he shoots it anyway, and it's nothing but cord." Led by the trio, Purdue won the Big Ten title in 1987 and 1988. People sensed the 1988 campaign would prove special. That year's team was the subject of two books—Mark Montieth's *Passion Play* and John Feinstein's *A Season Inside*. Purdue lived up to expectations, losing just three games in the regular season, even though Lewis suffered a broken foot before the season. But Purdue's dream ended with an upset loss against Kansas State, a team the Boilermakers defeated by 39 points earlier in the year. Lewis says when he gets together with Mitchell and Stephens, they never talk about that game. "That one haunts me, but unlike the state championship game, there's no singular moment. It's just the whole second half of that game, it was like we did everything wrong." Just like in high school, Lewis couldn't write the perfect ending after a nearly perfect career.

Lewis played some CBA ball and in an under-six-foot-five league, which is how he ended up in Dayton. Today Lewis works for the grocery supply company Victory Wholesale Group. He keeps connected to basketball as an assistant coach for a local school. The shooting star now preaches defense. The jump shot still lives when he occasionally runs up and down the court. That pretty much only happens at Purdue alumni games, where he's still capable of knocking down threes, although primarily worried about walking off with his Achilles intact. "Haven't lost my shooting ability. Now, am I as consistent? Because of the legs, I don't have that. Shooting's all about the legs. I don't have the same lift."

But of all the shots Lewis has made—he scored 4,004 combined points in high school and college—it's the one that fell off in the final seconds of the 1983 state title game that lingers in the background. The location of the ring and medal he received for the runner-up finish remains a mystery, and Lewis has no interest in tracking them down. Lewis says there are thoughts about how making that shot "might have changed my life to another level than what it is now. I just thought of myself in this little bubble—I never thought outside of it so when that happened, I was crushed." But, he adds, "I think it's just part of life, because I think about all of the other great things that happened to me."

Everything's different now in Anderson. Consolidations and closings eliminated rivals Highland and Madison Heights—schools that made Anderson the toughest basketball city in the state. The Wigwam's glory days ended, and the facility was actually set for destruction until city officials reached a deal with a private company in 2014 that guaranteed the gym will survive, although a portion of it will be turned into housing. Nothing can restore basketball to its former stature in Anderson. The community isn't what it once was, and Lewis can't help but wonder what could have been if his shot went down. "It would have been more than me," he says. "That's the thing that I always regret about that shot, is that it would have been for so much more. The town's been waiting for a state championship. To have the ball in your hands at that time to win it all, it's just . . ."

Bobby Plump knows what it's like having the ball in your hands, and the ripples that follow one shot. "The most important thing that happened in '53 and '54, not only did it raise the expectations of the players, it raised the expectations for all the students," he says, "because they looked at this and said, 'If they can win the state tournament, maybe there's things that I can do.'" Plump estimates "no more than sixteen" kids total left Milan for college the previous four years, but "seventeen out of thirty" from his class went off to school. "In '54, it inspired people to try something different."

Even if Lewis made his shot, it wouldn't have become as iconic as Plump's. Anderson was a big school, not small. Hollywood wouldn't have made a movie out of it (probably). And it wouldn't have brought jobs back. But it would have lifted the city, whether for just a moment or a decade. The shot bounced off and an entire community felt the pain. That Anderson cafeteria worker quoted in *SI*, Belinda Kinder, said of the state defeats, "Each time it takes people weeks to get over it. Some people have to go to the doctor. It's like a death." So maybe Lewis's shot could have inspired some students in Anderson to try something different, just like Plump's jump shot did for kids in Milan. That seems implausible, a shot from a teenage basketball player altering the futures of people who weren't even on the team—but it's no more implausible than 5,000 people owning season tickets for high school basketball. Jump shots change lives in Indiana, the makes and the misses, from Oscar to Bird to Alford to Rayl to Mount to Plump to Lewis and a thousand more, in big cities and small towns throughout the state. Indiana didn't invent the jump shot. But Hoosier Hysteria was built by it.

PART THREE

GUNNER'S PARADISE

TEN

1970s: NO CONSCIENCE REQUIRED

Floppy-haired, long-armed Pete Maravich scored more points than anyone in Division I basketball history, and on February 7, 1970, in a game against Alabama, the superstar with the haunted eyes scored the most points in a single game in his college career. Maravich—Pistol Pete—lit up the Crimson Tide for 69 points. To get there he took 57 shots, hitting 26. It was the quintessential Maravich performance—electric and absurd, over the top but somehow still not enough. Alabama held off Pistol Pete—and his LSU teammates who tagged along for the trip—106–104.

For a time—from the late 1960s through the mid-1970s—shooters and high scorers ruled basketball, especially in college, and performances like Maravich's became, if not common, expected from certain players. The jumper became fully weaponized, creating scoring totals never before seen in basketball—and ones that haven't been seen again. The words "unconscious" and "no conscience" became the favorite words when describing shooters. These players—superstars who averaged 35 or 44 points—attempted 30 or 40 shots every game, hitting jumpers from distances that left fans cheering, opponents muttering, and sometimes even their own teammates complaining. The NCAA Division I record book lists the twenty-six highest single-season scoring averages. Seventeen came between 1968 and 1978, and most of the time it was a great jump shooter setting the record. And of the top seven players with the highest career scoring averages, five of them finished their careers between 1970 and 1973. Coaches let shooters loose and many times ordered the players to act like they were the only ones on the court. It usually gave their teams the best chance to win, but if the team came up short, the shooters got labeled as losers. Transcendent talents, they enjoyed the type of freedom that's unfathomable in today's game. And often, their jump shot is what allowed their teams to win, even as writers and critics simply thought of them as nothing but gunners.

These baby boomers started practicing their shots in the late '50s and early '60s, when the jumper emerged as a legitimate play in basketball. But it was still an era when not everyone took advantage of the shot, when you didn't see every kid on the playground working on it. For those who practiced it more than other players, and were blessed with natural talent, their jumper put them ahead of their time when they reached college. Seeing this, their coaches built programs around their skills, with those jump shots the focal point.

Jump shooting phenoms like Rick Mount, Calvin Murphy, Austin Carr, Dwight Lamar, and Travis Grant put up eye-popping numbers in college while Bob McAdoo did the same thing in the NBA. And then there was Pistol Pete, who wrecked defenses and scorebooks until injuries and his demons wrecked his career.

Call it the golden era of the jump shot. Not because these players always shot with great accuracy—as Maravich showed against Alabama and so many other times, they often didn't—but because they lit up scoreboards and enjoyed an offensive freedom that soon went the way of the set shot. No coach today designs an offense that demands one player take 35 shots every game. Efficiency rules. Teamwork. But during this golden era, the fundamentals of the jump shot combined with the athleticism of the players, creating scoring machines whose numbers still amaze. None more so than the ones put up by Pete Maravich.

"Maravich, for all the points he scored, I would never consider him a great shooter." These are the words of columnist Peter Vecsey, who, in addition to covering Maravich's pro career, watched a teenage Pistol Pete play high school ball in North Carolina. "He was a scorer, a volume scorer, a volume shooter, but, yeah, no three-pointers back then and he averaged 44 a game in three years? Pretty unbelievable."

Maravich's ball-handling and passing skills are as exciting to watch today as they were when he was a college kid in his famous drooping socks, wearing the white uniforms of LSU. Every few months I'll call up Pistol Pete videos on YouTube and lose myself in highlights. The between-the-legs bounce pass on a fast break. The behind-the-back flips in a half-court setting. The around-the-head dish for a layup. Sadly I'm too old to go out in the backyard and impersonate these moves anymore, and too young to have watched Maravich pull them off in his prime.

Maravich's dad, Press, put a basketball in Pete's hands as a kid. Pete learned those tricks at a young age, perfected them as a teen. He famously dribbled a ball into town, took it into the movies, bounced one on a bike and while riding in a car. At night in bed, before Maravich drifted off to sleep, he practiced his shooting with a basketball, releasing it off his fingertips while alone in his room, perhaps already dreaming of the days when he'd do the same thing in front of millions. All of that work and practice—a little kid once asked Press how long it took Pete to learn his tricks, and Press said, "All his life"—created a basketball machine, one designed to entertain and thrill. But mostly, one designed to shoot and score.

Maravich's career college average of 44.2—that pretty unbelievable number—remains the centerpiece of his legend. For three straight seasons he averaged at least 43.8 points per game—no one else in Division I has ever averaged that much in even one season. He also owned one of the great nicknames in sports, although carrying the name Pistol placed even more pressure on Pete, creating a mythical character who had to shoot 40 times a game and score 44 points if he wanted to live up to the moniker.

Years before Pete played college ball, Press coached at Clemson and suggested outlawing the jump shot, believing finesse could return to the game. He echoed other jump shot critics. Ambivalence about the shot disappeared by the time Pete first rose up from 25 feet to launch his jumper. Press built his offense and the LSU program around Pete's talent, specifically his shooting ability. In *Pistol*, Mark Kriegel described the LSU offense:

By Press's calculation, Pete would have to shoot 40 times a game for LSU to have a chance of winning. Not only did the theory violate every strategic principle of the game, it had never been done. Shooting at such an absurdly rapid rate—better than a shot a minute—would prove physically and psychologically grueling. Pete's number 23 might as well have been replaced with a bull's eye. As a coach, Press understood the burden this would place on his son; as a father, he could live with it. "He's got more pressure on him than any kid in America," he said.

Later, his fellow coaches—some of them his closest friends—believed Press became too concerned with Pete's numbers. Press's response? "I wish he'd shoot a thousand times." If Pete ever played in a four-overtime game, he would have come close. In his first game as a sophomore Maravich took 50 shots. That year he took 51 shots against Kentucky, and in the next game attempted 57 more against Vanderbilt, both games ending in LSU losses, despite Pete scoring 52 in the first one and 54 in the second.

No one combined flair with fundamentals like Maravich, and no one kept pace with his scoring. As a senior, Maravich broke Oscar Robertson's career NCAA scoring record, setting the mark with a 23-foot jump shot in a victory over Ole Miss, an "arching missile," one writer called it, two of his 53 points. For all the records he broke—he scored 3,667 points in three years—and memories he created, Maravich couldn't lift LSU to the NCAA tournament, during the era when only the SEC champion qualified. He never won an NBA championship. Purists said it made sense—of course someone like Maravich, a one-man show, could never win big. Perhaps a more well-rounded Maravich might have experienced a bit more team success. Those criticisms overlook what he accomplished, especially at LSU, a moribund program before his dad unleashed his creation. LSU went 6–20 and 3–23 the two years before Pete played varsity. Over three seasons with the Tigers, LSU went 14–12, 13–13, and finally 22–10. In *Family Weekly* magazine, John Musemeche once wrote, "Shooting has always been Pete's mania. It has, in fact, brought criticism. But Pete's teammates come to his rescue. 'When Pete's shooting, we win,' says one of the LSU starters. 'That's what the game is all about—winning. We'd be crazy if we didn't give the ball to Pete.'"

Pete himself carried the burden of being a superstar without a team title, a magician who couldn't make the criticisms disappear. In 1977, seven years into his pro career, three years before his retirement, he said, "I think some people are destined to become losers, and some people are destined to become winners. Sometimes I feel that maybe I'm destined to never win an NBA championship." Maravich's words matched those said years earlier by Jerry West—who was as efficient as Maravich was theatrical—after one of his devastating Finals defeats. West eventually got his championship, but Maravich never did, a fact that tortured him even after retirement.

Maravich discovered some semblance of peace years after he left the game when he became a born-again Christian. Perhaps only the zeal Pistol Pete displayed toward basketball as a kid could match the fervor of the recently converted. On January 5, 1988, in a gym in California, Maravich died at the age of forty on a basketball court, in a game that included Dr. James Dobson, founder of Focus on the Family and an evangelical leader. Maravich's last words, spoken seconds before he collapsed and died of a rare heart disorder—he was born without a left coronary artery, which should have killed him twenty years earlier—were "I feel great."

His legacy grew after his death. People remembered the moves and the shots, each of them improbable, if not impossible. Fans looked back at his prodigious scoring numbers, those 50- and 60-point games that Maravich somehow made routine. In that *Family Weekly* story from 1969, Press told the writer Musemeche about working with Pete at a young age, about the first time Pete Maravich shot the ball, just a boy pushing the ball toward the rim, long before he became Pistol Pete, the man with the jump shot that shattered records. "He was about as interested as going to the dentist," Press said. "I set up a hoop and coaxed him into shooting. He thought it was too easy. He missed the first time and the second. Then he got mad and kept at it. He was hooked."

And basketball was never the same.

During the peak of Maravich mania, Press addressed criticisms of his Pete-centric offensive system. "Pete Maravich would be Pete Maravich whether he played for me or anybody else," Press said. The alternative history of Pete Maravich playing for a shooting-is-a-sin coach is intriguing—and depressing when you think about all the wonders fans would have been robbed of if Pete never became Pistol. But Press Maravich was not alone during that era in creating entire systems around the talents of one shooter.

Throughout those years, coaches—some of them rebels who flouted the rules and conventions, others old purists who changed their strategies when gifted with a great jump shooter—placed power in the hands of twenty-year-old marksmen. The shooters didn't disregard their coaches—they followed their directives. They were told to shoot, in offensive systems designed to maximize their shot attempts. These coaches recognized some players possessed shooting skills foreign to everyone else on the team. Few coaches in 1955 could have run these offenses—owing to a lack of sufficient great jump shooters and because of the era. Conformity reigned, on the court and off, making it impossible to imagine many coaches allowing stars to go off. By the late 1960s—blame or credit LSD, rock 'n' roll, hippies, LBJ, Nixon—times had changed. It couldn't last forever. Even by 1980 it became impossible to imagine several players shooting 40 times a game while their teams scored 100 points. For a time everything came together. It was system basketball—a phrase too often associated with boring, slowdown offense—that was fundamentally sound, but always aggressive.

Austin Carr starred during that era and says, "Scoring in a system is totally different than taking the ball and saying, 'Give me the ball and get out of the way.' If I got the ball, and I wasn't open, my next play I had to give it up and then go back through whatever the next side of the play was. So I would get it back, but I first had to give it up."

Carr set high school scoring records in Washington, D.C., and went to Notre Dame, bringing basketball excitement to a football school. One of the great midrange shooters of his generation, Carr combined that shot with an ability to bully defenders, despite standing just six-foot-four. His career average of 34.6 only trails Maravich among Division I players. Always moving without the ball—the system called for it—Carr rarely took wild shots. Unlike Maravich—a career 43.8 percent shooter at LSU—Carr was incredibly accurate, hitting 52.9 percent for his career. All along he obeyed the orders from Notre Dame coach Johnny Dee, who let everyone know the team's first option was also first among equals. "We tried to get him about 32 to 36 shots a game," Dee once said. "We weren't going through a batting order where everybody had to take the same amount of turns."

Carr now works in community and business development for the Cleveland Cavaliers, the team that took him with the number one pick in the 1971 NBA draft. He spent nine years with the Cavaliers, and today he's also the analyst on Cleveland's telecasts. With his energetic voice and quick laugh, Carr has become known for his love of all things Cavs and his catchphrases. To many fans, that's all they know. Carr's the guy who yells "Throw the hammer down!" after a dunk and "Get that weak stuff outta here!" after a block. But at Notre Dame he was a superstar, a player who didn't impress with flash, just with the final results.

On the June 2014 day I met with Carr in a small conference room at Quicken Loans Arena in downtown Cleveland, he had spent the morning at an event in nearby Independence, the kind of goodwill appearance he frequently makes. Carr remains a face of the franchise. When he returned to his cubicle at Cavs headquarters, reporters inundated Carr with calls. That day, Miami Heat superstar and Ohio native LeBron James revealed his intention of becoming a free agent. He hadn't signed with the Cavs—that came later—but by announcing his desire to explore free agency, James set off a frenzy in Cleveland, a city desperate for his return, four years after he departed. Tampering rules prevented Carr from saying much of anything about LeBron.

As much as I wanted to ask about the possible return of the King, I resisted, content to talk about the days when Carr ruled all he surveyed. Carr maintains an impressive physical presence, despite feet and knees ravaged by breaks and tears—during our talk he used his arm to demonstrate his defense on Jerry West. He obviously doesn't look the same—a bald dome has replaced the Afro—but when he talks about his high-scoring days he comes alive, as if he's in a locker room after a 45-point game.

In high school, Carr played at D.C.'s Mackin, a private school Carr's dad insisted he attend because he didn't want him in the public school system. Year after year Mackin lost to DeMatha, until Carr's senior year, when Mackin won a city championship. For Carr, that 1967 title completed a quest he began three years earlier, when head coach Paul Furlong spotted the freshman shooting baskets. "I don't know if I was a great shooter that early," Carr says, "but I had a work ethic, and I always wanted to be the best player on the floor every time. So there were two things I had to have: good fundamentals and stamina, because you're going to need that if you're going to score a lot of points like I did." Carr learned to shoot on D.C.'s playgrounds, where he battled the city's best, in parks that featured top high school and college players. During the off-season, pros and D.C. natives like Dave Bing and Elgin Baylor stopped by for games. By tenth grade, Carr and his friends traveled around "trying to control the playgrounds," playing day and night. "You had to learn the pull-up jumper there," Carr says, "because you couldn't go inside too many times or you'd get hurt. Guys would just foul you, and you'd have to take the ball out of bounds. You could get into a game where there was a lot of tension, and you'd get fouled ten times. So you had to learn to shoot before they could foul you. You shot the pull-up or used a pick to catch and shoot."

Carr's college choice came down to North Carolina and Notre Dame. It proved a difficult decision for basketball reasons—the Tar Heels were a national power while Irish fans tolerated basketball mediocrity while fantasizing about football greatness—and personal ones. The Carrs came from Carolina. "My mother said I was conceived in North Carolina, but born in Washington." Carr's dad, Austin Sr., helped with the decision. A Catholic who wanted his son exposed to the education at Notre Dame, Dad got his way.

With Carr, a program that made three NCAA tourneys in the decade before his arrival made three consecutive appearances from 1969 to 1971. And it was in the NCAA tournament when Carr ensured his spot in college basketball history. Six times in the NCAA tournament a player has scored 50 or more points in a game (no one's done it since 1987). Carr did it three times. Of the twelve highest-scoring games in NCAA tourney history, Carr has five of them. In seven career tournament games he averaged 41.3 points, nearly eight points higher than the next player. That average includes the first tourney game he ever played, when he scored only six points against Miami of Ohio because of a broken foot he suffered in the game. His average in the other six postseason games? An astounding 47.2. He scored 52 against Kentucky on 22 of 35 shooting, and 45 against Iowa on 21 of 39 shots. Against Texas Christian University in 1971 he scored 52 in a 102–94 victory, and made 20 of his 34 field goals.

His masterpiece came against Ohio in the 1970 tournament. Carr broke Bill Bradley's single-game scoring record with 61 points in a 112–82 victory. He made 25 of his 44 shots, mesmerizing Ohio with short pull-up jumpers and long-range bombs. As always he moved effortlessly, his Notre Dame jersey hanging loose. Throughout his career he never kept the shirt tucked, a fashion statement as distinctive as Maravich's famed floppy socks. Early in the game, Coach Dee threatened to remove Carr because he couldn't stop Ohio guard John Canine. With Ohio leading 20–14, Canine and Carr both had 12 points. Canine went scoreless the remainder of the half while Carr scored 35 over the first 20 minutes. Notre Dame led 54–41 at halftime and cruised in the blowout. He knocked his final jumper in from 20 feet. The shot hit the back of the rim, went nearly as high as the top of the backboard, and fell through, giving him 61 points.

Notre Dame ran a double-stack offense, created by assistant coach Gene Sullivan, who often directed the Irish's practices while Dee sat at half-court smoking cigars. The offense called for one guard on the outside with four players inside. Carr started low and broke out for a pass, where he could shoot or take his man off the dribble. "We ran all kinds of variations from that," Carr says. "Crossing the lane, pick downs, we just ran our system. In order to shoot the ball as many times as I did, I had to do it within the system. So I had to be moving properly, making the right move, so I could be open. I didn't want to take a shot where my teammates were going to be screaming at me for not passing the ball."

Others noticed Carr's unselfish play, even as he put up numbers associated with selfish players. Kansas coach Ted Owens raved, "He never takes a bad shot, he never forces because he passes off when he feels he's in a bad position. Carr has few equals as a team player." Each Austin Carr game became a clinic in how to slice apart a defense. "The midrange game is what I excelled on," he says. "Once I saw you overcommit—bang!—I'm there. To me, if you're going to be a great jump shooter, you've gotta be able to score from everywhere. Low baseline, top of the key, corners. That's how I practiced, impromptu shots coming from anywhere. If you noticed, a lot of my shots I take one dribble, two dribbles, turn around and shoot it. But that's what the defense gave me—so I took it."

Remarkably, for a player with the second-highest average in major college basketball history—Carr averaged 38.1 as a junior and 38 as a senior—he never led the nation in scoring. In 1970, he lost the title to Maravich. And in 1971, another gunner from the South, Johnny Neumann with Mississippi, averaged 40.1. But few matched Carr's consistency. He displayed his endurance as he ran defenders ragged. During one 1970 game against Butler, a flu bug left the Irish with a depleted roster. Dee told Carr, "Auggie, we only have seven players, so I think it's time we need a good game from you tonight." Carr responded with 50. The Irish won 121–114.

Carr enjoyed battling the best. As a junior, in a ten-day span he scored 43 points against top-ranked Kentucky, 43 against third-ranked South Carolina, and 24 against second-ranked UCLA. Then, in his senior year, against UCLA, the number one team and on its way to its fifth straight national championship, he scored 46 points as Notre Dame upset the Bruins 89–82. Curry Kirkpatrick wrote in *Sports Illustrated*, "He got rebounds, made steals, embarrassed four defenders, fouled out Sidney Wicks and finished with 15 of the last 17 Irish points. What Austin Carr did, as any old Golden Domer could have told us, was wake up the echoes and shake down the thunder all by himself." Wicks, taken second in the 1971 draft, behind Carr, fouled out while trying to guard the Irish star. "I told you, Coach," Wicks yelled at John Wooden. "I told you not to put me on him. I told you."

Cleveland took Carr with the top pick in the 1971 draft, an honor Carr learned of while sitting in art history class. Over the course of his career injuries—broken feet and torn knee ligaments, some of them suffered in the summer before his rookie year, others when he was a seasoned veteran—kept NBA fans from discovering if Carr could have duplicated his outrageous college feats. Bill Fitch, Carr's first pro coach, stated, "When he was healthy, I'd put him right there with the eleven or twelve other guys I have in the Hall of Fame." Great shooters need healthy legs. They need them for balance and lift. Carr managed to dominate at Notre Dame with fractured feet, but when his knees went, it was too much. "It started out as cartilage, it ended up as ligaments," he says. "And back then they didn't know anything about it. They just sewed you up. I was carrying my leg instead of using my leg."

Despite all of those tribulations Carr still averaged more than 20 points per game in each of his first three years, although his shooting percentage never approached what it was during his college years. He retired as Cleveland's all-time leading scorer, a mark that stood for nearly fifteen years. He also played a key role on one of Cleveland's favorite teams, the 1976 squad that made it to the Eastern Conference Finals. When he's out in public at an event or walking the street, people in Cleveland are as likely to talk about that team as they are the LeBron James–led Cavaliers. "It was like the first girlfriend," Carr says. "You just don't forget."

Even if it's sometimes easy to forget just how good Austin Carr was in his prime.

A few years after Pete Maravich left LSU for the NBA, another college player with shooting range that extended to Texas put his name in the record book for a school in Louisiana. Dwight "Bo" Lamar came to Southwestern Louisiana from Columbus, Ohio, in the fall of 1969. He became the only player to ever lead small colleges in scoring and then do the same thing when Southwestern Louisiana joined the big boys and became a Division I school. Two different scoring titles at two different levels, all thanks to his looping jumper, which the six-foot-one Lamar developed against players with superior height. "I was always shooting over people," he once said. "So I had to get the ball in the air. You either did that or got it slapped down your throat."

Lamar didn't handle the ball or pass like Pistol Pete—no one did—but Louisiana Tech coach Scotty Robertson once declared, "Maravich can't touch Lamar as a shooter." Robertson wasn't alone in thinking college basketball hadn't seen a gunner like Lamar. "Bo Lamar is the purest shooter

I've ever seen," Jerry Tarkanian said. "He's a great player, and his uncanny range virtually makes it impossible to play a zone against Southwestern."

Growing up in Ohio, Lamar made a name for himself at Columbus North, before transferring to Columbus East as a senior. At East, Lamar joined a team that was likely the best high school team in the country. The center, Nick Conner, excelled at Illinois. Lamar's backcourt mate, Ed Ratleff, became an Olympian and All-American at Long Beach State. Lamar joined Ratleff on the All-American team in 1972. Everyone expected Ratleff's greatness—a six-foot-six all-around maestro—but East's coach Bob Hart later said, "Lamar—it never dawned on me he would develop into an All-American. He's been a pleasant surprise."

Lamar didn't even average 20 points per game as a senior in high school, but when he arrived in Louisiana, Southwestern Louisiana coach Beryl Shipley unleashed him. Hart believed, "If Lamar was playing with a team that stressed discipline he might average only 20 or 25 points a game. But his team lets him have a free hand, and he's done a great job."

Shipley certainly believed in giving his players, especially Lamar, freedom. Shipley's career ended because the NCAA believed he—and other coaches—gave Lamar and the other players much more. As the Cajuns prepared for the 1973 postseason tournament, the NCAA announced it discovered approximately 125 violations. Shipley supposedly said, "Was that all they could find?" One report claimed Lamar "was handed $100 after a hot game in 1972." It didn't specify which hot game, since any game Lamar played qualified. The program eventually shut down for two years. Shipley admitted he skirted the NCAA's laws, but more than anything he was done in by the changes he brought to Louisiana and the South. Many parties wanted him to fail, and it had nothing to do with believing in the purity of NCAA bylaws. In 1966, he recruited the first black players into a major college in Louisiana. People hated him. For years the Gulf States Conference relied on unwritten rules that prevented teams from even playing against schools with black players; forget allowing them on an actual team. Shipley was a rule breaker—but his most important legacy was as a groundbreaker. Shortly before his 2011 death, Shipley told *Sports Illustrated*'s John Ed Bradley, "I didn't care about any damn rule book. I just tried to do what was right for the boys, what I had to do."

And with Lamar shooting, Shipley's vision of basketball dominance came to fruition. The Cajuns played in Lafayette, which *Sports Illustrated* wrote at the time "may be the No. 1 fun city in the nation." Lamar loved Westerns, his favorite being *The Wild Bunch*. That also served as an accurate description of the Ragin' Cajuns. Southwestern Louisiana scored 100 points five straight times during the 1973 season. Lamar led what was then called the college division (analogous to the current Division II and III combined) with 36 points per game in 1971. The next year Southwestern Louisiana went to the university division—today's Division I—and he led the country with 36.3 points per game. Along the way he made Southwestern Louisiana a household name, even though that success put the school in the NCAA's crosshairs. The Ragin' Cajuns made it to the NCAA tournament in 1972 and '73, thanks to Lamar and Roy Ebron, an inside power. Twice Southwestern Louisiana advanced to the round of 16, including in 1973 when the Ragin' Cajuns beat Houston 102–89 before losing to Kansas State 66–63.

Lamar and the Cajuns even got the best of his former high school teammate. At the 1971 Bayou Classic, Southwestern Louisiana beat Ratleff and Long Beach State—ranked sixth—90–83. Lamar scored 38 and shared the Most Outstanding Player trophy with Ratleff. When I spoke with Ratleff, he laughed when talking about Lamar's scoring—and shooting. During Southwestern Louisiana's recruitment of Ratleff, the coaches told him he could come down and shoot as much as he wanted. "Bo went there and took advantage of that," Ratleff says. "He shot like crazy. I don't blame him, because he was a great shooter."

A natural entertainer on the court and a sharp dresser off it, Lamar preferred colorful, outrageous outfits. Following one game, reporters saw him dressed in plain jeans. They asked him, "Did Coach Shipley tell you to dress like that so people wouldn't believe all those stories about your salary?" Lamar smiled and responded, "I tell you what, baby. Come catch my act when we're not traveling in cars. I'll show you something you won't ever forget." Forty years later, the people of Louisiana haven't forgotten those magical Cajuns.

Southwestern Louisiana's success helped prove the shooters of that era weren't just in it for themselves, although none of them would ever say scoring a lot of points ever hurt when it came to landing cash, cars, coats, or women. Notre Dame won with Austin Carr, Purdue won with Rick Mount, and Southwestern Louisiana won with Lamar. His performances left rivals flustered, even as they watched in admiration.

Against Louisiana Tech in a February 1972 game, Lamar scored 51 in a 111–101 victory. After the defeat, Scotty Robertson—the coach who thought Lamar was a better shooter than Maravich—pointed at Lamar and said, "There's your game. We did the job we wanted to on the other players. If we had held him to 30 points, we would've won by 11. If we had held him to 40 points, we would've won by one. They beat us with one guy." That happened a lot during that era. It was a good time to be alive for great shooters who teamed with coaches who encouraged an offensive freedom that bordered on madness. Those shooters weren't one-man teams, but as Lamar and his peers showed, one man could defeat many teams.

My first conversation with Archie Talley lasted two hours, forty-seven minutes. At one point Talley spoke for seven minutes uninterrupted. About a week later, Archie called at six at night. My wife picked up the phone. Thinking it was a telemarketer, she told Archie I wasn't home and hung up. When she later asked if I knew someone named Archie, I said yes. She called him and apologized. Talley took it in stride—and spent the next fifteen minutes telling Louise about his own troubles with telemarketers. I eventually got on the phone and we spoke for another two hours.

If I'd wanted the conversation to go in that direction, Talley probably could have talked about the telemarketing industry—the flaws, annoyances, pitfalls, ethics—for five hours. Instead we talked about shooting. Archie Talley makes his living talking, although usually in front of crowds. For thirty years he's worked as a motivational speaker, talking to groups and in schools while performing ball-handling demonstrations.

Talley played NAIA ball at Salem College in West Virginia, after growing up in Washington, D.C. Thirteen times a college player has averaged more than 40 points in a season. Talley averaged 40.8 for Salem in 1976. In the nearly forty years since, only one player has averaged 40, and that came in 1987. Talley was the last of a dying breed, the unapologetic gunner who, with his coach's encouragement, fired when ready—and he was always ready. His coach, Don Christie, said, "I only have three words of coaching advice for Talley: Don't stop shooting." Talley didn't stop shooting or talking, making him a fan's dream—and a reporter's. During Talley's postseason tourney in 1975, a West Virginia columnist wrote, "He's Muhammad Ali without the shouting. When they hold that Great Press Conference in the Sky, there will be a lot of people like Archie Talley. But at the West Virginia Conference tournament, there is only one."

The man earned the right to talk. Chris Wallace, a West Virginia native and longtime NBA executive, has said, "To this day, he is the best long-range shooter that I have ever seen." As Talley thrilled fans in the 1970s, Charleston sports editor Bob Baker wrote, "Even on the road, almost every place we went, the crowd was for Archie. He just has to be the most popular basketball player in West Virginia—and the most exciting—since Jerry West." Over a six-day span in his senior season, Talley exploded for four 50-point games.

When he started playing in D.C., Talley learned to shoot with a rubber dodge ball. Without access to a real basket, Talley used the red paint he dug out of the trash bin from his apartment building—the janitors threw it away—and put a dot the size of a baseball on a swing pole. On his own, he shot at that dot from 30 feet. "I'm hitting it square on," he says, "even as a little kid." After a few years, around fourth grade, Talley moved from the dot on the swing pole to the monkey bars in the playground. Still without a real rim, and still using a rubber ball, he shot on that equipment. "It couldn't hit anything on the sides or anything in the middle, or it would bounce out. I was shooting that thing from 30 feet, too. That's how I developed my touch—on the monkey bars and the dot."

Shooting came easy after that. However, attention from college recruiters didn't follow. Coaches thought he was too small, too skinny to play at the next level. Only Salem offered him a scholarship. The school didn't regret the decision. A six-foot-one dynamo, Talley often pulled up from

30 to 35 feet, at least according to witnesses and Archie himself. All told, Talley scored 3,720 points. He flourished in the clutch, thanks to a resting heart rate the Salem team physician said was a remarkable 35. In situations where others panicked or lost their cool as the pressure mounted, Talley's body helped him maintain his poise. "Joe Louis is the only other athlete I ever heard of who had a pulse rate below 40," Dr. Fred Spencer said at the time. An NBA career didn't materialize for Talley, but he forged a professional living overseas, taking his jump shot and outrageous scoring exploits across the pond. In a German pro league, he scored 116 points in one game. Talley's talking days began when his playing days ended. And as he approaches sixty with the energy of the eighteen-year-old kid who stepped onto the Salem campus, his passion for shooters comes through in every moment of every conversation. So here's Archie on the jump shot.

"You don't really need a perfect-looking shot, elbow in and all that kind of stuff. It's good to teach that, but I watch your wrists, because if you don't shoot the ball with your wrists, you're in trouble. But if you shoot it with your arms, I'll watch you and say, 'He's knocking them down today. He probably won't score tomorrow.' I'm not watching the shot. I'm watching what you do with your body, what you're looking at with your eyes. I watch balance a lot, because that is very, very important.

"Some guys need screens. Which, there's nothing wrong with that. But when you talk about great shooters, they don't need nothing. I mean nothing. A guy comes up and screens for me, I said, 'Man, get out of here. You're in my way.' Most of the time I was picked up either full-court or three-quarters court. Definitely by half-court. One guy just guarded me the whole time, then when I got across half-court, I was trapped and double-teamed. I would score 50 on stuff like that. They're playing traps and zones and all that kind of stuff. I never respected the zone. Most shooters would tell you that. If you're ready to shoot before you get the ball in your hands, no zone can guard you."

Archie knows what fans remember.

"America's all about scoring. You've got to put the ball in the hole in basketball. You've got to score touchdowns, man, in football. You've got to hit home runs, man, in baseball. You've got to score in this country.

People can say all that other diplomatic stuff about defense wins the game. But people remember scorers. Long after we're gone.

"I didn't set out to average 40. That just came along. That was the chemistry. Everyone had roles. We had a guy that rebounded very well. We had a guy that passed very well. You have guys that can score and can play, but that wasn't their role. That was my role.

"No one ever told me anything about shooting. Nobody ever, nothing. It was a gift from God. I could always shoot, always. You've got to have your wrist to guide the ball toward the target, shooting off your fingertips. Those are fundamentals. That had to be a gift of God, because I was never taught that. Nobody ever taught me about the wrist and the fingertips. Your palms should never touch the ball, because you don't have as much balance. You could still make it with your palms, but you won't make it consistently."

I guided Talley back to a favorite topic, offense versus defense. Can anyone stop great shooters, great scorers? When you say someone's unstoppable, is that literally true?

"I do value defense, I do. But if you're a great scorer and shooter, there's nothing you can do unless I miss on my own. I knew the guy in front of me, there was nothing he can do. Nothing he can do. Meaning, you can't stop me from shooting. I don't care what defense you play. Play my left, play my right, I don't care. It doesn't matter. I don't know who arbitrarily said, 'Defense wins championships.' I don't know. I'm quiet about it when people ask me publicly, but I'm like, 'Who said that? Who said that was true?' Because that's not true. I teach, and I know—a great offensive player could beat the great defensive player all day long. All day long. Because the offensive player has the advantage. He knows what he's going to do."

Talley knew what he was doing. So did every star in the golden era of the jumper. Writers and fans ridiculed them for not playing team basketball, for not playing winning basketball. They were called selfish and single-minded. But many of them combined scoring with winning, and those who didn't . . . how do you blame the guy scoring 35 every damn night? If anyone needed proof that a dominant shooter could also win, one more remarkable player from that decade—who also took 30, 40, and even 50 shots each night—provided it. He scored more than anyone. He won more than anyone. A flesh-and-blood human, his name was Travis Grant. But to his fans, teammates, coaches, and vanquished foes, he was The Machine.

ELEVEN

THE MACHINE

The first thing to know about Travis Grant is his nickname was not "Machine Gun." It was "The Machine." The second thing to know is his career destroys arguments about whether a prolific scorer can also be a prolific winner. When Grant left Kentucky State in 1972, he had scored more points than anyone else in college basketball history—including Pete Maravich—and the Thorobreds won three consecutive NAIA championships.

Grant earned his nickname in his first game at Kentucky State, when he hit either nine or 10 consecutive shots. A Kentucky State fan yelled, "He's a human machine," or, simply, "He's a machine!" Memories differ. The name stuck through Grant's career, which he finished with 4,045 points. The last of those points came in the 1972 NAIA championship game, when he scored 39 as Kentucky State defeated number one Wisconsin-Eau Claire.

Once he turned pro, writers and his own coach altered Grant's nickname. The Machine transformed into Machine Gun. "It was 'Machine,'" Grant confirms for me, and it was much more fitting. "Machine Gun" implies wild shots, scattered, with little control over the end result. Four misses probably follow every make. That wasn't Grant at Kentucky State. "The Machine" connotes efficiency, the same motion repeated time and time again, thousands of times during the summer, hundreds of times in practices, over and over in games, the end result preordained from the moment he caught the ball and rose off the floor—from five feet, 15, 25,

or beyond. That was Grant. During his four years on the Frankfort campus, Grant never shot below 60 percent, despite taking most of his shots
from the perimeter. One year he hit 70 percent.

But perhaps the most important thing about Travis Grant's career is
that it altered college basketball history. His jumper carried Kentucky
State to those three titles, and in turn, those titles helped carry basketball
into a new era. Dan Klores made *Black Magic*, a 2008 documentary that
profiled the teams and players who changed the game at historically black
colleges and universities. *Black Magic* included a brief feature on Grant
and Kentucky State's reign. Klores talked about how the Thorobreds' performances convinced college basketball powers they needed black players. He told Louisville's *Courier-Journal*, "I don't believe it's an accident
by the time Kentucky State is [beating] people it's a clear signal—yet a further and final signal—to the majority of institutions that, 'We've got to
get black kids.'"

Today, forty years after they made history—and changed it—the Kentucky State players gather for reunions. I spoke with Grant a week after the
2014 affair. Grant owns a deep voice. Coupled with his six-foot-eight frame
and serious nature, it proved intimidating to wayward students who dealt
with him when he roamed the halls as an assistant principal. The reunions
began after coach Lucias Mitchell died in 2010. Conversation focuses on
Mitchell, a disciplinarian who lorded over brutal practices but served as a
father figure to many players, including Grant, who doesn't remember
much of his own dad after he left the family when Travis was about five.

One reunion took place at Grant's home in the Atlanta area, and a few
players shot baskets on his hoop. He doesn't go out and re-create his heroics. But as the alcohol flows, stories about Grant's shooting skills pop
up. With so many to choose from, how could they not? Teammates talk
about that first game when he became The Machine. Or the 75 points he
scored in one game, or the 60 he scored in the NAIA tournament. They
talk about the time he scored 68 against George Gervin, the future four-
time NBA scoring champ. They could talk all weekend about The
Machine's jump shot, the only problem being they'd need more than
three days to recount the memories. "We used to focus on making sure
that Travis got his shots because we knew if he got his shots, that would

give us a big lead," says Elmore Smith, a dominant seven-foot teammate who went on to an NBA career that saw him set a single-game record for blocks. "We talk about how if we could have, we would have gotten him the ball more."

For his part, Grant prefers talking about the team accomplishments. A lot of guys have scored a lot of points over the years, he'll say, but they haven't won three straight titles. He's proud of his individual records, but maybe his nonchalant attitude about his shooting can be traced back to an old quote he gave. "I should be a good shooter. I've had enough practice at it." Plenty of players practiced a lot—but very few shot like The Machine.

The Grants of Clayton, Alabama, didn't have much during Travis's youth. His mom, Mattie Mae, raised Travis and his four sisters. She cleaned and cooked in the homes of white families. Unable to afford a regulation basket or a real basketball, Grant cut out the bottom of a five-gallon can and nailed it to the front of his house. He used a tennis ball or rubber ball or anything he could find, developing a shot "that no coach ever tried to change." Basketball took him out of Clayton and helped him take his mom out of that old family home. When Grant signed with the Lakers in 1972, he returned to Clayton in his Cadillac Eldorado, picked up his mom, and drove around paying off her bills. He then bought her a new home. His mom never saw him play—she always worked, bringing in what little money she could for the kids—and that's why Grant says his ability to help his mom when he made it to the NBA is "still the best thing that ever happened to me."

If Grant's home court wasn't the ideal place to become a shooter, his school wasn't much better. Until Grant's eighth-grade year, his school played on an outdoor court. Grant watched games for a dime. The team played indoors by the time he excelled at Barbour County High School, and about fifty colleges recruited him. By that time Grant had developed into an unstoppable force, putting up games of 68 points and dominating from the outside.

Lucias Mitchell wanted Grant for several years, first when he coached Alabama State, and then at Kentucky State. Mitchell arrived in Frankfort and found a program in disarray. He told *Sports Illustrated*, "They didn't want to practice, they didn't want to work on fundamentals, they didn't want to run, they didn't want to study. They wanted to tell the coach what to do, and I wasn't about to stand for that." Grant and his teammates talk about their coach and his techniques forty years later because Mitchell did everything in his power to make sure his players practiced. He worked on fundamentals. More than anything Mitchell ran his players. The Thorobreds ran in games—pressing and averaging more than 100 points every night—but they ran even more in practice. "We viewed him some-times as a maniac," Smith says with a laugh. For fifteen days before they practiced in the gym, the Thorobreds ran outside in yellow sweat suits, up and down the Kentucky hills. They did pull-ups on the football goal-posts, and tried keeping up with Mitchell's demands. Once practice started in the gym, the team went for two and a half to three hours. If a player came a minute late, Mitchell unleashed his anger, and, well, I'm not sure what happened to those poor souls—both Grant and Smith laughed and the conversation drifted off when they mentioned tardy teammates, as if everyone swore a pact to never again mention the fate of those players. "I never got used to that kind of training," Grant says, "but that's why, even though we pressed all the time, I played a large percentage of the game and didn't get tired."

Grant and Smith teamed up with six-foot-eight William Graham for the best frontcourt in the NAIA and maybe the best frontcourt anywhere in the country. Smith and Grant "didn't get any preferential treatment," Grant says about Mitchell, "but I think he understood he couldn't just ship us away home like he did some of the other players."

Kentucky State ran a motion offense, designed to get Grant the ball. Another offensive system invented for a special talent. He scored 75 points in a game against Northwood Institute—Kentucky State won 141–93, and Grant made 35 of 50 shots—and next time out went for 59 in a 159–79 victory. "When he's hot, he's inhuman," Mitchell said, a perfect endorse-ment for The Machine. Grant's shooting percentage separated him from other prolific scorers. From that first game, when he earned his Machine nickname, what went up, almost always went in. As a sophomore Grant hit 70 percent of his shots. One game that year he made 16 of 17 from the floor. Grant always faced junk defenses, which involved one opposing player shadowing him all around the court while everyone else played zone. Mitchell once said he put Grant farther out on the court to "counteract the diamond and one" and other Machine-centric defenses teams came up with when he was closer to the basket. The tactic blunted the effectiveness of the defenses, but not Grant's—the shots fell from 20 feet as easily as they did from 10. Grant's teammates "weren't rushing to take a shot," he says. "They waited for me to get open again. They probably went overboard trying to make sure they got me the basketball."

Kentucky State coasted to national titles in 1970 and '71. Smith scored 35 to lead the Thorobreds over Central Washington for its first title, and Grant erupted for 43 in Kentucky State's 102–82 victory against Eastern Michigan for its second crown. At that time, Mitchell and his players set their eyes on even bigger prizes, believing they were among the best teams in the country, regardless of size—and certainly the best team in their basketball-crazed state. Grant and his teammates traveled to Lexington for pickup games against University of Kentucky players. "They couldn't play with us," Grant says. Bigger schools refused to play Kentucky State in official games, because it put them in no-win situations. Beat Kentucky State and it's no big deal because you were expected to win. Lose, and it's humiliating, because no one should lose to a school from a lower division. Add in the racism in college basketball at the time, and Kentucky State didn't have any chance of hunting bigger game.

If the 1971 Kentucky State team was the school's best, the 1972 championship was its greatest title. No longer the overwhelming favorite, the Thorobreds lost Smith and Graham, but retained Grant. By winning three titles in a row, Kentucky State achieved something only Tennessee A&I and UCLA previously accomplished. Wisconsin-Eau Claire players and coaches thought 1972 was their year. In the previous two seasons, Eau Claire lost four times—two of the defeats came against Kentucky State. Coach Ken Anderson was on his way to 631 career victories, but all he wanted was to win the final game of the 1972 campaign. Early in the season, Kentucky State traveled to Wisconsin for a tournament. The Blugolds walloped the Thorobreds 101–81, destroying Kentucky State's press, but not its confidence. Grant endured a rough tournament in the Wisconsin cold. He got ejected in the opening game for an elbow to the face of an opponent, prompting Coach Mitchell to tell the ref, "You are putting my 50 points a game beside me on the bench. Ridiculous. This is basketball; basketball is elbows." He only made 11 of 30 shots while scoring 32 points in the 20-point defeat against Eau Claire, an outcome that hardly surprised Anderson, who said before the game, "If we play our best and they play their best, we will win."

Kentucky State lost five games in 1972, but none after January. Late in the year, against fifth-ranked Eastern Michigan, the Thorobreds showed why they remained a threat to win it all. Led by George Gervin, Eastern Michigan marched into Frankfort as a favorite. Gervin, the Iceman and future Naismith Hall of Famer, had a nice game, with 22 points. But Kentucky State took a 50–39 halftime lead. In a strange tactical decision, Eastern Michigan switched to a zone in the second half. Grant, who had 18 in the opening half, scored 50 in the second half, his 68 points leading Kentucky State to a 121–76 victory. Gervin didn't hold a grudge—he presented Grant with a medal during Travis's induction into the National Collegiate Basketball Hall of Fame.

In an NAIA district tournament game, with one of his perfect jump shots, Grant became the highest scorer in college basketball history, passing Grambling's Bob Hopkins, who scored 3,759 points.

Grant diversified his game in 1972. With Smith no longer in the middle, Grant posted up more and added a hook shot. But the jump shot was as smooth as ever—Grant scored 39.5 points per game as a senior—and Kentucky State rode that shot to the NAIA tournament in Kansas City. The event is the oldest college national tourney—it was played before the NIT or NCAA tournaments—and during the 1970s became a must-see for fans. The tournament lasted a week. Teams needed five victories to claim a national championship, a grueling affair, making Kentucky State's three-year run even more impressive. People in Kansas City worshipped the tournament. Sellout crowds of 10,000 jammed into Municipal Auditorium. Office pools popped up in Kansas City for the NAIA tourney, years before brackets became a March obsession. Thirty-two teams descended on Kansas City, but in 1972 only three had a chance of winning: Eau Claire, Stephen F. Austin, and Kentucky State. For Eau Claire, Municipal Auditorium became a home arena. Between 4,000 and 5,000 Eau Claire fans showed up in the city—"a virtual occupation," *Sports Illustrated* called it. "They swarmed over Civic Plaza in downtown KC and undoubtedly and unequivocally set a national small-college all-time record for partying and nonstop cheering. The local cops were so impressed with the gang's voluntary collection of huge heaps of beer cans that they were considering writing a letter of commendation to the college."

In this crazed atmosphere, Kentucky State started its march toward a third title behind another record-breaking effort by The Machine. Minot State out of North Dakota played the patsy in the opening round as Grant set a tournament record with 60 points—43 of them in the second half, proving, as he did against Eastern Michigan, that sometimes he used the first 20 minutes of a game to get loose. Or maybe The Machine simply enjoyed toying with mortals. He roamed the baseline against Minot, going 27 of 47 from the floor and receiving a standing ovation from the 10,410 people in attendance when he came out of the game, a 118–68 victory. Kentucky State cheerleaders chanted, "Don't you be so mean, Machine. Don't you be so mean." He ignored the pleas for leniency. After the Minot game, legendary basketball figure Dick McGuire—a scout at the game—called it "a hell of an exhibition." Grant made 22 of his final 32 shots, "many from the deepest corner, what would have been three-point territory in the American Basketball Association," according to *The Washington Post*. Following the game, Grant said, "I didn't feel I had an unusual game. It was my usual performance," and he tells me, "I had a stretch in just about every game where I wouldn't miss for a long time."

Against St. Thomas, Kentucky State led 39–14 before nearly squandering the game. The Tommies' seven-foot-three center, Bob Rosier, anchored the middle, but in the first half Kentucky State's six-foot-seven Sam Sibert blocked an incredible 15 shots (feel free to doubt the number, but it's worth noting newspapers at the time, and *Sports Illustrated*, both reported it). St. Thomas eventually took shots that didn't connect with Sibert's hands and cut the deficit to three. Kentucky State held off the Tommie rally and won 66–57 behind Grant's 38 points. In the semifinals, Kentucky State rallied from an eight-point deficit against Stephen F. Austin. Grant scored 13 points in a row in the second half before fouling out, although the Thorobreds were able to hang on, thanks to his 33 points.

That set the stage for the rematch everyone in the NAIA wanted: Eau Claire vs. Kentucky State. "We've been waiting for them for a long time," Mitchell said. "We're ready." So was a tournament record crowd of 10,801 fans. Entering the game, Eau Claire didn't have a player among the top fourteen scorers in the tournament. Grant, meanwhile—who set a five-game record with 213 points in the tourney—entered the final averaging 43.5. It was the ultimate team against the ultimate individual weapon—men versus Machine. The Blugolds—with only one loss—took an early 13–5 lead and harassed Grant in the first half. Like they did in the holiday tournament, the Blugolds rotated defenders and double-teamed him, forcing Grant into missing 16 of his first 22 shots. "They tried to keep the ball out of my hands," Grant says. "I guess it worked for a while. And then it didn't work."

Grant put together a personal 10-point run to give Kentucky State the lead for good in the second half. He took over with a 20-footer from the top of the key, two shots from 12 feet, an 18-footer, and a baseline jumper. Four years of dominance summed up in a five-shot display. The Thorobreds won 71–62, clinching a third straight national title. Grant scored 39 points, the only Kentucky State player to reach double figures. Ken Anderson was right—Eau Claire probably had a better team. But Kentucky State had the best player—and when that one player was The Machine, that was enough. "I knew all along we could do it," Grant said. "But this title is the greatest of the three. This is the best one." Two players, both from Lipscomb University in Tennessee, broke Grant's career scoring mark in the 1990s (Philip Hutcheson scored 4,106 points, John Pierce 4,230). But Grant's combination of scoring and winning has never been duplicated. He scored 518 points in fifteen career games at the NAIA tournament and Kentucky State went 15–0. He won every player of the year award and received the Lapchick Trophy, given to the best college basketball player in the land, regardless of division. Forty years after he last played in a game in the city, people in Kansas City still talk to him and remember his performances when he's in town.

Grant didn't duplicate the success in the pros. Coming off an NBA title and 69 wins, the Lakers took Grant with the thirteenth pick in the 1972 draft. "They didn't really need me but just because I was there they took me," Grant says. "They weren't planning on me to come in and play. They weren't playing rookies as much." Grant only appeared in 33 games that first year, averaging 3.8 points. Still, even in that time he left an impression. A year later his Kentucky State teammate Smith came to the Lakers in a trade. Smith recalls, "Jerry West told me, 'I gotta admit, that's one of the purest shooters I've ever seen,'" when talking about Grant.

It took a trip to San Diego and the ABA for The Machine to reappear. Grant played for the Conquistadors and coach Wilt Chamberlain, who, if not the strongest when it came to on-court strategy, recognized scoring talent. Wilt was supposed to play for San Diego. A contractual legal dispute prevented that, keeping him in large, loud suits on the sideline. Grant enjoyed playing for Chamberlain, and it showed in the box score. He averaged 15.3 in 1974, and in 1975—even though Chamberlain no longer coached—Grant scored 25.2 points per game. In one game he scored 41 points in just 22 minutes. Leg injuries eventually derailed Grant's career. He only played four years of professional ball, the same amount of time he spent at Kentucky State.

When he left basketball, Grant worked in real estate. After moving to the Atlanta area, Grant went into education. A basketball coach for nineteen years, his players didn't know much about his previous accomplishments. Occasionally Grant showed them his Lapchick Trophy as inspiration, and even if they couldn't recite his career numbers at Kentucky State, they knew he'd once been a player. In a profile on Grant in *The Atlanta Journal-Constitution*, one player said, "Coach doesn't miss." While he was an administrator, some students learned of his past and called him The Machine. Grant played ball into his fifties. One year he went to the Senior Olympics. His team won the three-on-three event, a "real fast, tough game" where "the three-point shot is huge," he says. "I kind of enjoyed it because that was an easy shot for me."

Every shot was easy for The Machine.

TWELVE

BOB McADOO: THE REVOLUTIONARY

No one ever played basketball quite like Bob McAdoo, and no one's jump shot made people quite so mad, whether they were friend or foe. He was ahead of his time, a center who was one of the great outside shooters in history. *New York Times* columnist Harvey Araton wrote, "There was a freak-show aura about him, the sense that he could not be what a man his size, almost 6 feet 10 inches, was meant to be." His game was built around the jump shot. That jump shot angered the opposition because it was so unstoppable, and angered his coaches when they were forced to build an offensive system around it—but also when they lost its services. McAdoo's junior college was so terrified of losing him after one season, McAdoo believes, coaches sabotaged his mail to keep him from leaving. Fans at North Carolina taunted him with racist messages when he dared leave after one season in Chapel Hill. When Willis Reed coached the Knicks he vowed to build a team in his own tough-guy image but eventually gave in, constructed the team around McAdoo's game, and seemed to resent every moment. Rarely did McAdoo get the type of coaching support available to his era's shot-happy peers, who played for coaches who catered to great shooters. Players like Dirk Nowitzki and Kevin Durant are the heirs to McAdoo's game and style, but even forty years after he outshot everyone in the league there's still never been a center who performed like he did from the perimeter. And few players have been as unappreciated.

I spoke with McAdoo two months after the Spurs defeated the Heat in five games in the 2014 Finals, and a few weeks before McAdoo, an assistant coach with Miami since 1995, was reassigned, moving from the bench to a role as a scout. The move made McAdoo a behind-the-scenes figure in the Miami franchise and means even fewer people will hear about his accomplishments. During his time as an assistant, a few times each season the broadcast for a Miami opponent found McAdoo on the bench—his mournful eyes looking out through a pair of glasses, the long arms resting on his lap, clipboard in hand—and one of the announcers would mention McAdoo being one of the deadliest shooters in history. The broadcast continued, but at least some fans heard about one of the greats.

McAdoo won Rookie of the Year, three scoring titles, and the 1975 MVP. A key reserve on two title teams, he could have won a Finals MVP. McAdoo is the last NBA player to average 30 points and 15 rebounds in the same season—and that was a year he *didn't* win the MVP. With Buffalo, McAdoo turned an expansion franchise into a contender. Few people remember his days as a Knick—and even fewer recall them fondly—but he still owns the highest career scoring average in franchise history: 26.7. Apart from the numbers, McAdoo altered people's perceptions about NBA centers. He matched guys like Kareem Abdul-Jabbar point-for-point, despite doing most of his damage with his devastating midrange game and ability to get to the basket. While McAdoo didn't have the reputation as a player who intimidated others in the paint on defense, he finished in the top six in blocks three straight years with the Buffalo Braves. He crashed the boards, finishing third in rebounding one season, fourth in another. While critics ridiculed McAdoo's defense, in 1974 Walt Frazier said, "Near the basket, he's almost a Bill Russell."

But it was the jump shot people remember. It made him an evolutionary figure. Today tall players are encouraged to develop their outside touch. They're celebrated, not scorned. Players like Nowitzki and Durant—and Larry Bird before them—stand six-nine or taller, like McAdoo, and they have better range. But no one shot like he did while playing center. In a 1976 cover story, *Sports Illustrated*'s Curry Kirkpatrick argued, "The point here is that there were others in the Kareem mold (Chamberlain, Bill Russell) and there are imitation Cowenses too—witness Denver's Dan

Issel and Phoenix's Alvan Adams. But there has never been another Bob McAdoo."

McAdoo was born to shoot jumpers. When he scored 41 points after returning from a toe injury that sidelined him for a dozen games in 1978, the AP wrote, "They say you can get Bob McAdoo out of bed and he'll hit a jump shot for you. Get him out of sick bay and he might hit several." Same with the wedding altar. On the afternoon of February 16, 1973, McAdoo married his first wife, Brenda. That night he scored 22 points against the Knicks.

Calling McAdoo one of the best big men shooters is accurate, but the adjective does a disservice. Mack Calvin played in the ABA and bounced around the NBA. During his time with the Nuggets, he said McAdoo displayed the most confidence in his shooting ability of anyone he'd watched. "Pete Maravich is a terrific scorer," he told the *Sporting News*, "but I don't think that he has as much confidence in his shooting ability as Mac does." Opponents often talked about the futility of putting a hand in McAdoo's face, a sound fundamental tactic that provided radar for McAdoo. Or maybe he was just insulted anyone thought five fingers in front of his eyes could distract him. After he tied Billy Cunningham's regular season Spectrum record with 46 points in a 1974 game, Cunningham admired, "I can't think of one or two shots when he wasn't contested—had a hand in his face. He shot like nobody was there."

The Celtics, winners of two titles in the decade, operated a McAdoo fan club and did everything but mail a weekly newsletter. Paul Silas said, "There's no way I could guard him. He's six-ten and jumps out of the sky. I bump him, and he still shoots over me." John Havlicek called McAdoo the "best pure shooter I've ever seen." After McAdoo went off for 52 against the Celtics in 1974, Don Nelson said, "I don't think I've ever seen a better shot anywhere. His release is unbelievable." According to the *Sporting News*, which didn't want to offend the sensibilities of its box-score-loving readers or America's youth, Celtics coach Tommy Heinsohn complained of McAdoo, "The bleep never misses." And, McAdoo tells me, "They asked Bill Russell about me being the best big man shooter and he said, 'Big man shooter? That's the best shooter, period.'"

McAdoo's height and size "kind of trumped everything," he says, "because I could always shoot over anybody. If they put a bigger guy on me, I could go around them. If they put a smaller guy on me, I was going to shoot over them."

The McAdoo jump shot was hardly beautiful, even if the results were. Tony Kornheiser described McAdoo's shooting hand as "resembling a seal's flipper. Sometimes the ball rotates perfectly and glides to the hoop like a seagull. Sometimes it has no rotation and moves like a guided missile. Most of the time it goes through cleanly, touching only cord and making a swishing sound. It is almost boring." At the age of seventeen, McAdoo played in a camp in Laurinburg, North Carolina. Jerry West attended. McAdoo says West came up to him and said, "Son, you've got one of the ugliest shots that I have ever seen, but I wouldn't change it at all because you make it." Impossible to duplicate or impersonate, it would be criminal to teach the McAdoo jump shot. His arms snapped down quickly, like he was putting a weapon back in its holster before he ran back on defense. Sometimes McAdoo kicked both legs back as he rose for a jump shot, occasionally they'd scissor, the left leg going in front of the right, making him look like the world's tallest Olympic hurdler. *Sports Illustrated*'s Bruce Newman called McAdoo's jumper "an awkward-looking shot from which he pulls his hands back so fast it looks as if he's burned his fingers." Elmore Smith played one year in Buffalo with McAdoo. It was only after the Braves traded Smith that McAdoo flourished, once he played center. Smith says McAdoo's "jumper was so nice we used to call him 'Face,' because if you got too close when he brought his hand down after releasing the ball, he would hit you in the face." The "Face" nickname had another meaning. Early in his career McAdoo enjoyed reminding defenders they were inferior against his offense, telling them, according to Kornheiser, "In your face" whenever another shot found the net.

When McAdoo rose for a jumper, "I never focused on just the front of the rim," he says. "I focused on the two sides of the rim on my jump shot." Upon McAdoo's selection to the Naismith Memorial Basketball Hall of Fame in 2000, his former coach Pat Riley said, "The mechanics can be taught, but the touch comes from the soul—and he had the greatest touch in a big man I've ever seen." But McAdoo gets lost to history. McAdoo was the only former MVP winner left off the NBA's top 50 players of all time, a list the league revealed on its fiftieth anniversary in 1996. Eighteen years after the omission, the decision baffles McAdoo. "It's ridiculous," he says. Part of the issue might be geographical. McAdoo spent his first four full seasons in Buffalo, an expansion team that played an exciting brand of basketball under Jack Ramsay at the start of McAdoo's career but devolved into dysfunction by the end of his stint.

"Our Buffalo franchise, I left and then they disbanded," McAdoo says. "Who knew about Buffalo anymore? Buffalo wasn't a franchise anymore so it's almost like I got lost in all that stuff too." Couple that with the three or four years McAdoo spent in NBA purgatory—if not hell—on bad teams and with dysfunctional franchises with no direction, and it's easier to see why McAdoo's accomplishments have, for some, faded from memory. An occasionally divisive figure, he and his legacy are still debated. Then again, that's often the case with revolutionary characters.

McAdoo played all sports in Greensboro, North Carolina—and was a champion high-jumper—but as he grew physically, so did his dominance on the basketball court. During his early days he played inside. Frustrated by zones, McAdoo ventured outside. "It wasn't discouraged," he says of his shooting. "Coaches discourage you if you aren't making them. That wasn't me." McAdoo led his high school team from Greensboro Smith to the state tournament. An opposing coach called Smith "the jumpingest team in the state," and a reporter admired McAdoo's ability to nearly dunk the ball flat-footed, thanks to his long arms.

Instead of attending an ACC school or his hometown North Carolina A&T, McAdoo ended up in Indiana, playing for junior college power Vincennes. McAdoo played with future pros Roy Simpson—who stood about six-nine and made an intimidating front line with McAdoo—and Clarence "Foots" Walker. One rival coach called Vincennes the UCLA of junior colleges. Vincennes rolled to the national title in McAdoo's freshman year, dominating Missouri's Moberly in the tourney final in Hutchinson, Kansas, behind McAdoo's 27 points.

"Our team could have beaten the majority of Division I teams," McAdoo says. "The talent was better at Vincennes than it was at Carolina, and we made it to the Final Four." Don't just take McAdoo's word. One of the refs in Vincennes's title victory also officiated in the Big Eight and told a reporter, "Vincennes University could play basketball in any league, including the Big Eight, Big Ten or whatever." McAdoo averaged 25 points as a sophomore at Vincennes, but the season ended with an upset loss. Everyone knew McAdoo would take his game to a bigger level, but after his first year he thought he'd leave the UCLA of junior colleges for the real thing. "My original plan was to go for one year and then transfer to UCLA," he says. McAdoo says he didn't receive recruiting letters that year and learned later the coach intercepted the mail. A 1974 *Sports Illustrated* story mentioned longtime North Carolina assistant John Lotz expressing surprise that McAdoo never responded to his recruiting letters. When McAdoo said he didn't get them, Lotz supplied carbon copies. "When you win a national championship, they're going to do whatever they can to hold the team together," McAdoo says, "so you'll go your whole two years."

McAdoo returned to North Carolina, becoming the first junior college player recruited by Dean Smith. Before arriving in Chapel Hill, McAdoo represented the U.S. in the Pan Am Games. The U.S.'s failure to win a medal wasn't the most shocking thing about the event. That title belonged to the performance of the junior college player who excelled on the international level. McAdoo averaged 11 points and hit a game-winning shot in an overtime victory over Brazil. "I was a JUCO All-American," McAdoo says, "but people don't take you seriously. They're just looking at the NCAA All-Americans. You talk about the jump shot? That's when it was really on display. Nobody had seen anybody my size shoot like that."

The Tar Heels went 26–5 in McAdoo's lone season, as he averaged 19.5 points and 10 rebounds. Tar Heel fans didn't quite know what to make of the McAdoo-led squad, a team that featured a tall player who shot better than the guards. Curry Kirkpatrick wrote, "They are led by two sore backs in backcourt, a 'Ukrainian mystic' at forward, and a tall, dark stranger named McAdoo everywhere else, and they are accompanied by the shortest cheerleader on record, Miss Annis Arthur, an honest-to-goodness dwarf. As they say in Chapel Hill, it is the year of the big man and the tiny lady: they also say McAdoo can do."

McAdoo impressed with his versatility—his quickness that was rare for a man his size, and the shooting ability that proved even more special. He toyed with North Carolina State's seven-foot-two giant, Tom Burleson. *The Daily Tar Heel* reported McAdoo "reclined for those jumpers time and again over" Burleson.

North Carolina's quest for the national title ended when Florida State upset the Tar Heels 79–75 in the Final Four, despite McAdoo's team-best 24 points and 15 rebounds. At the end of the season, McAdoo—who had also been pursued by Virginia in the ABA—became an NBA hardship case, confirming the worst fears Tar Heel fans carried with them: They'd only get sweet-shooting 'Doo for one year. Certain fans did their best to sway McAdoo. Following Carolina's victory in the ACC Tourney final over Maryland, a bizarre scene took place in the locker room. *Daily Tar Heel* writer Mark Whicker saw an "an apparent alumnus" lecturing McAdoo "about the evils of pro basketball" while telling him to "stay down there at Carolina. You know your mother wants you to. You'll be a lot happier." The begging didn't work. Dean Smith's first junior college player became Dean Smith's first player to leave early for the pros. "It was chaos," McAdoo says. "Dean Smith was the one guy who said, 'Bob, look, if they're going to offer you this, I would suggest you leave,' but nobody knew that. Everybody was upset. I was ten years ahead of Jordan and Worthy doing it. I guess I helped clear the way for those guys because I caught hell for leaving." Hell included racial taunts from fellow students after he turned pro. "I had notes put on my car," he says. "I had milk spilled on my car."

Buffalo took McAdoo with the second pick in the 1972 NBA draft. The Braves entered the league in 1970 and won 22 games each of their first two years. With McAdoo, Buffalo's fortunes didn't immediately improve, even with the Rookie of the Year and new head coach Jack Ramsay—the Braves only went 21–61 in 1973. It proved a frustrating season for McAdoo, especially the first half. Always a center, McAdoo played small forward with the Braves. He scored 20 points in his first game, but for the next two months he hardly showed the form that made him a Hall of Famer—or even Rookie of the Year. McAdoo suffered games of two points, three, four, five, two again, and even zero. But McAdoo's jump shot could only be kept down for so long. He scored a career-best 29 points on December 16, 1972, and his first 30-point game arrived two weeks later. From

December 28 until the end of the season, he only scored under double figures twice and exploded for games of 41 and 45. "I should have started
from day one," McAdoo says. "But the old coaches didn't believe in just
throwing a rookie out there. You had to earn your stripes."

General manager Eddie Donovan did his part to help McAdoo by draft-
ing point guard Ernie DiGregorio, a passing sensation, and trading center Elmore Smith to the Lakers. The move brought Jim McMillian to
Buffalo, but also opened up the center position for McAdoo, who unleashed his entire arsenal. McAdoo won his first scoring title in 1974,
with 30.6 points per game, 15.1 rebounds, and 3.3 blocks. Buffalo—with
the new players, along with guard Randy Smith developing into an explosive threat—went 42–40 and made the playoffs for the first time. The
season ended with a six-game playoff loss against the Celtics, the eventual NBA champion. Game 6—when Boston finished the series with a
106–104 victory—went down in maddening fashion for Buffalo. McAdoo
scored 40, taking over in the final minute with a dunk to bring the Braves
within two points. Trailing 104–102 with 10 seconds left, McAdoo stole
an inbounds pass and dribbled in for another dunk. His defensive abilities were again on display on Boston's final possession. First he blocked
John Havlicek's shot, but the ball went to Boston's Jo Jo White. McAdoo
challenged that shot. This time, referee Darell Garretson called a foul as
time expired. It was a borderline call. And there was still one second left
when the whistle blew. McAdoo did bump White. Fans' views on the call
depended on their beliefs about how much refs should let go at the end of
games. The clock, however, wasn't in dispute—Buffalo deserved one more
second, even after White made two free throws to give Boston the victory. The next day's newspaper included a photo showing a second on the
clock at the time of the call. Ramsay told Tim Wendel—author of a history of the Braves franchise—that Buffalo wanted the ball at midcourt
after White's free throws for "just one chance. With the way Mac was
shooting the ball. I mean anything could have . . ."

McAdoo epitomized cool, from the facial hair to the calm, expressionless play—nothing fazed him, a trait often mistaken for indifference. He

was cooler than ever in the decisive Game 3 in the opening round of the
Eastern Conference Playoffs in 1976, when Buffalo faced the 76ers in Philadelphia. The teams split the opening two games, setting the stage for
Game 3 in the Spectrum, a place the 76ers went 34–7 during the regular
season.

Buffalo fell behind 64–55, but Buffalo's star center found the range in
the second half. McAdoo scored a game-high 34 points to go along with
22 rebounds. Still, Buffalo trailed by two points with six seconds left, the
franchise's best chance at advancing in the playoffs beginning to disappear after the 76ers took the lead on a Fred Carter shot. Years later, Ramsay wrote about setting up a play for McAdoo "to get the ball just inside
the top of the foul circle. Mac drove the ball from there, pulled up and
was fouled on a six-foot jumper with one second left to play." Coming from
Ramsay, the play sounds clinical, the call obvious. But here's Rich Podolsky in Delaware County's *Daily Times*. "Buffalo inbounded to Bob Mc-
Adoo who drove and threw up a wild one-hander. [Clyde] Lee stood firmly
planted under the basket while McAdoo charged after his miss. Both went
up, the whistle blew. Although the TV replay clearly showed Lee having
position inside, [referee Jake] O'Donnell said he 'went over the top.'" The
controversial call enraged Philly players, coaches, and fans. But only one
person took action.

As McAdoo stood at the free throw line, a fan along the baseline yanked
on the guy wires anchoring the backboard to the floor. The basket swayed.
O'Donnell screamed at the vigilante. When McAdoo took the ball back
from the referee, he eyed the rim—and saw it still shaking. "I should have
asked them to wait," McAdoo says, "but I didn't. I just focused." Shooting in conditions fit for a playground in Greensboro, McAdoo made both
free throws, sending the game into overtime. Buffalo won 124–123, a victory that would have been one of the most controversial defeats in NBA
history—a fan interfering with a basket!—if not for the fact Buffalo's fate
rested in the hands of one of the coolest shooters ever.

A quiet guy, when McAdoo did talk he expressed confidence. Reporters
love a good quote, but it can't be too good—it can't be too honest or a

player gets accused of arrogance. Following the 1974 season, *Daily Tar Heel* writer Chan Hardwick asked McAdoo, did he expect to "have trouble next year with the new, big centers in the league? Walton, Burleson?"

"I'm not worried because they have to guard me too. And I know for a fact that I will give them more trouble than they will give me."

Profiles during his playing days always included a plethora of honest lines, the type writers become excited about the moment a subject says them because the reporter knows just how great they'll look in tiny print. When Curry Kirkpatrick wrote about McAdoo for *Sports Illustrated* in 1976, Ramsay said McAdoo would become the greatest player in NBA history. McAdoo told Kirkpatrick, "That would be a nice goal, but it doesn't matter what any coaches or writers or any damn-body else thinks except me. I think I'm the greatest already." In defense of his own oft-criticized defense, McAdoo said, "Well, who are these supposedly superduper defensive people in the league, anyway? If I can get 35 and 40 on these guys any time I want, how good can they be?"

By 1975, McAdoo thought of himself as the NBA's best player—and he was right. People have criticized McAdoo's MVP selection in 1975, but that has to do with what Rick Barry did in the Finals, which didn't play a role in MVP voting. Barry seized control in the playoffs, leading Golden State to an improbable sweep of the Washington Bullets, the team that eliminated Buffalo. It's one of the great efforts in league history, cementing Barry's legacy. But in the regular season? McAdoo deserved MVP. A story line developed over the years, focusing on Barry's lack of popularity with the league's players, who voted on the award. Perhaps Barry should have finished higher in the voting—he was fourth, behind McAdoo, Cowens, and Elvin Hayes. But Barry's Finals brilliance doesn't detract from McAdoo's dominant regular season. The *Sporting News* also named McAdoo its Player of the Year in 1975 in a landslide vote, with McAdoo receiving 88.5 votes and Elvin Hayes coming in second with 33.5. (In the regular MVP voting, McAdoo earned 547 total points in the voting and 81 first-place votes, compared to 310 points for Cowens.) McAdoo's first three years in the league were so dominant, the media scrambled to adjust its awards system. Writing in the *Sporting News* about McAdoo's 1975 triumph, Bob Wolf explained, "The honor normally would carry with it a

Bulova Accuquartz wrist watch. But since McAdoo had won a Bulova watch as the *Sporting News'* Rookie of the Year in 1972–73, he will receive instead a portrait of himself in oil, done by nationally rated staff artist Bill Perry of the *Sporting News*." There's no statistical case for Barry in 1975, other than retroactive imaginary polling about how much his fellow players disliked him and how that factored into the voting. No case exists for anyone but McAdoo—not in the 82-game regular season.

The Braves won 49 games in 1975, one more than Golden State, good enough for the third-best record in the league after Boston and Washington. Both won 60 games. Both teams played in the East with Buffalo, while Golden State finished with the best record in the weaker West by going 48–34.

McAdoo led the league in scoring with a 34.5 average and was fourth in rebounds with 14.1, while Barry scored 30.6. In the forty seasons after that campaign, here are the players who exceeded McAdoo's 34.5 mark: Michael Jordan (1987 and 1988) and Kobe Bryant (2006). Despite operating on the perimeter, McAdoo was fifth in field goal percentage at 51.2—Kareem, dominating closer to the basket, was ahead of him at 51.3— and fifth in total blocks. He led the league in minutes, making McAdoo the one constant for a team ravaged by injuries. Ernie DiGregorio, the 1974 Rookie of the Year, played 31 games because of a knee injury, robbing McAdoo of his playmaker. Valuable forward Jim McMillian only played 62 games. And if advanced stats—which weren't in use then but are helpful when looking back—are your thing, McAdoo was second in player efficiency behind Kareem at 25.8, compared to Barry's 23.5, and was a runaway leader in Win Shares (17.8 compared to Barry's 12.7).

A relentless force, McAdoo never faltered. Remarkably, his lowest point total of the season was an 18-point outing—he was held below 20 points one other time. Over a four-game stretch in December he scored 42, 37, 44, and 49 points. In January, the Braves played on three straight nights. McAdoo went for 43, 32, and 43 points, and the Braves went 3–0. Buffalo didn't play a fourth straight day, but after one night off McAdoo erupted for 49 points. And he *still* hadn't enjoyed his best four-game stretch of the year. That finally occurred in March, when he put together a 51-point outing, followed by games with 49, 42, and 48 points. If those numbers weren't good enough to win an MVP, it raises the question: What else was 'Doo supposed to do?

One victim that year, Seattle coach Bill Russell, appeared in shock after McAdoo scored 49 points. "He takes the 17-footers you want him to take," Russell said. "But they all go in."

McAdoo put all of his talents on display in Game 4 of the playoffs against the Bullets, a series the Braves lost in seven. McAdoo received his giant league MVP trophy at Game 4, and then he showed why it belonged in his hands. Washington tried four defenders on McAdoo, all of them helpless. He even embarrassed Wes Unseld, one of the game's great defensive players. Aside from a handful of dunks, McAdoo relied on his mid-range jumpers. Early in the game he took two dribbles with his right hand, moved into Unseld, went up over the Washington big man, and drained a 15-footer. Next time he took two dribbles with his left hand to the baseline for another 15-footer. Showing some variety, McAdoo took a pass, spun along the baseline, kicked his left leg three feet in front of the right, and drained a fadeaway. A free throw line jumper rolled around the rim as TV analyst Oscar Robertson yelled, "You can't let that young man get his hands on the ball!"

At the start of the second half, after he scored 20 points in the first two quarters, McAdoo left Unseld behind with a pump fake, ventured into the lane, and hit an easy-for-him jumper over another Hall of Fame big man, Elvin Hayes. The Braves won 108–102 behind McAdoo's 50-point show.

Even after his eruption, his critics—and teammates—picked apart the game. McMillian said, "When Mac gets 45 or more points, we usually get beat. It happens seven out of ten times." And a bitter Elvin Hayes—his vision clouded by images of McAdoo jumpers—scoffed, "It doesn't matter what he does. He scored over 50 against Boston and they lost. He scored over 50 against Houston and they lost." Let the record show McAdoo scored 40 or more points twenty-one times during the 1975 season. The Braves went an outstanding 15–6 in those games—a respectable 5–3 when McAdoo scored more than 45. Instead of hurting his team or leading to a loss "seven out of ten times," those McAdoo explosions helped the Braves come out on top in games they otherwise had no business winning.

Unfortunately for the Braves, Washington won the series in seven games, despite McAdoo's 36 points in the finale.

In history, McAdoo's MVP gets dismissed because of the loss to Washington, since Golden State swept the Bullets. But that's unfair. When the *Sporting News* previewed the 1975–76 season, it looked back on the previous playoffs. Bob Wolf wrote, "The Braves's feat of carrying the Washington Bullets to seven games in the quarterfinals without DiGregorio was one of the biggest—and most unsung—accomplishments of the year."

That ended the peaceful time in McAdoo's career. Even the 1976 season—which saw him lead the NBA in scoring for a third straight time—included a negative note. Buffalo owner Paul Snyder suspended McAdoo when he sat out with a sore back. At the time of the suspension, McAdoo had just welcomed his second child and was thinking of renegotiating his contract, prompting Kirkpatrick to write in *SI*, "These circumstances, plus the fact that the volatile Snyder (or The Cookie Monster, as the majority Nabisco stockholder is sometimes known) could even imply that McAdoo, a man who works as hard in practice as in games, who plays more minutes and shoulders a bigger burden than anybody in the NBA, was a loafer, made the suspension a landmark in the history of dubious decisions."

Snyder traded McAdoo to the Knicks, who won one playoff series in his two-plus years in New York. That wasn't good enough for Knicks fans. McAdoo's Knicks teams lived in the shadows of the title teams from 1970 and 1973, squads whose legacies haunt the franchise forty years later. Before taking over as coach in McAdoo's second season as a Knick, Willis Reed, the leader of those old championship teams, talked about how, in those glory days at the Garden, "Everyone had been a star, and, consequently, no one had been the star. That's basketball; that's how it should be played." By January 1978, Reed surrendered the offense over to McAdoo. "Reed put his money on practicality," Kornheiser wrote, "and gave the ball to McAdoo. As in, that's two for McAdoo." It was a familiar struggle for McAdoo's coaches. Jim O'Brien in the *Sporting News* wrote about McAdoo's time at North Carolina—years after McAdoo left campus: "[Dean] Smith wasn't the first, and he certainly wasn't the last coach, who had to make McAdoo an exception to previous rules or strategy. He is such a talented individual, with regard to shooting, jumping and rebounding, that he just dominates a team's attack." Imagine those skills causing distress for coaches, making them move out of their comfort zone. O'Brien's column ended with the line, "He may be the best shooter of all time." Too often, that possibility was a problem.

The McAdoo–New York Experiment ended in February 1979, when the Knicks traded him to Boston for three first-round picks. At the time of the deal, McAdoo was the NBA's third-leading scorer. John Y. Brown, a future governor of Kentucky, owned the Celtics. He ran the Braves until swapping franchises with Irv Levin (the '70s were strange). As the story went—one story, anyway—Brown cooked up the deal over drinks with Knicks owner Sonny Werblin. Among those not consulted? Boston general manager Red Auerbach. Years after McAdoo's Boston nightmare, Mike Littwin explained the story in the *L.A. Times*. Brown was with Phyllis George—a former Miss America who was on *The NFL Today*—at the time; the two eventually married. Littwin wrote, "The story goes that she asked Brown to get McAdoo for the Celtics. And John Y. reportedly told her: 'You want him, little lady. All right, you've got him.' Maybe it never happened, but it's a story that has made the rounds." According to the too-good-to-not-be-true tale, George knew about the deal before Auerbach or Dave Cowens, the Celtics coach. The Celtic legends couldn't have been more surprised than McAdoo, who heard about the trade in the middle of the night on a call from Harvey Araton, the future *Times* columnist who worked for the *New York Post* at the time. Araton later wrote that Auerbach "confirmed the story for me by shouting, 'Call John Y., he made the damn trade.'"

While frustrated by the end of his days with the Knicks—McAdoo thinks they would have been successful if they'd kept the team together—he enjoyed his time in New York. But in Boston—and then Detroit—"things started to fall apart," he says. McAdoo didn't have much chance of finding success in Boston, based on his welcome. Coaches, executives, and fans talk about a player fitting in with a team, but what's a team's responsibility in adjusting to a player? What kind of attitude was McAdoo expected to have in Boston when its most important figure—who didn't actually make the trade—didn't want him? A few years earlier, when the

Knicks grabbed McAdoo from Buffalo and someone asked Auerbach how he would fit in, Red said, "When you're that good, you don't have to adjust. They have to adjust to you." His feelings changed once McAdoo arrived in Boston.

McAdoo disappeared for a few years, at least away from the eyes of the rest of the basketball world. Bouncing from Boston to Detroit to New Jersey, he lost more of his reputation at every stop, picking up labels, the kind that are coded, impossible to shed, and were often based more on race than reality. Elgin Baylor told *Sports Illustrated* in a 1982 story about McAdoo, "Ever hear anybody call a white player a malingerer? Ever? Think about that." He battled injuries and front office executives who didn't believe the injuries were serious. Around 1981, columnists wrote about him again. Gone were the profiles filled with accolades and quotes from peers about his automatic jumper. The stories instead carried a where-are-they-now vibe, as if McAdoo last played in 1962 and reporters discovered him running a small pizza shop back in Greensboro. This was an MVP and three-time scoring champ who all but disappeared. His career looked like it'd be cursed by being stuck on good franchises going through bad times or bad franchises going through normal times.

McAdoo's career changed when Mitch Kupchak's was damaged forever. Kupchak signed with the Lakers but suffered a devastating knee injury early in the 1981–82 season. The Lakers looked at other players, but settled on McAdoo. Pat Riley later told *SI*, "Everything—his image, his problems with coaches—was discussed before we got him. We still felt he was the ideal guy. Everywhere else Mac had played, he was expected to carry the load every night. This team is too strong for any one player to be a disruption." McAdoo finally found a new basketball home, even if he wasn't always entirely comfortable being at home on the bench.

My favorite stories from McAdoo's time with the Lakers involve his belief in his own talents, no matter the sport or recreational activity. The bad years drained his spirit before he found redemption, but a lack of success did nothing to detract from his confidence on the court—or away from it. Magic Johnson revealed numerous McAdoo tales in his book *My Life*. The Lakers had a saying: "If you do it, Doo do it. But Doo do it better." McAdoo told teammates no one in the league could beat him in ten-

Wyoming's Kenny Sailors, a player people consider the father of the modern jump shot, launches his jumper in a 1946 game against Utah State.

1946 UNIVERSITY OF WYOMING YEARBOOK, PROVIDED COURTESY OF THE PRIVATE ARCHIVES OF KENNY SAILORS.

The Boston Celtics of the 1950s and 1960s were the greatest dynasty in NBA history, and Bill Sharman's picture-perfect jump shot on offense served as the ideal complement to Bill Russell's intimidating defense.

HERB SCHARFMAN / *SPORTS ILLUSTRATED* / GETTY IMAGES

Dwight "Bo" Lamar used his jump shot to become the only player in college basketball history to lead two divisions in scoring while carrying Southwestern Louisiana to unprecedented heights, which ended when the NCAA temporarily shut down the school's hoops program.

GEORGE LONG / *SPORTS ILLUSTRATED* / GETTY IMAGES

Jerry West's jump shot was one of the NBA's defining shots of the 1960s, and Mr. Clutch was never better than when shooting in the final seconds of a close game.

Indiana schoolboy legend Rick Mount earned nationwide fame when he made the cover of *Sports Illustrated* as a high school senior, and his famous jump shot carried Purdue to the 1969 Final Four. More than forty years later, Mount still makes his living with the jumper.

Injuries robbed Austin Carr of the chance at NBA stardom, but during his college days at Notre Dame, no one shot like the Washington, D.C., native, who scored a NCAA tournament record 61 points against Ohio in 1970.

HEINZ KLUETMEIER / *SPORTS ILLUSTRATED* / GETTY IMAGES

Blackballed by the NBA after getting caught up in a gambling scandal, former New York City high school legend Roger Brown found redemption and stardom with the ABA's Indiana Pacers, thanks to his sharpshooting eye and unlimited range.

COURTESY OF PACER SPORTS & ENTERTAINMENT

With his unique shooting form, unique game, and unmatched jump shot, Bob McAdoo was a basketball revolutionary who didn't always receive the credit he deserved.

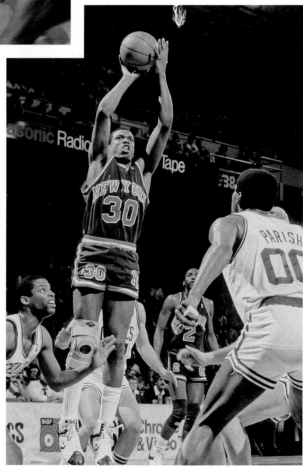

Former New York Knick Bernard King possessed the quickest jump shot in the NBA, and not even a devastating knee injury could stop him.

Larry Bird's all-around brilliance made him one of the greatest players ever, but his jump shot provided many of the most memorable moments in the Boston legend's career.

STEVE LIPOFSKY / WWW.BASKETBALLPHOTO.COM

Mark Price's dad taught him how to shoot, and following his retirement, the former Cleveland star created a shooting lab that helps the next generation of shooters learn the craft.

STEVE LIPOFSKY / WWW.BASKETBALLPHOTO.COM

Michael Jordan's aerial theatrics often overshadowed his shooting touch, but a series of jump shots created and solidified his legacy while also sealing his reputation as perhaps the greatest player ever.

Ray Allen made more three-pointers than any player in NBA history, but the lessons he learned as a military kid in California helped him develop into a standout shooter.

nis. He challenged Norm Nixon, one of the league's fastest players, to a race, with the winner, in McAdoo's words, "getting a million dollars in cash." Swimming? McAdoo was Spitz in sneakers. Baseball? Good glove, great bat. But, Magic wrote, the other players found a weakness when they asked about bowling. "I don't bowl," McAdoo said. Magic wrote, "By now the whole bus was involved. Three or four guys called out in unison, like a chorus: 'Doo don't bowl?' We were still laughing when Doo said, 'No. But give me a week and I'll bowl three hundred.'"

Playing for the Lakers—reviving his career, overcoming the stigma of the lost seasons, winning two championships—benefited McAdoo's career and reputation, even if it wasn't enough for the Top 50 committee. But it wasn't a one-way street. "I brought something they needed," he says. "I was the one ingredient that they needed that kind of took them over the hump at that time."

When you look at L.A.'s roster and see names like Kareem, Magic, Wilkes, Nixon, and Cooper, it sounds strange to say the team needed another ingredient. But as with his boasts from the prime of his career, the man speaks the truth. McAdoo was only thirty when he joined the Lakers, playing his first game with the purple and gold on December 29, 1981. The Lakers unleashed an unmatched weapon, even in a league that featured superteams stacked with superstars: a former MVP and one of the great scorers who could replace—or play on the court with—the highest scorer in NBA history, Kareem. McAdoo only averaged 9.6 points per game in the regular season. Once the playoffs started, the McAdoo who tormented the league in the 1970s emerged. In fourteen playoff games his lowest point total was nine. He averaged 16.7 in the postseason, with five games over 20. Following McAdoo's performance against the Spurs in Game 1 of the Western Conference Finals—in which he scored 21 points in 28 minutes—San Antonio coach Stan Albeck said, "If we're going to do anything in the playoffs, we have to find an answer for Bob McAdoo." Albeck never solved the McAdoo riddle. The Lakers swept the Spurs in four games. "He's the guy who beat us," George Gervin said.

McAdoo scored 26 points in the Game 4 clincher against the Spurs and sent the Lakers into the Finals, a performance that looked similar to his 50-point playoff outing against the Bullets seven years earlier. The superstar turned supersub went on a midrange rampage, again playing the game in his groundbreaking way. Only now L.A.'s short purple shorts with the white drawstring dangling in the front replaced Buffalo's short white ones. The pulled-up socks were now plain white instead of striped, and a respectable '80s mustache replaced the fearsome mutton-chops. McAdoo scored 26 in a variety of ways. He drilled jumpers off of passes—his hands again snapping down after the release—and hit jump shots after taking two or three dribbles, a defender tight against him, as helpless as he'd be if he was 15 feet away from McAdoo. Early in the second half, McAdoo set up on the right block. He caught an entry pass from Kareem, turned, and shot a jumper against Mike Mitchell. The Spurs forward put a hand in McAdoo's face, like so many defenders before him. McAdoo's height and size again trumped everything against the six-foot-seven Mitchell. This time the ball rotated perfectly on his 16-foot jumper and fell easily through the net. Calling the game for the Lakers, Chick Hearn said, "I don't blame Mitchell for shaking his head. He did everything a human could do." He did. But, as always, 'Doo do it better.

McAdoo's performance carried over into the Finals, where he averaged 16.3 points in 27.5 minutes per game, helping the Lakers to a six-game victory over Philadelphia. He shot 56.9 percent from the floor—no rotation player shot better. With the 76ers rallying in the third quarter of Game 6, McAdoo produced the key defensive play, blocking Julius Erving at the basket with L.A. leading by a point. On the other end, Kareem dunked. Philadelphia never did lead after the, yes, Russellesque play. Many people thought 'Doo deserved the Finals MVP, which went to Magic. Months later, prior to the 1982–83 season, Philadelphia and McAdoo engaged in contract talks before he returned to L.A., where he played for three more seasons. Sixers coach Billy Cunningham talked about the challenges the team faced if McAdoo moved. With Moses Malone, Julius Erving, and Andrew Toney, Philadelphia had offensive talent. Like the Lakers a year earlier, and like so many of McAdoo's coaches, Cunningham wondered if McAdoo's scoring could fit on the team. "It would be very delicate," he said. "And yet, when I remember last year against Los Angeles, the difference that stands out in my mind is Bob McAdoo."

McAdoo's NBA career ended in 1986 after he did eventually play one season in Philadelphia. But his playing days continued. Dragging his jumper to another continent, he traveled to Europe and played past his fortieth birthday, with the same predictable results: lots of scoring and titles. McAdoo married an Italian woman, Patrizia, and he still travels overseas to visit in-laws. Beyond the family connections, Europe remains a special place. "Professionally, I enjoyed my six years in Italy more than any block of basketball in my whole career," he says. His old coach Riley once said of that special career, "Bob played the game to the very last ounce of his jump shot." And even in the golden era of the jumper, when his fellow scoring and shooting wizards put up record-breaking numbers at all levels, that jump shot made McAdoo a basketball revolutionary.

PART FOUR

THE MODERN GAME

CHAPTER

THIRTEEN

1980s: SMALL FORWARDS, BIG SCORERS

On the spring day he engaged in one of the greatest scoring duels in NBA history—when he matched Larry Bird shot for shot, scoring from every dead spot on the old parquet floor in the Boston Garden, with shots that hit nothing but net and ones that went gently off the glass—Dominique Wilkins ended the game needing to miss. In Game 7 of the 1988 Eastern Conference Semifinals, Wilkins scored 47 points for the Atlanta Hawks. With Atlanta trailing 118–115 with one second left in the game, Wilkins made the first of two free throws and missed the second on purpose, giving the Hawks a chance at an offensive rebound and a potential tie. Instead Boston grabbed the rebound and the victory, advancing to the Eastern Conference Finals behind Bird's 34 points, 20 of them in the final magical quarter.

In a way, the final 12 minutes of that game symbolized much of the decade, an era that saw unprecedented scoring feats from small forwards like Wilkins, Bernard King, Alex English, Mark Aguirre, Purvis Short, Adrian Dantley, and Kiki Vandeweghe. Each played with a unique personal style, but all of them excelled from 12 to 20 feet with their midrange jumpers. They won scoring titles and numerous playoff series. But for all their greatness, the small forwards rarely got the best of the two teams that controlled the decade: the Celtics and Lakers. Magic Johnson and his Hall of Fame teammates stood in the way in the West. And as Wilkins learned, Larry Bird and his Hall of Fame teammates blocked the way in the East.

Yet the lack of NBA championships for those forwards—the Lakers and Celtics won eight titles that decade—does nothing to detract from the records they left behind. The NBA of the '80s featured high-scoring teams who flew up the court, right up until the end of the decade, when the Detroit Pistons slowed down, beat everyone up, and captured two titles. But before the Bad Boys ascended, one position produced amazing scorers whose jump shots carried their franchises to unprecedented heights, even if they never achieved championship ones.

Those players were part of the last generation who played without the three-pointer as kids. Growing up they didn't shoot from long range. Every basket counted for two, so they worked on their jump shots from 20 feet and closer. They used the midrange jumper, a shot that is all but disappearing in a game ruled by the three-pointer. When these players became prolific scorers, the three-pointer existed more as a rumor than a weapon. The entire league treated the three-point line—which came into the league for the 1980 season—as if the painted line 23 feet, 9 inches from the basket contained deadly toxins. Bernard King led the NBA in scoring in 1985, averaging 32.9 points. He made one three-pointer all year. When Alex English led the league in 1983 with 28.4 points per game, he made two threes. English is the perfect example of what the midrange jump shot could accomplish. He scored more points than any other player in the 1980s, becoming the first player in NBA history to score at least 2,000 points in eight straight seasons. Wilt Chamberlain didn't do it; neither did Oscar Robertson. English did, but from 1980 through 1989 he made a total of 16 three-pointers. "The three-pointer was still a novelty. It was like cheating," says Bob Ryan, who covered Bird and was perhaps the game's most famous scribe during the decade that was perhaps the most famous in NBA history. Even Bird—winner of three straight three-point contests—took his time falling in love with the shot. Bird made 58 in his rookie year, but over the next several seasons only made 20, 11, 22, and 18 threes.

Instead the high scorers knocked in shots from inside 20 feet. And the variety of their shots! They ranged from the perfect to the imperfect, from the sublime to the . . . how in the hell did they shoot like that? While players like Dale Ellis and Danny Ainge displayed textbook form, the type coaches and parents want kids studying, the shooting forms of guys like Jamaal Wilkes and English were the *Catcher in the Rye* of jump shots—something to be feared, hidden away, and possibly banned. Because they didn't gravitate to the three-pointer from the time they could chuck the ball toward the basket, the forwards of the 1980s became creative geniuses. Form wasn't as important—it was about whether they got the ball in the basket, through whatever method worked. King owned the quickest release, especially on his turnaround jumper from the baseline, where it looked like he caught the ball and shot in one motion. Wilkins might have been the greatest in-game dunker ever, but as he's said whenever someone focuses only on his jams, "It's hard to get 26,000 points on dunks." He mixed in jumpers that caressed the backboard with violent dunks. Vandeweghe perfected a graceful stepback. Short's jumper rose like a balloon before drifting down toward the net. Dallas star Aguirre hauled around an ass the size of Texas and put it to good use, punishing defenders in the post by backing up and drilling his turnaround jumper. English extended his arms like he was trying to touch the rim with his hands from 15 feet away.

Year after year these players put their names at the top of the scoring charts. English led the league in scoring in 1983, with his Denver teammate Vandeweghe second. In 1984, the top five scorers were Dantley, Aguirre, Vandeweghe, English, and King. Bird was seventh. The next year, King led, followed by Bird. Short, English, Wilkins, Dantley, and Aguirre occupied spots four through eight that season. Wilkins won in 1986, with Dantley, English, Bird, Short, and Vandeweghe following him. By the late 1980s guards started dominating. Michael Jordan won his third straight scoring title in 1989 and of all the great scorers from earlier in the decade, English was closest to the top, finishing sixth. But Jordan tightened his stranglehold on the scoring title, and the up-and-down style from the 1980s—which gave those forwards the chance to flourish—disappeared.

Because the forwards didn't win numerous titles (Aguirre got two rings with Detroit as a role player) and because their styles of play didn't awe like those of Jordan, Magic, or Bird—one of them in the air, the other two with some of the most inspired passing ever seen—their talents are easily overlooked. But King, English, and the rest—along with their varied shots—are as much a part of NBA history from that memorable decade as the Celtics, Lakers, and Jordan. They showed what the jump shot could do at the highest level in the soft hands of its greatest shooters. The legacy lives on, long after their pet midrange shot faded away.

At their best they matched weapons with the decade's MVPs. For those few glorious seasons when he scored in a way that occasionally rivaled Wilt Chamberlain, Bernard King proved he belonged with the best. *New York Times* columnist Ira Berkow wrote, "No one ever has accused King of doing anything other than trying to be the best basketball player in the NBA. If he didn't succeed at it—if there was Magic and Bird and maybe Moses [Malone] above him—he got very close."

Unlike Bird and Magic, who for much of their careers played on rosters with fellow Hall of Famers, the great shooting forwards often operated as a lone star. During the 1986 season, the champion Celtics could have put a lineup on the court with nothing but Hall of Fame players—Bird, Kevin McHale, Bill Walton, Robert Parish, and Dennis Johnson. That season Boston defeated Atlanta and Wilkins in five games in the playoffs, and the Hawks' second-leading scorer was the pedestrian Randy Wittman, career average of 7.4.

The same held true for the others. But while they didn't have Hall of Fame teammates, they utilized those sweet jump shots. Short, a longtime Golden State Warriors star, played nine years before he made the playoffs. He relied on a rainbow jumper that spent so many seconds in the air writers penned three-paragraph odes to its beauty in the time it took to come back down through the net. When I spoke with Bob Ryan, we predictably spent half of our hour-long conversation discussing Bird's exploits, but his enthusiasm for the great shooters wasn't restricted to Larry Legend. "You go talk to anybody, and say, okay, I'm going to give you a category," Ryan says. "Arc. When you think of arc, who do you think of? I promise you, if you ask people, eighty-eight and a third percent of respondents would say Purvis Short. . . . Incredible arc. It looked like a little parachute opened when the ball came down."

A few days before I spoke with Short, I e-mailed him a twenty-minute YouTube clip that consisted almost exclusively of Purvis Short jump shots. Rainbow jumpers, high-arcing shots that all but skimmed the top of NBA arenas before plummeting back to earth. Short hadn't seen it before and said he enjoyed it, thirty-year-old clips of a jumper he learned in high school.

Short's prep coach in Mississippi, Johnny Hurtt, taught him the rainbow. Hurtt made Short shoot over a broomstick, forcing his prize pupil to make 15 to 20 shots in a row from 15 to 20 feet. "I had to develop the concept of arc and get it ingrained," Short says. "He was a firm believer in the higher the arc you put on a shot, the softer it is." If that's true, then no one possessed a softer shot than Short, who starred at Jackson State—where his older brother Eugene also excelled as a player—before entering the NBA in 1978. Golden State won the NBA title in 1975, but by the time Short arrived fortunes had plummeted. The Warriors suffered through mismanagement and bad luck. For a few years Short played with fellow prolific scorer Bernard King—the team barely missed the playoffs two straight seasons—but the Warriors got rid of King. His departure created an opening for Short, and he averaged 22.8 in 1984, 28 in 1985, and 25.5 in 1986.

To this day Short credits Hurtt for his shooting lessons, calling him one of the two great fundamental basketball teachers he worked with. The other is Pete Newell, who ran a camp Short attended eleven of his twelve NBA seasons. At Newell's camp, Short learned the importance of footwork. While the height on Short's jumper captured the eyes of fans, the critical work took place on the ground. "He made scoring easy," Short says. "After my rookie year I started working with him, and my scoring from my first year to my second year and every year after that continued to rise. He was the reason why."

Short shot more three-pointers than many of his contemporaries—he made 47 in 1985—but, he says, for the most part "all of our scoring took place probably 17 feet on in. Kiki [Vandeweghe] used to always say that your offensive game should be much like a great baseball pitcher. They have pitches for different situations. We should have offensive moves, solutions for many defensive situations. We never worried how we were going to be played."

The three-pointer "was just being incorporated into the game, and the team was trying to figure out how best to use it," he says. "We would use it if you got down a lot, but it was still not something, at least when I came in, that was really encouraged. It's kind of a last resort. If it was one of those nights when everything was going in, you shot a few." Against San Antonio in January 1984, Short savored one of those nights, scoring 57 points on 24 of 38 from the floor. And in November of that year, he pumped in 59 against the Nets, making 20 of his 28 shots. In the midst of his scoring binge, Philadelphia coach Billy Cunningham said, "Anyone who doesn't consider Purvis Short among the top three or four small forwards in this game either has his head in the sand or should consider putting it there."

Scoring came easy, winning proved harder. Finally in 1987, Golden State made the playoffs for the first time with Short, although injuries limited him to 34 games. He recovered for the playoffs and scored 32 in Game 4 of the first-round series against Utah, leading Golden State to a 98–94 victory. The win evened the series at 2–2, and the Warriors won the fifth game. Their season ended the next round—against the Lakers—but Short savored his playoff moment.

After his NBA career, Short played in Israel, where others mimicked the rainbow he brought over from America, the shot he learned in Mississippi two decades earlier. "Once you understand the fundamentals of it, it's easily incorporated into your shooting because you're not trying to change the way you're comfortable shooting. That's one of the great lessons Coach Hurtt taught me. For any shooter to be a great shooter, he has to be comfortable."

No one looked more comfortable on the court than Alex English, although his jump shot occasionally appeared awkward. English proved what so many of the small forwards of the 1980s showed: A player didn't have to do everything well, as long as he developed a deadly jump shot.

At a young age English picked up the nickname Flick. Different stories emerged about the origin. Some said he looked clumsy, afflicted, and his friends shortened it to Flick. But it also described that jump shot, which he pulled off with a simple flick of his wrist.

For the first three and a half years of his career English toiled in Milwaukee and Indiana, never averaging more than 16.9 points. But in Denver, playing in Doug Moe's record-breaking motion offense, English became an All-Star. Between 1981 and 1989, his lowest scoring average was 23.8. He won just one scoring title, but was always around 26 points per game, year after year.

At 190 pounds and with the waist of a supermodel, English looked delicate on the court, yet between 1981 and 1991 he played in at least 79 games every season. On his jumper English fully extended his arms and often appeared to fall toward the basket, making him seem even taller than six-foot-seven. The shot worked in traffic—he avoided block attempts—or alone from 18 feet. English's feathery touch racked up points, almost all of them out of the spotlight. English rarely penetrated; the Denver offense didn't require it, and it didn't play to his strengths. Moe said, "He's not good at putting the ball on the floor so therefore he doesn't put the ball on the floor." English shared that trait with many of the great forwards. King, English, and Short all moved to their spots with one or two dribbles (they would have been perfect weapons in the Iowa girls six-on-six game and could have possibly challenged Denise Long's scoring marks). The pigeon-toed English once told sportswriter Jack McCallum, "I guess what my game has is kind of an off-balance flow."

Throughout his career, English developed a reputation for being a thoughtful, concerned citizen. Prior to the 1985 All-Star Game, he organized a cash drive by the players, convincing his peers to give up their shares from the game—$2,500 from the winners, $1,500 from the losers— and contribute the money to an Ethiopian relief fund. He even starred in a quintessential saving-the-world movie from the 1980s, *Amazing Grace and Chuck*, an occasionally absurd film about a boy concerned with nuclear bombs who ropes a pro basketball player into his movement. The movie star bit seemed strange for an under-the-radar player like English, but the themes of the movie fit perfectly with his worldview. English also produced several books of poetry, writing about everything from nature to switching teams in the NBA.

Early in the decade, Denver paired English with Kiki Vandeweghe, giving the Nuggets a pair of graceful scorers (along with sweet-shooting center Dan Issel). The six-foot-eight Vandeweghe credits Jerry West with giving him "eighty percent of the basis of my game in about ten minutes in his driveway," when Kiki was a kid. His dad, Ernie, a former pro player, worked as a team doctor in the NBA. One day out in L.A., West provided the younger Vandeweghe with a shooting lesson. "That shows how much knowledge he has," Vandeweghe tells me. "Ten minutes of his time stuck with me my entire career."

As with Short, Vandeweghe's footwork, much of it taught by Newell, provided the foundation for his game and the stepback jumper Newell believed Kiki invented, although others did actually shoot it earlier. Especially in his first few years, before back problems and other injuries, Vandeweghe relied on his drives to the basket. But as his career progressed, Vandeweghe found it tougher getting all the way to the rim. So he adapted. On drives, he put his foot down with the weight on the back leg and then stepped back from his opponent for a jump shot. He once compared it to a spring, as it allowed him to rise up over defenders caught on their heels. Done correctly, it's impossible to defend. "The first couple of times I tried it, Pete said, 'Hey, where did you think of that?' and it was just by necessity." Going against players like Kenny Carr and Kermit Washington at Newell's camp, Vandeweghe needed a shot against their physical defense. It's a shot most of the great scorers use in today's NBA. "Dirk does it, Carmelo does it, Kobe does it. It's a matter of knowing how to do it, and why and when. And then if you know that, then it's a few little tricks and you can get it off against anyone." Denver traded Vandeweghe to Portland for half its roster before the 1985 season. Two years later, as Portland players and coaches talked about the importance of playing better defense, Vandeweghe said, "It seems that every team has at least one outstanding scorer, and most of them happen to play small forward. I don't think anyone can stop a scorer one-on-one. I don't think one defender can stop me from scoring."

The same held true for English, even after Vandeweghe departed and defenses focused more on him. The Nuggets enjoyed plenty of team success. They just never reached the ultimate goal. English's best chance at making the Finals came in 1985, when the Nuggets lost to the Lakers in five games in the Western Conference Finals. English sat out the final game with a fractured thumb, the supreme scorer reduced to an observer, a giant white cast stopping him in a way no defender could.

It seemed English could go on scoring 20 points per game every season until he started collecting Social Security. Everything looked so easy, which made the ultimate end of his Denver career so hard to take. The Moe-English relationship, which produced those points for Denver, ended badly in 1990. Moe cut English's playing time, English complained to the press, Moe retaliated in the media, and for the first time in a decade Alex didn't average at least 20 points. But twenty-five years later, Denver fans fondly recall the Moe-English Nuggets, teams that ran the opposition off of the high-altitude court. The smooth forward went into the Hall of Fame in 1997. During his induction speech he surely didn't break a sweat, since he never seemed to on the court. English made scoring look easy, thanks to his extended right arm and a flick of his wrist.

Moe once said of English, "He was a guy who couldn't dribble, couldn't pass, couldn't do a lot of things, yet was terrific." That description also applied to Bernard King. He wasn't a great passer, never put the ball on the floor much. But when healthy, teams had no answers against him. Bird—born three days after King in 1956—said in 1984, "I don't understand how Bernard does it. He's in heavy traffic—guys all over banging him and waving their arms—and he gets the shot off, not just any shot, but the shot he wants, and he cans it. Time after time. He's the best scorer I've ever seen or played against."

King grew up on the playgrounds of Brooklyn. Columnist Dave Kindred described him as a "child filled with a rage to win because victory on the asphalt made him feel like a man." Substance abuse and arrests damaged his college career at Tennessee and early NBA days. He won SEC Player of the Year three times—but his demons threatened to derail everything. Finally, when he returned home to play for the New York Knicks, he found personal peace and professional greatness. King's best year came in 1984, stretching from one season into another. In January, King scored 50 points on back-to-back nights, the first player since Chamberlain in 1964 to accomplish the feat. He carried the Knicks into the playoffs, leading them to a dramatic five-game victory over Detroit. For that series, King averaged 42.6 points and scored 44 in the decisive Game 5, despite battling the flu. King played with dislocated middle fingers on each hand, yet it hardly seemed to bother him. Boston defeated the Knicks in seven games in the conference semifinals, but only after King terrified Celtics fans, who watched in disbelief as one man nearly single-handedly took down a team with four Hall of Famers in the lineup. He scored 44 to force Game 7. In the final game he struggled early and watched as Bird delighted Boston Garden with 39 points, 12 rebounds, and 10 assists. It was the closest King got to the NBA Finals. He finished second to Bird in the MVP voting in 1984, although the *Sporting News* named King as its top player.

At the start of the following season, his hot streak continued. On Christmas in 1984, King scored 60 against the Nets. In those years no one scored like King. And certainly no one shot like him. Early in King's career he preferred posting up only on the left side for his turnaround jump shot, but throughout his career he expanded his arsenal. The fadeaway appeared, followed by dominance on the right block. He later developed a shot Ira Berkow described as being "a push shot that is neither a hook, a jumper or a flip, but distillation of all three." Dallas coach Dick Motta said King didn't see the rim on half of his shots. People often credit shooters who barely need a "sliver of daylight" to get their shot off. King didn't even need that. He didn't need any space for his jumper, which he shot on the way up. "The mechanics of King's quick release are all wrong, according to the shooter's bible," Phil Elderkin wrote, "which preaches that a player sacrifices control firing up the basketball before his body has reached its apex. But to Bernard that suggestion has as much credibility as an old wives' tale."

King also carried that rage he first displayed on the hot Brooklyn playgrounds. He rarely spoke during games, and smiled even less, as if he thought any display of happiness meant the refs deducted two points from him. Instead he observed. He analyzed. Then he struck. Big or small, defenders were helpless. When a smaller man guarded him, King simply spun and shot over him. "Most guys spin on their toes. But if you spin on your heel you're closer to the basket, and I think you are in a position to shoot faster," he said. Teams got physical with King, hoping to disrupt him, but he loved battling a defender who bodied him. It let him know where the defender was, and then King knew exactly which trick to fetch from his oversize bag.

But at the peak of his powers King suffered a brutal injury on March 23, 1985, when he tore his knee against the Kings. Surgeons first worried about helping him properly walk again. King missed nearly two years of action—then returned for a handful of games for New York at the end of the 1987 season. But his hometown days were finished. Many figured the same was true for his career. Instead he created an inspirational second act in Washington, averaging more than 20 for three straight seasons with the Bullets, peaking at 28.4 per game in 1991. After scoring 45 points one night in January 1991, King, thirty-four at the time and on his ninth basketball life, temporarily took over the league scoring lead from Michael Jordan. The man who defended him that night, Clippers forward Ken Norman, said, "I'd rather guard Jordan than Bernard King. With Jordan you get help. With Bernard he is going to catch it and control it before you have time to double team. . . . And when he comes off a screen, well, a couple times I wanted to ask him, does he ever miss?"

Washington general manager John Nash said he didn't have a "favorite King move because he never seems to take two shots the same. He improvises so much and his release is so quick that, even when you know he's going to shoot, he can still get it off."

That improvisation, the "spontaneous creativity" as King called it, was "ninety percent deliberate—a re-creation of something I've practiced over and over. The other ten percent, I don't know where it comes from. Those are the big, big nights." A big night occurred on January 31, 1991, when King exacted revenge, scoring 23 points in the fourth quarter, 49 in the game, to lead the Bullets to a 107–98 victory over the Knicks in Madison Square Garden, in front of the fans who adored him as much as they did when he put up similar numbers for the home team. The Bernard King of 1991 wasn't as explosive as the Bernard King of 1984—and he still wasn't a great passer, didn't dribble much, and didn't grab a lot of rebounds.

But he showed just how great one player with one jump shot could be in the NBA.

No one identifies Dominique Wilkins with the jump shot. Instead he's known for his dunks. The windmill. The double-clutching, two-handed jam. The offensive rebound dunk with one hand. But during many of his 40- or 50-point games, Wilkins only dunked once or twice in the whole game. By the time he battled Bird in that Game 7 showdown in Boston in the 1988 playoffs, his all-around skills made him one of the game's best. Wilkins used the summer to steal from great players. He took Bob Love's jump shot, Earl Monroe's spin, watching tapes provided by the NBA. "Guys were able to do multiple things offensively," he tells me of his era. "We could post up. We could shoot the three. We could go off the dribble. We could shoot the midrange. I loved coming off screens at the elbow and getting shots." He learned to control his physical skills, which occasionally threatened to overwhelm his game. "Sometimes I jumped too high and shot the ball too long," he says.

Wilkins took after King in not having to see the rim. One writer called Wilkins perhaps the greatest bank shooter of his generation. "I got a spot on the glass. If I get the right arc on the shot, it's going in." His athletic ability allowed him to make the type of jump shots others found impossible. On fast breaks, everyone remembers Wilkins finishing time and again with a powerful dunk, but no one was better at stopping on a moment's notice after catching a pass and instantly rising from 12 to 15 feet for a pull-up jumper. After suffering a ruptured Achilles in 1992 at the age of thirty-two, Wilkins evolved. In 1993, he made 120 three-pointers— on a solid 38 percent—after previously having a career high of 85 threes in a single season. On dunks, no one attacked rims like an in-his-prime Wilkins—he seemed to hold a grudge against them, as if they'd somehow wronged his family years earlier and he'd returned to make them pay. But as he said, the only reason he scored 26,000 points in his career is because he became adept at hitting nothing but net with his jumper. Wilkins played with an obvious passion, similar to King's, but with less anger and more joy. Atlanta sportswriter Mark Bradley wrote, "You loved him not because of the whirls he authored and the dunks he delivered and the points he scored, though all those things were part of the charm. But you loved him most of all because he played as if every minute of every game was his last."

That's just what he did against Bird in their showdown—only, as always seemed to happen, Bird left as the victor. Atlanta took a 3–2 series lead against the Celtics in their 1988 series, but squandered a chance to advance with a one-point loss in Game 6. Bird struggled early in Game 7—he only scored 14 points in the first three quarters. Wilkins came out firing, hitting on his trademark dunks while displaying great range, creativity, and imagination. He knocked in three-pointers, and hit off the glass from 15 feet, all while being defended by Kevin McHale, one of the great defensive players. Dominique did everything in his power to pull a young Hawks team past an old Celtics team.

Entering the fourth quarter Boston held an 84–82 lead, before both teams got out of the way, and the final 12 minutes became a one-on-one challenge. Years later, in an oral history on the NBA Web site, Wilkins recalled teammate Kevin Willis telling him to not let Bird score anymore. "Bird's eyes got like *this big*. I knew it was going to be on then. It just woke him up." Bird, in perhaps his greatest performance, hit nine of 10 in the fourth quarter, throwing in three-pointers and left-handed flings that went in without a glance at the basket. After Boston took a 99–97 lead with 6:43 left in the fourth, Bird scored 11 of the next 15 for the Celtics, Wilkins 12 of the next 14 for Atlanta. Bird had the advantage of not having to guard Wilkins. McHale did his best against Wilkins, but because Dominique was at his best, McHale's efforts were mostly futile.

Yet it came down to Wilkins needing to miss that free throw with the score 118–116. It came down to Boston getting one more rebound, and the Celtics advancing one more time. In the oral history with NBA.com, Bird said, "I played in a lot of great games, and it's hard to rank them. They're all different, you know. I know I felt one thing after that game: It was the best one I ever played. I said, whoa, I can play."

And he could shoot.

CHAPTER

FOURTEEN

BIRD

For several days in the summer of 2014 I debated a question whose answer seems obvious. Was Larry Bird a pure shooter? I kept this debate internal—I drafted e-mails for friends and basketball writers asking for their opinions, but never sent them, for fear of their reaction and eventual abandonment. Instead I went back and forth with the question. Calling someone a pure shooter can be used as an insult, if "pure" becomes synonymous with "only" or is the first half of a compound sentence that begins "He's a pure shooter," and ends "but he can't play any defense or put the ball on the floor."

Bird belongs in the discussion on the greatest shooter of all time, but simply calling him a pure shooter might erase the way he controlled the game with his passing, rebounding, tenacity, team defense, and floor game. Is calling Larry Bird a pure shooter the ultimate compliment or an underestimation? Praise or pejorative? But then if Bird isn't a pure shooter, who the hell is?

Regardless of definitions and labels, Bird's greatness as a shooter can get lost when discussing his career. His all-around brilliance separated him from everyone else, from those other great forwards like Bernard King, Alex English, and Dominique Wilkins. He could dominate without taking a shot, but it was still that shot that made everything else possible.

At the height of his powers in 1986—when he dreamily talked with reporters about treating basketball like gymnastics, because he now thought in terms of degree of difficulty—Bird bragged, "It's pretty hard to guard somebody like me, especially if your range is unlimited." Bird could always just step farther and farther away from the basket to shoot his jumper, as if competing against his own boredom instead of the opposition. And with defenders venturing out to honor his deadly stroke, it opened up the rest of the floor, allowing him to drive despite facing opponents who almost always owned a quickness advantage. Teammate Robert Parish said Bird's "greatest asset is his very poison jumper," a grammatically odd phrase that perfectly described Larry Legend's shot. Very poison. Very good.

And it was a jumper, even if his feet barely left the court. On his release, he brought the ball behind his head, making him another of the small forwards from the decade who excelled despite not owning picture-perfect form.

Jack McCallum profiled Bird for *Sports Illustrated* in 1986. The piece argued Bird's place in history, and suggested he belonged at the top. The story carried the subhead, "In a glorious seventh season, Larry Bird of the Boston Celtics is demonstrating that he may be the NBA's best player of all time." McCallum wrote, "Owing to the extraordinary importance of the giant pivotman in the game, it is probably impossible to declare that, in his seventh season, the 6'9", 220-pound Bird, a forward, is greater than Bill Russell, Wilt Chamberlain or Kareem Abdul-Jabbar—that is, the greatest player of all time. Or maybe it isn't." At that point in the game's history, it still seemed impossible that any player other than one of the game's great big men could be considered the best ever. Russell, Chamberlain, and Abdul-Jabbar were so dominant close to the basket, on offense and defense, people doubted a perimeter player—someone who primarily relied on an outside jump shot—had any claim to the throne. But then along came Bird, combining passing and rebounding with his unmatched shooting skills. McCallum wrote about Bird's all-around game, but noted, "Above all, it is Bird's ability to hit a shot under pressure that makes him great. Scott Wedman may beat him in H-O-R-S-E now and then, and Ainge took him for $35 in a game two weeks ago in Seattle, but turn on the TV lights and put 15,000 hostile fans in the seats and Bird has no peer."

Boston sportswriter Leigh Montville believed "the Larry Bird jump shot, free and perfect, is the point where the entire Celtics' offense begins. That one shot is the hum in the background that other teams have to stop first, a night light that the Celtics always can use to ward off the dark, a reason for all the Celtics' success."

Go back for a moment to that battle against Dominique Wilkins in Game 7 of the Eastern Conference Semifinals. Following the shoot-out and his 20-point fourth quarter, Bird explained, "That's why I do all that shooting, in order to be able to have games like this. You want to feel in control. There is no better feeling than to be in control of a basketball game and know your shot's going to open up every other aspect of your game, as well as help other players."

Bird always improved his game, adding tricks and shots every year, yet in the big picture, little changed from his high school days to his professional ones. Growing up in French Lick and attending Springs Valley High School, Bird developed into the prototypical small-town Indiana legend. His high school coach Gary Holland called him "a perfect ballplayer. He shoots well, plays defense and is very unselfish, always looking for the other guy. He can also play anywhere on the floor and does whatever I ask. He's not very emotional; he just does his job." His college coach later said those exact same words—in a different order—and each of his pro coaches echoed them. The type of player Bird was at eighteen was the same type of player he was at twenty-eight. His size helped, putting the skills he developed as a small boy into the frame of a big man. He went from a scrawny six-one, 135-pound sophomore into a six-foot-seven senior star. By the time he reached the Celtics, he reached six-nine. His passing always stood out, along with his work under the boards—he averaged 30 points and 20 rebounds as a high school senior. But that jumper set up everything else in French Lick, just like it later did in Boston. In one memorable weekend as a high school senior, Bird exploded for games of 42 and 55 points.

Bird experienced some low moments in high school as well. In a showdown against Loogootee, which Springs Valley lost 66–63, Bird scored in the wrong basket, putting the ball in the opponent's side after a jump ball. Fortunately, the ref called traveling and it nullified the embarrassing wrong-way hoop. His high school career ended when Springs Valley lost to Bedford, a team that went 9–11 in the regular season. Bird only scored 15 points in his last game. He had a long memory for that disappointment, writing in his autobiography about a teammate's missed free throws late in the loss.

The young Bird failed to get attention in the southern part of Indiana, although one columnist championed him. Jasper sportswriter Jerry Birge produced numerous stories about Bird, imploring readers and writers to give him the respect he deserved. At the end of the year, Birge wrote, "We read with disbelief today when the Associated Press announced its All-State team, six players on the first team and nine on the second team, and it didn't include Valley's Bird! . . . I'd like to see all of the 15 players named ahead of Bird. They must be super players for some reason or another since none of them came close to the accomplishments of the blonde bomber from Valley." People think Bird received more accolades than he actually did back in high school. When I spoke with longtime Indiana high school coach Norm Held, Bird's name came up—how could it not when talking about great shooters in Indiana?—and Held mentioned Bird won co–Mr. Basketball in 1974. But he didn't. Roy Taylor and Steve Collier were named co-winners. Forty years after Bird's senior season, it did seem improbable anyone else would have won it.

The details of his college career became legendary after he became a legend himself, although they could have served as a cautionary tale for French Lick youth if he'd never succeeded. *"Don't drop out of college or you'll end up working sanitation like that Bird kid."* After attending Indiana, Bird only lasted a few weeks before he hitchhiked home. He eventually landed at Indiana State, a school with no basketball tradition that he transformed into an unlikely national power. Bird's jumper carried Indiana State—but he also displayed a well-known temper, a trait that helped him on the court, but sometimes got him in trouble away from it. Before the Final Four in 1979 a writer noted, "Bird, reports say, has been known to k.o. persons who anger him." After a regional final victory over Arkansas, Bird slugged a fan who grabbed his bad thumb and twisted it. "I dropped him to his knees with a punch to the mouth," Bird explained.

Years later he got into a bar brawl in Boston that may or may not have injured a shooting finger. Bird's magical college career ended when Magic Johnson and Michigan State handed Indiana State its only loss of the year in the 1979 championship showdown, in a game that served as the opening act for a rivalry that defined the next decade in the pros. For once, Bird's shot was off—he made seven of 21 in the defeat.

At the start of his NBA career, some people carried doubts about how good Bird could ever be—people expressed similar thoughts in high school and at Indiana State. Everywhere he went, it was the first question people asked about Larry Bird: Is he as good as the stats say? He wasn't—he was even better.

The remarkable thing about Bird is he never shot in the pros at his physical peak. He broke the index finger on his right hand during a softball game in May of 1979. It remained deformed, as if he injured it in an industrial accident. Later he played with excruciating back pain and injured his Achilles. The injuries altered his shooting technique and form, but they did little to mess with the final result. Bird himself once said, "I'm not a great shooter, I need to shoot and shoot and shoot to get it right. Some guys can stay off all summer, come back to a gym and get 50 points. I shoot so many wild shots, stuff like fadeaways and off-balance ones, that I need to play a lot to get a feel for the ball." (Bird, I think, meant he wasn't a great natural shooter, so he always worked at it. Perhaps it's an argument that he wasn't a pure shooter. But again, the phrase "pure shooter" seemingly becomes worthless if Bird doesn't qualify.)

Throughout his career, Bird cultivated a reputation as a supreme trash talker. His jump shot gave him the confidence to tell opponents what was coming or to ridicule them after another soft jumper fell through the net. Seattle forward Xavier McDaniel became a supporting actor in a devious Bird mind game. In a game at Seattle, Bird told McDaniel where he would take the game-winning shot in the final seconds. After a timeout, Bird walked out and hit his right-wing jump shot, just like he prophesied. Bird's confidence in the shot allowed him to challenge entire fan bases. Against Cleveland in the 1985 playoffs, Bird missed one game with an injury. When Cavaliers fans expressed their desire to see Bird in the next game, he snarled, "They don't want me. They don't want no part of me. It shows they don't know much about basketball if they're calling for me." He scored 34 in his return as Boston ushered the Cavs out of the playoffs.

Perhaps the most famous example of Bird's arrogance around his jump shot came during the 1986 three-point contest, the first year the NBA held the event. After asking the other contestants who was going to finish second, Bird went out and hit 11 straight threes in the final round to win. A year later, he expressed mock sympathy for runner-up Detlef Schrempf. "Can you imagine having $12,000 riding on one shot and missing it? I feel really bad about this." And in 1988 he won with his final shot, the red, white, and blue money ball worth two points. With the ball headed to the basket, Bird, in his green Celtics warm-up jacket, standing in the left corner at Chicago Stadium, put up his right, mangled index finger to indicate he already knew the shot's outcome. After the victory, he said, "It's been a little easier to win it each year. After winning the first two years the other guys know who the favorite is. I don't have to talk as much."

Before that 1988 three-point contest, Bird revealed some shooting secrets to Chicago writer Lacy Banks. "When I try to shoot, I let the feel of the flow of the ball out of my hands determine how much my fingers and palms are on the ball. It must be such that I get a good, smooth rotation on the ball, letting it flow out of my hands. That comes from years of practice and a certain style that you feel comfortable with."

While the 20-point fourth quarter against the Hawks in 1988 was probably his greatest moment—"I think he would hang his hat on that fourth quarter," Bob Ryan says—his most absurd effort came three years earlier, also against Atlanta. Bird set a Celtics scoring record with 60 points, hitting shots late in the game that had some Atlanta players falling off their chairs in disbelief and respect.

That 60-point game occurred in an easy Celtics win. But the Bird jump shot was at its most dangerous in tight games. He told Houston's John McClain, "Making a shot when it means something is the most fun in basketball. When you're down by one point in the closing seconds, you can count on one hand the guys in the building who would take that shot. That's a shot I like to take." In the final minutes of Game 7 of the 1981 Eastern Conference Finals—in a series Boston once trailed 3–1—Bird came down on the left side at the Garden and knocked in a 12-footer off the glass against the Sixers, giving the Celtics the lead. Boston won the game, the series, and eventually Bird's first NBA championship. "I hate to bank shots," he wrote in *Drive*. "Why I decided to bank that one I'll never know. I just don't like to bank and I certainly didn't want to bank from that far out. Who can explain why you do what you do at moments like that?" Bird often defied explanation.

During his 1985 MVP campaign, Bird's jumper ruined a long vacation for his coach, K. C. Jones. Against Portland in late January, Bird caught an inbounds pass, took one dribble, and drilled an impossible shot from the deep left corner at the buzzer in a 128–127 victory. He stood there accepting congratulations, but didn't show much excitement. This was practically routine, like hitting a first-quarter free throw. The shot gave him 48 points and gave Boston the best record in the conference at the time, meaning Jones had to coach the East squad in the All-Star Game. "I could have used the three days off," Jones joked, "but Larry messed it up by hitting that shot."

The Bird jump shot overcame opponents, and the elements. With the 1984 NBA Finals tied at 2–2, the Celtics and Lakers played Game 5 in temperatures around 100 degrees in Boston Garden. L.A.'s players struggled for air. Bird seemed oblivious to the torturous heat and humidity, hitting 15 of 20 from the floor, many of them midrange jumpers or three-pointers. To him it was like working out under the Indiana sun when he returned home each summer. On that night Bird again proved the Garden belonged to him; he owned the place, or at least took over the lease from Bill Russell.

At the end of Bird's career, which officially came in 1992, he played many games when it looked like he could barely run. Yet even in those final painful years, the jump shot created new memories for Celtics fans, and reminded them of so many old times. Facing the Pacers in a 1991 playoff elimination game, Bird slammed his head on the floor at Boston Garden and left the floor, only to make a dramatic return and lead the Celtics to victory in the climactic Game 5. Perhaps the most compelling image from that game—other than the disturbing shot of the right side of his head hitting the court—came when Bird collected the ball near the free throw line, faked a pass, pivoted, and drained a jumper for two of his 32 points, followed by a fist pump with his magical right hand.

Montville wrote a story for *The Boston Globe* in 1988 about a TV station taping a piece on Bird's pregame shooting, detailing how Bird worked out early with assistant equipment manager Joe "Meat" Qatato. Meat threw the ball, Bird shot it. A TV interviewer asked Qatato how many shots he'd seen Bird make in a row during those sessions.

"I never count," Qatato said. "I think it must have been about 30."

Bird also said he never counted, but believed, "I must have hit 50 or 60."

The interviewer told Qatato that Bird thought he hit 50 or 60 shots in a row.

"Fifty or 60?" Qatato said. "Never. Sorry, Larry, never."

So there you have it, straight from Meat: Larry Bird didn't make 60 shots in a row in warm-ups. And he missed half the shots he took in games, despite countless performances when it seemed like he made everything. But even with his all-around brilliance, the jump shot separated him from all of his peers, from all of his rivals—the jump shot he learned in Indiana and perfected in Boston. That jump shot wasn't the only thing that made him great. But the jumper, pure or otherwise, transformed him from Larry Bird into Larry Legend.

FIFTEEN

INSTRUCTORS: THE SHOOTER, THE LAB, AND THE REBEL

I'm sitting in the living room of a radical. We're talking in his remote headquarters in rural Ohio, in the middle of a forest, on a road it took me twenty minutes to discover despite written directions. The revolutionary lives in a modest home—and with a wolf that emerges from the woods with animal bones of unknown origins. I'm on the couch while the rebel leader rests on his recliner.

Paul Hoover is a basketball agitator, and all he's trying to do is change the way people teach and shoot the jumper. He's not bringing down the basketball world—he's trying to make it, in his eyes, better. But to hear him talk—and to hear others talk about him—you get the idea he's fixing to take down the government. One person called him a snake charmer, and people ridicule his methods and ideas. Online someone claimed his ideas are dangerous, another said they were garbage. "I'm the most hated man on the face of the earth," he tells me. "Are you kidding? You either love my stuff or you hate my stuff. There are no fence-sitters on this one."

I should note he laughed when talking about being the most hated person on the planet, but while Hoover occasionally jokes about his place in the basketball community, he's serious about the jump shot. Understanding how it works has become his obsession. "I guess I'm married to the jump shot," says the single Hoover. "You're not going to meet many fanatical people like me."

Hoover makes his living as a shooting instructor. He created the Pro Shot Shooting System, which, in its founder's words, is dedicated to "exposing basketball's lies and myths." Those lies and myths relate to how people teach the jumper. Hoover believes too many coaches use methods that have been around for five or six decades, but are useless in modern basketball. The game has changed dramatically, thanks to the jump shot, but the jump shot itself hasn't changed enough, according to Hoover.

I spent the Fourth of July with Hoover, talking about the jump shot and how he spreads his gospel. Shooting instructors are a fairly recent basketball phenomenon. In the early days of the jumper, coaches obviously taught the jump shot—as they still do—but few specialized in it. Today development coaches help players with dribbling, speed, strength, rebounding, and passing. Shooting often gets rolled up into all of that. In Hoover's mind, a shooting coach should focus on one thing in the job title: shooting.

People debate whether shooting coaches help. Former Golden State coach Mark Jackson once said, "I'm not really a guy that believes in 'em. I never had to work with one. To me it's repetition, putting the time in." For those who *do* teach the jump shot, Jackson's mind-set infuriates. What good is repetition if you're repeating a bad action or form? Basketball's different from other sports. Football teams hire coaches for every position, from the quarterbacks to the wide receivers to the kickers. Baseball teams use pitching coaches and batting coaches. But few basketball teams employ shooting instructors. Maybe it's because more mysticism surrounds the jump shot. Many basketball players and coaches believe you're either a shooter or you're not, and you're either one by the age of eighteen or you're not.

All shooting coaches believe there's value in their work. But the similarities end there. Shooting coaches teach different methods. They come from different backgrounds. They belong to different tax brackets. But they all love the jumper and can teach some secrets. We'll return to the radical Hoover in a bit. First, let's drop in on an early morning workout with one of the most famous shooting coaches, who might also be the greatest shooter in the country.

THE PURE SHOOTING SHOOTING INSTRUCTOR

It's the most basic question about shooting coaches: Do great shooting coaches have to be great shooters? Can you live by "Do as I say, not as I brick"? Hoover claims a coach's shot is irrelevant. He admits he's not a marksman, never was one. He walks around with a paunch. And he doesn't believe any of that affects teaching the shot. "I'm not worried about my shot. I'm worried about your shot. I don't care about mine. How's your shot?"

Dave Hopla's shot is usually perfect. For those who believe a great shooting coach requires a perfect shooting stroke, Hopla is their hero. Hopla is fifty-seven, although with his spiky hair and nonstop energy he seems a decade younger. He's worked as an NBA instructor for years, as a consultant and full-timer with the Toronto Raptors, as a coach with the Washington Wizards, and as an occasional instructor with longtime NBA coach George Karl, with stops in Seattle and Milwaukee. Most recently, he worked for two years as the shooting instructor for the New York Knicks. Those are his professional credentials. But for thirty-plus years, he's built his reputation as a coach on his abilities as a shooter. One year, as he traveled around giving speeches and demonstrations, Hopla drained 11,093 out of 11,183 shots, a percentage of 99.2. And these aren't righty or lefty layups. He takes jump shots, from 15 feet and beyond. At UCLA he once went 272 for 272, including 20 for 20 from the three-point line.

In his second season as a shooting coach with the Knicks, before a game against Miami, he bumped into Ray Allen, the man who's made more three-pointers than anyone else in NBA history. Hopla told him, "Ray, how does it feel to be the second-best shooter in the gym?" Prior to a Knicks game in Utah, Hopla left the ball boys sputtering by draining 75 consecutive three-pointers from the right corner. And Cal Ramsey, who had a brief pro career as a player and later served as a television analyst for the Knicks, told Hopla he was "the greatest shooter who ever stepped into the Garden" after watching him make 42 straight long-range shots. "I said, 'If you would have been here a few minutes earlier, straight on I just made 58 in a row.'"

I visited Hopla at a difficult time in his professional life. We met in May

2014, two weeks after Phil Jackson fired the Knicks coaching staff, including Hopla. One day I took the train from northern Manhattan to White Plains, where Hopla spent his mornings working on his jump shot. Instead of shooting at the Knicks training facility, Hopla took his jumper to the New York Sports Club, to shoot around with the common folk. I arrived at the gym at 8:35 in the morning and found Hopla deep into his workout. Another man shot at the same basket as Hopla, ignoring etiquette and the open hoops located on the other end of the gym, cramping the master's style. I imagined how much that annoyed Hopla, a creature of habit and routine, a shooting machine now dealing with an inconsiderate slacker messing up the assembly line. He confirmed as much when we talked. Not wanting my name thrown into the same category as the shooting intruder—whose ball bumped into Hopla's after another one of Hopla's jump shots ripped the nets—I said a quick hello, took a seat, and let him go about his work.

After the other guy exited, Hopla—who wore black shoes, black socks, a black T-shirt, and striped shorts—then put on a show. I watched him make 20 in a row from the top of the key, a high school three-pointer. A few minutes later he moved back to the NBA three-pointer, although no line in this gym marked the actual distance of 23 feet, 9 inches. From my angle, it looked like Hopla actually stood well behind where the NBA line would be located—call it more like 25 feet. Hopla made three of four from that distance, straight on. He then made 24 shots in a row from the same spot, although I was the only person in the gym impressed and incredulous. To Hopla this is routine, as easy as me taking 24 dribbles in a row without losing the ball. Two types of makes exist for Hopla: swishes and ones that go through the back of the rim. That's it. No lucky bounces or shots that slide in from the side. It looked like a scene in a caper movie when the robbers fool everyone by setting up security cameras that play on a loop, showing the same scene over and over. If you've seen one Dave Hopla jump shot, you've seen the next 30.

Hopla charts every shot. He learned the value of shot tracking when he was sixteen. A coach at a camp he attended told him to chart every attempt. "From that time I wrote everything. I didn't realize nobody else in the world did it." Notebooks fill Hopla's house, the written figures documenting the tens of thousands of shots he's taken in the decades since he received that advice. He marks the makes and misses from every session and every spot on the floor. If he wanted to know his percentage during a shooting workout from a specific day in January 2008, he could hunt down the appropriate notebook and see the results from the corners, wings, and three-point line. On each page he writes the date, and draws a small semicircle for the three-point line, along with his results outside that stripe and inside. Hopla doesn't understand how anyone shoots without a notebook—how would you ever know if you're getting better if you don't have tangible written evidence from every session? To help the new generation of players, who might not appreciate the power of a pen and paper, Hopla developed an app to track shots, the iHopla.

When Hopla ended his shooting in front of me and wrote in his notebook, he lamented not making 25 in a row from the NBA (and longer) mark. Twenty-four in a row felt like a failure. We spoke a bit about his workouts—some days he works off the dribble, other days on form shooting. No matter the format, the result is the same. "I never get bored because I try to always beat what my all-time highs are," he says.

Numbers drive Hopla. He gives a talk to corporations called "Numbers Are Everything and Numbers Are Everywhere."

"What's the first thing you did this morning when you woke up?" he asks me.

"Ate breakfast."

"You didn't look to see what time it was?"

"Yeah, I did."

"And then you had to check the time to see what time your train was, right? Everything you do. And then the gravestone—what's on there? Numbers, that's what motivates you. When you're born, ten fingers, ten toes, two eyes—they check it."

Numbers provide certainty, a foundation. His firing by the Knicks did the opposite, although it wasn't unexpected. Assistant coaches are nomads, wandering from job to job, state to state, hoping to stay on with an old head coach they've been with for a decade, hustling to land gigs with new ones. Hopla himself didn't get hired on a full-time basis by a team until he was forty-eight. But he always made his living with the jump shot, at camps, clinics, and corporate gigs.

Hopla doesn't dwell on the negative. In camps, speaking engagements, and everyday conversation he rattles off motivational phrases. He's Dale Carnegie with a, presumably, better 20-foot jumper, Tony Robbins with a sweeter bank shot. In his ever-present notebooks, an X means Hopla missed. He refuses to say "miss." His personal dictionary censors negative thoughts or words. "I never say that I'm doing good. I'm always doing great, fantabulous, fantastic." He gives a talk entitled, "Good Is Good, but It's Not Great." At camps he talks to kids about the importance of "a free shot. I don't call it a free throw or a foul shot because 'foul' is a negative. You go to McDonald's and you get foul French fries, are you going to eat them? No, they're negative, that's a negative word." During his clinics, Hopla recruits helpers who pass the ball, but don't dare say they rebound for him, because rebounders grab missed shots and even thinking about misses and rebounds brings a bad energy to a session.

After moving from New Jersey, Hopla went to high school in Baltimore. He played junior college ball and then NAIA at Chadron State in Nebraska. I asked Hopla if he could pinpoint a time when he became the shooting creature I watched. No. It just happened, if anything that takes tens of thousands of repetitions can "just happen." Hopla continued his career overseas, including in Northern Ireland. When he returned he ran a paint business for a time, but always improved his jump shot and made money with it. Eventually he made his living trying to teach others to shoot like him, as impossible as that seems. When he shoots in front of kids, the eager-to-please participants pretend they own the same dedication. One time Hopla asked if anyone shot every day. Hands went up.

"You shoot every day? Every single day?" Hopla asked one kid.

"Yeah."

"Did you shoot on my birthday?"

"When's your birthday?"

"If you shot every day you wouldn't have to ask. You'd have just said yes."

There are days Hopla himself doesn't make it to a basket. When Hopla and his wife scouted wedding locations in Maine, he liked the idea of a 3:00 P.M. ceremony, because "I have a friend of mine in Portland, Maine, who'd been dying for me to do a clinic. I said I could do a three-hour, nine-to-twelve clinic: an hour shooting, two-hour demo with drill work. It's like an hour drive." The idea didn't advance past the planning stage, so hoops did not interrupt the ceremony.

In his coaching Hopla keeps things simple and believes in repetition. He preaches pre-shot preparation. Put the palm up toward the passer, the elbow cocked in the letter L. The elbow, in his view, is the most important part of shooting. Keep that elbow in, under the ball, above the shooting foot, with the ball on the fingertips, never on the palm. If an elbow is set right, a player should only miss long or short. One other note: Please don't call the off-hand an off-hand. That's too negative. And calling it the guide hand makes it sound like a shooter's guiding the ball in, and that's not right, either. He calls it the balance hand.

As one of the most famous shooters and instructors in the country, Hopla constantly gets pitched devices. He maintains skepticism. "I had people ask me, 'How many times should the ball rotate?' I don't know." Gadgets and gizmos flow in, all of them from people hoping they'll have a product blessed by the jump shot master. "I've got a big ball. I've got a ball with hands painted on it. I've got a ball that sings like a bird so that you have good rotation on it." One contraption, a strap, reminded him of something that would aid in sexual performance but had little effect on anyone's jumper.

Following his workout in the White Plains gym, we spoke about Hopla's time with the Knicks, and the shooting drills he uses with players like Carmelo Anthony. He offered to put me through one. I'd packed for the occasion, with shorts under my jeans and my basketball shoes in my backpack. I didn't even get a practice shot so I wasn't prepared for an NBA-level workout, but I wanted to interact with Hopla the coach after watching Hopla the shooter in disbelief.

For the first drill, Hopla ordered me to stand just inside the three-point line while he manned the lane. I shuffled to my left and right, exchanging chest passes. Finally he barked out a spot I should run to, and I sprinted to the location—in this case, the right corner. He delivered a pass and I took a shot, my legs already heavy. My early shots carried a flat arc, but my jumper has always been flatter than many. Hopla thought the arc kept me from hitting the shots—I countered that it was due to my legs feeling like they weighed 100 pounds each—but on one of my jumpers he sprinted toward me with a hand in my face. That forced me to get a bit more air under my shot . . . and it went in. On later shots he widened my base, told me to spread my feet, and, again, the swishes followed. The teacher was correct; the student learned a lesson—and searched for oxygen.

Next, Hopla set up cones at midcourt and on the wings. I sprinted in from midcourt, took a pass, and shot a free throw line jumper. Returned to midcourt and then ran to the wing for another jumper. Then we repeated it on the other side. Finished it by running in from midcourt for a layup, although Hopla said I was welcome to end with a dunk.

Later he talked about the time he put a young, pre-NBA Kobe Bryant through the same drill—another player with a flat jumper, I told Hopla; he didn't see the similarities. They scheduled the session for 5:30 in the morning. Kobe arrived at 4:45. "He pulls up, shoots the jump shot, gets his ball, comes around the left. Boom. Comes around the right and makes three shots in a row. Dribbles out to midcourt, comes dribbling in, takes off from the free throw line. Ball hits the back of the rim on a dunk. The ball goes all the way down to the other end. Most guys would be like, 'I can't.' They would stop. He sprints down there. He grabs it, dribbles down, throws it down, and says, 'What's my time? I want to do the drill again, and I'm not missing the dunk.'"

When it comes to pure shooting, not even the greats like Kobe can match Hopla in absurd displays. I asked him if Ray Allen could beat Hopla in H-O-R-S-E. "Certain days he'd beat me with the threes," he says.

Before we left to grab pizza for lunch, I asked him for a game of P-I-G or H-O-R-S-E. "Hey, pick your poison," he says. We went with the five-letter game. In the first contest I hung with Hopla for a few minutes, although this wasn't exactly Rayl against Mount in an Indiana driveway. At one stage I fought off a letter by draining five straight shots after his inevitable makes, including one from deep in the corner, slightly behind the backboard—that shot Jerry West is still so good at. But I never got a letter on him; I suggested we consider his shots misses if he didn't finish with swishes. In his book *Basketball Shooting*, Hopla wrote about visualizing swish shots. "It requires more focus and concentration, and you'll eventually discover that when shots rattle in, you won't feel satisfied." While he accepted rattled-in shots as real makes—and got real letters against me—I could sense his disappointment with any shot that hit the rim. The second game was even less competitive. His steady barrage of 22-footers proved impossible to keep up with. When my last shot rimmed out I shook his hand and meekly walked off the court. I can imagine Hopla getting bored with writers or campers or fans wanting to face him in shooting contests—he expressed enthusiasm but inside probably felt like an old, tired gunfighter putting his drink down at the bar to walk out of the saloon to face another challenger on the dusty streets in the Old West.

When we said our good-byes, Hopla walked off with his professional future as a shooting coach clouded by uncertainty. He savors the opportunity that comes with working with the best in the world, players with unmatched skill, shooters who are so good they might even be able to one day match Dave Hopla in a shooting contest. No matter where he lands as a coach, his reputation as a shooter will stay intact.

Earlier during our lunch, Hopla talked about how mad he got when he'd walk into the gym, put on a display, and "a guy would say, 'You're a pretty good shooter.' Pretty good? Pretty good? I'll show you pretty good. Good is forgotten."

And as anyone who's watched him shoot knows, a Dave Hopla exhibition is unforgettable.

SHOOTER'S LAB

One month after I watched Hopla make jump shooting look as easy as breathing, I witnessed something equally improbable: Mark Price losing a free throw competition.

The fifty-year-old Price looks pretty much the same as he did as a freshman at Georgia Tech and during his days with Cleveland. He maintains the same features and perfectly coiffed hair that looks like it was gene-tically engineered as the ideal object for an elderly aunt to tousle at Thanks-giving. Surely his wife and four kids spot signs of aging—a new line or a bit of weight on his face, or a brown hair that isn't as dark—but other-wise he looks like the guy who jetted through defenses, a six-foot shoot-ing and playmaking sensation.

When Price retired in 1998, he owned the highest career free throw percentage in NBA history, making 90.4 percent of his attempts. (Today he sits in second place, behind Steve Nash.) Yet on a June day in a facility located about thirty minutes outside Atlanta, I stood in the doorway of a gym and saw Price miss two straight free throws in a battle against a kid who was about twelve. The showdown took place at Price's camp at the Suwanee Sports Academy. I was visiting the Mark Price Shooting Lab, a 3,000-square-foot gym nestled in the 100,000-square-foot complex.

But I also took in the free throw exhibition that concluded the camp. The scene looked like something out of a Duke home game when Price attended Georgia Tech and battled the Blue Devils in front of the Cam-eron Crazies, except these kids kept their shirts on, and the blood-alcohol levels remained at zero. Dozens of campers sat around the court scream-ing, encouraged by the instructors and Price. The kid at the line taking on Price might be the greatest free throw shooter his school has ever seen. Maybe he's beaten every kid in a hundred-mile radius. The weekly news-paper brags about him. It doesn't matter. There's no way he'd beat Price in a free throw competition, I thought. But . . . damn, the kid was good. He calmly knocked down his free throws. Price did the same—until one of his free throws bounced off the back of the rim. The campers pounded on the floor. Price's blond-haired foe knocked in another shot. And Price missed again. One of the greatest shooters in basketball history choked two straight free throws. It was all very suspicious.

Price smiled when I expressed shock at the misses. He mentioned "keeping the customers happy" and laughed and said he seems to lose more often than he wins at his camps. There's no definitive proof Price purposely botched the challenge, other than his entire basketball history. Maybe it was his unlucky day.

But it is difficult to comprehend him missing shots because if anyone deserves a shooting lab named after him, it's Price. His shooting stroke took him from obscurity in Enid, Oklahoma, to stardom at Georgia Tech, and to NBA All-Star status in Cleveland. Price's dad, Denny, taught him how to shoot. Denny lit up high school scoreboards himself in Norman, Oklahoma, and later played at the University of Oklahoma before starting a long career as a coach. In 1955, Denny set the state tournament record with 42 points as he led Norman to the title. Twenty-seven years later Mark tied his dad's record in a state semifinal victory, although on that night, too, he missed a free throw that could have potentially let him pass Denny. From Enid to Cleveland, Denny Price was always the only one who corrected his son's shot. One day in May 1993—during a season when Price made the first-team All-NBA squad, next to Hall of Famers Michael Jordan, Charles Barkley, Karl Malone, and Hakeem Olajuwon—Denny hopped in a van with three friends from Enid and traveled to Chicago to help with Mark's shooting stroke during a series against the Bulls. "Don't make it look like I have all the answers," he told Cleveland writer Bud Shaw. "But I can usually tell when something's wrong with Mark's shot." Denny explained how he'd studied Mark's shot from the time he was five and shooting underhanded. "I suppose it's like guys on the pro golf tour. No matter how successful, they all have instructors who study their swing and offer advice. When Mark is having trouble, he'll ask me what's wrong."

More than twenty years later, Price tells me, "I was always kind of my dad's guinea pig as a kid. He would come home and say, 'Let's try this,' so I was always messing around with my shot. It ended up working out okay."

Price left Oklahoma for Georgia Tech, a desperate program led by a young coach named Bobby Cremins. The year before Cremins took the job, Tech went 4–23. The previous coach fled basketball and became a professional golf caddie. Cremins says when he took the Tech job he was "young and stupid. Thank God I wasn't smart because otherwise I probably would have been too nervous to take the job." The turnaround began with the little guard from Oklahoma. Tech landed Price thanks to assistant coach George Felton, who attended seventeen of Price's games during his senior year at Enid. "I didn't know what the hell George was doing at first," Cremins tells me. "I said, 'Where the hell is Enid, Oklahoma?' Then I saw him play, and I couldn't believe it."

Cremins famously sported an entire mop of gray hair by the time he turned thirty, making the hyperactive boy wonder look like a sixty-year-old veteran of the sidelines. But with Price directing his attack, it's doubtful a single new gray strand popped up in four years. Price made life easy.

In 1983, thanks to an experimental and criminally short three-point line—17 feet, 9 inches out—Price became the first freshman to lead the ACC in scoring. He also made Georgia Tech relevant. Price teamed with New York City players John Salley and Bruce Dalrymple and turned Tech from a laughingstock into a power. The Yellow Jackets won the ACC tournament and advanced to the region finals in 1985, a year that ended in agony for Price, as his stroke abandoned him in a 3-for-16 shooting performance against Georgetown. A fun-loving center who never met a reporter's recorder he couldn't hijack, Salley once said of his soft-spoken costar, "He's not the average white point guard. He plays like he's six-five—a Larry Bird type. If coach was to let him go, he'd have 40 a night on anybody."

Price was an actual choirboy off the court—his family, including his two younger basketball-playing brothers, sang at church—and he never drank, smoked, or cursed. At Tech, he once politely asked Cremins to watch his swearing around him. When he played in Cleveland someone made a Mark Price Candy Bar that included chocolate, caramel, and nuts, and came with an inspirational saying embedded in the wrapper: "With discipline and determination, you can overcome any obstacle."

Just as he did at Georgia Tech, Price spearheaded a remarkable turnaround in Cleveland, transforming one of the league's worst franchises into one of its best. With the Cavs, Price developed into an outstanding all-around shooter, not just someone who made shots while spotting up on the corner or wing. He beat players with his dribble, his drives, and his pull-up jumpers. On offense his fellow point guards credit him with basically inventing how players split the defense on a pick-and-roll, and his arsenal included one-footed floaters. But the jump shot drove his game, from midrange or long-distance—he finished his career with a 40.2 percentage from the three-point line.

And he showed his toughness. After tearing his ACL in 1990, Price attacked his rehab and came back strong. Only one challenge proved insurmountable: Price lost five times to the Chicago Bulls in the playoffs. On two occasions, Michael Jordan finished off Cleveland with a jumper. First with The Shot, his hanging, buzzer-beating jumper over Craig Ehlo in Game 5 of the 1989 playoffs, and then with a turnaround in Game 4 of the 1993 playoffs. "You look back and it's like, what else could you possibly do?" Price says of the 1989 heartbreak. "You're up with three seconds to go and a guy hits an incredible shot. I never really had many regrets because I felt in a lot of ways we did all we could do."

Initially Price's retirement from the NBA in 1998 led to his complete departure from the game. He dabbled in business, spent time with his family, played tennis. But he couldn't have expected to give up the game his dad taught him. "Basketball kept drawing me back in." Price worked in player development, and then focused on shooting, consulting, and instructing NBA players. Giving his name to the shooting lab also kept him involved with his best-known skill. Price once told *The New York Times* he thought of the lab as being "the A.A. of shooting. You show them, and they go, 'I've got a problem.'" Price tells me, "I enjoyed teaching it, even though I don't expect guys to be able to shoot like me." Price worked as an assistant with the Charlotte Hornets, after living that nomadic coaching lifestyle with stops in places like Orlando and Golden State. Finally, in March 2015, he earned a top job, taking over as head coach at the University of North Carolina at Charlotte.

Even with his coaching career taking him to North Carolina, he maintains his relationship with his Georgia shooting lab. Price has worked with, he estimates, about twenty players at the facility. In 2007, Suwanee's director of basketball operations, Dan Searl, said Price "gave us all his input on shooting philosophy, what it takes to become a great shooter. We took all of his knowledge and packaged it into a shooting lab and added the technology to it."

Bruce Kreutzer, a sixty-four-year-old basketball lifer, handles much of the behind-the-scenes shooting work at the Price Shooting Lab. Kreutzer won a state title as a coach in North Carolina, travels to Europe in the summer to work with players, and served as the shooting consultant for the NBA Development League. Like Price and Hopla, he looks ten years younger than his age; perhaps the jump shot holds the secrets of youth—pure shooting equals pure skin? I walked into the lab—also known as a gym, albeit one with a low ceiling—to meet with Kreutzer. Red banners hang on the walls with "Price Points," tips on field goal shooting and free throws. "Practice spot shooting, shooting off the pass and shooting off the dribble." "Have feet and hands ready."

Because the lab utilizes technology, Kreutzer, like Hopla and all shooting coaches, receives pitches from folks promoting the gadgets. Kreutzer says, "Basketball's almost gotten to the point where it's about as bad as golf. Some of the devices are okay, but I'm pretty much an old-school guy. We have a minimal amount of things, but there are some devices that help out, and help give a better visual." Two of those technologies became lab mainstays.

The Noah shooting system measures arc and helps with depth, displaying a player's shots in different colors. Kreutzer showed me how it worked with footage from a Price demonstration, when the lab namesake fired 25 shots. With Noah, the player and instructor see the consistency on the arc—some colors show a higher shot, some a lower, some right in the sweet spot. On Price it was almost all green, showing his consistency, while a stray yellow arc popped up on shots that weren't quite perfect. "If you shoot it between 43 degrees and 53 degrees, you're going to get to use all 18 inches of the rim," Kreutzer says, which gives players a better chance at a shooter's roll. Price, ideally, shot between 42, 43, and 44 degrees. Anything below 43, "The cylinder actually starts to shrink." The same holds true if a shot goes too high.

The Dartfish uses cameras to track a player's shot frame by frame. Kreutzer can also now take that on the road, through a program on his phone, meaning he doesn't have to haul two cameras and a tripod.

The lab offers kids, starting at about the age of ten, five one-hour sessions, which cover everything from shooting off the dribble to transition shooting. Even before he got a full-time assistant's job with Charlotte, Price mostly worked with the NBA guys, while Kreutzer handles all levels, from kids to the pros.

Kreutzer doesn't put all his belief in the Noah, but he babies the machine. When he searched for some data on a former player for the University of Georgia women's basketball team, another shooter's information popped up instead. Kreutzer griped about somebody else using his equipment, sounding very much like a dad complaining about one of his kids misplacing a shovel in the garage.

He estimates he's worked with about forty NBA players over his career. "All of them have gotten better. The problem with that is they don't always stay with it. It's usually the guy that's in his last year of his contract looking for another, and all of a sudden he's improved so now you don't see him again." Too often Kreutzer saw a former pupil abandon the lessons they learned at shooting school and revert to old ways, their pride keeping them from returning for more help with their jumper. Every shooting coach I spoke with expressed bewilderment that NBA teams don't invest more in shooting development. Part of the disbelief is surely motivated by very personal reasons—they'd all welcome high-paying job opportunities at the highest level of the sport. But the reluctance of pro—and major college—teams is out of touch with other sports. Going back to baseball, if only five or six teams employed pitching coaches in the Major Leagues, it would seem strange. Kreutzer says, "It amazes me that an NBA team is worth two billion dollars, and they're not going to spend $150,000, $200,000 to have somebody help their players shoot the ball."

In many ways Kreutzer has a lot in common with many of the players he coached. He relates to the guys in the NBA Development League looking for another shot—or just one shot—at the highest level. When he auditioned for the shooting consultant gig with the NBADL, he said, "I'm the poster child for chasing a dream," but now he admits, "I'm getting to that point in my life that I've chased the dream for so long, you wonder what's next." As a coach at all levels, he's felt the frustration of working as an assistant and being passed over when the head spot opens up. "It's a business of insanity," he says.

Kreutzer holds out hope of returning to the NBA, despite the league's seeming reluctance to embrace full-time shooting coaches, and despite his own contemplation about the rigors of the career. Coaching took him away from his wife, son, and daughter for many years. When his son considered coaching, Kreutzer originally told him, "What do you want to do that for? Look at the life. Of course it wasn't that bad. I tell people my life's been a holiday because I'm doing exactly what I love to do."

Just like Mark Price is doing what he was born to do. His dad once said, "The reason Mark is in the NBA is because he practiced. When other kids spent their summer sitting in the sun or chasing girls, Mark was in the gym." Often he battled his father in the gym. Mark and his brothers, Matt and Brent, fought against each other, and their dad. "They were serious battles," Mark says. "And my dad was probably the worst, most physical out of everybody." Denny once told longtime Ohio sportswriter Terry Pluto, "I'd never let them win. Some people told me that I should once in a while, but I told them that the day was coming when the boys would beat me. I think Mark was a sophomore in high school when he beat me. I never played him again after that."

Denny stopped competing against his boys, but he never stopped loving his time on the court with them. On July 7, 2000, with Mark and Brent in Enid, Denny went to the town's YMCA to watch them. Denny, at sixty-two and still owning what he once claimed was the best shot in the family, joined his boys on the court. After a couple of trips up and down, Denny held on to another player. The boys thought he was fouling someone to slow the game, but he suffered a fatal heart attack. At his funeral at Emmanuel Baptist Church, Mark said, "My daddy wasn't perfect, but my dad was the best man I ever knew."

Denny Price didn't get to see Mark follow his path into the NBA and college coaching ranks. But he saw him take his lessons and become one of the best shooters of all time. The Mark Price Shooting Lab exists as a testament to one of the NBA's greats. But it's also a tribute to an old Oklahoma dad.

THE REBEL

When I set up a time to meet with Paul Hoover at his Ohio home, he suggested the Fourth of July.

"You're not doing anything?" I asked.

He laughed. Beer, brats, and fireworks weren't on the menu at the Pro Shot estate. It was all basketball. When I found the location through a series of winding roads outside Athens in southern Ohio, I encountered numerous houseguests and a gym filled with players going through workouts. Hoover rents his house. He moved there because the owner of the land had previously built a gym for his daughter inside a large facility in the backyard. The gym has three baskets. College and NBA banners hang on the walls, which are also adorned with posters of shooters—no dunks. Out in the yard sits Hoover's truck, decorated with an ad for Pro Shot in the back window that reads, "The revolution is here."

Here's Hoover's revolutionary belief about the jump shot: Coaches should teach players to shoot the same way the best players in the world shoot. That's it. Watch the greatest shooters. Show players videos of those shooters. Teach them the same techniques.

It sounds simple. It sounds right. Hoover thinks so. Many others think it's crazy. Those differences in opinion, along with Hoover's skills as a presenter, make him one of the most engaging shooting coaches in the country and one of the most controversial.

I first heard about Hoover and the Pro Shot Shooting System from a former co-worker named Dean Witter who lives near Madison, Wisconsin. Dean coaches youth teams in the area, and Pro Shot put on a clinic for his kids. He became a fan, and he included some links to Hoover's videos. The YouTube videos captured my interest. They're fun and sarcastic, filled with clips from movies and television shows. Classic rock songs provide the sound tracks. Although he hates his own voice, Hoover narrates the videos. Mostly they contain clips of NBA and college players making shots, with Hoover describing the mechanics. "We show the best players in the world," he says. "I don't want to show a twelve-year-old shooting."

One video even references Shirley Jackson's classic short story and stoning horror "The Lottery." Hoover uses it to question why people do things in basketball simply because of tradition. A small village partakes in a tradition for no apparent reason, just like the basketball world does when it comes to shooting.

So what else do these videos show? A few key components of Hoover's system, some of which go against long-held shooting beliefs:

The dip: This happens on a catch. The player doesn't go straight up. Instead he drops the ball a few inches, say, from the waist to the thigh, then rises for the jumper. In video after video, Hoover shows great NBA players doing this on shots they take off of the pass.

The turn: Square your feet! Hoover thinks this is an antiquated lesson from the set shot days, when players really did need ten toes facing the basket when they fired with two hands. In one of his videos about the turn, the video begins with Thunderclap Newman's "Something in the Air," and Hoover's narration: *"In the late 1400s, explorer Christopher Columbus proclaimed to the world that the world was round."* He then interjects a shot of a scene from *Peanuts* with kids laughing. *"And people laughed at him. They argued the world is flat. Columbus was right. The world is round. Five hundred twenty years later, Pro Shot has proclaimed to the basketball world that great shooters turn their feet when they shoot. In other words, great shooters square their shooting shoulder and hip to the basket. And the world laughs."* Hoover then tosses in a clip of laughter from *Goodfellas.* *"But the best players do shoot with their feet turned. And they have been doing so for over fifty years."*

Hoover tells me, "If you ask every high school coach, 'What do you think about Steph Curry's shot?' 'Oh, it's great!' 'Would you like your kids to shoot like Steph Curry?' 'Absolutely!' 'Do you know Steph Curry turns when he shoots?' 'No, he squares!' Nope. We call it cognitive dissonance."

Sweep-and-sway: More so on longer shots, the player's feet come forward and their shoulders go back. This really developed with the advent of the three-pointer. The strange forms of earlier eras worked when the game took place inside 20 feet, and when everyone knocked down 15-footers. Players could go straight up and down and remain effective. They could get by with awkward hitches. With longer shots, that no longer worked for many players. Those small forwards of the 1980s didn't shoot threes for the most part so they could use different strokes. Or take Michael Jordan. "When he came in, he was not a sweep-and-sway. He was a straight up-and-down shooter. Once again, he wasn't raised on the three-point line. Did anybody teach him this? I don't know. Maybe the sweep-and-sway, you can either teach it or it takes you a long time to get it or you naturally will."

Hoover simply wants younger players to take what the pros are doing and use it themselves. It's the way the game has evolved; why wouldn't coaches want their players to evolve like the pros? "They don't shoot straight up and down from long-distance," he says, while acknowledging there are always exceptions to this and all of his beliefs. "They may shoot straight up from 10. They don't need those shoulders." In other words, a flick of the wrist—think of Alex English effortlessly shooting his midrange shot—isn't enough in today's game. From farther out on the court, Hoover says, power comes from the shoulders going back and the feet coming forward.

The eyes: Most coaches believe you should lock your eyes on the rim. Hoover thinks it's fine to follow the flight of the ball. Why? Because his videos show shooters like Steve Kerr, Ray Allen, Steve Nash, and Reggie Miller doing just that.

The hop: This contrasts to a move called the one-two. On a one-two, a player steps into the shot, compared to the self-explanatory hop. Hoover believes this leads to a quicker release. With defenders seemingly getting longer and tougher every year, he believes it will become the dominant move in time. The hop has a fluidity, Hoover thinks, and provides balance.

One-motion versus two-motion: Two-motion shooters are guys like Jordan and Kobe Bryant, who jump higher and release the shot nearer to the top of their jump. Kids used to always hear coaches say to not shoot on the way up. "We have to shoot on the way up," says Hoover, a one-motion advocate. "Everybody has to shoot on the way up to a certain extent, but two-motion is because you're jumping so high you have to pause."

One coach told Hoover there's no point in teaching the turn, the dip, and the sweep-and-sway. Players just do it. "I don't understand what the hell that means," he says. "You can teach anything. I really believe that. I get college coaches all the time say, 'We can't improve our shooting, we just have to go get better shooters.' What are you talking about? You're dealing with some great athletes, and you're basically giving up on them?"

As much as Hoover enjoys teaching his beliefs, he loves just as much talking about other concepts around the jumper. The phrase "cognitive dissonance" doesn't come up in a lot of discussions with most basketball coaches, but those are two of Hoover's favorite words. It all relates to what he calls "the fog." "The great shooters," he tells me, "don't drill how they shoot. When somebody says, 'I was a great shooter,' I almost feel like saying, 'I'm sorry, you must not know much about shooting then.' They just do it." With the fog, great shooters don't know how to describe their form. A great shooter might say he squares his feet . . . but then Hoover shows five minutes of video showing how that player always turns them. A great shooter might tell young players to go straight up and down on their jump shot . . . but then Hoover shows five minutes of video proving that player always sweeps-and-sways. "This fog is a fascinating thing. Where you think you're doing one thing, and you're doing something else. Then you keep telling everybody else about what you think you're doing, and so you're messing people up." In one of Hoover's videos, he shows Stephen Curry talking about not dropping the ball down lower than where he catches a pass, followed by video of Curry doing it time and again. Same with Kevin Love talking about squaring up to the basket, followed by videos of Love turning his feet and aligning his shoulders. Hoover shows Pete Maravich discussing the importance of having your toes pointed toward the front of the rim, followed by video of Maravich shooting— and always turning his feet.

The forty-nine-year-old Hoover gets resistance from many quarters. A local high school coach refuses to let his players see Hoover for training. "He thinks I'm the Antichrist." One shooting coach wrote to him and said, "I don't need your e-mails." Hoover says, "I'm like, 'Dude, I wish all the shooting coaches would send me e-mails because I would know what my competition is doing, but I would also maybe get some ideas.' But there are a lot of people that don't want those."

Growing up in Orange County in California, Hoover got a coaching gig for a local rec team while still in school. Within a couple of years he coached at a high school. Eventually he became fascinated with shooting. He watched another longtime shooting coach, but soon came up with his own novel concepts.

Then he created the Pro Shot Shooting System. The name is key. It's not the Paul Hoover Shooting System. First, he doesn't have the name recognition to pull it off—"I'm not Rick Mount. And if I put my name and I don't show up for a camp it doesn't look good." But it drives home the concept that he wants players learning from the top players—the pros. A lot of people tell him, "Kobe can do it, Jordan can do that, but my players can't do that." Hoover says, "Basketball is the only thing like that in the world. It's the only sport. I've had people say, 'A twelve-year-old should shoot like a twelve-year-old.' What does that even mean? Does that make any sense?"

Hoover attracts followers with his prolific video output on the Internet, drawing them into his shooting web with music, highlights, and quips. But to fully win over converts he takes Pro Shot on the road and uses in-person instruction to show players and coaches what's possible with his system. Hoover guesses he stays on the road thirty-five weeks out of the year. When Hoover hires coaches, he doesn't look for great shooters, but great instructors. At camps, Pro Shot instructors haul out a forty-two-inch television and show videos of great shooters. They break the jumper down, usually starting with the dip. Pro Shot has done camps in forty-seven states—coaches have yet to hit Hawaii, Alaska, and, for reasons Hoover can't figure out, New Mexico. They do well in the Dakotas, Minnesota, Wisconsin, and out east. But not Indiana, home to so many great shooters. "Indiana is very traditional. They don't like change. I was watching *Hoosiers* today where they said, 'We don't like change here.' That's pretty much Indiana."

Hoover's love of all things shooting seems unmatched. And the loyalty of his coaches and players is just as passionate. They all eagerly shared stories about how the sweep-and-sway changed their shot or how they used Hoover's methods despite resistance from their own coaches, whether in the States or halfway around the world.

One thing I appreciate about Hoover's teaching is his own willingness to change, to tweak his beliefs if the evidence warrants. He wrote an e-book and updates it with new information. The book's title, *Pro Shooting Secrets*, seems simple enough, but the subtitle reveals its author's beliefs: *The Only Shooting System That Unlocks the Hidden Truth Behind Today's Greatest Shooters*. Like his videos, Hoover's book contains shots at the basketball establishment, bewilderment at the old ways, and confidence in the new ones. It's a fun book, unlike so many how-to shooting texts that work great as sleep inducers.

Because it's an e-book, Hoover can update information frequently, if he reconsiders the mechanics, as he did in an October 2014 video. It's an intriguing piece for anyone who thinks Hoover comes off as arrogant with his teachings. The video contains a different tone. Instead of the movie clips and music, the video features Hoover in his backyard gym. A somber opening makes it feel more like the president preparing to address the American people in the Oval Office. In the video, Hoover talks about "the finger." Hoover has discussed how Kobe Bryant uses his right index finger on his shot and delivers a pinch on his follow-through. Hoover still believes in the importance of the index finger on the player's release, but in the new video he spoke about hearing from players, coaches, and parents of players who weren't effective with the method, which Michael Jordan used in a similar manner.

"I'm kind of known as the finger guy," he says in the video. Pro Shot even made T-shirts focused on the finger. After years of believing the release was the most important part of a shot, Hoover now felt, "The key is this—it's about shooting alignment. The most important thing is my hip, my elbow, my shoulder, and my follow-through have to be aligned to the basket." Not the feet, never the feet—"We don't believe in that at all." But Hoover stressed that players could use the pinch, or two fingers, or maybe four down, putting their hand through the rim. "The release is huge, but it's where your body is aligned."

Hoover talks about misses as often as he does makes, because those reveal what's wrong with a jumper. Good shooters should never miss on the left or right. If they do, that's all about alignment, and if that's messed up, everything's messed up. "To be a great shooter, you've gotta be a straight shooter," Hoover says in a video. "If you can't shoot straight, you can't shoot."

Paul Hoover doesn't shoot as straight as many other instructors—he's not going to beat Dave Hopla or Mark Price in H-O-R-S-E. But when *talking* about the jump shot he's a straight shooter. In a decade, we might know if that was enough for a rebel to change basketball.

SIXTEEN

1990s AND BEYOND: LAND OF THE THREE

Howard Hobson lived for nearly eighty-eight years and became one of the great coaches of his era, but he didn't live long enough to see his favorite shot dominate basketball. In 1939, the NCAA held its first national tournament. Hobson coached Oregon to the championship. He entered the Naismith Hall of Fame in 1965. But to see Hobson's lasting impact, turn on any basketball game. Whether it's high school, college, or the pros, you'll see teams launching dozens of three-pointers. The three-point shot rules, in the same way big men dominated for decades. And seventy years ago, six months before the end of World War II, Howard Hobson—who died in 1991 at eighty-seven, a month before his birthday—dreamed of a future with the three-pointer. He championed the shot, believing it could change the game. It took sixteen years for any pro league to follow his lead and thirty-four years before the NBA made it an official part of its game.

Today it's unfathomable to picture basketball without the three-pointer, but for nearly the first hundred years of the game, it was unthinkable for the game's leaders to imagine the game with it. Because of the three-pointer, the jump shot has completely taken over basketball. Sometimes it seems like the three threatens to overwhelm the game. There are writers, fans, and coaches who think the shot's become too popular. Even I wonder about this. The three-pointer has always sparked feelings of uneasiness.

On February 7, 1945, New York City rivals Fordham and Columbia played with a three-point line, in an experimental game for Hobson's ideas about scoring. The game featured a three-point line from 21 feet, and the free throw lane widened to 12 feet from six. In addition, on free throws, players had the option of taking shots from the three-point line. Any make counted for two points instead of one. Hobson wrote a book called *Scientific Basketball* in 1949, the results "of a study of 460 college basketball games in which various performances were recorded. A period of thirteen years is covered, from the 1936–37 season through the 1948–49 season." In Chapter 10, Hobson—who did graduate and doctoral work at Columbia and teamed up with Columbia alum Julian Rice to sponsor the contest—described the circumstances surrounding the Columbia-Fordham game and why he believed in the importance of the three-pointer.

> *The home run is the most spectacular play in baseball. Parks have been built for particular hitters so that the fans will see an occasional home run. The baseball has been made more lively so that the home run will be more possible. Correspondingly, the long field goal is the most spectacular play in basketball. In spite of this fact, it is used sparingly in many sections of the country. The home run in baseball, of course, is worth more than the single. In basketball, however, the long field goal from, let us say, forty feet out, counts the same as the field goal under the basket. Since the data indicate clearly that it is much more difficult to score from the longer areas, why should not goals from the longer areas be worth more than goals under the basket?*

Columbia won the game 73–58. Under normal scoring, Columbia would have won 59–44. Following the game, *Columbia Spectator* writer Ed Gold quoted Norm Skinner, who scored 26 points that game: "It's nice having that three-point rule during the final five minutes of the game because that means you always have a fighting chance to take the contest." Columbia made 11 three-pointers out of 26 attempts while Fordham hit nine of its 18 attempts. Many confused, overeager players got called for traveling because they stopped dribbling and backed up behind the line. Some of the fans in attendance completed surveys about the rules. By a margin of 148–105, they liked the three-pointer. Writers at the game didn't share the feelings. Louis Effrat of *The New York Times* wrote, "At this stage it seems safe to predict that the optional plan will be permitted to die a natural death. There is more than enough confusion in basketball without adding to it by modifying the present rules." The *Spectator* noted, "There is no longer any emphasis on team play because the lay-up shot, which used to be the basis for any squad's attack, now counts less than an ordinary pop set shot."

In 1978, as the NBA contemplated installing the three-pointer, Hobson, long removed from his coaching days but still remembering his old experiment, told the UPI he wrote to Commissioner Larry O'Brien and said "making the three-point basket a permanent part of the game will help eliminate the violence he and basketball fans are concerned about in the NBA. It's like putting two heavyweight boxers in a telephone booth and telling them not to clinch. The three-point plan would tend to draw the defense out, decrease the use of the zone, relieve congestion near the basket, add a spectacular play for the fans and would give the team behind a better chance to catch up."

When NBA executives, coaches, and owners debated the shot, Red Auerbach said, "I say leave our game alone. Putting in the three-point play reminds me of a team that trades four, five, and six players every year. Everybody starts panicking." Warriors owner Franklin Mieuli—who flouted tradition when he drafted Denise Long a decade earlier—stormed out of the meetings. He supposedly had tears in his eyes when owners talked about the implementation of the three. In his mind, the three-pointer was "immoral. Everyone else from kids on the street on up will give two points for a field goal, but the NBA will give three for outside shots. We are going to destroy the team concept."

Few NBA teams or players knew what to make of the shot. In writing about the small forwards of the 1980s, I noted the reluctance of even the best shooters when it came to the three. The Atlanta Hawks took only 75 three-pointers that first year the NBA used it. They made 13. The world champion Lakers only attempted 100. In the 1980 Finals—when the Lakers beat Philadelphia in six games—L.A. didn't make a single three-pointer in four attempts. The Sixers made one of their 16 attempts. In Boston's six-game victory over Houston in the 1981 Finals, the Celtics made three three-pointers in the series out of 16 attempts, even with Larry Bird on the team (he made one of two). The greatest Celtics team of them all won the title in 1986 with Bird at the top of his game and the league, but in a six-game Finals Boston only made 12 threes. Even during the Finals in 1991, the year Howard Hobson died, Michael Jordan's Bulls made five three-pointers out of 21 attempts in a five-game victory over the Lakers. The game took place inside the line, and it seemed many players weren't yet aware they received an extra point for shots outside it.

The good three-point bombers took the shot for certain teams, but no one else fired it up. Consider the Utah Jazz. Guard Darrell Griffith set a league record in 1985 with 92 three-pointers. He was hurt the next season, and in 1986 Utah didn't make a three-pointer until the *twenty-third* game of the year. The 1983 Spurs took a mere 308 three-pointers, but that led the league. It wasn't until the 1994 season—fourteen years after the introduction of the shot—that the NBA leader made more than 190. In the new century, the shot exploded in popularity and importance. The 2013 Knicks shot 2,371 as a team. Stephen Curry made 286 threes in 2015, two years after he made a record 272.

And compare the present-day Finals to those in the past. In the 2014 series between the Spurs and Heat, which the Spurs won in five games, San Antonio made 55 out of 118 attempts while the Heat went 46 for 116. In short, the long shot reigns.

At first, the NBA didn't want people thinking the league borrowed anything from the ABA, its old rival, one reason the three-pointer struggled to gain acceptance. Starting in the 1967–68 season, the ABA brought the three-pointer to the masses. An early game featured a full-court shot by Indiana's Jerry Harkness with his team trailing Dallas 118–116. The teams prepared for overtime, until the refs informed everyone the game was over, thanks to the lengthy three-pointer. But if it took teams time to adjust to life with the three-pointer, some players adapted immediately, overjoyed at finding a home for their unique shooting skills. Even if a player did little more than shoot, he earned time on the court. A true gunner named Les Selvage went 10-for-26 on three-pointers in a single game.

Sports Illustrated's Frank Deford assessed the new league and its new shot early in its debut season. Writing in November 1967, Deford observed:

> *Selvage is hardly 6'1", much smaller than Oscar, with a build that is not prepossessing and a little-boy face. But he is strong enough to make the long jump shot. He has hit with 47 of 107 three-pointers (.439), while inside the arc he is only 36 for 111 (.324). "His wrists are so strong," [Anaheim] Amigo Coach Al Brightman says, "I think maybe Les would make more shots in close if he would try banking the ball." When the Amigos come out for pregame practice, Selvage embarks immediately for his dominion out past the arc. He pops them in from out there while his teammates mill around in closer, trying their more prosaic shots. The scene is reminiscent of a pregame football warmup, with Selvage the field-goal specialist, blithely tuning his sensitive skills, quite apart from all the mundane shoulder-knocking. . . .*
>
> *For its part, the NBA remains unmoved by any three-point ideas. The rulesmakers have never even considered it. Eddie Gottlieb, an NBA rules committeeman who has spearheaded many of the innovations that have, literally, saved the pro game, says, "What is it but an admission that you are dealing with inferior players who can't do anything but throw up long shots? Is length the only criterion for excellence? I would say that out of every 40 or 50 shots, at least 20 are more difficult than a simple long shot. If it is worth three points to make a standard long jump shot, well then, a twisting, driving hook, going full speed to take the pass, cutting between two big defenders— why, that must be worth six points. You encourage mediocrity when you give extra credit to this sort of thing."*

The ABA showed the game's grumps how teams and players could take advantage of the three-pointer, but it wasn't the first professional league to experiment. Abe Saperstein, who started the Harlem Globetrotters, created the American Basketball League, an eight-team outfit that started in 1961 and only lasted about a year and a half. But during that time, Saperstein brought the three-pointer to the ABL, with encouragement from Bill Sharman, who coached Cleveland to the championship in the debut season. Saperstein wanted to call it "the 25-foot home run." Papers called three-pointers 25-footers during the ABL's brief existence, but Sharman said in a 2008 interview about the history of the shot that the actual distance was close to the 23 feet, 9 inches that became the standard in the NBA. Before the first season, Saperstein said, "The sports fan likes the bonus thrill—the home run wallop in baseball, the long touchdown pass in football and the knockout punch in boxing. The bonus thrill in our league will be the three-point basket." Saperstein also touted the three-pointer's ability to help the little guy. In today's game, the three-pointer has evolved to the point where it's practically eliminated the traditional big man, as very few post players dominate solely in the paint. Everyone wants to shoot the three, including the giants. But when the three-pointer first started, the shot was a safety vest for short players. The few spectators who attended ABL games enjoyed the shot. According to an AP story from 1962, "Chants of 'hit a home run, hit a home run' or 'go, go, go for the long one' were common among fans at ABL games." Sharman said only two of his players could make a three-pointer so he didn't encourage his team to shoot it, but, "Psychologically, it's a big weapon."

Those psychological benefits became obvious long before anyone saw just how useful the shot could be as an every-possession weapon. For decades, teams used the three primarily when trailing or when putting a game out of reach. In *Drive*, Bird wrote, "I'll tell you when it is a particularly good time to use it. You're the road team, you've got maybe a five-point lead with a couple of minutes to go and you're wide open. That's when I love to crank that thing up there because if you make it you simply *destroy* a team at that point."

The shot still destroys teams—occasionally because no one on a team can make it—but now it happens from tipoff to buzzer. Even those who benefit sometimes still regard the three-pointer through the same lens as those who opposed it thirty-five years ago. Spurs coach Gregg Popovich, a sideline genius who changed his team's system so it utilizes the three-pointer and rode the shot to the 2014 championship, has said, "I hate it. It's changed the game. It makes it tougher to cover that much room defensively on the court, so you do have to pay attention to it defensively. It's a heck of a weapon. . . . To me it's not basketball, but you've got to use it. If you don't, you're in big trouble."

When the Big Ten dabbled with the three-pointer in 1983, with a line from 21 feet, Bob Knight said, "I think it's horseshit. The three-point rule should be taken to the Lincoln Park Zoo and placed between the reptile cage and the lion's cage and all the kids visiting the zoo should get a chance at the three-point shot." Three years later, the entire NCAA adapted the rule, putting the line at 19 feet, 9 inches. Knight still expressed disgust. "The thing I don't like about the three-point shot is that if I have good shooters and you don't, then it affects you negatively and affects me positively. And I don't think anything should be done that doesn't affect both teams the same." But by 1986, Knight had one of college basketball's great shooters on his roster: Steve Alford.

An Indiana legend, Alford won Mr. Basketball at New Castle in 1983. Alford's dad, Sam, who also coached New Castle, taught Steve to shoot. "I shot off the wrong side of my head," Alford, who now coaches UCLA, tells me. "And then after my freshman year my dad corrected it and got the ball on the right side, and really my shooting took off from my sophomore year on." Playing without the three-point line in high school, Alford still averaged 37 points per game as a senior. On the final day of his school career, Alford played two games, scoring 57 points in the first game, 37 in the second.

By his senior season at Indiana, Alford earned a reputation as the sharpest shooter in the land. That season he took advantage of the three-pointer, the shot his volatile head coach still couldn't stand. As much as Knight loathed the three-pointer, he also knew Indiana possessed a dangerous weapon in Alford. "He and the assistants spent a lot of time trying to tinker with my defense," Alford says, "but I think they were smart enough to leave the jump shot alone. I had that part down." Averaging 22 points in 1987, Alford hit 53 percent of his three-pointers. He hardly needed to make adjustments for the new line. "You just paid attention to pivoting a little bit, so you didn't step on the line. So just learning how to pivot, and use it, and, unfortunately, I only got to use it for one year."

In that one season he led Indiana to the national championship. The 1987 Final Four featured an intriguing mix of coaches when it came to their views about the three-pointer. Knight still cursed it, even after Alford embraced it. Rick Pitino's Providence took more three-pointers than any other team in the country. Syracuse's Jim Boeheim peered into the bedrooms of reporters and sneered, "A lot of fans and a lot of you writers like the three-point shot. Then again, a lot of you writers also like X-rated movies." Indiana defeated UNLV 97–93 in the semifinals, despite only making two of four three-pointers. UNLV made 13 of 35. Afterward Knight said, "I believe basketball should involve passing and a lot of other things rather than just throwing it up. I have an aversion to basketball of that kind."

But in the title game against Syracuse, Knight watched Alford make seven three-pointers—accounting for 21 of his 23 points—as the Hoosiers won 74–73 on a late jump shot by Keith Smart. At the postgame press conference, Knight again discussed the three-point shot. "I sit here, look at the box score, and the thing that I like least of all in basketball is the three-point shot. And we make three more points from the three-point shot than Syracuse does, and that's the difference in the ballgame. So, uh, thanks, Ed."

"Ed" was Ed Steitz, the man most responsible for the NCAA introducing the three-point shot on a national basis for the 1987 season. Like Howard Hobson, Steitz believed in the power of the three-pointer. A visionary who refused to live in the past, Steitz helped the NCAA bring back the dunk and utilize a shot clock. But the three-pointer became his legacy. People called him "the Three Stooge" for his love of the shot. He sought opinions from coaches, even those who hated the shot. Mike Krzyzewski complained, "This is a revolutionary change, and I don't think it's good for the game right now. We've just had a year of no chaos and now we're introducing chaos." Don Haskins, a groundbreaking coach who started five black players and led Texas Western to the history-making NCAA championship victory over Kentucky in 1966, wanted nothing to do with the three-pointer and didn't let workers paint a three-point line on the court for his team's preseason pickup games. It's hard to imagine any rule change in today's game that could spark such strong opinions, except, perhaps, if someone suggested *removing* the three-point shot. Now that would create chaos. Steitz died in 1990, but in 2011 his son Bob told ESPN.com writer Dana O'Neil, "It's neat for me to see how the game has evolved. I think my dad would be pleased but not surprised. He really believed it would work."

That evolution created a new type of player: the three-point specialist. Players developed entire careers based on their ability to shoot. Teams stationed them in the corner and waited for them to knock in a few threes, to stretch the defenses, allowing the superstars more room to operate, whether it was the big guy in the middle or guards with their penetration. Sometimes these players excelled on defense, but often they were on the court simply for offense.

In *The Art of a Beautiful Game*, while writing about pure shooters, Chris Ballard observed: "Pure shooters are held in such esteem, they change a game without even taking shots. Put a player like [Reggie] Miller, or three-point specialist Jason Kapono, on the floor, and the opposition must be aware of him at all times. His defender can't sag off or gamble for steals; if Kapono stands 25 feet from the basket, that's where his defender stands."

The frustrating thing for one of the greatest pure shooters ever—a man who became a specialist as his career progressed—was that in his younger days he was capable of doing everything on the court. "To me," says Dennis Scott from his Georgia home, "for the people that have watched my games throughout my whole career, I rest easy at night because they know I can handle the ball. They knew I had a post-up game. It's just that when I got to the NBA, the injuries may have taken that away. But God blessed me with such a shooting ability, that's how I was able to create my niche, and create the career I did in the NBA."

In 1996, Scott, on a star-studded, star-crossed Orlando Magic team led by Shaquille O'Neal and Anfernee "Penny" Hardaway, took advantage of the NBA's strange three-year experiment that moved the three-point line in from 23 feet, 9 inches to 22 feet and set a league record with 267 three-pointers. As of 2015, it remained the fourth-highest single-season total ever. At six-eight, Scott stroked one of the smoothest jumpers in the game, combining his size with an efficient, perfect form. Former LSU coach Dale Brown once said Scott could shoot from Jupiter, although another publication quoted Brown as saying Scott was good from Pluto. Either way, Scott's range always seemed otherworldly.

The forty-five-year-old Scott works as an analyst for NBA TV. We spoke a month after he suffered the most feared injury for any basketball player: a torn Achilles. Scott hurt it while playing ball with his kids. He grabbed a long rebound, made a spin move against his eight-year-old son, and went down. When Scott returns to play with his kids he'll probably limit his dribbling even more. A similar thing happened during his career, when injuries robbed him of his mobility, turning him more into a specialist than an all-around player. Scott showed his son a highlight reel of his school days, and the boy said, "Dad, that's not you," after watching Dennis dunk "maybe seven times." "I said, 'Yeah, that's me. I used to do that.'"

But from his days as a prep player at Flint Hill in Virginia when he was the top player in the country, to his All-American career at Georgia Tech, and his time in the pros, Scott's shooting stroke paid the bills. He made it look so easy, and he made it sound even easier. As a high school kid he said, "If Magic Johnson had my jump shot, he'd be incredible." Magic was Scott's idol. He laughs when I mention the old quote about the Laker god's push shot jumper. Scott felt comfortable critiquing the jump shot of one of the best players ever, because his faith in his own shot never wavered. Others believed in it too.

Back in high school, Scott played in a Philadelphia league run by a famous basketball fixture in the city named Sonny Hill. Scott loved throwing behind-the-back passes, dribbling between his legs, putting on a show. Hill pulled him aside.

"Son, do you want to make a little bit of money, or do you want to make a lot of money?"

"Why?" Scott asked.

"You dribble the ball too much, and you pass it too much. You're one of the best sixteen-year-olds at shooting the basketball I've ever seen. Shoot a little more, not all that dribbling and passing trying to be like Magic Johnson. Magic Johnson's Magic Johnson. And you're Dennis Scott."

And Scott was a shooter.

"My high school coach, Stu Vetter, he likes to take a lot of credit for it, but I was already shooting that well before I got to Flint Hill," Scott says. "I say, 'Coach, that's why you wanted me to transfer, because I was already shooting the ball so well.' "

A 1987 graduate, Scott didn't play with the three-point line at Flint Hill. High schools only started using it the following season. But at Georgia Tech, Scott found the distance, 19 feet, 9 inches, laughable. "When I would pull up, my teammates would be yelling, 'Layup.' " Scott's size made the jumper look easy, even when his big body occasionally made things difficult. New York scout Tom Konchalski once said Scott had "the body of a blacksmith, but the touch of a surgeon." Scott battled weight issues at various times—at his heaviest he weighed 259 pounds, but by his record-breaking junior year he dropped down to 220. Back home his friends called him "Legs 'n' Butt." The weight never gathered in his gut—it was all in his ass and thighs. "For me, being a big guy, my release always looked softer, because I always used my legs. I always used my big butt. I always used my hips. The Reggie Millers, the Ray Allens, they're a little slimmer. Their shot may be quicker. They may use their toes, or get into their shots faster, where I may need a half second more, because I used my whole body, especially when I was shooting real deep threes."

Scott's best season came his junior year at Georgia Tech, when he averaged 27.7 points and led the Yellow Jackets to the Final Four. *Sporting News* named him Player of the Year. He scored 40 points in Georgia Tech's 93–91 victory over Minnesota in the region final. The easygoing Scott enjoyed playing to the crowd, especially road ones that simultaneously jeered him and appreciated his jumper. At Duke that season, a student, egged on by a fraternity watching in the stands, challenged Scott to a shooting contest during warm-ups. Scott suggested each of them take five shots. The student could shoot from anywhere he wanted. He missed each one, including a layup, a free throw, and a three. Time was running out on the warm-ups. Duke players drifted onto the court, Georgia Tech players walked back to the locker room. Feeling merciful, Scott decided he'd only take one shot. "I walk out to half-court," he says. "I look back at the fraternity, take one dribble, turn back, shot it. I look up and said, 'This thing's going in.' Before the ball hit the net I started walking toward the locker room." The shot dropped. Scott bowed to the students, and strolled off. The student who challenged Scott that day was Seth Davis, who has enjoyed a long career in basketball—as a writer for *Sports Illustrated* and analyst for CBS, not as a shooter.

Scott's shooting was the main reason Orlando took him with the fourth pick in the 1990 draft. By the time Orlando became a powerhouse with Shaq and Hardaway, back and knee injuries robbed Scott of some of his lift and mobility, limiting his contributions. He sometimes expressed frustration with his role as the designated shooter, but no player was better suited for it. In addition to setting the single-season record for threes, Scott established a single-game record when he knocked in 11 three-pointers against the Hawks in 1996. It seemed inevitable Orlando would eventually win an NBA title behind O'Neal's awesome power, Hardaway's backcourt brilliance, and Scott's unmatched shooting. But the Magic only made the Finals once, and that ended in a four-game loss at the hands of the Rockets. Shaq left for Los Angeles, injuries derailed Hardaway, and Scott finished out his career as a wounded hired gun, battling injuries in five more NBA cities.

Today Scott's NBA TV colleague Rick Kamla credits Scott as being one of the main players who made the three-point shot relevant. By the time Scott started bombing away, it was no longer considered a gimmick shot or bad basketball. Scott helped show just how powerful a weapon the three-pointer was in the hands of a sharpshooter. People have approached Scott and said, "My coach never let me shoot threes until you started shooting them and showing everybody it was cool." He says, "It makes me feel good, to let people know, 'You may not be athletic, but if you can shoot the ball, and you keep your man in front of you, you can play basketball somewhere.'"

During our interview, Scott talked about telling his doctor he wanted to recover from the Achilles injury enough so he could at least play in a church league. He could play zone on defense, spot up for threes on offense. That's what middle-age ballplayers do, and it's a fitting fate for a man who once dreamed of being Magic Johnson, but instead became one of the game's great three-point shooters.

When people list the most memorable shots in basketball history, a few plays always make the cut. There's Christian Laettner's buzzer-beater against Kentucky in 1992. Bryce Drew's March Madness three-pointer for Valparaiso in 1998. Michael Jordan against the Cavs in 1989, and the Jazz in 1998. There's Kareem Abdul-Jabbar's skyhook in the 1974 Finals against the Celtics. Magic's hook against the Celtics in 1987. And in June 2013, Ray Allen added one more shot that will always make the list, a three-pointer that might have been the greatest shot in NBA history.

In Game 6 of the 2013 Finals between Miami and San Antonio, Allen, in his first season with the Heat after a long career in Milwaukee, Seattle, and Boston, hit a game-tying three-pointer with 5.2 seconds left, sending the game into overtime. A miss would have given the Spurs the series victory in six games. Instead he drained it, Miami prevailed in overtime, and then won Game 7, clinching the franchise's second consecutive championship. *Grantland*'s Bill Simmons wrote, "There's never been a greater NBA shot. With all due respect to Jordan's iconic jumper against the '98 Jazz, Allen's shot had similar clutchness, bigger stakes and a higher degree of difficulty."

"Nothing's greater than Ray Allen's shot," Bob Ryan concurs. "It comes down to that moment, and you have the perfect guy, the man you want. That saved them. They're done, it's over. They're losing. I think that is the greatest shot."

One of the more amazing aspects of Allen's three-pointer that night—aside from the skill and awareness it took to sprint to the right corner and fire while rising up over Tony Parker—was the end result surprised no one. He's made more three-pointers than anyone else in NBA history, and his pregame preparation and workouts are as admired as any of the shots he's hit. In a story breaking down Allen's shot against the Spurs, *Sports Illustrated*'s Lee Jenkins described how "Allen invented a drill in which he lies in the key, springs to his feet and backpedals to the corner.

A coach throws him a pass. He has to catch and shoot without stepping on the three-point line or the sideline." Allen worked his entire basketball life for that one moment in the Finals, and he was ready for it because he's never stopped working on his jump shot.

When I met with Dave Hopla and we talked about his shooting clinics, he spoke about putting on demonstrations at the University of Connecticut, where Allen earned All-American status. Allen still has a home in the area, and if he's in town when Hopla gives a lecture, Allen "sits in the front row and is so focused." But Allen was always an eager student.

Out in California, I met Jeff Lensch, the man who taught Allen the jump shot, or at least put him on the right path toward finding the jump shot that will one day put him in the Hall of Fame. A military kid whose dad worked as an Air Force mechanic, Allen traveled around the world as a child, moving from England to Germany and cities throughout the United States. Allen's family spent time at Edwards Air Force Base in California, where Ray came under the tutelage of Lensch. In 2004, Allen told Percy Allen of *The Seattle Times*, "My coach that coached me in my first organized league at the youth center [Lensch] . . . I always tell him, he and those guys there were one of the main reasons why I was successful because they gave me a fundamental foundation. And I haven't changed since."

Lensch first saw Ray in fourth or fifth grade. Ray's siblings displayed athletic prowess. A sister played college volleyball. His older brother John was an outstanding player with great quickness "but didn't grow like Ray. I tell people, if anybody was going to be an athlete it was going to be John. I thought Ray, because he was very sociable, he was quiet, but he was able to interact with older people, very intelligent—he was going to be the businessman of the family. And he grew up to be an athlete and a businessman." Lensch showed me pictures of Allen's shot, and we watched a DVD of one of his seventh-grade games. In black-and-white photos, Allen stands at the free throw line in his sweatpants. His butt sticks out as he takes a deep crouch and prepares to shoot. He has skinny legs and a thin frame. There's also a picture of Allen shooting from straight on; his right arm comes through on his shot in a follow-through no one would coach. It looks like he's thrusting his arm out in celebration or throwing a jab in the boxing ring. But another picture—in color—shows Allen the NBA player, on a return trip to the base, where he spoke with the school's football team. By that time the ugly shot he first displayed for Lensch lived on only in old photos and videos, yet he never forgot those early lessons.

Allen used an unattractive form on free throws, looking nothing like a player who eventually became an 89 percent shooter from the line. Lensch recorded all of his players, once in November and then again in January. He showed them their flaws and tried correcting them, first by showing them the tape in his office, then on the court. Not everyone learned like Ray Allen. Over the years, because people know about his work with a young Allen, parents wanted him to teach their kids how to shoot the jumper. Sounds easy, right? Turn my kid into Ray Allen. "If I get a kid in high school, unless he or she is really dedicated and really wants to make a change and is willing to make a change, it's too late." But with younger kids he can teach the basics, like he did with Allen. "I can show them the placement of the hands, but most of the little kids will bring that other hand up so it's a two-hand push, and that was the thing with Ray."

Lensch has a DVD of one of Allen's seventh-grade games, which he transferred from an old videotape. Watching it, a viewer would never pick out the future NBA star, but Allen was the best player, a forward who handled the ball and often set up the offense. Allen's passing skills set him apart, even if teammates botched potential assists with missed layups. Although he never hesitated to shoot, Allen couldn't find the range from the wing or the baseline. He was a skinny seventh-grade kid with an occasionally frightful shot—Lensch always tried getting him to pull his elbow in. But his desire to learn was always there, something he carried with him throughout his career. He once told *The New York Times* he credited his curiosity to his world travels. "On a daily basis, I have, on the average, ten questions," he said. "Then I put everything I've seen in that particular day in perspective and understand everything. And down the line, I won't be confused about anything."

Allen's family moved after his seventh-grade year. The next time Lensch heard about him, Allen had signed with the University of Connecticut. Lensch didn't realize the kid with the push shot moved to South Carolina and became a top prep player. When Allen played for the Bucks, Lensch went to a game at the Staples Center when Milwaukee came to L.A. Armed with his pictures of a young, awkward Allen, he convinced the ushers he knew the Bucks superstar. He found Allen shooting alone on the court during warm-ups. He yelled, "Raymond!" Allen looked over and said, "Jeffrey." It'd been at least ten years since they'd seen each other, but the best shooter in the NBA remembered the coach who first helped him learn the secrets of the jumper. After that game, Lensch and Allen developed a friendship; Lensch has traveled to Boston and Miami for visits. He'll occasionally send an e-mail or Facebook message when he sees Allen have an off night shooting. Not that Allen needs help at this stage.

At the University of Connecticut, Allen was much more than a shooter—he was dynamic off the dribble, capable of exploding to the basket. "Shooting was not his forte," says longtime Connecticut coach Jim Calhoun of Allen's early years at the school. "When he got to college, because of his incredible legs, athleticism, and work ethic, he developed into, obviously in the NBA, the greatest three-point shooter in the game." As a pro, Allen put so much work into his shot he told a writer, "I just shoot the ball. Like, I don't question going to the bathroom, I don't question eating. It's just that simple for me."

It's simple. Spend thousands of hours on a court, going through the same drills time and again, on the practice floor and in the arena before the games. Combine it with a six-five frame, world-class hand-eye coordination, and great instincts—he's often talked about not even having to see the basket on his jumper since the rim is always in the same place. Allen's pregame shootaround became something others talked about with a sense of wonder. Usually arriving three hours before tipoff, Allen went through a routine that impressed observers and intimidated younger players if they worked out on the opposite end of the court. The veteran left nothing to chance, so that any shot he took during a game was one he'd taken a thousand times in practice, whether it was a wide-open shot from the wing, a pull-up jumper from 18, or a do-or-die three-pointer in the corner of Game 6 of the Finals. Following his three-pointer against the Spurs, Allen told Harvey Araton of *The New York Times*, "It's tough, but believe it or not, I work on it quite often. I try to put my body in precarious situations coming from different parts of the floor, different angles to try to get my momentum going moving forward. . . . When it went in, I was ecstatic. But at the same time, I was expecting to make it."

During Allen's days at UConn, Calhoun once made Allen carry a basketball everywhere he went, getting him used to the feel of the ball. He soon knew every inch of a basketball—when he received a pass, his fingers found the seams in an instant as he fired a jumper. "He's one of the great catch-and-shoot players who ever touched a basketball," Calhoun tells me. "It was almost unbelievable that Ray would go up, catch the ball, and the next instant he's up and squaring and shooting. That took . . . I don't say hours or days and months—years and years of having someone pass you the ball and shoot. You can never predict who will have that drive. Ray has it. Special, special shooter."

As Lensch knows, that wasn't always the case, but years of work made a singular moment—and the greatest shot in NBA history—possible.

Sometime in the past few years—most likely after watching a Houston Rockets game when they shot 40 three-pointers—I began to feel like the three was too much a part of basketball. Teams are shooting more threes, and there's no sign that it's ever going to stop. Someday soon a team might shoot 60 three-pointers on a regular basis.

Analytics have played a large role in the three-point movement. Teams know you can miss more threes than twos and still score just as many points. (Although as Steve Kerr, one of the best three-point shooters ever, told Jack McCallum in 2004, "All I know is it's not very appealing to watch so many missed shots. Even if 33 percent is good statistically, it is pretty ugly to see two out of three shots clang off the rim.")

The corner three has become the favorite shot in basketball because it's easy and brutally efficient. So my occasional queasiness over the shot has nothing to do with statistics or math. It's about aesthetics, not analytics. As much as I love shooting, both as a player and as a fan—and as an author who's writing a book about the jump shot—I grow bored watching a team that only shoots threes and drives to the basket. I love the versatility of players and teams that can score from all over the court. I enjoy watching a post player catch a pass and operate in the paint, with up-and-under moves or hooks or turnaround jump shots. I love watching a player who can knock in 20-foot jumpers with ease, a shot that's becoming increasingly rare in basketball—partly because fewer players are effective at it, but also because, percentage-wise, it's simply not as smart as a three-pointer. Coaches and analysts revile the "long two" as much as they once did the three-pointer. I miss players like James Worthy swooping to the hoop on a fast break instead of drifting to the three-point line. Every game threatens to look the same, every team a clone.

I'm hardly alone with these feelings, though my unease isn't as extreme as that of many. Bob Ryan doesn't like its increasing popularity, and Peter Vecsey says, "I was an ABA guy who loved the three-pointer. I've come to despise the three-pointer. The whole game is let's find the line, make sure you're behind it, take the three. A guy driving to the hoop has a layup, throws it out for a three-pointer. I'm going to throw up." But it's not just old writers or those clinging to the old ways—remember Gregg Popovich's words about hating the shot, even as he extended an NBA dynasty with it.

Could anything ever be done? *Should* anything be done? Eliminating it seems impossible, rightly so. But then how would you discourage teams from taking a shot that's—from a numbers standpoint—the right shot? Is that moral? Moving the line back a few feet would lead to more misses, but might not do anything about the attempts. Maybe you could borrow some rules from slow-pitch softball, where many tournaments put a limit on the number of home runs a team can hit in a game. In the same way a softball team might only get four homers per game, maybe basketball teams would only be allowed six made three-pointers per game. To channel the spirit of Phog Allen, maybe we could lower the basket to nine feet, make the tall freaks dominant around the rim again.

One year the NBA Development League experimented with only letting teams shoot three-pointers in the final three minutes of each quarter. David Leonhardt wrote in *The New York Times* about the long-distance shot, "Today's players attempt it, and miss it, so often that the sport is not the fluid spectacle it once was. Without the 3-pointer, the executives wondered, would players try harder to move the ball around and wait for an open shot?" Talking about the rule change during that 2005 season, Chris Alpert, the director of basketball operations and player personnel for the league, said, "What we're seeing is the reemergence of the midrange game, which is something of a lost art in the NBA." The NBA is aware of the possible issues with a game ruled exclusively by the three-pointer. *Grantland*'s Zach Lowe wrote in 2013, "David Stern surprised reporters after a Board of Governors meeting in April by revealing that league officials, owners, and the competition committee had been 'monitoring' the uptick in 3-point attempts." The NBA's concern? Same as mine: style. "The league," Lowe wrote, "does not want NBA basketball to look like a pickup game, and it is concerned that games with, say, 70 combined 3-point attempts would take on the feel of a ragged, me-first open gym game."

Howard Hobson would likely be amazed at these developments. The three-pointer—the shot he believed in way back in 1945, long before anyone understood the concept or its possible impact—might actually be too popular now. When I start complaining about the effect of the three-pointer—and see how, at its most basic level, I'm complaining about the influence of the jumper on the game—I realize I sound like old Jimmy Breslin in the 1950s when he warned the world about the jump shot wrecking basketball. I sound out of touch, like the coaches who first feared the jumper and threatened anyone who shot it with a benching. I need to accept it and welcome the new reality. The game's evolving, and the jump shot is again the driving force. Only this time the shots are even farther out on the court. The jump shot has again changed basketball—just like it has from the moment it appeared on Kentucky farms and in Virginia gyms. Shooters improved basketball in the past and made it what it is today. I guess I can trust them with basketball's future.

SEVENTEEN

THE GREATEST

One of my favorite baseball books of recent years was Tim Wendel's *High Heat: The Secret History of the Fastball and the Improbable Search for the Fastest Pitcher of All Time.* Wendel profiled many of the famous flame-throwers in baseball history—Bob Feller and Nolan Ryan among them—but he also wrote about the different ways baseball people have measured the fastball over the decades. Even today with the radar gun, discrepancies can appear when charting the fastest throwers. But at least with baseball and the fastball, actual numbers exist. We can see a player throws 98 miles per hour or 101 miles per hour—or we can at least see what a specific radar gun reveals, even if its readings are flawed.

When I started writing, I wanted to profile many of the great shooters, but also explore how the jump shot has changed basketball, from its introduction on farms and gyms scattered across the land to today's three-point dominance. And along the way, when I spoke with many of the great shooters, I asked them their thoughts about the best shooters they've ever seen.

But can you really find the greatest shooter? Can anyone earn that title when there's nothing like baseball's radar gun to help? In baseball it's possible to at least say certain pitchers have recorded the fastest pitches. How do you do that with the jump shot? There's no one gadget or one statistic that reveals all. Instead of an improbable search it becomes an impossible one.

The other problem with searching for the greatest jump shooter in history comes with defining what the word "greatest" even means in this context. Does "greatest" mean the most accurate three-point shooter in NBA history? That's Steve Kerr. When it comes to spotting up for three-pointers and knocking in long-distance bombs when superstars draw the attention of defenses, Kerr just might be the greatest. But aside from that specific classification, Kerr wouldn't be many people's choice for the greatest, not when he couldn't create his own shot and relied on the talents of others to get him so many open looks. Because if you have the greatest jump shot, shouldn't you be able to shoot it against tight defense, off the dribble or off the pass, against a single defender or over a double-team?

Consider Michael Jordan and Kobe Bryant, probably the two most explosive perimeter scorers who have ever played. Neither could beat Kerr in a stand-alone three-point contest, yet Bryant owns the NBA record for most three-pointers in a game with 12. And a signature Jordan moment happened when he drained six three-pointers in the first half against Portland in the 1992 Finals and reacted with a famous shrug. Both players made jump shots that most players can't even imagine during their dreams, much less pull off in a real game. Both are two of the great mid-range shooters to ever play. And Kobe might have put together the greatest individual shooting display ever when he scored 81 points against Toronto in 2006. He made 28 of 46 field goals that night, including seven three-pointers. The combination of outside shots he made has never been equaled in a single game, from turnaround jumpers at the top of the key, to bank shots from eight feet, to pull-up three-pointers from well beyond the arc. If a game came down to the final two seconds and a team threw the ball in, the coach would want Kobe or Jordan to get the shot, because they could create good looks—and get a quality jumper off—without needing much time and against tight defense. They're two of the greatest shooters in those moments, not just because they can make it, but because they can even attempt it. So how does that quality fit in the overall discussion of the greatest shooters?

Eras also present problems. They're impossible to compare. As I've written about, rules of the day dictate how players develop their shots. Consider Golden State's Stephen Curry. No matter how we define "greatest," he'd enter the debate, making his case with one perfectly launched shot

after another. Of the players I spoke with—whether they play today or retired years ago—Curry's name came up over and over again, along with
Kevin Durant's. With Curry, much of it revolves around his three-point
shooting, although he's deadly inside the arc as well. His unparalleled
shooting made him the best player on the best team during the 2015 season. Curry developed a delightful new trick, running back to the other
end of the court seconds after shooting an ultimately successful three-
pointer, turning his back to the ball as it was halfway to the basket, an arrogant gesture that told everyone in the arena he didn't even have to watch
the ball because he knew it would find the net. When I watched Curry accept his MVP trophy for the 2015 season, I thought about Red Auerbach's
list of offensive plays that changed the game, from Kareem's hook to Sam
Jones's bank shot. If the late Celtics legend had ever watched Curry play, I
wondered, would he have added his three-pointer to that illustrious list?
The game has seen dozens of great three-point shooters—but basketball's
never seen a three-point shooter who dominated like Curry. Yet if Curry
played in the 1960s, when the three-pointer didn't exist, he would not have
developed the same type of game. So it's impossible to compare his shooting against that of a player like Jerry West. Just as it's impossible to know
how West or any other player from back then would do in today's game.
They didn't develop long-range shooting because the three didn't exist, but
if they started playing in the 1980s they would've added it to their game—
but in turn, that would have detracted from their midrange games.

How about Durant? He makes every jumper look smooth, no matter
the distance. His six-nine size and wingspan give him an advantage over
every defender, and it seems obvious he would dominate in any era. But
in a different time a player his size wouldn't have been given the freedom
at a young age to develop the outside skills—a coach might have planted
him on the inside and lectured Durant if he left the lane.

What Durant has shown is that there's still no greater shot than the
jumper. No player thrills like an unconscious shooter. In the summer of
2011, during the NBA lockout, Durant played in streetball games across
the country, leaving wreckage behind at every stop. I saw him in my neighborhood in northern Manhattan, at the Dyckman tourney, when I
watched in awe as a man his size moved like a man a foot shorter. A few

days earlier, at famed Rucker Park, Durant scored 66 points in a performance that enthralled viewers who watched the video replays and nearly destroyed those who actually witnessed it in the park. At one stage Durant drained five straight three-pointers as Rucker's two announcers walked courtside and screamed into their microphones, with one of them repeating "I am!" over and over, bestowing Durant with biblical, godlike abilities. This was not a night for understatement. After one late Durant three-pointer ripped the net, the crowd swarmed the Oklahoma City superstar in the New York night. It was an unofficial game with nothing at stake. Yet in fifty years, when people compile Durant's video résumé, when they debate his place among the greatest shooters of all time, that game will make for useful evidence supporting his claim as being the best. Partly because the greatest shooters can light it up from any distance, and on any court.

Discussion about the greatest shouldn't be limited to America's shores. Brazilian legend Oscar Schmidt put on his most famous performance at the 1987 Pan Am Games against the United States, when he scored 46 points in the gold medal game. He never played a minute in the NBA, but when it comes to pure shooting few have been better than the man who entered the Naismith Hall of Fame in 2013 after an introduction from Larry Bird himself. In 1989, Schmidt engaged in one of the great shootouts—one that compares to Bird vs. Wilkins—when he scored 44 against Croatian sensation Drazen Petrovic in a European game. Petrovic scored 62 points and led Real Madrid to a 117–113 victory. Petrovic, whose life was cut short in a 1993 car accident, actually played in the NBA, unlike Schmidt, and during his brief time in the league he established himself as a premier shooter. If the "greatest" label includes international accomplishments, Schmidt and Petrovic both belong in the discussion.

"Infinite possibilities." That phrase by John Christgau followed me throughout this book. He talked about it because his own search for the first jump shooters in the game threatened to veer off in so many directions. Infinite possibilities make any definitive hunt for the first shooters impossible. The same holds true when searching for the greatest.

So maybe instead of finding the greatest, it's easier to answer a different question, one you might hear fans debating at a bar or a game.

If your life was on the line, and you needed one person to make a jump shot to save it, who would you choose? Assume the diabolical mastermind who came up with this sick game and is deciding your fate will set some parameters for this life-or-death jumper. The shot will come from 20 feet, so anyone in the game's history is eligible—set it at 25 feet and it eliminates a lot of shooters from the first century of the game. This gesture allows you a wider pool of candidates who will hold your fate—and the ball—in their hands. But, to make things tougher, a defensive player will challenge the shot. The shooter has to fire over someone with a raised arm. In an act of mercy, the madman says the shooter can come off the dribble or receive a pass.

So who do you pick? Don't worry—any player you choose shoots while in the prime of his career (science does incredible things). So maybe you want Rick Mount dribbling into the corner and launching one of his leaping lofters. Maybe you want Bob McAdoo kicking his legs back—after all, as defensive players testified, McAdoo liked it when a defender put a hand in his face. Anyone would take Curry, a player whose shot is so pure that in twenty years we might have a definitive answer to the question of who was the greatest shooter of all time. But how do you turn down Michael Jordan? He might not care about your life, but he'll want to claim the million bucks he's wagered on the outcome. The Bulls put their fate in his jumper so many times, why wouldn't you? And don't forget Larry Bird. If he ever heard about this event he'd trash-talk anyone you picked and you'd instantly regret not going with the Celtics legend. Imagine the fun of Bird launching a shot, and as it's still in the air, your life in the balance, seeing him raise an index finger—or maybe a middle one to your executioner—because he knows it'll fall and he's saved your life.

One jump shot—who do you got? Me? I'd go a different direction. Ignoring the legends, I'd take the shot myself. As I've learned while talking to dozens of memorable shooters for this book, a shooter has to *believe* he's the greatest to ever be included in the discussion *about* the greatest. Every shooter from Kenny Sailors to Kevin Durant has wanted the ball in his hands if a game came down to one jumper. Call it self-confidence or delusion, but writing about the history of the jump shot has made me believe I'd want that one shot. I could take all of the lessons I've learned from talking to the best. I grew up shooting a jumper—might as well go out doing the same. All of the jump shooting legends would understand.

And so with my life in the balance I'd walk onto the court and sneer at the man deciding my fate, letting him know he should have made this a tougher challenge. I'd grab the ball and step into the shot with a left-handed dribble. I'd rise against that defender with the form I learned years ago. I'd keep my elbow locked in, the ball on my fingertips. I'd rise one more time and release the ball, holding a fundamentally perfect follow-through. I'd watch the rim. I'd fall back to earth, my fate resting on the ball's path to the basket. I'd watch and wait—and wish I'd chosen Jerry West.

ACKNOWLEDGMENTS

This will sound cheesy and unbelievable, but it's true: The idea for *Rise and Fire* came to me in a dream. During one of my regular nightly visions of past basketball games, I had a thought: Write a book about the history of the jump shot. Several years later, Bob Miller at Flatiron Books helped turn that fleeting idea into a reality. He enthusiastically supported the book, from his first e-mail expressing interest to an early lunch where he helped me come up with an idea for the structure to his continuing championing through the research and writing. The Flatiron is one of the coolest buildings in New York City, and its tenant Flatiron Books is one of the coolest—and best—publishers for any writer, thanks to Bob and everyone else. Jasmine Faustino is a regular wonder woman at Flatiron, and her editorial insights were sharp and invaluable. She also kept me from going on too many thousand-word detours. It'd be a pleasure to work on another book with her and torment her with more tangents. And thanks to designers Karen Horton and Pete Garceau for their work on the cover, which I loved from the moment I saw it. In PR, thanks to Steven Boriack and Marlena Bittner.

I'm grateful to everyone who agreed to an interview for this book, and a full list is available in the bibliography. Special thanks to several folks who went out of their way to help.

Paul Hoover took time out of his Fourth of July to welcome me to his Ohio home/headquarters.

During my dinner with Troy Lewis in Dayton, Ohio, we started the meal and conversation in the middle of a packed restaurant. Five hours later we were the last ones in the place, and I could have spent many more hours listening to him talk about his career and the insanity of high school basketball in Anderson, Indiana.

When I was in high school, Joel McDonald was a god in Minnesota basketball, and more than twenty years later it was a pleasure reminiscing with him about his career. He also helped me set up interviews with his entire family. Thanks to all the McDonalds for meeting, from New York to Minnesota's Iron Range.

Jimbo Rayl not only had a role in the greatest movie of all time—*Hoosiers*—he also set up my meeting with his parents, Jimmy and Nancy Rayl. Thanks to the Rayls for showing me the Kokomo, Indiana, sites, although I still regret not taking Jimmy up on his idea of getting my wife something from Opalescent Glass.

I introduced myself to Rick Mount cold at his shooting camp, but he graciously opened up his schedule and his home to me just a day later and regaled me with his insights on the jump shot and its influence on his life.

I tracked down Bobby Plump, one of the most famous athletes in Indiana history, by wandering into his financial planning company one late summer afternoon, where I found him in his back office. He invited me over to his restaurant, Plump's Last Shot, for an interview a few days later, and sitting with him talking about his famous jump shot from 1954 was certainly one of the highlights of the book.

Bill Schrage arranged my interview with Kenny Sailors, and also served as a patient, wise guide to the way basketball was played in the 1930s and '40s. He provided me with numerous old stories and pictures that helped me understand Kenny's era and jumper, and also sent a video of Kenny in action.

John Simms and Janice Young at West Virginia State helped me with information on Wendell Smith's college days.

Numerous NBA media relations people lined up interviews and meetings. Jon Steinberg with the Atlanta Hawks helped me chat with Dominique Wilkins. Tad Carper and B. J. Evans with the Cavs arranged my Austin Carr interview. Rob Wilson with the Heat lined up a talk with Bob McAdoo. And Golden State's Raymond Ridder helped me set up an interview with one of the best ever—Jerry West. At Turner Sports, Audrey Brees arranged my Dennis Scott interview.

Ted Green took time from finishing up his documentary on Slick Leonard to talk about his film on Roger Brown during a fun lunch in Indianapolis.

During my time in Georgia, Bruce Kreutzer walked me through the technology at the Mark Price Shooting Lab while talking about his own adventures in the world of jump shooting. Mark Price himself patiently chatted with me before rushing out to finish final preparations for his daughter's wedding.

Dave Hopla met with me during a difficult moment in his professional life, but he allowed me to sit in on his incredible shooting workout and then spent several hours discussing his shot and those of top players around the world. All while we ate good pizza.

Bevon Robin, Jack Ryan, and Keydren Clark are three of the best shooters on New York City's streetball scene, but they're also great basketball minds, and it was a blast not only watching them perform, but talking with them about their careers and the jumper.

Thanks to Matt Zeysing and his staff at the Naismith Memorial Basketball Hall of Fame for their help during a road trip I took to dig through some files. Similarly, Becky Beavers and her staff helped me during my trip to the Indiana Basketball Hall of Fame.

Dean Prator and Ryan Polomski allowed me to sit in on several interviews as they filmed their Raymond Lewis documentary, and it was a pleasure watching them work. I think their finished product will be one of the best basketball films in recent memory.

Jeanette Lietz and her husband, Doug, spent an entire day with me in their Estherville, Iowa, home, talking about Jeanette's teenage years. Jeanette's old high school rival, Denise Rife, did the same in a Wichita restaurant and Starbucks, along with her husband, Dan, sister Dana, and Dana's husband, Jim. In Northern California, John Christgau, just months after losing the bottom part of his leg after an infection threatened his life, took me into his home, served me a great turkey sandwich, and offered up his insights and memories about the early jump shooters he wrote about so brilliantly in *The Origins of the Jump Shot*. In Southern California, Jeff Lensch came down from Edwards Air Force Base to fill me in on the early life of Ray Allen.

Bob Kuska served as a tour guide for the early days of basketball and connected me with the great and entertaining Archie Talley. And thanks to Ray LeBov, a basketball historian who put me in touch with Kuska.

For photos, thanks to Steve Lipofsky, Scott Sawyer at Getty, and Ted Green.

Copy editor extraordinaire Fred Chase provided smart edits and great suggestions, and he only tried a few times to push through propaganda about the 1970s Knicks.

Kevin Van Valkenburg delivered a clutch late assist to the manuscript, and I hope to return the favor when he writes a book about Tiger Woods's nineteenth major championship victory.

Just as they did on my book *Keeping the Faith*, my parents, Pat and Cees Fury, let me use one of their vehicles as I spent a few days traveling around the Midwest. But this time they also helped with research on some of the jump shot pioneers, and they unearthed a few of the facts in the book's early chapters.

I bounced some ideas off of my uncles Mike Fury and Jerry Fury, and in addition picked up lessons from them during countless games at my grandpa's farm. My uncle Steve Brake helpfully answered a farming question that popped up as I finished the book.

Finally, thanks to my wife, Louise Fury, who is also my agent and managed to sell this book despite being a South African who doesn't know the difference between a jump shot and a dunk. She makes my dreams, about basketball books and everything else, come true.

BIBLIOGRAPHY

BOOKS

Allen, Forrest C. *Better Basketball: Technique, Tactics, Tales.* New York: Whittlesey House, 1937.

Ballard, Chris. *The Art of a Beautiful Game: The Thinking Fan's Tour of the NBA.* New York: Simon & Schuster, 2009.

Bird, Larry. *Drive: The Story of My Life.* With Bob Ryan. New York: Doubleday, 1989.

Caponi-Tabery, Gena. *Jump for Joy: Jazz, Basketball, and Black Culture in 1930s America.* Amherst: University of Massachusetts Press, 2008.

Christgau, John. *The Origins of the Jump Shot: Eight Men Who Shook the World of Basketball.* Lincoln: University of Nebraska Press, 1999.

Fox, Stephen. *Big Leagues: Professional Baseball, Football, & Basketball in National Memory.* Lincoln: University of Nebraska Press, 1998.

Guffey, Greg. *The Golden Age of Indiana High School Basketball.* Bloomington, Ind.: Quarry Books/Indiana University Press, 2006.

Hobson, Howard: *Scientific Basketball.* New York: Prentice-Hall, 1949.

Hoose, Phillip M. *Hoosiers: The Fabulous Basketball Life of Indiana.* Indianapolis: Guild Press of Indiana, 1995.

Hoover, Paul. *Pro Shooting Secrets: The Only Shooting System That Unlocks the Hidden Truth Behind Today's Greatest Shooters.* E-book, Columbus, Ohio: Paul Hoover, 2014.

Hopla, Dave. *Basketball Shooting.* Champaign, Ill.: Human Kinetics, 2012.

Johnson, Earvin "Magic". *My Life.* With William Novak. New York: Fawcett Books, 1992.

Krenz, Joel B. *Gopher State Greatness: A Thirty-Year History of Minnesota Boys High School Basketball.* Richtman's Printing, 1984.

Krider, Dave. *Indiana High School Basketball's 20 Most Dominant Players*. Bloomington, Ind.: Rooftop Publishing, 2007.

Kriegel, Mark. *Pistol: The Life of Pete Maravich*. New York: Free Press, 2007.

Lazenby, Roland. *Jerry West: The Life and Legend of a Basketball Icon*. New York: Ballantine Books, 2009.

Mallozzi, Vincent M. *Asphalt Gods: An Oral History of the Rucker Tournament*. New York: Doubleday, 2003.

McElwain, Max. *The Only Dance in Iowa: A History of Six-Player Girls' Basketball*. Lincoln: University of Nebraska Press, 2004.

Miller, Ralph. *Ralph Miller: Spanning the Game*. With Bud Withers. Champaign, Ill.: Sagamore Publishing, 1990.

Peterson, Robert W. *Cages to Jump Shots: Pro Basketball's Early Years*. New York and Oxford: Oxford University Press, 1990.

Pieratt, Marty, and Ken Honeywell. *Bobby Plump: Last of the Small Town Heroes*. Indianapolis: Good Morning Publishing, 1997.

Pluto, Terry. *Loose Balls: The Short, Wild Life of the American Basketball Association*. New York: Simon & Schuster, 1990.

Porter, David L., ed. *Basketball: A Biographical Dictionary*. Westport, Conn.: Greenwood Press, 2005.

Sachare, Alex. *When Seconds Count: Counting Down Basketball's Greatest Finishes*. Champaign, Ill.: SportsMasters, 1999.

Sharman, Bill. *Sharman on Basketball Shooting*. Englewood Cliffs, N.J.: Prentice-Hall, 1965.

Sutton, Stan. *100 Things Hoosiers Fans Should Know & Do Before They Die*. Chicago: Triumph Books, 2012.

Tarkanian, Jerry. *Runnin' Rebel: Shark Tales of "Extra Benefits," Frank Sinatra, and Winning It All*. With Dan Wetzel. New York: Sports Publishing, 2005.

Washburn, Jeff. *Tales from the Indiana High School Basketball Locker Room: A Collection of the State's Greatest Basketball Stories Ever Told*. With Ben Smith. New York: Sports Publishing, 2013.

Wendel, Tim. *Buffalo, Home of the Braves*. Traverse City, Mich.: SunBear Press, 2009.

West, Jerry, and Jonathan Coleman. *West by West: My Charmed, Tormented Life.* New York: Little, Brown, 2011.

Wideman, John Edgar. *Hoop Roots: Basketball, Race, and Love.* Boston: Houghton Mifflin, 2001.

Wolf, David. *Foul! The Connie Hawkins Story.* New York: Warner Paperback Library Edition, 1972.

NEWSPAPERS, MAGAZINES, AND ONLINE STORIES

Albom, Mitch. "Today's Thought: Bird's Greatest Hits May Be Yet to Come." *Detroit Free Press,* June 1, 1986. http://mitchalbom.com/d/journalism/193/todays -thought-birds-greatest-hits-may-be-yet-come.

Allen, Percy. "The Sonics' Ray Allen: Developing a Shooter's Touch." *Seattle Times,* February 15, 2004. http://community.seattletimes.nwsource.com/archive/?date =20040215&slug=rayallen15.

Alvarez, Lizette, and Michael Wilson. "Up and Out of New York's Projects." *New York Times,* May 29, 2009. http://www.nytimes.com/2009/05/31/nyregion/31projects .html?pagewanted=all.

Anderson, Dave. "Sports of The Times; Cousy and the All-Time N.B.A. Team." *New York Times,* November 2, 1980. http://query.nytimes.com/mem/archive/pdf?res=9 D0DE0DA1038E432A25751C0A9679D94619FD6CF.

——. "Sports of The Times; How Ethiopia Touched a Poet." *New York Times,* February 3, 1985. http://www.nytimes.com/1985/02/03/sports/sports-of-the-times -how-ethiopia-touched-a-poet.html.

Angelopolous, Angelo. "Rayl Splinters Cage Marks as Newest Hoosier Hotshot." *Sporting News,* February 7, 1962.

Angelopolous, Jimmie. "Cheers Mounting for Purdue's Rick." *Sporting News,* January 13, 1968.

Araton, Harvey. "Heat's Allen Knows All About Hitting Big 3-Pointers." *New York Times,* June 19, 2013. http://www.nytimes.com/2013/06/20/sports/basketball/heats -allen-knows-all-about-big-3s.html?_r=0.

——. "Sports of The Times; McAdoo's Low Profile Was Higher Calling." *New York Times,* June 16, 2006. http://www.nytimes.com/2006/06/16/sports/basketball /16araton.early.html?_r=0.

Archdeacon, Tom. "Roger Brown Finally Gets His Due." *Dayton Daily News,* February 27, 2013. http://www.daytondailynews.com/news/sports/basketball/roger -brown-finally-gets-his-due/nWbw4/.

Archibald, John. "20,000 Points Locked in Vault—Will Banker Pettit Decide to Quit?" *Sporting News,* November 28, 1964.

Armour, Terry. "United Against the Center: Bulls Still Miss Stadium." *Chicago Tribune,* January 6, 1997. http://articles.chicagotribune.com/1997-01-06/sports /9701060069_1_bulls-united-center-scottie-pippen.

Associated Press. "76ers Cry Foul." *Danville Bee,* November 22, 1969. http://www .newspapers.com/image/46693393.

Associated Press. "ABL's 3-Point Bucket Idea Might Spread." *Post-Crescent,* April 15, 1962. http://www.newspapers.com/image/22773344.

Associated Press. "Ailing McAdoo hits 41." *Kokomo Tribune,* December 18, 1978. http://www.newspapers.com/image/2572177.

Associated Press. "All-Star Prep Squads Chosen." *Miami Daily News-Record,* March 21, 1955. http://www.newspapers.com/image/30222386/.

Associated Press. "Austin Carr Surprise First Pick in NBA Draft." *Warren Times-Mirror and Observer,* March 30, 1971. http://www.newspapers.com/image /51394578.

Associated Press. "Basketball Hall of Fame Selects 7." *Gettysburg Times,* February 22, 1982. http://www.newspapers.com/image/46213079/.

Associated Press. "Basketball Hall of Fame: Thomas Leads Strong Class." *Boca Raton News,* October 13, 2000. https://news.google.com/newspapers?nid=1291&dat =20001013&id=6ilUAAAAIBAJ&sjid=Y44DAAAAIBAJ&pg=5728,2892083&hl =en.

Associated Press. "Bevo's 113 'Unbelievable' to Frank Selvy, Nation's No. 1 Basketball Scoring Champion." *Oneonta Star,* February 4, 1954. http://www.newspapers .com/image/47277642.

Associated Press. "Bird's 48 Propels Celts Over Blazers." *Sarasota Herald-Tribune,* January 28, 1985. https://news.google.com/newspapers?nid=1755&dat=19850128 &id=GXAeAAAAIBAJ&sjid=_mgEAAAAIBAJ&pg=6560,3043156&hl=en.

Associated Press. "'Blue Collar' Havlicek, Jones Enter NBA Hall." *Bloomington Pantagraph,* May 1, 1984. http://www.newspapers.com/image/72880647.

Associated Press. "Blugold, Kentucky State Shootout No. 2 Tonight Is for NAIA Crown." *Ironwood Daily Globe,* March 18, 1972. http://www.newspapers.com/image /55236461.

Associated Press. "Boston Slips Past Philadelphia 109–107 to Win Series." *Danville Register,* April 6, 1962. http://www.newspapers.com/image/23274861/.

Associated Press. "Carr Gives 50-Point Show, Notre Dame Beats Kentucky." *Monroe News-Star,* December 30, 1970. http://www.newspapers.com/image/32275750/.

Associated Press. "Celtics Even Series With 119–105 Win, Home Tomorrow." *Portsmouth Herald,* April 17, 1962. http://www.newspapers.com/image/56522090.

Associated Press. "Celtics Tie Lakers, 2–2, Via Jones' Dramatic Shot." *Fitchburg Sentinel,* April 30, 1969. http://www.newspapers.com/image/45351871.

Associated Press. "Claim Dwight Lamar Already Is a Better Player Than Pete Maravich in His College Days." *Gettysburg Times,* February 15, 1972. https://news .google.com/newspapers?nid=2202&dat=19720215&id=OupTAAAAIBAJ&sjid =BjkNAAAAIBAJ&pg=2328,3276326&hl=en.

Associated Press. "Cousy Blasts the Jump Shot; Demands Aggressive Players." *Lewiston Daily Sun,* March 22, 1963. https://news.google.com/newspapers?nid=1928&dat =19630322&id=xhYgAAAAIBAJ&sjid=X2YFAAAAIBAJ&pg=1623,2053185&hl=en.

Associated Press. "Denise Hits 51 in Opener." *Des Moines Register,* October 20, 1969. http://www.newspapers.com/image/8674366/.

Associated Press. "Denise Long Sought by Warriors." *Colorado Springs Gazette,* May 11, 1969. http://newspaperarchive.com/us/colorado/colorado-springs/colorado -springs-gazette/1969/05-11/page-27.

Associated Press. "Despite Complaints, NBA Says Ball Better." *Washington Post,* October 3, 2006. http://www.washingtonpost.com/wp-dyn/content/article/2006/10 /03/AR2006100301190_pf.html.

Associated Press. "Dream World Long Gone for Denise Long." *Estherville Daily News,* February 23, 1972. http://www.newspapers.com/image/588480/.

Associated Press. "Duke Coach: 3-Point Shot to Lead to Chaos." *Santa Cruz Sentinel,* April 3, 1986. http://www.newspapers.com/image/70663232.

Associated Press. "Ex-Tech Coach a Caddy." *Gadsden Times,* July 9, 1982. https:// news.google.com/newspapers?nid=1891&dat=19820709&id=56cfAAAAIBAJ &sjid=WdYEAAAAIBAJ&pg=958,1398511&hl=en.

Associated Press. "Fulks Breaks BAA 1-Game Point Mark." *Kokomo Tribune*, February 11, 1949. http://www.newspapers.com/image/2416431.

Associated Press. "Fulks Sets Pro Cage Point Mark." *Dixon Evening Telegraph*, April 3, 1947. http://www.newspapers.com/image/7564036.

Associated Press. "Girl Intrigued by Draft Idea." *Bridgeport Post*, June 5, 1969. http://www.newspapers.com/image/60694004/.

Associated Press. "Glass Backboards Newest Allen Beef." *Valley Morning Star*, March 15, 1942. http://www.newspapers.com/image/51445574.

Associated Press. "Glenn Roberts Is Wizard Shooting Basketball Goals." *Danville Bee*, January 12, 1933. http://www.newspapers.com/image/45706864.

Associated Press. "Greer's Smile Reveals Feelings on Point Mark." *Pottstown Mercury*, February 2, 1971. www.newspapers.com/image/42376544.

Associated Press. "Hawks' Pettit Fractures Arm, Will Play With Cast." *Milwaukee Sentinel*, February 17, 1957. https://news.google.com/newspapers?nid=1368&dat=19570217&id=6dUpAAAAIBAJ&sjid=5g8EAAAAIBAJ&pg=4273,1646683&hl=en.

Associated Press. "High School Girl Picked by Warriors." *Spokesman-Review*, May 8, 1969. https://news.google.com/newspapers?nid=1314&dat=19690508&id=CrZWAAAAIBAJ&sjid=fukDAAAAIBAJ&pg=5709,3070436&hl=en.

Associated Press. "Hot Shooting Loyola Wins." *Benton Harbor News-Palladium*, December 28, 1962. http://www.newspapers.com/image/21210051.

Associated Press. "Inventor of Glass Backboard Fighting for Job as Teacher." *Lewiston Evening Journal*, March 31, 1950. https://news.google.com/newspapers?nid=1913&dat=19500331&id=HokpAAAAIBAJ&sjid=NWcFAAAAIBAJ&pg=3742,8084660&hl=en.

Associated Press. "Jury Out on Three-Point Basket." *Palm Beach Post-Times*, October 27, 1979. https://news.google.com/newspapers?nid=1964&dat=19791027&id=e6lUAAAAIBAJ&sjid=lzsNAAAAIBAJ&pg=3433,3451044&hl=en.

Associated Press. "Kentucky State Whips Eau Claire." *Tucson Daily Citizen*, March 20, 1972. http://www.newspapers.com/image/18894895.

Associated Press. "Lamar Keeps Winning Converts." *Reading Eagle*, January 11, 1972. https://news.google.com/newspapers?nid=1955&dat=19720111&id=Z6QhAAAAIBAJ&sjid=1pkFAAAAIBAJ&pg=2911,311584&hl=en.

Associated Press. "Lamar Playing for Pay?" *Anniston Star,* February 11, 1973. http://www.newspapers.com/image/19384478/.

Associated Press. "Long Practices Pay Off for Bernard King." *Kentucky New Era,* December 26, 1984. https://news.google.com/newspapers?nid=266&dat=19841226&id=xQksAAAAIBAJ&sjid=cG0FAAAAIBAJ&pg=2937,7674855&hl=en.

Associated Press. "'Lucky Old Sun' Unlucky For Brandeis Hoop Team." *Newport Daily News,* January 4, 1954. http://www.newspapers.com/image/59278025.

Associated Press. "Marines Trounce Dow Chemical." *Ogden Standard Examiner,* March 8, 1944. http://www.newspapers.com/image/27101314.

Associated Press. "McAdoo Has Hot Hand." *Reading Eagle,* November 27, 1974. https://news.google.com/newspapers?nid=1955&dat=19741127&id=7Q0rAAAAIBAJ&sjid=LZoFAAAAIBAJ&pg=2475,4124970&hl=en.

Associated Press. "McAdoo Scores 49." *Reading Eagle,* January 22, 1975. https://news.google.com/newspapers?nid=1955&dat=19750122&id=tQ5XAAAAIBAJ&sjid=MkMNAAAAIBAJ&pg=4409,3571724&hl=en.

Associated Press. "McAdoo's 50 Keys Win." *Pittsburgh Post-Gazette,* April 19, 1975. https://news.google.com/newspapers?nid=1129&dat=19750419&id=7KlRAAAAIBAJ&sjid=h20DAAAAIBAJ&pg=5603,2330573&hl=en.

Associated Press. "Mikan Issued Challenge by Joe Fulks." *Nebraska State Journal,* January 27, 1949. http://www.newspapers.com/image/42103489.

Associated Press. "Milan Opens Gates for Victory Celebration." *Kokomo Tribune,* March 22, 1954. http://www.newspapers.com/image/17823115.

Associated Press. "Missouri Cager Masters Shot Defying All Legal Guarding." *Moberly Monitor-Index,* February 18, 1932. http://www.newspapers.com/image/19562690.

Associated Press. "NBA Continues to Debate 3-Point Goal." *Kokomo Tribune,* October 27, 1979. http://www.newspapers.com/image/2730588/.

Associated Press. "'Out-of-Shape' Wizard a Near-Perfect Shooter." *Lawrence Journal-World,* January 14, 2008. https://news.google.com/newspapers?nid=2199&dat=20080114&id=epcyAAAAIBAJ&sjid=sOcFAAAAIBAJ&pg=6260,2124500&hl=en.

Associated Press. "Philadelphia Cager Sets Scoring Mark." *Times Recorder,* February 11, 1949. http://www.newspapers.com/image/19394223.

Associated Press. "Race in Big Six Will Be Settled at K.U. Tonight." *Maryville Daily Forum,* February 27, 1932. http://www.newspapers.com/image/87479065.

Associated Press. "Rapid Rick Goes for Warm Miami." *Kokomo Tribune,* July 3, 1966. http://www.newspapers.com/image/44753652/.

Associated Press. "Rick Mount Guns Down Penn in ECAC Tourney." *Delaware County Daily Times,* December 30, 1969. http://www.newspapers.com/image /22402775.

Associated Press. "Selvy Almost Unanimous Choice for All-America." *New London Evening Day,* February 26, 1954. https://news.google.com/newspapers?nid=1915 &dat=19540226&id=9GApAAAAIBAJ&sjid=1nIFAAAAIBAJ&pg=1858,4271236 &hl=en.

Associated Press. "Spiders Play With Caution to Lick Wasps." *Danville Bee,* February 14, 1935. http://www.newspapers.com/image/13185323.

Associated Press. "Three-Point Basket Won't Help Colleges, Says Indiana's Knight." *Los Angeles Times,* April 20, 1986. http://articles.latimes.com/1986-04-20/sports/sp -1190_1_college-students.

Associated Press. "Three-Pointers Fall Short of Final Two: Banks Scores 38 the Long Way, but Indiana Beats UNLV." *Los Angeles Times,* March 29, 1987. http://articles .latimes.com/1987-03-29/sports/sp-990_1_banks-scores.

Associated Press. "Two Players Break 50 Points as Ole Miss Outguns LSU in 'Unbelievable' Shoot-Out." *Lexington Herald-Leader,* March 6, 1989.

Associated Press. "Use Glass Backboards at State Net Tourney." *Huntington Press,* March 12, 1926. http://www.newspapers.com/image/40264328.

Associated Press. "Warsaw Upsets Top-Ranked Michigan City Rogers." *Kokomo Tribune,* March 18, 1984. http://newspaperarchive.com/us/indiana/kokomo/kokomo -tribune/1984/03-18/page-22.

Associated Press. "West: 'We Blew It.'" *Tri-City Herald* (Richmond, WA), April 30, 1969.

Baker, Chris. "Supply and Demand Is Working Even in These Times of Tight Money." *Los Angeles Times,* June 7, 1991. http://articles.latimes.com/1991-06-07 /sports/sp-186_1_tight-demand-times.

Banks, Lacy J. "Pure Shooter Bird Preaches Practice." *Chicago Sun-Times,* February 5, 1988. http://www.highbeam.com/doc/1P2-3868920.html.

Barnes, David. "Anderson Guns Down Marion, Blackmon." *Kokomo Tribune,* March 27 1983. http://newspaperarchive.com/us/indiana/kokomo/kokomo-tribune /1983/03-27/page-32.

Barry, Jack. "Celts Rewrite Book as Four-Time NBA Kings." *Sporting News,* April 25, 1962.

———. "Charmin' Sharman All-Sports Star Man." *Sporting News,* March 19, 1958.

———. "Sam Jones—Celts' Successor to Ol' Pro Cousy." *Sporting News,* February 8, 1964.

———. "Will Fulks' Point Mark Be Broken?" *Sporting News,* February 11, 1959.

Baumgartner, Stan. "Fulks, Relaxed as Rag, Wiping Up BAA Again." *Sporting News,* January 28, 1948.

Bell, Daryl. "Prep Star Scott Can Find Flaws With Idols, Self." *Richmond Times-Dispatch,* December 1, 1986.

Benner, Bill. "A Pair of Itchy Trigger Fingers." *Sporting News,* March 21, 1988.

Berkow, Ira. "Basketball; A Hard Case From the Streets Makes Good." *New York Times,* December 3, 2003. http://www.nytimes.com/2003/12/03/sports/basketball -a-hard-case-from-the-streets-makes-good.html.

———. "The Mysterious Moves of Bernard King." *New York Times,* December 24, 1984. http://www.nytimes.com/1984/12/24/sports/the-mysterious-moves-of-ber nard-king.html.

———. "Royals Oscar Robertson—Best Ever In Basketball." *Chillicothe Constitution-Tribune,* January 4, 1968. http://www.newspapers.com/image/17397477.

———. "Sports of The Times; Bernard King of the Bullets." *New York Times,* November 3, 1987. http://www.nytimes.com/1987/11/03/sports/sports-of-the-times -bernard-king-of-the-bullets.html.

Bilovsky, Frank. "A Doormat No More—It's Penn the Cage Power." *Sporting News,* January 23, 1971.

Birge, Jerry. "Bedford Wins Washington Regional Crown." *Dubois County Daily Herald,* March 11, 1974. http://www.newspapers.com/image/32742456.

———. "Keeping Score." *Dubois County Daily Herald,* January 22, 1974. http://www .newspapers.com/image/32807147.

———. "Keeping Score." *Dubois County Daily Herald*, January 30, 1974. http://www
.newspapers.com/image/32808203.

———. "Keeping Score." *Dubois County Daily Herald*, March 7, 1974. http://www
.newspapers.com/image/32742355/.

———. "Keeping Score." *Dubois County Daily Herald*, March 27, 1974. http://www
.newspapers.com/image/32743517/.

Blytheville (ARK) Courier News. "Hawks (Pettit) Hang Celtics, Take Crown." April 14,
1958. http://newspaperarchive.com/us/arkansas/blytheville/blytheville-courier
-news/1958/04-14/page-9.

Bondy, Filip. "Stranger in Paradise." New York *Daily News,* April 6, 1995. http://www
.nydailynews.com/archives/sports/stranger-paradise-article-1.686461.

Bouchette, Ed. "Keady's Boilermakers No. 2 in Polls, but No. 3 in Indiana." *Pittsburgh Post-Gazette,* March 7, 1988. https://news.google.com/newspapers?nid=1129
&dat=19880307&id=i9RRAAAAIBAJ&sjid=8m0DAAAAIBAJ&pg=6610,1958757
&hl=en.

Bradburd, Rus. "Still a Sharp Shooter." *Charleston Daily Mail,* November 21, 2007.
http://www.highbeam.com/doc/1P2-11299800.html.

Bradley, John Ed. "An Accidental Hero Beryl Shipley, 1926–2011." *Sports Illustrated,*
May 2, 2011. http://www.si.com/vault/2011/05/02/106063234/an-accidental-hero
-beryl-shipley-1926—2011.

Bradley, Mark. "Appreciation: Wilkins Worked to Earn Our Love." *Atlanta Journal-
Constitution,* April 1, 2006.

Bradley, Michael. "All He Did Was Win." *Slam,* February 25, 2013. http://www
.slamonline.com/nba/sam-jones-all-he-did-was-win/.

———. "Leading Man." *Slam,* October 8, 2013. http://www.slamonline.com/college
-hs/college/travis-grant-points-ncaa-basketball/.

Breslin, Jimmy. "College Basketball Jumping Away From Form and Finesse." *Gastonia
Gazette,* February 13, 1956. http://www.newspapers.com/image/4312027.

Briggs, David. "Tiger Might Have Invented Jumper: Cooper Often Regarded as Shot
Innovator." *Columbia Daily Tribune,* April 24, 2011. http://www.columbiatribune
.com/sports/mu_basketball/tiger-might-have-invented-jumper/article_2be3ad7c
-7037-5fc3-bcc2-82e5c7c665d6.html.

Brown, C. L. "They Made 'Magic' in Frankfort, KY." *Louisville Courier-Journal,* March 17, 2008.

Bullard, Charles. "Denise to Quit Basketball." *Des Moines Register,* June 30, 1970. http://www.newspapers.com/image/18968351/.

Burnes, Bob. "Bob Pettit: NBA Answer to Musial." *Sporting News,* February 15, 1964.

Butler, Tom. "No Alarm—Rick Beats the Clock." *Wisconsin State Journal,* March 16, 1969.

Caple, Jim. "Real-Life 'Hoosiers' and Their Fabled Gym." ESPN.com, June 1, 2010. http://sports.espn.go.com/travel/columns/story?id=5219787.

Carr, Howie, and Mark Whicker. "Nissalke: 'McAdoo Is Super.'" *Daily Tar Heel,* February 9, 1972. http://www.newspapers.com/image/67799308/.

Casady, Fred. "Spotlite of Sports." *Anderson Daily Bulletin,* March 22, 1954. http://www.newspapers.com/image/10970776.

Chapin, Dwight. "Hank Changed Entire Game." *Spokesman-Review,* April 7, 1976. https://news.google.com/newspapers?id=piBOAAAAIBAJ&sjid=cu0DAAAAI BAJ&pg=6873%2C2563681.

———. "Jerry, Lakers Finally Made It: West Was Wrong—Glory Knocked Again." *Milwaukee Sentinel,* May 9, 1972. https://news.google.com/newspapers?nid=1368 &dat=19720509&id=boZRAAAAIBAJ&sjid=XBEEAAAAIBAJ&pg=7234,2455595 &hl=en.

Chicago Sun-Times. "Austin Carr's Legacy." March 15, 1987. http://www.highbeam .com/doc/1P2-3815576.html.

Christopulos, Mike. "McGuire's Lament: 'Just Wasn't Meant to Be.'" *Milwaukee Senti-nel,* March 17, 1969. https://news.google.com/newspapers?nid=1368&dat=19690317 &id=AqpRAAAAIBAJ&sjid=fBEEAAAAIBAJ&pg=7164,3765115&hl=en.

Collins, Bob. "Shootin' the Stars." *Indianapolis Star,* February 8, 1959. Accessed from Jimmy Rayl's file at Indiana Basketball Hall of Fame.

Columbia Spectator (Columbia University). "Columbia Downs Fordham, 73-58, Under Changed Basketball Rules." *Columbia Spectator,* February 9, 1945. http:// spectatorarchive.library.columbia.edu/cgi-bin/columbia?a=d&d=cs19450209-01 &e=——en-20—1—txt-txIN——#.

Coyle, Vince. "Cubettes Bow to Everly, 105-79." *Ames Daily Tribune,* March 13, 1968. http://newspaperarchive.com/us/iowa/ames/ames-daily-tribune/1968/03-13/page -15.

———. "Long Nets 93; UW Wins 114-66." *Ames Daily Tribune,* March 14, 1969. http://newspaperarchive.com/us/iowa/ames/ames-daily-tribune/1968/03-14/page -17.

Crowe, Jerry. "Crowe's Nest; How Basketball Became Three-Dimensional." *Los Angeles Times,* May 6, 2008. http://articles.latimes.com/2008/may/06/sports/sp-crowe6.

Currence, Stubby. "Pedie Jackson Pilots Emory and Henry Wasps to 1934 Virginia Cage Title." *Bluefield Daily Telegraph,* March 4, 1934. http://www.newspapers.com /image/13180580.

Curtright, Guy. "A Scoring 'Machine.'" *Atlanta Journal-Constitution,* January 23, 2000.

Daley, Arthur. "Sports of The Times; Confessions of a Coach." *New York Times,* October 21, 1954. http://query.nytimes.com/mem/archive/pdf?res=9502E7DE113 FE33BBC4951DFB667838F649EDE.

Deford, Frank. "Basketball's Bright Star in Indiana." *Sports Illustrated,* February 14, 1966. http://www.si.com/vault/1966/02/14/608095/basketballs-bright-star-in-indiana.

———. "The Last Drop in the Bucket." *Sports Illustrated,* May 12, 1969. http://www .si.com/vault/1969/05/12/610773/the-last-drop-in-the-bucket.

———. "Shooting for Three." *Sports Illustrated,* November 27, 1967. http://www.si .com/vault/1967/11/27/609758/shooting-for-three.

———. "A Teddy Bear's Picnic." *Sports Illustrated,* February 7, 1972. http://www.si .com/vault/1972/02/07/565942/a-teddy-bears-picnic.

Delaney, Ed. "Arizin's Famed Jump Shot Was Discovered by Accident." *Sporting News,* December 13, 1950.

DelNagro, Michael. "McAdoo About Something Boffo in Buffalo." *Sports Illustrated,* March 18, 1974. http://www.si.com/vault/1974/03/18/619274/mcadoo -about-something-boffo-in-buffalo.

Denlinger, Kenneth. "Machine Apt Name for Travis Grant." *Milwaukee Sentinel,* March 17, 1972. https://news.google.com/newspapers?nid=1368&dat=19720317&id =-W1QAAAAIBAJ&sjid=sxAEAAAAIBAJ&pg=7084,712967&hl=en.

Denny, Dick. "Brown the Unsung Ace of Fast-Stepping Pacers." *Sporting News,* January 31, 1970.

———. "Rick Mount: He's Tireless and Terrific." *Sporting News,* February 22, 1969.

Des Moines Register. "Denise Long 'Hoops' It Up With Johnny Carson on TV." May 21, 1969. http://newspaperarchive.com/us/iowa/des-moines/des-moines-register/1969/05-21/page-14.

DeSimone, Bonnie. "On or Off the Court, Mark Price Likes to Lead, Not Follow . . . and Chart His Own Course." *Plain Dealer,* February 13, 1994.

Deveney, Sean. "Olympics 2012: Team USA Not the Only Ones Struggling to Find Range at Basketball Arena." *Sporting News,* last modified July 30, 2012. http://www.sportingnews.com/olympics/story/2012-07-30/olympics-2012-team-usa-basketball-results-schedule-kevin-love-france-tunisia.

Effrat, Louis. "18,316 See Wyoming Quintet Beat St. John's in Overtime." *New York Times,* April 2, 1943. http://query.nytimes.com/gst/abstract.html?res=9F05E2DB1730E53BBC4A53DFB2668388659EDE.

———. "Columbia Defeats Fordham, 73 to 58." *New York Times,* February 8, 1945. http://query.nytimes.com/gst/abstract.html?res=9D02EED6173FE731A2575BC0A9649C946493D6CF.

Eggert, Bill. "Attucks Brings City Its First State Title." *Indianapolis Times,* March 20, 1955. Accessed from Oscar Robertson's file at Indiana Basketball Hall of Fame.

Eifling, Sam. "Bill Sharman Became a Legend for (and by) Thanking Everyone." *Deadspin,* October 26, 2013. http://deadspin.com/the-late-bill-sharman-became-a-legend-for-and-by-thanki-1452811277.

Eisenberg, Jeff. "No. 3 in The Untouchables: Frank Selvy Scores 100 Points in a Game." *The Dagger: College Basketball Blog,* June 13, 2012. http://sports.yahoo.com/blogs/ncaab-the-dagger/no-3-untouchables-frank-selvy-scores-100-points-130024684—ncaab.html.

Elderkin, Phil. "Flashy Forward Bernard King a Leading Depositor in NBA Baskets." *Christian Science Monitor,* November 5, 1984. http://www.csmonitor.com/1984/1105/110505.html.

———. "Sam Jones Latest to Crash Superstar Status." *Sporting News,* February 13, 1965.

———. "Sam Slipping—Poor Celtics Pay the Price." *Sporting News,* February 15, 1969.

Ellis, Gary. "Verbum Dei Gets Another CIF Title." *Independent Press-Telegram* (Long Beach, CA), March 14, 1971. http://www.newspapers.com/image/30504431.

Enright, James. "Footnote to Mark Rayl Point Binge." *Sporting News,* February 14, 1962.

———. "Rayl Real Catch as Indiana Cager." *Sporting News,* January 18, 1961.

Evans, Bob. "Sideline View." *Clovis News-Journal,* March 1, 1970. http://www.newspapers.com/image/7285447/.

Farmer, Neal. "Did *Hoosiers* Inspire Indiana to Title?" *Houston Chronicle,* April 2, 1987.

Farmer, Sam. "He Missed a Shot at Changing NBA History." *Los Angeles Times,* June 17, 2010. http://articles.latimes.com/2010/jun/17/sports/la-sp-0617-frank-selvy-20100617-20.

Fehrman, Craig. "The End of an Era in Indiana." *New York Times,* March 24, 2012. http://www.nytimes.com/2012/03/25/sports/farewell-to-wigwam-and-heyday-of-high-school-basketball-in-indiana.html?_r=0.

Feinberg, Paul. "The Phantom." *Slam,* January 1995. http://www.slamonline.com/nba/original-old-school-the-phantom/.

Felser, Larry. "McAdoo Can Do It All, but Who's Watching?" *Sporting News,* January 11, 1975.

———. "Unheralded Bob McAdoo Scourge of the NBA." *Sporting News,* March 23, 1974.

Finch, Frank. "Ex-Point King Selvy Sparks Lakers' Defense." *Sporting News,* February 14, 1962.

Finn, Gerry. "Solving the Sam Jones Riddle." *Springfield Union,* May 4, 1984. Accessed from Sam Jones's file at Naismith Memorial Basketball Hall of Fame.

———. "Will Sam Jones Turn Back on Hall, Too?" *Springfield Union,* February 28, 1984. Accessed from Sam Jones's file at Naismith Memorial Basketball Hall of Fame.

Finney, Peter. "NBA Hall of Famer Bob Pettit Has Seen Coaching Searches Up-Close Before." *Times-Picayune,* May 26, 2010. http://www.nola.com/hornets/index.ssf/2010/05/nba_hall_of_famer_bob_pettit_h.html.

Fitzgerald, Ray. "Super Shot Pops Hall." *Boston Globe,* April 25, 1976. Accessed from Bill Sharman's file at Naismith Memorial Basketball Hall of Fame.

Ford, Bob. "The Goal Rush." *Kokomo Tribune,* December 19, 1958. http://www .newspapers.com/image/41843016/.

———. "Mount Exciting! Top Draw Since Kats' Jimmy Rayl." *Kokomo Tribune,* November 24, 1965. http://www.newspapers.com/image/44784486.

———. "The Skinny Kid Gave Us Thrills." *Kokomo Tribune,* November 20, 1983. http://newspaperarchive.com/us/indiana/kokomo/kokomo-tribune/1983/11-20 /page-17.

Fried, Joshua. "Shooting Star: Hank Luisetti scored big, and changed the game." *Stanford Alumni Magazine,* March/April 2003. https://alumni.stanford.edu/get/page /magazine/article/?article_id=36959.

Friedman, David. "Hal Greer: Productive, Consistent, and Durable." *Hoop,* January 2006. http://20secondtimeout.blogspot.com/2009/06/hal-greer-productive -consistent-and.html.

Frisk, Bob. "Joe Fulks—a Superstar in Simple, Gentle Times." *Daily Herald,* March 26, 1976. http://www.newspapers.com/image/44589311.

Gold, Ed. "On the Sidelines." *Columbia Spectator,* February 9, 1945. http:// spectatorarchive.library.columbia.edu/cgi-bin/columbia?a=d&d=cs19450209-01 &e=——en-20—1—txt-txIN——#.

Goldpaper, Sam. "N.B.A. Leaning to 3-Point Goal." *New York Times,* June 13, 1979.

Goldstein, Joel. "Explosion II: The Molinas Period." *ESPN Classic,* special to ESPN.com, November 19, 2003. http://espn.go.com/classic/s/basketball _scandals_molinas.html.

Gordon, Devin. "Attack of the Killer Basketball!" *Newsweek,* December 17, 2006. http://www.newsweek.com/attack-killer-basketball-105827.

Gould, Herb. "Carr's 61: It All Fell in Place." *Chicago Sun-Times,* March 15, 1987.

Grayson, Harry. "Jump Shot Leaves Fans Yawning as Cage Scores Mount." *Rhinelander Daily News,* January 24, 1957. http://www.newspapers.com/image/10310444.

———. "This Is the Era of Offensive Basketball, and Furman's Frank Selvy Epitomizes Best." *Santa Cruz Sentinel,* February 16, 1954. http://www.newspapers.com /image/58954072.

Gustin, Carl. "Blackmon vs. Lewis." *Pharos-Tribune,* March 28, 1983. http://www
.newspapers.com/image/13513535.

Gwinnett Daily Post. "Shooting Lab Mixes Technology, Basketball." June 30, 2007.
http://www.gwinnettdailypost.com/news/2007/jun/30/shooting-lab-mixes
-technology-basketball/.

Hafner, Dan. "Baylor, West Sparking Speedy Laker Voyage." *Sporting News,* December 13, 1961.

———. "Nimble West Outshines Hoop Giants." *Sporting News,* January 30, 1965.

Hager, Don. "Greer-the-Vet Key for 76ers." *Charleston Daily Mail,* February 16,
1966. http://www.newspapers.com/image/36771554.

Hall, John. "Luisetti Record Falls; SC's Sharman Betters Yardley by One Point."
Stanford Daily, March 6, 1950. http://stanforddailyarchive.com/cgi-bin/stanford?a
=d&d=stanford19500306-01.2.19&e=———en-20—1—txt-txIN———.

Hannen, John. "Mount Nips Warriors; Purdue Mideast Ruler." *Toledo Blade,*
March 16, 1969. https://news.google.com/newspapers?nid=1350&dat=19690316&id
=pYEyAAAAIBAJ&sjid=rAEEAAAAIBAJ&pg=4908,6954406&hl=en.

———. "Take Dee's Word: Austin Carr Is the Best in the Land." *Toledo Blade,* December 2, 1970. https://news.google.com/newspapers?nid=1350&dat=19701202
&id=3CYxAAAAIBAJ&sjid=zAEEAAAAIBAJ&pg=7196,651598&hl=en.

Hardwick, Chan. "Robert McAdoo Satisfied With His NBA Success." *Daily Tar Heel,*
July 16, 1974. http://www.newspapers.com/image/67894347.

Hart, Micah. "Nique vs. Bird: An Oral History of the NBA's Greatest Playoff Duel."
NBA.com, May 20, 2013. http://www.nba.com/hawks/features/nique-bird-oral
-history-full-version.

Hart, Tommy. "Looking 'Em Over." *Big Spring Daily Herald,* March 15, 1961. http://
www.newspapers.com/image/11487724.

Harvin, Al. "People in Sports: Cowens Center of Attention on the Court or Driving a Cab." *New York Times,* April 15, 1977. http://query.nytimes.com/mem/archive
/pdf?res=9A0CE5DF1E3BE334BC4D52DFB266838C669EDE.

Haugh, David. "Dee Built N.D. Program, Successful Men." *South Bend Tribune,*
April 27, 1999.

Heffernan, Jim. "Arizin Saga—Dance Floor to Court Ball." *Sporting News,* February 18, 1959.

——. "With Greer to Steer, 76ers Can Go Like 60." *Sporting News,* February 22, 1964.

Hersom, Bob. "Close Enough to Perfect: Faith, Family Sustain Free-Throw Shooting Star Mark Price." *Daily Oklahoman,* December 3, 2000. http://newsok.com/close -enough-to-perfect-faith-family-sustain-free-throw-shooting-star-mark-price /article/2722082.

Heyman, Jo. "Kiki: He's the NBA's Renaissance Man." *Daily Breeze,* March 24, 1987.

Hirsch, Stuart. "Wigwam Saved From Wrecking Ball." *Herald Bulletin,* August 28, 2014. http://m.heraldbulletin.com/news/article_6602ec96-2f09-11e4-a65f-0019bb 2963f4.html?mode=jqm.

Hubbard, Jan. "Long-Distance Connection." *Dallas Morning News,* February 5, 1986.

——. "NBA All-Stars: The King and His Court." *Sporting News,* May 7, 1984.

Hunter, Bill. "Bulldogs Battle Smith Here Tomorrow Night." *Daily Times-News,* January 27, 1969. http://www.newspapers.com/image/53061717.

Janoff, Murray. "Handy Hal-Hot-Shot of NBA All-Stars." *Sporting News,* February 3, 1968.

Jares, Joe. "A Coach's Garden of Curses." *Sports Illustrated,* February 22, 1971. http:// www.si.com/vault/1971/02/22/554321/a-coachs-garden-of-curses.

——. "Voodoo Might Help." *Sports Illustrated,* March 24, 1969. http://www.si.com /vault/1969/03/24/559090/voodoo-might-help.

Jauss, Bill. "Gene Sullivan 1931–2002: Coach, Builder, and Rebel; Sullivan Helped Develop Programs at Loyola, DePaul." *Chicago Tribune,* February 22, 2002. http:// articles.chicagotribune.com/2002-02-22/sports/0202230054_1_irregular -heartbeat-northwest-side-notre-dame.

——. "Meet the Man Who Beat DePaul With One Hand." *Chicago Tribune,* July 1, 1985. http://articles.chicagotribune.com/1985-07-01/sports/8502120542_1_one -hand-one-hand-rich-basketball-tradition.

Jemail, Jimmy. "The Question: Do You Think That Old-Time, Low-Scoring Basketball—Before Hank Luisetti Popularized the One-Hand Jump Shot—Was a Better and More Interesting Game Than It Is Today?" *Sports Illustrated,* December 9, 1957. http://www.si.com/vault/1957/12/09/605740/the-question-do-you-think -that-old-time-low-scoring-basketballbefore-hank-luisetti-popularized-the-one -hand-jump-shotwas-a-better-and-more-interesting-game-than-it-is-today.

Jenkins, Lee. "Anatomy of a Miracle: Ray Allen's Shot in Game 6." *Sports Illustrated,* December 18, 2013. http://www.si.com/nba/2013/12/18/ray-allen-miami-heat-29 -seconds-nba-finals-game-6.

Johnson, Roy S. "Unusual Strategy, Instincts Serve Nuggets Well." *New York Times,* December 2, 1985. http://www.nytimes.com/1985/12/02/sports/unusual-strategy -instincts-serve-nuggets-well.html.

Kasey, David A. "2 Kokomo Stars Glitter at MSA." *Kokomo Tribune,* June 27, 1988. http://www.newspapers.com/image/2518294.

———. "Jim Rayl: A Fitting Hall of Fame Choice." *Kokomo Tribune,* December 1, 1988. http://www.newspapers.com/image/2347452.

———. "Legendary Rayl Finally Put in Proper Place." *Kokomo Tribune,* March 24, 1989. http://www.newspapers.com/image/17419433/.

———. "'Rocket' Leads New Class Into Hall of Fame." *Kokomo Tribune,* March 27, 1992. http://www.newspapers.com/image/20120587/.

Kindred, Dave. "What Makes King Run?: Five Arrests in 18 Months Taint Cage Star." *Toledo Blade,* July 25, 1977. https://news.google.com/newspapers?nid=1350 &dat=19770725&id=OwtPAAAAIBAJ&sjid=YgIEAAAAIBAJ&pg=6878,4608416 &hl=en.

Kingsport Daily News. "Jerry West 'Jumps' East Stars, 112–110." January 20, 1972. https://news.google.com/newspapers?nid=1241&dat=19720120&id =IUUPAAAAIBAJ&sjid=8IUDAAAAIBAJ&pg=6197,501795&hl=en.

Kirkpatrick, Curry. "Head Over Heels in Love." *Sports Illustrated,* March 13, 1972. http://www.si.com/vault/1972/03/13/576411/head-over-heels-in-love.

———. "An Irish Carr Moves Into High Gear." *Sports Illustrated,* February 1, 1971. http://www.si.com/vault/1971/02/01/554257/an-irish-carr-moves-into-high -gear.

———. "Latest Biggie Among the Mighty Smalls." *Sports Illustrated,* January 10, 1972. http://www.si.com/vault/1972/01/10/554410/latest-biggie-among-the-mighty -smalls.

———. "Shoot If You Must . . . I Must, Says McAdoo." *Sports Illustrated,* March 8, 1976. http://www.si.com/vault/1976/03/08/559139/shoot-if-you-musti-must-says -mcadoo.

———. "A Time to Bless the Beasts and Freshmen." *Sports Illustrated,* November 27,

1972. http://www.si.com/vault/1972/11/27/619145/a-time-to-bless-the-beasts-and
-freshmen.

Kitchell, Dave. "Rayl Helped Make Kokomo 'King of Basketball.'" *Kokomo Tribune,*
February 28, 1979. http://www.newspapers.com/image/2598795/.

Kornheiser, Tony. "Knicks: Behind Big Mac Attack." *New York Times,* January 30,
1978. http://query.nytimes.com/gst/abstract.html?res=9F04E5DA1E3EE632A2575
3C3A9679C946990D6CF.

Kritzer, Cy. "Ken Sailors' Play Helps Wyoming to Sail to Cage Titles." *Sporting News,*
April 8, 1943.

Kuska, Bob. "Talley the Terminator, He Gave You Buckets." *DC Basketball.* http://
www.dcbasketball.com/Talley-the-Terminator.php.

Layden, Tim. "Rick Mount: This Indiana Schoolboy Star Flopped as a Pro, and
Is Only Now, at 54, Coming to Terms With Life After Hoops." *Sports Illustrated,*
July 2, 2001. http://www.si.com/vault/2001/07/02/306832/rick-mount-this-indiana
-schoolboy-star-flopped-as-a-pro-and-is-only-now-at-54-coming-to-terms-with
-life-after-hoops.

Leighton, Tim. "High School Basketball: Bob McDonald, the Good Shepherd."
St. Paul Pioneer Press, January 21, 2014. http://www.twincities.com/sports/ci
_24952317/high-school-basketball-bob-mcdonald-wrapping-up-six.

Leonhardt, David. "Keeping Score; The Lost Art of Shooting Is Being Found." *New
York Times,* February 27, 2005. http://www.nytimes.com/2005/02/27/sports
/basketball/27score.html?pagewanted=print&position=&_r=0.

Levitt, Ed. "Sex and the Hoop." *Oakland Tribune,* February 11, 1970. http://news
paperarchive.com/us/california/oakland/oakland-tribune/1970/02-11/page-41.

Littwin, Mike. "Georgetown Wins as Price Is Wrong for Georgia Tech." *Los Angeles
Times,* March 24, 1985. http://articles.latimes.com/1985-03-24/sports/sp-30262_1
_georgia-tech.

———. "Lakers—'This McAdoo's for You.'" *Victoria Advocate,* May 23, 1982.
https://news.google.com/newspapers?nid=861&dat=19820523&id=FmVf
AAAAIBAJ&sjid=GV4NAAAAIBAJ&pg=6904,6105123&hl=en.

———. "A League of His Own: Former Pacers Star Roger Brown Left Behind a Legacy as the Ultimate ABA Player." *Sports Illustrated,* March 17, 1997. http://www.si
.com/vault/1997/03/17/224218/a-league-of-his-own-former-pacers-star-roger
-brown-left-behind-a-legacy-as-the-ultimate-aba-player.

Longman, Jere. "High School Basketball; A Scorer's Mentality Lives On." *New York Times,* December 21, 2002. http://www.nytimes.com/2002/12/21/sports/high-school -basketball-a-scorer-s-mentality-lives-on.html.

Louisiana Sports Hall of Fame. "Greg Procell." http://www.lasportshall.com /inductees/basketball/greg-procell/?back=inductee.

Lowe, Zach. "Life Beyond the Arc." *Grantland,* December 17, 2013. http://grantland .com/features/the-reliance-3-pointer-whether-not-hurting-nba/.

Maly, Ron. "Everly Wins State Title, 65-55." *Des Moines Register,* March 13, 1966. http://www.newspapers.com/image/7432332.

———. "Olson Duels Long in Title Game." *Des Moines Register,* March 16, 1968. http://www.newspapers.com/image/7879486/.

———. "Union-Whitten Wins It: 113-107!" *Des Moines Register,* March 17, 1968. http://www.newspapers.com/image/7880293.

Marine Corps Chevron. "Marine Cagers Await USC Trojans." December 18, 1943. http://historicperiodicals.princeton.edu/historic/cgi-bin/historic?a=d&d =MarineCorpsChevron19431218-01.1.17&e=——en-20—1—txt-IN——#.

McCallum, Jack. "'As Nearly Perfect As You Can Get.'" *Sports Illustrated,* March 3, 1986. http://www.si.com/vault/1986/03/03/628910/as-nearly-perfect-as-you-can-get.

———. "English Is Spoken Here." *Sports Illustrated,* December 9, 1985. http://www .si.com/vault/1985/12/09/622650/english-is-spoken-here.

———. "Not by a Long Shot." *Sports Illustrated,* December 13, 2004. http://www.si .com/vault/2004/12/13/8215560/not-by-a-long-shot.

McCarter, Mark. "ASHOF Class of 2014: Travis Grant Was Most Prolific Scorer in NCAA Hoops History." *Huntsville Times,* May 14, 2014. http://www.al.com/sports /index.ssf/2014/05/post_614.html.

McCarthy, John. "NAIA Hall of Famer Travis Grant=Incredible Story." *Play NAIA Blog,* January 21, 2011. http://www.playnaia.org/blog/2011/01/naia-hall-of-famer -travis-grant-incredible-story/.

McClain, John. "Celtics' Bird: The Master of the Court." *Houston Chronicle,* June 1, 1986.

McDermott, Barry. "A Legend Searching for His Past: Raymond Lewis Was Considered the Greatest Basketball Talent in LA But He's Still Waiting to Play in His

First NBA Game." *Sports Illustrated,* October 16, 1978. http://www.si.com/vault
/1978/10/16/823046/a-legend-searching-for-his-past-raymond-lewis-was
-considered-the-greatest-basketball-talent-in-la-but-hes-still-waiting-to-play-in
-his-first-nba-game.

McDill, Kent. "Female Referees Don't Concern Rodman." *Arlington Heights
Daily Herald,* October 29, 1997. http://www.highbeam.com/doc/1G1-69055272
.html.

McGinley, Terence. "Clifton Basketball Coach, Player Reunite." *North Jersey Record,* March 28, 2014. http://www.northjersey.com/community-news/celebrations
/basketball-coach-player-reunite-1.753142?page=all.

McKee, Sandra, with Ken Rosenthal. "King Reaching Rarefied Scoring Air of a Jordan." *Baltimore Sun,* January 11, 1991. http://articles.baltimoresun.com/1991-01
-11/sports/1991011174_1_bernard-king-scoring-king-played.

Mechem, Rose Mary. "Les Girls in Des Moines." *Sports Illustrated,* February 17,
1969. http://www.si.com/vault/1969/02/17/559641/les-girls-in-des-moines.

Miller, Hack. "Con Was First at One-Hand Shot." *Deseret News,* August 6, 1976.
https://news.google.com/newspapers?nid=336&dat=19760806&id=AM1SAAA
AIBAJ&sjid=HH8DAAAAIBAJ&pg=6595,1427455&hl=en.

Montieth, Mark. "Jerry Harkness Plays Game-Changing Role in Basketball History." NBA.com, September 18, 2013. http://www.nba.com/pacers/news/jerry
-harkness-plays-game-changing-role-basketball-history-part-2.

———. "A Legacy Preserved: Brown Gets His Due With Hall of Fame Enshrine-
ment." NBA.com, September 7, 2013. http://www.nba.com/pacers/legacy-preserved
-brown-gets-his-due-hall-fame-enshrinement-part-2.

Montville, Leigh. "Green Ghosts." *Sports Illustrated,* June 25, 2008. http://www.si
.com/vault/2008/06/25/105711055/green-ghosts.

———. "In Search of a Lost Jump Shot." *New London Day,* June 3, 1985. https://
news.google.com/newspapers?nid=1915&dat=19850603&id=q5hGAAAAIBAJ
&sjid=hvgMAAAAIBAJ&pg=2091,512217&hl=en.

———. "Pregame Shooting Pointless." *Boston Globe,* June 2, 1988. http://www
.highbeam.com/doc/1P2-8064700.html.

Moran, Malcolm. "College Basketball; UConn's Allen Is Worldly and Wise." *New
York Times,* February 19, 1996. http://www.nytimes.com/1996/02/19/sports/college
-basketball-uconn-s-allen-is-worldly-and-wise.html.

Morrow, Mark. "Oscar Robertson No. 1 When It Comes to Style." *Kokomo Tribune,* February 8, 1970. http://www.newspapers.com/image/44712001.

———. "Time Doesn't Take Away Desire, Ability." *Kokomo Tribune,* July 12, 1966. http://www.newspapers.com/image/44756668.

Murray, Jim. "Fans Overlook 6'9" Pettit." *Pacific Stars & Stripes,* March 21, 1964. http://newspaperarchive.com/jp/japan/tokyo/pacific-stars-and-stripes/1964/03-21/page-20.

———. "Lakers' Wild, Wild West." *Des Moines Register,* April 29, 1969. http://www.newspapers.com/image/7828746/.

———. "One Sam Jones Who Isn't 'Sad.'" *Hammond Times,* March 14, 1969. http://newspaperarchive.com/us/indiana/hammond/hammond-times/1969/03-14/page-42.

Musemeche, John. "LSU's 'Pistol Pete' Maravich: The Price He Pays for Stardom." *Tuscaloosa News,* February 23, 1969. https://news.google.com/newspapers?nid=1817&dat=19690221&id=cw4fAAAAIBAJ&sjid=NJsEAAAAIBAJ&pg=6044,5361177&hl=en.

Naismith Memorial Basketball Hall of Fame. "Glenn Roberts and the Genesis of the Jump Shot." http://www.hoophall.com/glenn-roberts-and-the-genesis/.

NBA.com. "Hal Greer Bio." NBA Encyclopedia, Playoff Edition. http://www.nba.com/history/players/greer_bio.html.

———. "Sam Jones Bio." NBA History. http://www.nba.com/history/players/sjones_bio.html.

Neddenriep, Kyle. "Milan 60 Years Later: 'We Didn't Realize What We'd Done. And I'm Still Not Sure We Do.'" *Indianapolis Star,* March 21, 2014. http://www.indystar.com/story/sports/high-school/2014/03/21/milan-years-later-realize-done-still-sure/6675287/.

Nevada Daily Mail. "Travis Grant Tallies 68." February 29, 1972. https://news.google.com/newspapers?nid=1908&dat=19720229&id=FV4fAAAAIBAJ&sjid=fdQEAAAAIBAJ&pg=2894,3036540&hl=en.

Newman, Bruce. "Back Home in Indiana." *Sports Illustrated,* February 18, 1985. http://www.si.com/vault/1985/02/18/622308/back-home-in-indiana.

———. "Mac Has Been a Real Blast From the Past." *Sports Illustrated,* May 24, 1982. http://www.si.com/vault/1982/05/24/627982/mac-has-been-a-real-blast-from-the-past.

———. "Now It's Bombs Away in the NBA." *Sports Illustrated,* January 7, 1980. http://www.si.com/vault/1980/01/07/824274/now-its-bombs-away-in-the-nba -traditionalists-may-blanch-but-pro-basketball-is-going-downtown-with-the-three -point-shot-the-celtics-especially-have-fired-shots-heard-round-the-nba-world-but -most-teams-have-yet-to-exploit-the-three-pointer-fully.

———. "Opposite Side of the Tracks." *Sports Illustrated,* November 20, 1985. http:// www.si.com/vault/1985/11/20/638200/opposite-sides-of-the-tracks.

Newspaper Enterprise Association. "Carr—Next Cage Point Champion?" *Daily Herald,* March 24, 1970. http://www.newspapers.com/image/8250018/.

Nugent, Frank S. "The Screen in Review." *New York Times,* review of *Campus Confessions*, September 23, 1938. http://www.nytimes.com/movie/review?res=9C07E6 D61531E03ABC4B51DFBF668383629EDE. Summary of *Times* review: http://www .nytimes.com/movies/movie/86532/Campus-Confessions/overview.

O'Brien, Jim. "Size and Shooting Skill Make McAdoo Super." *Sporting News,* February 25, 1978.

Olderman, Murray. "Bob Pettit Picked by Pros as Loop's Most Valuable Man." *Times—Tri-Cities Daily,* March 15, 1959. https://news.google.com/newspapers ?nid=1842&dat=19590315&id=0SIsAAAAIBAJ&sjid=F54FAAAAIBAJ&pg =3459,1776739&hl=en.

O'Neil, Dana. "Ed Steitz's 3-Point Dream Turns 25." ESPN.com, November 3, 2011. http://espn.go.com/mens-college-basketball/story/_/id/7178690/one-man -believed-adopting-3-pointer-college-basketball.

O'Riley, Francis J. "17,623 See Stanford Stop L.I.U. Streak at 43 Games; Georgetown Triumphs." *New York Times,* December 31, 1936. http://query.nytimes.com /mem/archive/pdf?res=9504E1DE143EE53ABC4950DFB467838D629EDE.

Paul, Jim. "Lamar Off to 'Slow Start' This Year." *El Dorado Times,* December 27, 1972. http://www.newspapers.com/image/35109062/.

Pennington, Bill. "College Basketball; In Search of the First Jump Shot." *New York Times,* April 2, 2011. http://www.nytimes.com/2011/04/03/sports/ncaabasketball /03jumper.html.

Peterson, Harold. "All the Smalls Were Tall." *Sports Illustrated,* March 27, 1972. http://www.si.com/vault/1972/03/27/576451/all-the-smalls-were-tall.

Pettit, Bob. "'Mind' Aided Bob Pettit Change His Game Tactics." *Daily News* (Virgin Islands), January 14, 1964. https://news.google.com/newspapers?nid=757

&dat=19630114&id=IQ5OAAAAIBAJ&sjid=660DAAAAIBAJ&pg=6853,856840
&hl=en.

Plaschke, Bill. "Urban Legend." *Los Angeles Times,* February 14, 2001. http://articles
.latimes.com/2001/feb/14/sports/sp-25258.

Pluto, Terry. "A Proud Papa Denny Price Shares His Son's Dream." *Akron Beacon
Journal,* May 5, 1988.

Podolsky, Rich. "Sixers Stopped by Refs." *Delaware County Daily Times*, April 19,
1976. http://www.newspapers.com/image/19368276.

Porter, David. "Paul Arizin Pioneered the Jump Shot While Playing in NBA." *Oska-
loosa Herald,* December 19, 2006. http://newspaperarchive.com/us/iowa/oskaloosa
/oskaloosa-herald/2006/12-19/page-9.

Powers, Ian. "Kenny Sailors and the Jump Shot Heard 'Round the World." New York
Daily News, March 23, 2014. http://creative.nydailynews.com/jumpshot.

Ralstin, Rick. "Jim Rayl 'MVP' in Rochester Tourney." *Kokomo Morning Times,* July
4, 1966. http://www.newspapers.com/image/32529024/.

Ralstin, Dick. "Lebanon Is Edged, 59–58, at Night by E. Chicago . . . After Mount
& Co. Edged Logan, 65-64." *Kokomo Morning Times,* March 13, 1966. http://www
.newspapers.com/image/32511487.

Ramsay, Dr. Jack. "Winning Game 5 on the Road Not Easy." ESPN.com: NBA Playoffs 2002, May 2, 2002. http://a.espncdn.com/nba/playoffs2002/columns/ramsay
_drjack/1377040.html.

Ramsey, David. "'Lethal Weapon 3' Wrecks Minnesota's Dream." *Sporting News,*
April 2, 1990.

Reed, William F. "Good Times Come to Cajun Country." *Sports Illustrated,* December
20 1971. http://www.si.com/vault/1971/12/20/667756/good-times-come-to-cajun
-country.

———. "Man of the Century Frank Selvy's 100-Point Game Secured Him a Spot in
College Hoops History." *Sports Illustrated,* February 6, 1995. http://www.si.com
/vault/1995/02/06/133238/man-of-the-century-frank-selvys-100-point-game
-secured-him-a-spot-in-college-hoops-history.

Reidenbaugh, Lowell. "Peerless Pettit Powers Hawks to Pro Cage Prize Over Celtics." *Sporting News,* April 23, 1958.

Reusse, Patrick. "Reusse: Chisholm's McDonald Nears 1,000 Career Victories." *Minneapolis Star Tribune,* December 17, 2013. http://www.startribune.com/sports /236134101.html.

Rist, Chuck. "Archie's Pulse 35!" *Charleston Daily Mail,* February 26, 1976. http:// newspaperarchive.com/us/west-virginia/charleston/charleston-daily-mail/1976 /02-26/page-20.

Roberts, Lee. "Of the Fish-Fries, Scott Is Hottest." *Wilmington Morning Star,* February 24, 1988. https://news.google.com/newspapers?nid=1454&dat=19880224&id =6c1OAAAAIBAJ&sjid=tBMEAAAAIBAJ&pg=5939,2820023&hl=en.

Rosenberg, I. J. "Georgia Tech's Triple Trouble." *Sporting News,* January 22, 1990.

———. "Nobody Beams 'Em Up Like Scott." *Sporting News,* March 26, 1990.

Rosenstihl, Jim. *Developing the Jump Shooter.* Accessed from Rick Mount's file at Indiana Basketball Hall of Fame.

Rusk, Larry. "Trailblazers Have Become UCLA of Junior Colleges." *Kokomo Tribune,* November 17, 1970. http://www.newspapers.com/image/44864916.

Ryan, Bob. "Banner Series in '57: Celtics Raised Their Game to Beat Hawks." *Boston Globe,* April 13, 2007. http://www.boston.com/sports/basketball/celtics/articles /2007/04/13/banner_series_in_57/?page=full.

———. "Braves Fans Regard Their Big Mac With Relish." *Sporting News,* April 19, 1975.

Sahadi, Lou. "Hal Greer of Marshall Fills Three Posts in Three Years." *Sporting News,* January 29, 1958.

Santa Cruz (CA) Sentinel. "Denise Meets Nate." June 8, 1969. http://www.newspapers .com/image/62647219/.

Scott, Nate. "Gregg Popovich Is So Old School He Hates Three-Pointers." *USA Today,* June 8, 2014. http://ftw.usatoday.com/2014/06/gregg-popovich-hates-three -pointers.

Sedalia (Mo.) Democrat. "M.U. Tigers Win 26-22 From the K.U. Jayhawks." January 31, 1932. http://www.newspapers.com/image/71780422.

Sharp, Bill. "Defense Only Slows Travis Grant." *Kansas City Times,* March 20, 1972. http://www.newspapers.com/image/56175487.

——. "Point Demon Grant Sparks Kentucky State, NAIA King." *Sporting News,* April 1, 1972.

Shaw, Bud. "It's Dad to Rescue as Price Struggles." *Chicago Sun-Times,* May 11, 1993. http://www.highbeam.com/doc/1P2-4169417.html.

Shirk, George. "Cunningham Shows Caution on McAdoo." *Philadelphia Inquirer,* October 13, 1982.

Simmons, Bill. "The Legacy of Game 6." *Grantland,* June 4, 2014. http://grantland .com/features/nba-finals-game-6-heat-spurs/.

Simpson, Kevin. "Denise Long, the Patron Saint of Girls Basketball, Is Now 33." *Los Angeles Times,* February 10, 1985. http://articles.latimes.com/1985-02-10/sports/sp -3529_1_denise-long.

Soldan, Ray. "Northwest, Enid Reach 5A Finals." *The Oklahoman,* March 20, 1982. http://newsok.com/northwest-enid-reach-5a-finals/article/1977581.

Spokesman-Review (Spokane, Wash.). "UCLA's Rushing for Home After Opening Road Scare." December 4, 1967. https://news.google.com/newspapers?nid=1314&dat =19671204&id=nWtWAAAAIBAJ&sjid=—gDAAAAIBAJ&pg=6962,1824359&hl=en.

Sporting News. "Auerbach Tabs Wilt as Only Player With Chance to Break Fulks' Mark." December 18, 1957.

Springfield (Mass.) *Daily Republican.* "Conn. Aggies in Win Over Local College Quintet." March 1, 1928.

——. "Conn. Aggies Out for Locals' Scalp." February 28, 1928.

——. "Springfield College Hoop Candidates Start." November 27, 1928.

Stankovic, Vladimir. "The Drazen and Oscar Show." Euroleague.net, Voices, March 12, 2011. http://www.euroleague.net/features/voices/2010-2011/vladimir -stankovic/i/83379/the-drazen-and-oscar-show.

Stein, Marc. "Leather Ball Will Return on Jan. 1." ESPN.com, December 12, 2006. http://sports.espn.go.com/nba/news/story?id=2694335.

——. "NBA Ball Controversy Reaches New Level." ESPN.com, December 8, 2006. http://sports.espn.go.com/nba/columns/story?id=2689744.

Stephens, James M. "Funeral Services for Smith." *Pittsburgh Courier,* December 9, 1972. http://www.newspapers.com/image/39212687/.

Sullivan, Jerry. "McAdoo Enlightens Young Heat With Courtly Wisdom." *Buffalo News*, October 17, 1996. http://www.highbeam.com/doc/1P2-22891963.html.

Sulzberger, A. G. "Handmade Hoops Put Clang Into New York Courts." *New York Times*, May 29, 2010. http://www.nytimes.com/2010/05/30/nyregion/30rims .html.

Sylvester, Curt. "Coach of the Year: Cavaliers Turning Things Around Under George Karl." *Beaver County Times*, February 26, 1985. https://news.google.com/newspapers ?nid=2002&dat=19850226&id=jV0vAAAAIBAJ&sjid=EdsFAAAAIBAJ&pg =1395,4994745&hl=en.

Templeton, David. "Obituary: Charles Wesley Diven, Jr./Oakmont Man Believed to Have Invented Basketball's Jump Shot." *Pittsburgh Post-Gazette*, June 16, 2008. http://www.post-gazette.com/news/obituaries/2008/06/16/Obituary-Charles -Wesley-Diven-Jr-Oakmont-man-believed-to-have-invented-basketball-s-jump -shot/stories/200806160141.

Thomas, Norman S. "Ye Sport Sandwich." *Lewiston Evening Journal*, January 31, 1938. https://news.google.com/newspapers?nid=1913&dat=19380131&id=p7U0 AAAAIBAJ&sjid=qmkFAAAAIBAJ&pg=5171,2454930&hl=en.

Thornley, Stew. "Minneapolis Lakers: Game With 12-Foot Baskets." Stew Thornley Web site, 1989. http://stewthornley.net/mplslakers_12foot.html.

Tierney, Mike. "Pro Basketball; Shooting Lab Makes Swishes Come True." *New York Times*, December 26, 2010. http://www.nytimes.com/2010/12/27/sports/basketball /27lab.html.

Timms, Landy. "A Miracle Revisited: Never Again May Spines Shiver as They Did When Frank Selvy Scored 100 Points." *Spartanburg Herald-Journal*, February 12, 1984. https://news.google.com/newspapers?id=Nm4sAAAAIBAJ&sjid=4c4EA AAAIBAJ&pg=5832%2C2627095.

Tipton Daily Tribune. "'Bobby Plump' Shot Overcomes Tipton." July 17, 1963. http:// www.newspapers.com/image/174712.

Togneri, Chris. "*Pittsburgh Courier* Writer Helped Jackie Robinson Break MLB Color Barrier." *Pittsburgh Tribune-Review*, April 12, 2013. http://triblive.com/news /allegheny/3786550-74/smith-black-robinson#axzz3WFyo6iMl.

Treadwell, Sandy. "A Most Conventional Win for the Thorobreds." *Sports Illustrated*, March 22, 1971. http://www.si.com/vault/1971/03/22/616942/a-most-conventional -win-for-the-thorobreds.

Tuscaloosa News. "Frank Selvy Not Bitter About Trade." February 17, 1958. https:// news.google.com/newspapers?nid=1817&dat=19580217&id=bfocAAAAIBAJ&sjid =CJoEAAAAIBAJ&pg=6757,2387079&hl=en.

United Press. "Crowd of 40,000 Welcomes Milan's Champions." *Logansport Pharos-Tribune,* March 22, 1954. http://www.newspapers.com/image/14870377.

United Press. "Frank Selvy Laughs About Brushoff Rupp Gave Him." *Brownsville Herald,* March 11, 1954. http://www.newspapers.com/image/23843674.

United Press. "'Phog' Allen Urges Boost in Height of Basketball Hoops." *Lubbock Morning Avalanche,* December 30, 1942. http://www.newspapers.com /image/6234901/.

United Press. "San Diego Marine Cagers Have Won 20 Straight Tilts." *Nevada State Journal* (Reno), January 13, 1944. http://www.newspapers.com/image /75299215.

United Press. "San Diego Marines Trim Southern Cal." *Tucson Daily Citizen,* January 29, 1944. http://www.newspapers.com/image/9800289.

United Press International. "53 Points ABA Record: Pacers—'We Rely on Brown.'" *Palm Beach Post,* May 21, 1970. https://news.google.com/newspapers?nid=1964&dat =19700521&id=i30yAAAAIBAJ&sjid=-bUFAAAAIBAJ&pg=2925,2379244&hl=en.

United Press International. "76ers, Celtics Win Eastern Semis." *Naugatuck News,* April 2, 1968. http://www.newspapers.com/image/4537065/.

United Press International. "76ers Clinch Second Straight Division Crown." *Lebanon Daily News,* March 9, 1967. http://www.newspapers.com/image/5429179.

United Press International. "ABL Excites Fans With 3-Pointers." *Huntingdon Daily News,* October 28, 1961. http://www.newspapers.com/image/5292486.

United Press International. "Big Ten Coaches Lukewarm About 3-Pointer." *Logansport Pharos-Tribune,* November 18, 1986. http://www.newspapers.com/image /16935974.

United Press International. "Carr Now Candidate for Naismith Honor." *Wilmington Star-News,* February 12, 1971. https://news.google.com/newspapers?nid=1454 &dat=19710212&id=DytkAAAAIBAJ&sjid=sQkEAAAAIBAJ&pg=4238,1823896 &hl=en.

United Press International. "Celtics Drop Lakers, 119–105." *Terre Haute Tribune,* April 17, 1962. http://www.newspapers.com/image/80247304.

United Press International. "Celtics Trade for McAdoo." *Beaver County Times,* February 12, 1979. https://news.google.com/newspapers?nid=2002&dat=19790209 &id=U18uAAAAIBAJ&sjid=wtkFAAAAIBAJ&pg=3812,2456508&hl=en.

United Press International. "Coach Calls Travis Grant 'Unbelievable, Inhuman.'" *Baltimore Afro-American,* March 25, 1972. https://news.google.com/newspapers ?nid=1715&dat=19720318&id=L7s9AAAAIBAJ&sjid=4SsMAAAAIBAJ&pg =2622,4647876&hl=en.

United Press International. "Connersville Wins State Basketball Title." *Logansport Pharos-Tribune,* March 27, 1983. http://www.newspapers.com/image /13513157.

United Press International. "Hobson Preaches 3-Pointer." *Eugene Register-Guard,* July 15, 1978. https://news.google.com/newspapers?nid=1310&dat=19780715&id =PchYAAAAIBAJ&sjid=7OEDAAAAIBAJ&pg=5330,4083430&hl=en.

United Press International. "Jerry West's Jump Shot Wins It for Lakers: 'Mr. Clutch' Up to His Old Tricks." *Beaver County Times,* April 18, 1973. https://news.google.com /newspapers?nid=2002&dat=19730418&id=lLMiAAAAIBAJ&sjid=ibMFAAA AIBAJ&pg=803,791333&hl=en.

United Press International. "Kentucky State, Eau Claire Paired in NAIA Championship." *Ellensburg Daily Record,* March 18, 1972. https://news.google.com /newspapers?nid=860&dat=19720318&id=QVlUAAAAIBAJ&sjid=1Y4DAAAA IBAJ&pg=7125,3857446&hl=en/.

United Press International. "Kentucky State Repeats NAIA." *Pocono Record,* March 20, 1972. http://www.newspapers.com/image/44299382.

United Press International. "Larry Bird Breaks Finger." *Logansport Pharos-Tribune,* May 10, 1979. http://www.newspapers.com/image/13918921.

United Press International. "Larry Bird Breaks Silence—for Team." *Roswell Daily Record,* March 21, 1979. http://www.newspapers.com/image/14923977.

United Press International. "Long Beach State Falls." *Bryan Times,* February 24, 1973. https://news.google.com/newspapers?nid=799&dat=19730224&id=hVgzAA AAIBAJ&sjid=WlIDAAAAIBAJ&pg=2887,3629846&hl=en.

United Press International. "Maravich's 'Good Loser' Label Grows Increasingly Tiresome." *Daily Herald,* May 25, 1977. http://www.newspapers.com/image /33320081/.

United Press International. "Robinson Backer Dies at Age of 58." *Pocono Record,* November 27, 1972. http://www.newspapers.com/image/44387320.

United Press International. "Russell Hero as Celts Capture Another Title." *Dispatch (Lexington, NC),* April 19, 1962. https://news.google.com/newspapers?nid=1734 &dat=19620418&id=KI4bAAAAIBAJ&sjid=XlEEAAAAIBAJ&pg=7142,2789658 &hl=en.

United Press International. "Some Still Don't Like It: Three-Point Shot Is a Big Weapon." *Lodi News-Sentinel,* March 27, 1987. https://news.google.com/newspapers ?nid=2245&dat=19870327&id=4Bc0AAAAIBAJ&sjid=qDIHAAAAIBAJ&pg =7123,3263323&hl=en.

United Press International. "Spurs Had Better Not Overlook McAdoo Again." *Sarasota Journal,* May 11, 1982. https://news.google.com/newspapers?nid=1798&dat =19820511&id=yOkhAAAAIBAJ&sjid=rY4EAAAAIBAJ&pg=3584,1115694&hl =en.

United Press International. "Three-Pointers Indiana's Forte." *Pharos-Tribune,* January 27, 1983. http://www.newspapers.com/image/13491437.

United Press International. "Travis Grant Becomes Top Basketball Scorer." *Redlands Daily Facts,* March 7, 1972. http://newspaperarchive.com/us/california/redlands /redlands-daily-facts/1972/03-07/page-13.

United Press International. "Travis Grant Thrills NAIA With 60 Points; Viks Win." *Ellensburg Daily Record,* March 15, 1972. https://news.google.com/newspapers?nid =860&dat=19720315&id=PllUAAAAIBAJ&sjid=1Y4DAAAAIBAJ&pg =3830,3654483&hl=en.

United Press International. "Warsaw Stuns MC Rogers." *Pharos-Tribune,* March 18, 1984. http://www.newspapers.com/image/13455201.

United Press International. "West Sparks Victory." *Panama City News-Herald,* January 19, 1974. http://www.newspapers.com/image/2008744.

Van Sant, Rick. "Two Stars Ex-Teammates." *Bryan Times,* March 15, 1972. https:// news.google.com/newspapers?nid=799&dat=19720315&id=oU8LAAAAIBAJ &sjid=a1IDAAAAIBAJ&pg=5892,4469423&hl=en.

Vecsey, Peter. "Oh, Boys, Was This a Classic Matchup." *New York Post,* March 14, 2010. http://nypost.com/2010/03/14/oh-boys-was-this-a-classic-matchup/.

Vetrone, Bob. "Warriors on Title Warpath as Arizin Joins Johnston." *Sporting News,* November 3, 1954.

Walsh, George. "Jones & Jones at Court." *Sports Illustrated,* March 20, 1961. http://www.si.com/vault/1961/03/20/580207/jones—jones-at-court.

Ward, Bill. "Basketball Fans Clearly Won't Be Shortchanged." *Minneapolis Star Tribune,* November 22, 1988.

Waterman, Frederick. "Auerbach Tabs Five as Game's Top Innovators." *Chicago Sun-Times,* April 19, 1987. http://www.highbeam.com/doc/1P2-3821467.html.

Weisberg, Sam. "Westford Man 'Invented' One-Handed Jump Shot." *The Sunday Sun* (Lowell, Mass.). November 9, 1975. http://www.newspapers.com/image/48138748.

Wells, Danny. "One and Only Talley Leads Salem With 38." *Charleston Gazette,* February 27, 1975. http://newspaperarchive.com/us/west-virginia/charleston/charleston-gazette/1975/02-27/page-24.

West, Evan. "Remember the Tigers." *Indianapolis Monthly,* March 2005. http://www.indianapolismonthly.com/news-opinion/remember-the-tigers/.

Whicker, Mark. "Great Year, Big Mac, and Good Luck." *Daily Tar Heel,* April 11, 1972. http://www.newspapers.com/image/67800004/.

White, Jr., Gordon S. "Boys High Tops Wingate, 62-59, and Reaches P.S.A.L. Final." *New York Times,* March 16, 1960. http://query.nytimes.com/gst/abstract.html?res=9F0DEEDD1331EF3ABC4E52DFB566838B679EDE.

White, Neil. "60 Years Ago, Furman's Frank Selvy Joined a Very Exclusive Club." *State* (Columbia, S.C.), February 8, 2014.

Whiteford, Mike. "West Virginians Who Made a Difference: Greer Broke Barrier, Won Hearts of Fans." *Sunday Gazette-Mail,* November 21, 1999. http://www.highbeam.com/doc/1P2-19009916.html.

Wilson, Brad. "Everly's Olson: One Down, Two Titles to Go." *Des Moines Register,* March 16, 1966. http://www.newspapers.com/image/7439476.

Wolf, Bob. "Braves Could Zip Past Celtics." *Sporting News.* October 11, 1975.

———. "McAdoo Sweeps Boards as No. 1 NBA All-Star." *Sporting News.* April 19, 1975.

REFERENCES, GUIDES, AND VIDEOS

Most of the statistics for NBA players came from the invaluable www.basketball-reference.com. Many college statistics came from www.sports-reference.com. Other pro, college, and high school stats came from newspapers, magazines, and

Web sites. Record books for NCAA Division I, Division II, and Division III basketball were also helpful, as was the NAIA record book. For a complete list of videos used in the research, please visit shawnfury.com.

INTERVIEWS

Gary Addington; Dana Alexander (Long); Steve Alford; Bill Boyd; Jim Calhoun; Austin Carr; Craig Carse; John Christgau; Brad Clark; Keydren Clark; Bobby Cremins; Paul Culpo; Randy Echols; Andy Enfield; Ed Ferguson; Howard Garfinkel; Dick Garmaker; Gerald Glass; Travis Grant; Ted Green; Carol Gunderson (Hannusch); Norm Held; Paul Hoover; Dave Hopla; Tom Konchalski; Bruce Kreutzer; Bob Kuska; Ray LeBov; Jeff Lensch; Troy Lewis; Jeanette Lietz (Olson); Doug Lietz; Cyndy Long; Bob McAdoo; Bob McDonald; Joel McDonald; Mike McDonald; Paul McDonald; Tom McDonald; Rick Mount; Ray Pavy; Bobby Plump; Ryan Polomski; Dean Prator; Mark Price; Judy Racek; Ed Ratleff; Jimmy Rayl; Nancy Rayl; Dan Rife; Denise Rife (Long); Bevon Robin; Johnny Rogers; Tony Rosa; Bob Ryan; Jack Ryan; Kenny Sailors; Bill Schrage; Dennis Scott; Dan Shaw; Purvis Short; Elmore Smith; Archie Talley; Sue Tesdahl; Dan Touhey; Kiki Vandeweghe; Peter Vecsey; Jerry West; Dominique Wilkins.

INDEX